LEADERSHIP PRACTICES FOR SPECIAL AND GENERAL EDUCATORS

Gloria D. Campbell-Whatley
University of North Carolina at Charlotte

James E. Lyons
University of North Carolina at Charlotte

PEARSON

Boston Columbus Indianapolis New York San Francisco Upper Saddle River
Amsterdam Cape Town Dubai London Madrid Milan Munich Paris Montréal Toronto
Delhi Mexico City São Paulo Sydney Hong Kong Seoul Singapore Taipei Tokyo

Executive Editor and Publisher: Stephen D. Dragin
Editorial Assistant: Katherine Wiley
Marketing Manager: Christine Gatchell
Production Editor: Mary Beth Finch
Editorial Production Service: Element LLC
Manufacturing Buyer: Megan Cochran
Electronic Composition: Element LLC
Cover Designer: Laura Gardner

Cataloging-in-Publication data unavailable at press time.

10 9 8 7 6 5 4 3 2 1

Cover image: nokhoog_buchachon/Shutterstock.com

ISBN 10: 0-13-299632-4
ISBN 13: 978-0-13-299632-7

CONTENTS

Where the Interstate School Leaders Licensure Consortium (ISLLC) Standards Are Addressed in This Book

ISLLC Standards	Chapter(s) Where Addressed
Standard 1: A school administrator is an educational leader who promotes the success of all students by facilitating the development, articulation, implementation, and stewardship of a vision of learning that is shared and supported by the school community.	Chapter 1 addresses leadership and the leader's principal roles, including developing and implementing an educational vision in concert with school stakeholders.
Standard 2: A school administrator is an educational leader who promotes the success of all students by advocating, nurturing, and sustaining a school culture and instructional program conducive to student learning and staff professional growth.	Chapter 1 addresses the leader's role in establishing a school culture, climate, and ethos that fosters student learning and staff professional growth.
Standard 3: A school administrator is an educational leader who promotes the success of all students by ensuring management of the organization, operations, and resources for a safe, efficient, and effective learning environment.	Chapters 13 and 14 address school finance/budgeting and school transportation, respectively; Chapter 12 addresses the management of human resources; coupled with Chapter 1, all these chapters address how school leaders should provide a safe, efficient learning environment for students.
Standard 4: A school administrator is an educational leader who promotes the success of all students by collaborating with families and community members, responding to diverse community interests and needs, and mobilizing community resources.	Chapter 6 addresses family involvement and school leaders' roles in building relationships with and working with diverse families and students; Chapter 8 also addresses collaboration with families and other agencies.
Standard 5: A school administrator is an educational leader who promotes the success of all students by acting with integrity, fairness, and in an ethical manner.	Chapter 1 addresses the need for school leaders to do the right and fair thing; Chapters 4 and 11 address assessments and evaluation, including acting with integrity, fairness, and in an ethical manner.
Standard 6: A school administrator is an educational leader who promotes the success of all students by understanding, responding to, and influencing the larger political, social, economic, legal, and cultural context.	Chapters 1, 2, and 13 address the legal, social, and economic context; Chapter 5 also addresses the legal issues, regulations, and mandates applicable to special education.

Reprinted with permission from Council of Chief State School Officers.

PREFACE

Since the United States Congress enacted the Education for All Handicapped Children Act in 1975, Public Law 94-142, school policymakers at all levels—federal, state, and local—and local school leaders and teachers across the United States have had the responsibility, mandated by law, to provide all children with disabilities a free appropriate public education (FAPE) in the least restrictive environment. This act ushered in a new era for children with disabilities and special learning needs and their families. However, ever since that time, school boards and school leaders have faced many challenges as they have tried to comply with the spirit and letter of this omnibus, albeit very noble, law. Research shows that the most protracted, contentious conflicts school leaders have with individual parents involve serving children with disabilities and special needs. Also, research shows that during the last 25 years, special education has consistently been the most litigated single area in public education, and school districts have won only slightly more than half of these cases. Moreover, collectively, local school districts have expended an enormous amount of their limited resources on defraying the legal costs to defend themselves after being charged with failing to provide a free and appropriate education to students with disabilities and/or special needs.

Given this history, one might wonder what has contributed to this state of affairs vis-à-vis special education. The answers are multifaceted. First, the federal statutes and regulations that govern special education policies, procedures, and practices are enormously complicated and are frequently revised. Also, since nearly every state has a complementary statute and regulations that govern special education programs and services, this further adds to the labyrinthine volume of material with which local school districts must be familiar. Moreover, most local education agencies also absorb some of the costs for supporting special education programs and services, so they have enacted local district policies and procedures to govern and operate their programs. Hence, local school officials, leaders, and teachers must lead and manage special education programs and services through a tri-tiered voluminous set of statutes, regulations, guidelines, and practices. Given the level of complexity involved, few, if any, school leaders would claim to be intimately familiar with all of them.

Second, the level of funding to support special education programs and related services has never been sufficient to cover the need in the vast majority of school districts. Thus, districts are seldom able to employ the number of teachers, teacher assistants, and paraprofessionals needed to adequately serve students with disabilities and special needs. Moreover, given the paucity of funding, most districts are seldom able to adequately provide the array of related services that students with disabilities need to maximize their opportunities to learn and develop.

Third, time is the most important resource that local school leaders have and they face a myriad of responsibilities that consume it. They are so busy that they seldom are able to devote the needed amount of time to addressing the needs of students with disabilities and special needs individually and collectively. Neither are they able to devote the time needed to work with special education teachers, regular classroom teachers, counselors, psychologists, and families who have children with disabilities. Additionally, the daily demands on their time limits their ability to keep current on special education regulations and guidelines.

These factors led us to conclude that a book was needed that would specifically address the type of problems, challenges, and issues that regular and special education leaders frequently face on a day-to-day basis as they lead and administer special education programs and serve students with disabilities and their families. Given the ubiquitous struggles school officials frequently encounter in leading and supervising special education, the content and focus of the book is intended to serve as a resource for both practicing and future school leaders in both general and special education. It is purposely written to be easily readable, practical, authentic, and not overly theoretical. Recognizing that it is not always easy to decipher the federal statutes and regulations that govern special education, the chapters are written so that that the reader can "cut to the chase" and readily get the gist of pertinent issues that relate to special education.

In each chapter, a vignette is presented that reflects a typical issue that a principal and/or special education director is likely to encounter in a school setting. The chapter then discusses the issue in a comprehensive manner, citing appropriate statutes and regulations where appropriate, to provide the reader background knowledge relative to the specific issue in question. At the end of the chapter, a resolution or suggested approach is provided for the issue addressed in the vignette. In short, the book is structured to help the reader learn how to problem solve issues he or she is likely to face when dealing with students who have disabilities or special needs. For example, Chapter 14, which addresses transportation (a related service for some children with disabilities), gives a building principal some very useful knowledge and insights regarding how to properly handle a field trip or off-campus extracurricular activity in which one or more students with a physical disability is involved. In addition to the legal, practical, logistical issues involved, the chapter is written to include issues of sensitivity, fairness, empathy, and parental perceptions.

This book is also written to reflect the ISLLC standards adopted by the National Policy Board for Educational Administration. These standards were developed and deliberatively designed to incorporate the knowledge and indicators of that knowledge that should be acquired by preservice graduate students and in-service school practitioners. Most chapters in the book include content that is drawn from the standards.

It is our sincere hope that the readers of this book will enjoy it as much as the authors of the chapters enjoyed writing and rewriting them. More important, it is our hope that the readers will acquire new and additional knowledge from the book that will equip them to more effectively serve children with disabilities and special needs and their families and to help these students develop to their fullest potential. They deserve no less.

Finally, we offer our sincere thanks and appreciation to the all the authors who contributed chapters to this book. Collectively, they added immensely to the knowledge and expertise that is reflected in this work. These authors included our faculty, colleagues, and graduate students at the University of North Carolina at Charlotte: Dr. Jim Bird, Dr. Mickey Dunaway, Dr. Richard Lambert, Dr. Ya-yu Lo, Dr. Christopher O'Brien, Dr. Lee Sherry, and Dr. Richard White. Other authors included Dr. Nancy Aguinaga, Southeast Missouri State University; Dr. Louise Allen, South Carolina State University, Dr. Heather Britt, Kennedy Charter Public School; Dr. Loury O. Floyd, North Carolina Agriculture and Technical University; Dr. Victoria Knight, University of Kentucky; Dr. Ann McColl, Esq., North Carolina State Board of Education; Dr. Khalilah O'Farrow, North Carolina Department of Public Instruction; Dr. Dawn A. Rowe, the University of Oregon; Dr. Cheryl T. Smith, University of North Carolina at Greensboro; and Dr. Ozalle Toms, University of Wisconsin at Whitewater. We also extend our gratitude to Ruth Klein, LeMoyne College; and Jennifer Naddeo, Loyola University Chicago, for their helpful comments and suggestions.

Gloria Whatley-Campbell, Ed.D.

James E. Lyons, Ph.D.

CONTRIBUTORS

Chapter 1   EDUCATIONAL LEADERSHIP: AN EVOLVING ROLE

Dr. James E. Lyons
Department of Educational Leadership
University of North Carolina at Charlotte

Dr. Gloria Campbell-Whatley
Department of Special Education and Child Development
University of North Carolina at Charlotte

Chapter 2   LAWS AND POLICY AFFECTING SCHOOLS: GOING BEYOND COMPLIANCE

Dr. Ann McColl, Esq.
Legislative Director
North Carolina State Board of Education

Dr. Irene Meier
Director of Special Education Instruction
Fairfax County Public Schools

Chapter 3   SCHOOL REFORM AND THE STANDARDS-EMBEDDED CURRICULUM

Dr. Louise Anderson Allen
Department of Educational Leadership
South Carolina State University

Chapter 4   ASSESSMENT AND THE IEP PROCESS

Dr. Gloria D. Campbell-Whatley
Department of Special Education and Child Development
University of North Carolina at Charlotte

Chapter 5   DISCIPLINE: FUNCTIONAL BEHAVIOR ASSESSMENT AND BEHAVIOR INTERVENTION PLANS

Dr. Gloria D. Campbell-Whatley, Dr. Ya-yu Lo, and Dr. Richard White
Department of Special Education and Child Development
University of North Carolina at Charlotte

Chapter 6   BUILDING ETHOS AND INTERPERSONAL RELATIONSHIPS WITH FAMILIES AND STUDENTS

Dr. James E. Lyons
Department of Educational Leadership
University of North Carolina at Charlotte

Chapter 7   TRANSITIONING FROM EARLY INTERVENTION TO ADULTHOOD

Dr. Dawn Rowe
Department of Secondary Special Education and Transition
University of Oregon

Dr. Lee Sherry
Department of Special Education
University of North Carolina at Charlotte

Chapter 8   RESPONSE TO INTERVENTION AND INCLUSION: FACILITATING COLLABORATIVE ARRANGEMENTS

Dr. Gloria D. Campbell-Whatley
Department of Special Education and Child Development
University of North Carolina at Charlotte

Dr. Loury Ollison Floyd
Department of Curriculum and Instruction
North Carolina Agricultural & Technical State University

Dr. Khalilah S. O'Farrow
Regional Trainer, EC Delivery Team
North Carolina Department of Public Instruction

Dr. Cheryl T. Smith
School of Specialized Education Services
University of North Carolina at Greensboro

Chapter 9   LEADERSHIP IN A MULTICULTURAL SETTING

Dr. Gloria Campbell-Whatley
Department of Special Education and Child Development
University of North Carolina at Charlotte

Dr. Khalilah S. O'Farrow
Regional Trainer, EC Delivery Team
North Carolina Department of Public Instruction

Dr. Ozalle Toms
Department of Special Education
University of Wisconsin at Whitewater

Chapter 10   UNIVERSAL DESIGN FOR LEARNING: ACCESSING THE GENERAL CURRICULUM WITH EFFECTIVE TEACHING AND DIGITAL TECHNOLOGIES

Dr. Christopher O'Brien
Department of Special Education and Child Development
University of North Carolina at Charlotte

Dr. Nancy Aguinaga
Department of Special Education and Child Development
Southeast Missouri State University

Dr. Victoria Knight
Department of Special Education and Rehabilitative Counseling
University of Kentucky

Chapter 11   PROGRAM EVALUATION METHODS FOR EDUCATIONAL LEADERS

Dr. Richard G. Lambert
Department of Educational Leadership
University of North Carolina at Charlotte

Dr. Heather Britt
Director of Freshman Academy English
Kennedy Charter Public School
Charlotte, North Carolina

Chapter 12   HUMAN RESOURCES

Dr. Gloria D. Campbell-Whatley
Department of Special Education and Child Development
University of North Carolina at Charlotte

Dr. James E. Lyons
Department of Educational Leadership
University of North Carolina at Charlotte

Chapter 13   SCHOOL FINANCE

Dr. James J. Bird
Department of Educational Leadership
University of North Carolina at Charlotte

Chapter 14   SCHOOL TRANSPORTATION

Dr. David M. Dunaway
Department of Educational Leadership
University of North Carolina at Charlotte

ABOUT THE AUTHORS

Dr. Gloria Campbell-Whatley is an Associate Professor in the Department of Special Education and Child Development at the University of North Carolina at Charlotte, where she teaches graduate students and has served as the graduate coordinator. She received her doctorate of education degree at the University of Alabama at Birmingham. Prior to entering the professorship, in Birmingham City Public Schools, she served as an elementary teacher, special education teacher, and a transition teacher on special assignment at the University of Alabama at Birmingham. Dr. Campbell-Whatley has delivered numerous national and international presentations, workshops, and strands. Her specialty is infusing diversity into higher education and K–12 curriculum and she also offers solutions for behavior problems, response to intervention, and social skills training in public schools. Dr. Campbell-Whatley has written over 40 articles, book chapters, research reports, and modules related to multicultural education, and has published two books on behavior. Her research focus is diversity, social skills and behavior, and administration in special education. In her career, she has served as a program specialist for for Special Education Programs in the Birmingham City Public Schools in Alabama, and has been on the Council for Exceptional Children National and International Board.

Dr. James E. Lyons has served as a faculty member and administrator at the University of North Carolina at Charlotte since 1979. During this time, he has taught hundreds of students who have become successful school leaders in North Carolina and beyond. Prior to entering the professorship, he served as a high school teacher, principal, and school management consultant for the Ohio Department of Education. In recognition of the excellent quality of the professional consultation services he provides and his graduate-level teaching, Dr. Lyons was awarded the University of North Carolina at Charlotte's faculty service award in 2005; he was awarded the College of Education's Excellence in Teaching Award in 2007; and he was a finalist for UNC Charlotte's Bank of America Excellent Teaching Award in 2009. As the author of over 40 articles and book chapters, he has been widely recognized for his research and scholarship. Dr. Lyons received the doctor of philosophy (Ph.D.) degree from The Ohio State University.

CHAPTER 1

Educational Leadership

An Evolving Role

JAMES E. LYONS

GLORIA D. CAMPBELL-WHATLEY

INTRODUCTION

Special education programs and services are administered through a bureaucratic structural arrangement whereby federal, state, and local general and special education leaders share joint responsibility for providing a free and appropriate education to students with disabilities and exceptionalities in the least restrictive educational environment. In the vast majority of cases, the day-to-day responsibilities for leading, supervising, and managing special education programs and services are carried out by public school principals who are often general school leaders with limited formal training in special education. Since the enactment of the landmark Education for All Handicapped Children Act (PL 94-142) in 1975, there has been a continuing struggle in schools and school districts across the United States as parents of children with disabilities have sought to help their children get the appropriate education and related services that this act and its various amendments mandated. For over 30 years, many parents of students with disabilities have alleged that they have had to engage in protracted and often contentious struggles with unresponsive school officials when pursuing special education and related services for their children. During the last 25 years, special education has consistently been the most litigated area in public education, and school districts have won only slightly more than half of the cases that have gone to court. Given that courts have ruled in the parents' favor in 45 percent of the cases during this time, this suggests that more effective leadership needs to be exercised by school leaders, particularly principals, to see that special education programs, practices, and procedures are in compliance with the laws and regulations that govern them. The laws and regulations cited in this chapter are important guidelines for assuring that student needs are met.

Numerous current and past reforms in education have changed the face of education, especially for children with disabilities. In the United States in the mid-1970s, parents of children with disabilities had fought for years to address many of the problems they had encountered with the public education system. School programs for children with disabilities were often housed in segregated settings, away from mainstream public education, and these children were often provided inadequate or minimal educational services. The Education for All Handicapped Children Act (EAHCA, also known as EHA), PL 94-142, enacted by the Congress in 1975, dramatically affected most general education leaders and classroom teachers, as the law mandated that children with disabilities were entitled to a free appropriate public education (FAPE) in the least restrictive environment (LRE). This landmark act ushered in a new era for children with disabilities as well as their parents. Specifically, the act mandated that students with disabilities had to be provided access to a free and appropriate public school education, which meant access to regular classes and school activities. Passage of the law, however, marked only the beginning of changes that were needed to better serve students with disabilities (Bartlett, Weisenstein, & Etscheidt, 2002; Podemski, Marsh, Smith, & Price, 1995).

Congress has since amended and reauthorized the EHA in 1990, 1997, and 2004. These revisions included changing the name of the law to the Individuals with Disabilities Education Act (IDEA) in 1990 (PL 101-476) and the Individuals with Disabilities Education Improvement Act (IDEIA) in 2004 with PL 108-446. Before enactment of IDEA laws, children were served in special education classrooms in resource or separate classroom settings; in fact, before the EHA, 80 percent of students with disabilities were placed in separate facilities (Idol, 2006). Since then, educational trends have progressed toward creating and adapting regulations to include children with disabilities into general education programs and the general curriculum to a much greater extent (Idol, 2006). Currently, approximately 7 million students—12 percent of the school population—are labeled as "exceptional" and are receiving an array of special and general educational services (http://nces. ed. gov/; www.nichcy.org/Pages/Home.asp).

Perhaps not surprisingly, school officials, parents of students with disabilities, and legal scholars began to debate what constituted a FAPE immediately after passage of the EHA (Osborne, 1992; Osborne & Russo, 2010). There are legions of documented cases over the years wherein parents or guardians of children with special needs and disabilities have alleged that school officials have been unresponsive, slow, dismissive, arrogant, or uncooperative in addressing the needs of these students and their parents. Nevertheless, over 30 years later, parents still complain that, if their concerns are addressed at all when they are brought to school officials, they are often dismissed with only brief consideration. Research shows that the most protracted, contentious conflicts school officials have with individual parents involve serving children with special needs (Trainor, 2010; Zirkel, 2005). Moreover, during the last 25 years, special education has consistently been the most litigated area in education (Katsiyannis & Herbst, 2004; Osborne & Russo, 2010), and school districts have won only slightly more than half (55 percent) of these cases (Zirkel, 2005). Thus, in nearly half (45 percent) of the cases, the courts have ruled against school officials, which strongly suggests that more effective leadership is needed in this area. Court cases still abound arising from the interpretation of special education laws and regulations regarding student behavior, curricular modifications, high-stakes testing, reform standards, and parental rights (Bateman, 2007; MacLaughlin & Rhim, 2007).

RATIONALE FOR THIS BOOK

Given this history of ubiquitous struggles to provide appropriate education for all students with special needs, we have written this book with two fundamental purposes in mind. First, it is intended to be a clarion call to action to current and future general and special education school leaders to effectively address this crucial issue and become more proactive and responsive to meeting both the spirit and letter of the law. In particular, we argue that new proactive leadership, particularly transformational leadership, is needed to transform the efforts to improve special education in schools today. Parents should not have to engage in protracted and contentious struggles with unresponsive school officials to obtain the type of education and services to which their children have been legally entitled for nearly 35 years. Second, this book is intended to provide both practicing and future school leaders, in both general and special education, with the most crucial fundamental and practical knowledge they need to administer special education programs and services. Even if they genuinely wish to do the right thing with and for students with special needs, education professionals must be equipped with the requisite knowledge to effectively do it.

Although we have progressed with the delivery of services to learners with disabilities in U.S. schools, many other challenges strongly suggest that continuing improvements are still gravely needed. Specifically, we still have problems with overidentification of students with special needs, assessments, referrals, disproportional representation of minority students, appropriate discipline practices, appropriate programming, early intervention, curricular adaptations, and response to interventions—to list a few of the many recent concerns and challenges that school leaders persistently tackle in the administration of special education programs and services (Anthun & Manger, 2006; Epley et al., 2010; Harry & Klinger, 2007; Sugai, Guardino, & Lathrop, 2007).

As the requirements for serving students with disabilities and special needs have been revised over the years, school leaders have continuously struggled to make appropriate programming decisions about special education. In particular, they have been expected to weave special education programming into inclusive school settings and offer equal access to the general school curriculum to students with disabilities and exceptionalities to the maximum extent possible. Moreover, since the passage of No Child Left Behind Act of 2001, they have had to address issues relating to the testing of students receiving special education and related services to determine if they are making adequate yearly progress (Browder, Wakeman, & Flowers, 2006; Riley, 2010). Many of the issues and challenges that leaders face are outlined in Box 1.1.

BOX 1.1

Challenges and Issues for School and Special Education Leaders

- How to be a transformational leader
- How general and special education leadership personnel may cooperatively and effectively work together
- How to establish and sustain a wholesome, positive school ethos, climate, and culture
- How to work more effectively with exceptional students and their parents
- How to become more knowledgeable of statutes and regulations governing special education
- Knowing the age ranges of children and youth who qualify to receive special education services

LEADERSHIP STRUCTURE FOR SPECIAL EDUCATION

Special education is a program—funded with federal, state, and local monies—that is normally administered through local public school districts. Consequently, like most federal education funding, federal monies are funneled through state education agencies to local school districts. Therefore, state education agencies carry out the administrative responsibilities for allocating these federal special education funds along with state special education funds to local school districts. For assuming this responsibility, state education officials are allowed to retain a percentage of the federal funds received to defray administrative costs and to monitor, supervise, and assist local school districts with special education programs, professional development, and related services. In a similar vein, local school districts are also permitted to use a portion of their special education funding allocation for administrative costs and program coordination, and to assist individual schools in providing special education programs and services to students. This creates a bureaucratic structure whereby both general education and special education leaders jointly share responsibility for administering special education programs and services.

This structure, however, can present challenges if and when general and special education leaders do not cooperatively and harmoniously work together to seamlessly weave special education into the fabric of U.S. schooling, wherein special education is cut from the same cloth as general education (Crockett, 2002; Crockett, Becker, & Quinn, 2009). School principals are the general education leaders with the most important supervisory responsibility for leading and administering special education programs and services in their buildings. Yet, it has been noted that most states require aspiring principals to have little knowledge related to special education, and many principals do not believe they have sufficient knowledge of special education law and express a need for additional preparation in special education (Davidson & Algozzine, 2002).

This book is intended to be a resource that proposes tangible illustrations that both special and general educational leaders, especially aspiring and in-service principals, can employ to understand the legal foundations, appropriate instruction, learning characteristics, appropriate assessments, accountability systems, human resource functions, and schoolwide conditions in both special and general education programs. Although the book focuses on special education leadership practices, it has also been written to address the efficacy of general education school leaders and offer proactive solutions to encourage the practice of inclusive problem solving to create a better learning community for all children (Heufner, 2000; Schwarz, 2007). When school leaders make successful learning and educational advancement of students their first priority, all participants and stakeholders in the educational enterprise will ultimately benefit.

The vignette in Box 1.2 demonstrates how both special and general education leaders are responsible for meeting the needs of children with disabilities. Amendments to IDEA in 1997 encouraged and reinforced accountability and greater collaboration between general and special education to improve public education for children with disabilities (Crockett, 2002; Crockett et al., 2009; Dipaola, Tschannen-Moran, & Walter-Thomas, 2004; Scherer, 2003). A better understanding of special education law can foster greater cooperation between special and general education leaders. Being familiar with federal and state statutes and regulations will better equip school leaders to plan and administer special education programs and services for students. For both general and special educators, leadership roles include, but are not limited to, specialized curriculum modifications, the institution of sound discipline methods, specialized instructional and assessment models, and appropriate parent communication (Barlett et al., 2002; Dipaola et al., 2004; Halvorsen, 2009; Hancock & Lamendola, 2005; Podemski et al., 1995). Although their responsibilities may vary somewhat, both special and

BOX 1.2

Vignette: *"A Time for Leadership"*

Toby Johnson was born with a spinal condition that left him paralyzed on his left side. His parents found financial assistance through a fraternal organization and used the resources to acquire the assistance of a special therapist for 18 hours a week at Toby's home. Additional occupational therapy began when he was 1 year old. A state-of-the-art electronic wheel chair was purchased with organizational funds as well.

The next year, the organizational funds were depleted and Toby's therapy was discontinued. One evening, Mr. and Mrs. Johnson were attending a party and met someone who also had a child with a disability. During the conversation, the woman said the local school had resources to assist her child, and since Toby was now 3 years old, Mrs. Johnson should contact the school and ask for assistance. The following Monday, Mrs. Johnson called the school and asked for a meeting to discuss school services. The assistant principal told Mrs. Johnson she would get back to her. After two weeks, Mrs. Johnson received a letter from the assistant principal stating that Toby would be accommodated when he entered kindergarten at age 5 at the special cooperative school located in the adjacent county. Mrs. Johnson filed the letter and completed an application for private assistance with a civic organization.

When Toby began school at age 5, he required special daily assistance with bodily functions. He needed urinary catheterization twice each day, help with eating lunch, and assistance with books, materials, and computers to function in each of his classes. The principal and three teachers met with Toby's parents and designed an individualized education plan. Toby's parents requested continued occupational therapy for 18 hours a week at home. The case conference committee met all of the Johnsons' requests for services but denied the continuation of the occupational therapy, substituting one-on-one work with a teacher's assistant. Trying to persuade the committee, Mrs. Johnson, listed the significant gains Toby made with his therapist, but she could not persuade the committee to continue his occupational therapy. A relative who joined the conference was overheard whispering to Mrs. Johnson at the door, "Perhaps you need to talk to an attorney."

After the conference, the principal contacted the special education director to discuss the outcome of the conference. The director told the principal that there might be some problems with compliance with IDEA. The principal asked, "What do we need to be doing for the child?" The director asked, "Where are the records on the Johnson case? Do you have copies of all correspondence sent to the mother? Who talked to her?" The principal replied, "Are we possibly in legal jeopardy here?"

Mrs. Johnson saw her attorney, who said, "We clearly have some options here. Please think it over; what do you want us to do to for Toby, Mrs. Johnson?"

As you read through this chapter, we suggest that you ponder answers to these questions:

1. Were any errors made by the school administration? What do you think they were?
2. What can the school do now?
3. Who should be involved in finding solutions for these issues?
4. What action can be taken by the school to ensure compliance in the future?
5. What were the underlying reasons that legal blunders were made? What can be done to correct these problems?

general education leaders have joint responsibility for providing an appropriate education for students with exceptionalities, disabilities, and special needs.

Special Education Leaders

Although roles vary from school system to school system, special education leadership positions most often include director, coordinator, or education specialist in special education. Because these positions are usually staff positions, they normally do not have direct line reporting authority over principals and teachers at the building level. Rather, district-level special education leaders usually and typically have responsibility for providing general oversight and support for special education programs and services on a districtwide basis. Their duties generally include keeping abreast of federal and state laws and local policies affecting special education, managing special education funding and budgets, and providing support and assistance for principals and special education teachers. In contrast, building principals normally have direct, day-to-day responsibility for administering and supervising special education programs, services, and teachers in their schools, and working with parents of students referred to and receiving special education services and support. Many times, however, the general school policies, procedures, and guidelines that principals follow in serving general education students differ from and may even conflict with special education regulations, procedures, and guidelines. For example, in the vignette involving Toby, the school was not aware that it was out of compliance. In most situations with general education students, home services are not usually provided and services are not customarily provided for a 3-year-old; however, with special education children, there is a wide range of related services and accommodations that are common for students with disabilities. (See Chapter 2, "Laws and Policy Affecting Schools: Going Beyond Compliance," and Chapter 7, "Transitioning from Early Intervention to Adulthood.")

Children without disabilities coexist in the same environment with students not receiving special education services, yet two sets of laws and policies may be operating according to the needs of the child. It is advisable that both special and general education leaders be aware of procedures that govern students with and without disabilities, and be able to work within the confines of the rules and procedures in order to have a positive effect on the education of all children (Crockett et al., 2009; Zaretsky, 2004).

Strong communication skills are suggested for special education leaders, as their duties require the ability to interrelate effectively with senior-level school officials, state education officials, school building principals, teachers, and members of the school board. Assisting and communicating with parents and working with community organizations and agencies (i.e., vocational rehabilitation and employment agencies) are also a large part of the job, as information about special education programs and services should be regularly disseminated to them. Also, developing procedures and policies related to program development and evaluation are usually included in the duties of a district-level special education leader. In large school systems, special education leaders might be supervising a team of psychologists, psychometricians, therapists, and/or specialists for each exceptionality area. In a smaller system, the position might have the responsibility of supervising a smaller staff, but it may require the performance of a number of multiple duties that are frequently assumed by other personnel in larger school systems. In all cases, however, the special education director is obliged to support the needs of students who may qualify for special education services in one or more of the 13 areas in which students may be classified. These areas are listed and discussed in detail in Chapter 4, "Assessment and the IEP Process."

The special education leader may also assist principals in recruiting, interviewing, and employing personnel, particularly teachers. Leadership in this area requires an ability to match teachers to specific classroom environments. Currently, there is a shortage of special education teachers, which results in the employment of large numbers of special education teachers with limited or probationary licenses (Billingsley, 2005, 2010). In order to fill these positions appropriately, it is essential that programs and teachers be evaluated for quality assurance in intervention and compliance. Because it is a legal teacher certification issue, special education leaders need to assure that those with appropriate training and resources continue to deliver the type of instruction that will meet the needs of children with disabilities (Crockett, 2002; Crockett et al., 2009).

In addition to monitoring compliance procedures, the special education leader will need to accurately prepare reports for federal and state education officials. Furthermore, the position requires knowledge of program budgeting, as special education programs are funded with a combination of federal, state, and local dollars. Thus, fiscal reports must be completed, submitted, monitored, and maintained on an ongoing basis.

In order to provide effective special education programs and services in a school district, both special education leaders and general education leaders, particularly principals, need to understand their respective roles, be willing to work collaboratively together, and jointly share the responsibility for meeting the needs of all students with disabilities or exceptionalities and their families. (See Chapter 8, "Response to Intervention and Inclusion: Facilitating Collaborative Arrangements.") Because the vast majority of principals do not have backgrounds and formal training in special education, it behooves them to work cooperatively with directors of special education in their districts to acquire the knowledge and expertise needed to administer special education programs and services at the building level where the children are served.

General Education Leaders

As noted earlier, some principals are unaware of and/or are uncomfortable with their knowledge of special education laws and regulations, and may forgo, neglect, or mishandle their responsibility for the supervision of the special education program. In some cases, they abdicate their personal responsibilities and allow them to be handled by other support staff such as the school psychologist or counselor (Billingsley, 2005, 2010; Crockett et al., 2009; McLaughlin & Nolet, 2004). For a number of reasons, it is generally best practice for building principals to develop the knowledge and expertise to provide the leadership needed to effectively manage and coordinate the special education programs and services provided to students in their buildings (Billingsley, 2005, 2010). Some tips are listed below:

- District-level directors/coordinators of special education are usually housed in the central office, and they are not readily available to assist in making the many day-to-day decisions required to administer programs in schools.
- The principal needs to be the resident expert in his or her building vis-à-vis special education regulations, programs, practices, and services.
- Most parents generally expect to interact directly with their children's teachers and the principal of the school they attend when the need arises to do so.
- Parents of students with disabilities or special needs have a right to expect that the principal of the school their children attend will have the expertise to competently address the needs of those children in the same manner as she or he would for all other students attending the school.

- Principals who have a clear understanding of special education laws and regulations will be able to interpret program requirements, and are more likely to embrace a philosophy that fosters the acceptance of students with disabilities (Dipaola et al., 2004).
- Principals will be involved in decisions that may lead to due process, and therefore they should be aware of compliance issues related to assessment, evaluation, service delivery, support services, modifications, accommodations, and other specifics of special education law. (See Chapter 2, "Laws and Policy Affecting Schools: Going Beyond Compliance.")

In the case of Toby, adequate interpretation of the law may have been too late. Although the parent requested continued occupational therapy for the student as he made significant gains, the services were inappropriately denied. After the school system had been out of compliance for not providing appropriate services earlier, assuring the parent that adequate services would now be provided for the child may have reduced the likelihood of this parent seeking legal counsel to obtain appropriate assistance for Toby.

As general education leaders, principals who develop a leadership style that facilitates collaboration and cooperation between general and special education teachers reduce the chances for conflict. Defining the parameters of the special education program as it relates to the school—such as scheduling, assistance with behavioral difficulties, and collaborative arrangements—aids general and special education teachers in mutual and shared problem solving. If the school leader participates and assists with these types of arrangements, the program will less likely be perceived as a separate entity, and is more apt to be an integral part of the general education system. Principals who provide logistical, academic, and emotional support to both general education and special education teachers have a stronger inclusionary and collaborative system because both sets of teachers face similar problems, stresses, and difficulties (Billingsley, 2005, 2010; McLaughlin & Nolet, 2004) .

It is crucial that specific laws regarding the behavior of children with disabilities be understood. Because there are a number of misconceptions about special education, many students are inappropriately referred (Anthun & Manger, 2006; Blatchley & Lau, 2010; Klinger & Harry, 2006; Lee-Tarver, 2006). Sometimes they are referred for academic difficulties and they really have behavioral problems or cultural differences (Gravois & Rosenfield, 2006). Behavior problems can even occur when students are not receiving appropriate academic intervention. Students are often referred and no varied strategies have been attempted. As the principal becomes more involved in the referral and assessment process, the probability increases that appropriate prereferral intervention strategies will be used before a student is referred.

In summary, both special and general education leaders:

- Need well-developed leadership skills to effectively discharge their responsibilities and duties
- Need up-to-date knowledge of the federal statutes and regulations that govern special education programs and services and they need to stay abreast of the state statutes and regulations where they are employed as well as local education agency policies that address special programs and services
- Are expected to provide assistance, advice, and counsel to school district officials, particularly superintendents and principals, who are likely to be general educational leaders
- Need to assure that school principals are sufficiently knowledgeable of special statutes, regulations, and practices in order that they may directly supervise the identification, referral, assessment, placement, and development of appropriate individualized education plans for students with disabilities and exceptionalities

- Need to be able to work effectively with parents of students with disabilities and handicaps to provide them the level of involvement (IDEA, 2004, Part B, Section 300.322) and procedural safeguards (IDEA, 2004, Subpart E, Section 300.500 through 300.536) required under the Individuals with Disabilities Education Improvement Act.

In the following sections, we address several areas that greatly affect the work of both general and special education leaders. These include leadership in general and transformational leadership in particular, school climate, culture and ethos, and school reform, as they impact special education and the delivery of special education services to students and their parents.

LEADERSHIP IN PERSPECTIVE

Although it has been exhaustively studied, particularly during the last century, leadership is still an elusive phenomenon. Even defining it has been difficult, as more than 350 definitions have been given for it (Bennis & Nanus, 1985). The common theme that seems to run through the definitions is that *leadership* is the process of influencing others to achieve a goal. Especially during the last 25 years when school reform efforts have been aggressively pursued, an increasing amount of attention has been devoted to leadership and the role of school leaders in school improvement. In fact, it is argued that leadership is the single-most important factor in the success or failure of institutions (Bass, 1990).

In their insightful book, *Leaders: The Strategies for Taking Charge,* Bennis and Nanus (1985) argue that managers seek to do things right, whereas leaders do the right thing. Bennis and Nanus's research, which was based on in-depth analyses of 90 successful leaders from a variety of fields and organizations, sought to identify common behaviors that contributed to their success. A premise of their book is that the wrong things may be done in an efficient and effective manner—to the detriment of the organization. By contrast, the effective leaders were seen as individuals who concentrated, first and foremost, on doing the right things. Specifically, they worked with and through their followers to develop a vision and they were found to be effective communicators generally and of their organization's vision in particular. Moreover, these authors were able to motivate and coordinate the efforts of their followers to achieve the vision.

Most school administrator preparation programs today emphasize the leadership role and responsibilities expected of principals, superintendents, and other school leadership personnel (Razik & Swanson, 2010). As a consequence, the managerial aspects of the role, although necessary, are emphasized less, as it is commonly now believed by educational scholars that standard cookbook, recipe approaches in the training of administrators are ill-suited for today's dynamic school environments. Rather, current preparation programs are more likely to emphasize the knowledge and skills needed to develop a vision, communicate with followers and stakeholders, problem-solve, and work effectively with people (human relations). Nevertheless, Kowalski (2003) argues that effective school leaders today, particularly superintendents and principals, should be able to lead and manage well. Also, school districts and schools are increasingly using models of distributed leadership in which they rely on a variety of individuals to perform leadership tasks. As a consequence, those who are able to comfortably share leadership functions with others make the best leaders (Hoy & Miskel, 2005; Marshall & Olivia, 2010; Short & Greer, 2002). Special education leadership is a prime example of this because those who work principally in this area are likely to have the most current knowledge and expertise in this area. Given the robust environment in which school leaders work today and will work in the foreseeable future as they practice their craft, leadership will be a *sine qua non.* Thus, to enter the profession, entry-level school leaders in regular and special education need to possess good leadership skills when appointed, and continue to hone and develop those skills through continuing professional development.

TRANSFORMATIONAL LEADERSHIP

Since the early 1980s, transformational leadership has been a type of leadership that has increasingly been advocated by scholars of leadership theory. James McGregor Burns (1978) is generally credited with introducing the concept of transformational leadership and having it embraced as a major contemporary leadership approach. Building on the work of Burns, Bernard Bass (1985) further defined this leadership model and helped in getting it widely accepted as a leadership approach in social organizations. In short, in transformational leadership, Hoy and Miskel (2005) assert, "Leaders are proactive, raise the awareness levels of followers about inspirational, collective interests, and help followers achieve unusually high performance outcomes" (p. 397). Transactional leaders engage in "transactions" with followers by exchanging rewards for their services and attempting to provide for their immediate self-interests by satisfying their material and psychological needs. Transformational leaders, however, seek to inspire followers to develop high standards and ethical and moral conduct and to transcend their own self-interests for the sake of the organization and its goals. Moreover, transformational leadership is concerned with improving the performance of followers and motivating them to develop their fullest potential (Northouse, 2007). In other words, transformational leaders are committed to going beyond the call of duty and they seek to develop those values and beliefs in their followers. Moreover, they are committed to the greater good of the organization and they are also committed to providing a high level of service to clients who are served by the organizations or organizational units they lead. Transformational leaders are highly committed to their work, and they instill these values and commitments in their followers. We argue that transformational leadership is highly appropriate for and is strongly needed today by school leaders in general and by those who serve learners with special needs in particular.

LEADERSHIP DEVELOPMENT

To successfully discharge their responsibilities, all educational administrators need to understand leadership theory, principles, and practices. Therefore, they need to have the necessary prerequisite formal education to become knowledgeable in these areas. This formal education is nearly always completed through a university preparation program through which the license to hold an administrative position is acquired. Since school administrator preparation programs normally equip graduates with only entry-level knowledge, skills, and attitudes required in leadership roles, continuing (in-service) professional development is necessary to further develop school leaders' repertoire of leadership skills. Although this is true of all administrators due, in part, to the complexity and dynamic nature of the educational environment today, it is particularly true of special education leaders who need to stay abreast of rapidly changing statutes (federal and state), regulations, and guidelines that characterize special education programs. A broad array of resources are available to facilitate school leaders' continuing professional development, including university coursework, on-line courses, workshops, professional associations, guided reading, site visits, conferences, and more. It is best, however, if school leaders see the inherent value for continuing their professional development and becoming life-long learners to improve their effectiveness rather than having it mandated by an external body or source.

LEADERSHIP AND MANAGEMENT NEEDED

Scholars have devoted much time and effort studying management, management practices, and leadership during the twentieth century. During the first half of the century, these studies focused principally on management in industrial settings, mainly addressing how to make workers more productive and efficient in performing manufacturing tasks. As school districts grew larger in cities and across the United States, primarily through consolidation, the same management practices used in industrial organizations were adopted by school boards and incorporated into how the schools were administered (Callahan, 1962; Razik & Swanson, 2010). Consequently, most programs for the preparation of educational leaders focused primarily on management principles and practices until the 1950s. Around that time, professors trained in the social sciences were added to the most influential educational administration departments. They began incorporating the findings of social science research into the curriculum, particularly the human and social elements of organizational life (Campbell, Fleming, Newell, & Bennion, 1987). As a consequence, leadership theory, principles, and practices along with human behavior were emphasized to a much greater degree in preparation programs for school leaders. However, it is imperative that effective leaders be good managers, so management principles and techniques continued to be emphasized, also. This is still the case today, as Hanson (2003) argues that management concentrates on making decisions about how things should be done—that is, work is directed toward controlling and using resources. Additionally, it is necessary that effective managers employ, supervise, and evaluate employees and manage the day-to-day activities in their organizations.

Since the 1980s, however, with the implementation of school reform initiatives, much more emphasis has been placed on leadership and the role of leaders in working cooperatively with school stakeholders to increase school effectiveness and student achievement. Thus, most preparation programs for school leaders now emphasize leadership to a greater extent than management. Similarly, school leaders today are expected to provide strong leadership while they simultaneously unobtrusively manage the administrative aspects of the organization. To effectively carry out their leadership and managerial responsibilities, however, school administrators must be familiar with the concepts of school climate, culture, and ethos, which are addressed in the following section.

CREATING A SCHOOL CLIMATE AND ETHOS

Schools and school districts both have ethos, cultures, and climates that greatly affect personnel, policies, and practices. Although the culture, climate, and ethos found in school districts and schools are distinctive, unique, and context specific, they are almost indefinable and powerful in terms of how they collectively influence human behavior in educational organizations (Green, 2010; Owens, 1998). *Culture* is generally defined as the values, belief systems, norms, and ways of thinking that are characteristic of people in an organization (Owens, 1998); whereas *climate* is generally defined as the characteristics of the total school environment (Marshall & Oliva, 2010; Miskel & Ogawa, 1988). Although the terms *organizational culture* and *organizational climate* are frequently used interchangeably, technically they are different. Organizational culture is defined as the social or normative glue that holds an organization together and expresses the values and beliefs that (organization) members come to share (Smircich, 1983). Organizational climate is deemed to be a subset of culture, and consists primarily of human interactions in the organization. In individual schools, it is the quality and frequency of interactions among staff members, between staff members and students, between and among students, and between staff members and parents and the community.

Although scholars of culture generally refer to it as "the way we do things around here," it is normally deemed to be one of four factors that determine the organizational climate. Including *culture,* Tagiuri (1968) describes the other three dimensions as ecology, milieu, and the social system. He defines *ecology* as the physical and material factors in the organization (i.e., age, size, design, and condition of the building(s) and technology used by employees). *Milieu* is the social dimension of the organization, including the number of people and what they are like demographically. The *social system* refers to the organizational and administrative structure of the organization, including how the school system (or school) is organized, how decisions are made and who makes them, communication patterns, work groups, and so on. Collectively, these four dimensions make up the organizational climate in all organizations, including schools. Depending on the overall efficacy of these dimensions, the school climate may be positive, wholesome, open, and effective, or, at the other extreme, it may be negative, closed, toxic, and ineffective.

Ethos is a term that is sometimes used interchangeably with both *culture* and *climate,* although most organizational theorists distinguish between all three of these. Culture and climate are often thought of collectively as an organization's ethos. *Ethos* is frequently defined as an organization's distinguishing characteristics, tone, or guiding beliefs. Given this definition, the sum total of an organization would be its ethos. This would include its structure, personnel, leadership, management practices, decision-making systems, communication patterns, beliefs, values, history, traditions, and customs.

For any organization, including school districts and individual schools, to function effectively over time, a reasonably healthy culture, climate, and ethos, created and sustained, serves as the glue that nourishes shared values and behavioral norms. Moreover, they establish the "public face" of the organization that both internal and external stakeholders perceive. When the ethos of the organization is positive and effective, usually a mutually beneficial symbiotic relationship will exist between the organization and its stakeholders. In a school a positive mutually beneficial symbiotic relationship means that administrators, teachers, students, and parents are able to resolve conflicts, solve problems, and work productively together for school improvement.

Why are ethos, culture, and climate so important in school settings? It is because they provide an unwritten set of informal norms that inform what actions are appropriate in most situations and they serve to guide employee action and behavior (Deal & Kennedy, 1982). Also, they serve to provide meaning to individuals in the organization and engender a sense of commitment that goes beyond self-interest (Smircich, 1983). Consequently, if school leaders wish to develop a healthy, vibrant, and positive environment, encouraging an attentiveness to the ethos and culture promotes a positive climate for their school districts and schools. When these are wholesome and positive, and they become part and parcel of the fabric of the school, ethos, culture, and climate will powerfully affect human relationships and teaching and learning.

SCHOOL ORGANIZATION AND SOCIAL SYSTEMS: DEFINING THE LEARNING COMMUNITY

Like most formal organizations in western societies, school districts and individual schools have well-established, self-perpetuating organizational structures that endure over time, regardless of the turnover of personnel. School districts and individual schools have formally appointed leaders, professional staffs, and support personnel. In public schools, there is a superintendent who is the chief executive and administrative leader of the district, who reports to a board of education that establishes policies to govern the district and that hires, evaluates, and fires the superintendent. The superintendent is responsible for the general leadership of the school district and supervision of all district-level administrative, supervisory, and support personnel. Additionally, he or she recommends the appointment and dismissal of other school-based personnel and directly or indirectly appoints, supervises, and evaluates building principals.

Similarly, public school principals serve as formally appointed leaders and chief administrators for all personnel (professionals, para-professionals, and students) assigned to their schools. In that capacity, they are held responsible for providing both long-term and day-to-day leadership and supervision for teaching and learning as well as the managerial responsibilities of operating the school, such as handling the budget, employing staff, procuring materials, and managing the care and maintenance of the school facility. Perhaps most important, however, school principals are responsible for creating and sustaining a learning community in cooperation with teachers, students, parents, and the community. A general understanding of social systems theory, in addition to the knowledge and ability to create and foster a continuing learning community supports a positive effect (Gallagher-Browne, 2010; Owens & Kaplan, 2003).

In its most simple form, a *social system* is an organization or a relationship that is established by two or more individuals to accomplish some goal in a stable manner. When the accomplishment of the goal requires collective effort, organizations are created specifically to coordinate activities necessary to accomplish the goals and to furnish incentives for others to join to help (Hoy & Miskel, 2005). Public school districts represent the epitome of complex, well-established social systems—established and maintained to accomplish the explicit goal of educating students. Large, complex organizations like the public schools are formal organizations that are expected to operate in perpetuity and continue on beyond the term of service of individuals who may work in them at any given time. They normally establish stable organizational structures, roles, reward systems, formal codified official policies, and rules and regulations to govern work and employee behavior. Also, they nearly always develop and maintain very elaborate regulations and procedures for recruiting, employing, evaluating, disciplining, and discharging employees. Although they are formal, complex, bureaucratic organizations, they still, nevertheless, have well-entrenched social systems embedded within them.

On a smaller scale, each public school that is a part of a school district is also an autonomous social system, with all the attendant attributes and characteristics. In schools, and other organizations, the people who inhabit them are the central part of the social system. In addition, there is a formal structure denoting rank and statuses, there are special roles, there are explicit goals, there are interdependent parts and relationships, there are rewards for special accomplishments, and there are regulations, rules, norms, and sanctions for their violation. Social systems are also political because there are individuals and groups with different amounts of power, so those with more power can exercise it on those with less power. One of the most powerful aspects of a social system is its normative element. Through it, informal norms become sufficiently powerful that they prescribe appropriate behaviors that become so well known and embraced by members of the organization that informal sanctions such as ostracism and ridicule are often experienced by those who violate these norms (Hoy & Miskel, 1996).

IMPLEMENTING A SHARED VISION

To work effectively together, best practice dictates that both regular and special education leaders have a shared vision regarding the undergirding philosophy, values, beliefs, programs, and delivery models that will characterize special education services offered. In order to achieve this shared vision, a well-established ethos and climate maintained by district and school-level administrators fosters a collaborative, harmonious work environment (Crockett et al., 2009). Trust, mutual respect, candor, and ongoing two-way communication are necessary elements to establish the type of organizational climate in which these will be established and maintained. Regular and special educators are to work cooperatively to provide effective programs and services to students with special needs and their families. They will therefore need to have mutual respect for the expertise that they have about educational policies, programs, and practices that are necessary to coordinate regular and special education programs and the work of regular and special education teachers. If and when these leaders do not have a shared vision, it will be difficult, if not impossible, to effect unity of effort in developing appropriate programs for students with special needs and achieving and sustaining effective teaching and learning in classrooms. Also, most critically, conflict is likely to be a recurring phenomenon when general and special education leaders do not have a shared vision and similar goals and aspirations for special education programs, practices, teachers, and students.

SCHOOL REFORM

Frequently there are laws written that are not special education laws but they greatly affect children with disabilities. Legislation passed in 2001, the No Child Left Behind (NCLB) Act, a reauthorization of the Elementary and Secondary Act of 1965, redefines the federal role in K–12 education. It was designed to help close the achievement gap between disadvantaged and minority students and their peers. The NCLB Act is based on four basic principles: (1) stronger accountability for results, (2) increased flexibility and local control, (3) expanded options for parents, and (4) an emphasis on teaching methods that have been proven to work. The act has created a stir that will increase standards driven educational systems linked to increased assessment. State tests aligned to standards are the fundamental cornerstone of the federal and state accountability laws (Elmore, 2002). Many states have tied monetary awards and penalties to test scores. Public media and exposure of test scores has been intense—in some cases praising schools with high scores and criticizing schools with scores below the state average or expected average (Browder, Ahlgrim-Delzell, Courtade, Gibbs, & Flowers, 2008; Meek, 2006; National Research Council, 1999; Orlich, 2004; Yeh, 2006). Greater accountability of students' achievement and higher graduation rates is the goal.

The possible negative effect the act will have on children with disabilities has been examined (Browder et al., 2006). Meier (2001) and Walsh and Matlock (2000) note that students with disabilities should not be held accountable for standards-based test scores, since there are serious promotion and retention issues related to assessment. The National Research Council (www.nationalacademies.org/nrc/) on Measurement in Education, and the American Association of Research Association (www.aera.net/) strongly support the premise that if students are to be held to standards that have an effect on graduation, promotion, and retention, the content should be covered effectively and well. Schools that tie graduation rates to test scores should take great care to align the curriculum with tests and ensure that all students with disabilities have ample time to acquire knowledge and skills contained within the standards (Little & Houston, 2003).

The probability of the act negatively affecting students with disabilities is compounded when alignment of the IEP to the curriculum is not a current practice in our schools. Similar studies by Dailey (2002), Dailey & Zantal-Wiener (2000), and Roach (2000) revealed that the vast majority of special education teachers lacked guidance about how to align IEPs with the standards; consequently, most IEPs are not aligned with standards. Special education teachers were usually not involved in schoolwide discussions about standards and tended to use the IEP rather than the standards as a guide for instruction. As a result, pedagogy, standards, and content were not aligned with the standards.

BOX 1.3

Advice for School and Special Education Leaders

- Become familiar with normative roles and responsibilities of general and special education leaders in PK–12 education.
- Develop, refine, and practice strong, effective transformational leadership skills.
- Become keenly knowledgeable of the statutes, regulations, and guidelines governing special education programs, practices, and services at the federal, state, and school district levels.
- Develop a fundamental understanding of social systems theory and organizational ethos, culture, and climate and how they influence human behavior in school settings.
- Become familiar with ongoing school reform initiatives and how they affect general and special education programs, practices, services, personnel, and students and their families.

However, there are efforts to find means of assessment and IEP alignment for children with disabilities to be included in school reform efforts, as well as in state and districtwide assessments (Browder et al., 2006; Meek, 2006). Suggestions include out-of-grade-level testing, where the child is allowed to test with those several grade levels below. Partial testing, where a student receives only a portion of the test, is another way to modify exams. Additionally, testing could focus on particular subject areas such as math or English. Other methods include portfolios, performance assessments, and direct measures. On the positive side, some studies have demonstrated that students with disabilities can perform in the same range as their peers when provided suitable accommodations and have reported scores in the same range as their peers with adaptations (discussed in-depth in Chapter 4) (Browder et al., 2008; Fewster & MacMillan, 2002; Johnson, Kimball, Brown, & Anderson, 2001; Thurlow, Lazarus, Thompson, & Morse, 2005). The school and special education leaders can jointly develop plans to assist general and special education teachers to work together to align the IEP to the curriculum in order to address the stipulations of the law. Shared accountability and responsibility is the goal (Goertz & Duffy, 2001; Jorgensen, 1977). Box 1.3 illustrates some key points for school and special education leaders.

Summary

The environment in which public education at the PK–12 level is offered today is complicated and complex. School leaders who work in this environment face many ever-evolving reforms, initiatives, mandates, and challenges as they seek to educate students for whom they are responsible. Arguably, one of their most challenging responsibilities is to lead and effectively manage programs for children who have disabilities and special needs due to the many laws, regulations, and guidelines that govern special education. The legal mandate to provide an appropriate education in the least restrictive environment often tests the mettle of even the most experienced school leaders, let alone those who are relatively new to their positions. Some of the most persistent, vexing problems for both general and special education leaders are identification of students with special needs, assessments, referrals, disproportional representation of minority students, appropriate discipline practices, programming, early intervention, curricular adaptations, response to interventions, testing children with disabilities under No Child Left Behind, and obtaining adequate resources (teachers and dollars) to serve children with special needs. Other legal tips are outlined in Box 1.4.

BOX 1.4

Legal Issues

The legal issues underlying the vignette of this chapter center on when local school officials are required to begin providing services to children with disabilities and their families, and the types of education and related services that schools are legally obligated to provide under IDEA. There are provisions in the law that clearly specify what is required of school officials in serving students with disabilities and handicaps. Relevant provisions for this vignette include Child Find.

Child Find (IDEA 2004, Section 300, Part B, Section 300.111): This component of the law requires states to rigorously identify, locate, and evaluate all children from birth to age 21 who are in need of early intervention or special education services. This places the obligation on local school officials to identify all children, including infants under age 2, homeless children, and children who may be wards of the state who may need early intervention and/or health and related services. Unless another entity in the state has been designated as the lead agency in Child Find, the state must carry out this function through local school districts. Most of the specific information regarding serving very young children, however, is found under Part C, Section 635, of IDEA, which addresses the Early Intervention Program for Infants and Toddlers with Disabilities. Specific disabilities for which special services should be provided are listed under Section 303.21, Infant or Toddler with a Disability. By the child's third birthday, an individualized education plan or an individualized family service plan (IFSP) must be developed to promote school readiness (Section 300.124—Transition of Children from Part C to Preschool Programs). This is to ensure that children have a smooth transition from early intervention programs to preschool programs and subsequently to early intervening services in grades K–3 and later if needed (IDEA 2004, Section 300.226).

The following are some websites addressing special education statutes and regulations with which both general and special education leaders should be familiar:

- http://idea.ed.gov/explore/home (primary site for the U.S. Dept. of Education Office of Special Education Programs)
- http://idea.ed.gov/download/finalregulations.pdf (Website of the Final IDEA regulations)
- http://idea.ed.gov/download/statute.html (website of the statute passed by the 108th Congress authorizing Public Law 108-446, the Individuals with Disabilities Act of 2004)
- www.nichcy.org/Pages/Home.asp (website of the National Dissemination Center for Children with Disabilities)

Far too often, parents of children with disabilities and special needs have alleged that school officials have been uncooperative, unresponsive, or arrogant when parents have sought assistance and support in addressing the needs of their children. Given the frequency with which the courts have ruled in favor of the parents or their children, the evidence indicates that some changes are needed in school leaders' behavior. Accordingly, we believe that schools leaders of today and tomorrow should answer the call to action and make a paradigm shift relative to leadership in special education.

To function effectively in this milieu, individuals in these roles should first and foremost be effective transformational leaders who are able to induce their subordinates and school stakeholders to cohesively work together for the benefit of all children and especially those children who have special needs. Thus, they must be vigilant, effective advocates for *all* children. In addition, they need to possess the repertoire of knowledge, competencies, and skills expected of all leaders: leadership skills, organizational skills, communication skills, planning skills, decision-making skills, resource management skills, and conflict resolution skills. Most particularly, as noted by Bennis and Nanus (1985), they should first be committed to doing the right thing and they should be committed to doing things right. Additionally, professional educators need to possess the ability to create a school ethos and climate that fosters the development of effective educational programs and the ability to administer them smoothly. The leader's job is not to know the solutions to all problems; the charge is to organize the environment so that people within can find solutions (Barth, 1991).

This book presents and examines innovative techniques while suggesting a combination of skills for general education and special education leaders that will result in proactive solutions. Subsequent chapters will explicitly explain, define, and interpret issues and laws while providing a modem of discussion through situational vignettes. The resolution to the vignette in this chapter is outlined in Box 1.5.

Chapter Questions

1. How do the roles of special education leaders differ from the roles of general education leaders? How are they alike?
2. What are the steps for creating a healthy school climate and ethos?
3. When defining a learning community, what are the most important factors?
4. What is the difference between management and leadership? What is meant by doing the right thing versus doing things right?
5. What are the negative effects of No Child Left Behind for special education students? What are the positive effects?
6. What legal obligations do school leaders have for serving infants and toddlers with disabilities? Who holds primary responsibility for identifying them and seeing that they are assessed?

CHAPTER 2

Laws and Policy Affecting Schools

Going Beyond Compliance

ANN McCOLL

IRENE MEIER

INTRODUCTION

Laws related to serving children with disabilities are unquestionably complex and often subject to various interpretations. There are multiple federal laws that can relate to serving these children, including the Individuals with Disabilities Education Improvement Act (IDEA; 1997, 2004), the Americans with Disabilities Act (1990), and Section 504 of the Rehabilitation Act (1973). Local educational agencies (LEAs) are guided in implementing these laws through a layer of federal agency regulations, guidelines, and memoranda, as well as layers of state laws and regulations. It is no wonder that many school leaders get mired in compliance and lose sight of the opportunities presented by these laws to meet the needs of these students so that they can maximize their achievement. This chapter is intended to help break through a compliance mentality to a leadership approach to laws affecting schools. How a leader addresses these laws can have a huge impact on the entire school and school culture. There are several challenges and issues that will be discussed throughout the chapter. They are summarized in Box 2.1.

Several legal challenges that face school and special education leaders will be explored, covering topics such as (1) highly qualified teachers, (2) transition services, (3) complaint resolution, (4) alternative methods for evaluating learning disabilities, and (5) universal design for learning. The related law statues are shown in Figure 2.1.

BOX 2.1

Challenges and Issues for School and Special Education Leaders

- Knowledge of the key tenets of state and federal regulations governing students with disabilities
- Ability to monitor the implementation of these regulations to ensure that students with disabilities receive a free appropriate public education in their least restrictive environment
- Knowledge of legal procedural safeguards that protect the rights of parents and children with disabilities
- Knowledge of disciplinary strategies that have proven effectiveness in reducing out of school suspensions
- Understanding of roles and responsibilities as a local educational agency (LEA) representative at an IEP meeting
- Ability to hire highly qualified staff, monitor for effectiveness, and provide appropriate professional development
- Knowledge of a response to intervention model
- Ability to provide students with disabilities access to the general curriculum through the use of universal design strategies
- Ability to move past a focus on compliance to a focus on positive student outcomes

The Individuals with Disabilities Education Act, Section 504 of the Rehabilitation Act, and the Americans with Disabilities Act are the major federal laws relating to disabilities and the schools. The No Child Left Behind Act also has provisions related to special education. In this chapter, the primary focus is on the IDEA and the 2004 amendments. Here is a list of laws addressed in this chapter. The references are to IDEA as amended unless otherwise note.

FIGURE 2.1 Laws at a Glance

Free appropriate public education	**20 U.S.C. §§ 1401(9); *Board of Education v. Rowley*, 458 U.S. 176 (1982)**
Least restrictive environment	20 U.S.C. § 1412(a)(5)
Individualized education plan	20 U.S.C. § 1414(d);
Highly qualified teachers	20 U.S.C. § 1401; 20 U.S.C. § 7801(11) (NCLB)
Transition services and goals	20 U.S.C. § 1414(d)(1)(A)(i)(VIII)(aa); 20 U.S.C. § 1401(34)(A)
Specific learning disability	20 U.S.C. § 1401(30)
Nondiscrimination in evaluation	20 U.S.C. § 1412(a)(6)(B)
Alternative evaluation of learning disability	20 U.S.C. § 1414(b)(6)
Eligibility for identification	20 U.S.C. § 1414(b)(5)
Components of reading instruction	20 U.S.C. § 1208(3) (NCLB)
Universal design	29 U.S.C. § 3002(19) (Assistive Technology Act of 1993); 20 U.S.C. § 1401(35); 20 U.S.C. § 1412(a)(16)(E)
Resolution	20 U.S.C. § 1415(f)(1)(B)
Mediation	20 U.S.C. § 1415(e)
Due process complaints	20 U.S.C. § 1415(b)(6)(A); 34 C.F.R. § 300.348
State investigations	20 U.S.C. §§ 1411(e)(2)(B)(i), 1412
Use of state funds	20 U.S.C. § 1411(C)(vi); 20 U.S.C. § 1411(e)(C)(iv); 20 U.S.C. §§ 1411(e)(C)(3), 1413(a)(4)(A)(iii)
Use of local funds	20 U.S.C. § 1413(f)
Congressional findings	20 U.S.C. § 1400(c)

HIGHLY QUALIFIED TEACHERS: TURNING A CHALLENGING LEGAL REQUIREMENT INTO AN OPPORTUNITY

In the last reauthorization of the most prominent federal law for serving students with disabilities, Congress required that teachers certified in special education also must be deemed competent by the state in core academic subjects (IDEA, 2004). Most school and special education leaders know this to be a challenge, as it is already difficult to obtain special education teachers.

Context of the Law

It is worth noting the significance of this requirement in regard to the history of this law. In the 1997 reauthorization of IDEA, special education teachers were required to meet state licensure requirements in special education but there were no federal requirements related to competency in academic subject areas. No Child Left Behind (NCLB; 2002) shifted the federal agenda by emphasizing accountability for meeting state standards in tested subjects through improving teacher quality and requiring the use of scientifically based research methods. The NCLB law requires teachers to meet state standards of "highly qualified" if they teach the core academic subjects, identified as English, reading or language arts, mathematics, science, foreign languages, civics and government, economics, arts, history, and geography. This shift in focus to accountability for results and greater emphasis on teacher quality and scientifically based practices is reflected in the 2004 authorization of IDEA. For example, compare the difference in the congressional findings as stated in 1997 and 2004:

> **IDEA 1997:** Supporting high-quality, intensive *professional development* for all personnel who work with such children in order to ensure that they have the skills and knowledge necessary to enable them –
>
> (i) to *meet developmental goals* and, to the maximum extent possible, those challenging expectations that have been established for all children; and
> (ii) to be prepared to lead productive, independent, adult lives, to the maximum extent possible.
>
> **IDEA 2004:** Supporting high-quality, intensive *preservice preparation* and professional development for all personnel who work with children with disabilities in order to ensure that such personnel have the skills and knowledge necessary to improve the *academic achievement* and functional performance of children with disabilities, including the use of *scientifically based instructional practices,* to the maximum extent possible.

Thus, NCLB (2002) and the 2004 reauthorization of IDEA are significant in making special education programs consistent with the overall educational reform agenda: In order for students with disabilities to perform well on state tests, they must have access to the same quality of instruction in the core academic subjects by having highly qualified teachers who use scientifically based practices.

The Individuals with Disabilities Education Act (2004) requires special education teachers to be "highly qualified" if they teach "core academic subjects." This reauthorization draws on the definitions for these terms in NCLB (2002). Also, IDEA follows NCLB in establishing the means by which veteran and new teachers demonstrate competence, with some nuances related to whether the special education teacher exclusively teaches students who are tested on alternative achievement standards and whether competence in one of the core subjects has already been established through licensure (IDEA, 2004). Veteran teachers who lack licensure in the academic subjects must demonstrate competence through successful completion of a state evaluation prepared specifically for the purpose of demonstrating competence in core academic subjects (i.e., High, Objective, Uniform State Standard of Evaluation, or HOUSSE). New teachers, with limited exceptions for when teaching multiple core subject areas, must demonstrate competence by obtaining appropriate licensure in the core academic subject areas as well as licensure as a special education teacher (IDEA, 2004).

Challenges in Meeting the Requirements

There are three major challenges in meeting the highly qualified requirement: (1) the existing teacher shortage in special education would make it difficult to find new teachers who have met all of the licensure requirements, (2) veteran teachers may be resistant to taking the state exam and may need additional training to meet content standards, and (3) principals will be challenged in minimizing the anxiety around the requirements. Sometimes principals become concerned because they are often told of new mandates after the fact and pass that feeling of anxiousness to their teachers. Instead, leaders can obtain the facts from their personnel department on state licensure standards so they can assist their staff in meeting these requirements.

Creative Solutions for Special and General Educators

- Inclusion encourages teachers to educate students with disabilities in general education classes. Coteaching provides collaborative efforts for these teachers, thereby providing students with appropriate course content as well as adaptive methodologies. In a cotaught classroom, the models may range from one teacher (either general or special educators), to one assistant, to a true team approach where both teachers take turns teaching the course content. Inclusion is also consistent with the IDEA least restrictive environment requirement to provide students with disabilities access to the general curriculum to the maximum extent possible. Using coteaching practices can increase student access and success while maintaining highly qualified staff in the core academic subjects.
- To be competent, the special education teacher must develop enough familiarity in core content to be able to effectively partner with the general education teacher. The general education teacher should be strong in core content in order to develop a partnership with the special educator while having some understanding of disabilities and alternative methods for instruction.
- Professional development of both general and special educators would bring these teachers together as a team focused on instruction. Cross-training in content and adaptations at the preservice level would also facilitate coteaching efforts.
- Collaboration among general and special education leaders at the central office tends to facilitate more joint professional development, expectations for school-level collaboration, and more partnerships between general and special education teachers. In addition, the expectations of the building-level administrator set the tone for the two disciplines working in isolation or in collaboration.

TRANSITION SERVICES AND THE LAW

Since 1994, IDEA has included requirements for transition services for children with disabilities. With the reauthorization in 2004, Congress changed the child's age in which schools needed to begin this planning from age 14 to age 16 and shifted emphasis from work training to postsecondary educational goals. Several states have opted to exceed the federal requirement of age 16 and have kept the age at 14 or even younger.

Context of the Law

It is important to recognize the significance placed in special education laws on the individual plans provided for students. The transition plan for a student is a part of the individualized education plan (IEP). Although Congress has tried to reduce "paperwork and requirements that do not assist in improving educational results," the IEP is still the vehicle for ensuring the delivery of appropriate special education and related services (IDEA, 2004). The IEP (discussed at length in Chapter 4 "Assessment and the IEP Process") includes (1) measurable academic and functional goals; (2) a description of the special education, related services, supplementary aids and services, and program modifications or supports; (3) an explanation to support the extent to which the child will not participate with children without disabilities in the regular class and related activities; and (4) a statement of any accommodations needed for participating in the statewide testing programs, or alternatively, an explanation of the use of an alternative assessment (IDEA, 2004). The transition plan is yet another facet of identifying appropriate education and services and is intended to help achieve the policy goals of IDEA of "helping children with disabilities achieve equality of opportunity, full participation, independent living and economic self-sufficiency" (IDEA, 2004).

What the Law Requires

The 2004 reauthorization of IDEA required local education agencies to include in the IEP a statement of transition services from school to work for exceptional children that would begin at age 16. The 1997 reauthorization became more specific and required that a statement of transition services begin at age 14 (Latham, Latham, & Mandlawitz, 2008). The 2004 reauthorization changed the age back to 16 years old and requires measurable postsecondary goals related to training, education, employment, and, where appropriate, independent living skills (IDEA, 2004). The plan also must identify the transition services needed to reach these goals. These services require a "results-oriented process . . . focused on improving the academic and functional achievement of the child with a disability" (IDEA, 2004). As a part of the IEP, the transition plan is to be developed as a part of the IEP team process and has all the procedural protections related to the IEP process and challenging IEPs (IDEA, 2004). Congress places great importance on the transition plan, finding that "providing effective transition services to promote successful post-school employment or education is an important measure of accountability for children with disabilities" (IDEA, 2004). The vignette in Box 2.2 provides an illustration of pending complications if appropriate procedures are not observed.

Connecting the Dots to Educational Reform

Although it might be possible to think of transition services (discussed further in Chapter 7, "Transitioning from Early Intervention to Adulthood") as simply one element of an IEP that therefore affects only a relatively small portion of the student population, a strong education leader will instead look for how these new requirements relate to other education reform initiatives. *Failing high schools* is a phrase so commonly used that most educators can immediately visualize the statistics behind the label: increased dropout rates, decreased graduation rates, low state test scores, and poor performance at the postsecondary level. As a result, scholars and practitioners are seeking strategies and new ways to conceptualize high schools (Cohen, 2001; Finn, 2002; McNeil, 2003). If leaders want to develop a cohesive approach to high schools, they will consider how these changes for transition services relate to serving all students. The shift in age from 14 to 16 raises questions about when decisions are made for children about their education.

BOX 2.2

Vignette: *"Breaking the Compliance Mentality"*

Donny is a 17-year-old twelfth-grade student with Down Syndrome who has a mild cognitive impairment, good social skills, and excellent parental support. He has been included in many general education classes most of his career and is an excellent trumpet player. Currently, he plays the trumpet in the high school band. Donny has been successful in school but his mother worries about what the future holds for him. There is some funding from the state for students like Donny to continue in a four-year college program, and Donny has expressed interest in playing the trumpet for a local college band. He works in the community as a stock clerk at the local grocery store and is supported by a job coach. His mother worries about her son working on his own and whether or not he will be able to live independently in the years to come.

Donny's mother arrived at the IEP meeting in which transition to postsecondary services was to be discussed. She came armed with stacks of information she had downloaded from the Internet. She had gone to national websites to learn more about transition services and then had visited local community and state websites to find out about particular programs and resources. She enthusiastically shared what she had learned. Donny also told the team how much he wanted to play the trumpet at the local college next year.

The assistant principal, serving as the LEA representative, listened for a while, and then said he had to leave in a few minutes to supervise the buses. Then, Donny's general education teacher said he had to conduct band practice. At that moment the exceptional children's coordinator explained that they had many documents to work through, so prewritten transition goals, objectives, and service descriptions had already been prepared in advance. Donny's mother had never seen these goals before and still had more to say about what she wanted for her son's future. Donny also had more that he wanted to say. As the teacher was passing out the forms and members of the team began reading, the parent slammed down her materials, and said in a voice shaking with emotion "I have never seen these goals before. You didn't ask me for suggestions. All you people care about is filling out your forms so you don't get into trouble. You don't even care about my son or his ideas for his future." She then walked out of the meeting.

1. How could the IEP team have avoided this unpleasant situation?
2. Who is responsible for ensuring that the meeting participants are available for the length of the meeting?
3. What is the role of the LEA representative in this meeting?
4. What could have been done prior to determine the student's employability and interest levels?
5. What is the purpose of an IEP meeting where transition goals are discussed?
6. Why would having pre-written goals and objectives cause the parent to feel this way?
7. How could the team members have changed their action to ensure a greater benefit for this student?

The answer varies from state to state or even by locality, but the key questions remain the same: (1) When are decisions made about high school course selection?, (2) How does course selection affect the nature of the diploma granted?, and (3) When are decisions made about whether students with disabilities participate in the testing program?

The original purpose of the 1997 change to age 14 was to help students make successful transitions to high school and then to work. If an LEA waits until a student is 16 to begin to develop a course of study, valuable time may be lost for the student (O'Leary, 2005). To examine the process further, O'Leary (2005) provides a framework for assessing the course of study for a student in a transition program. Leaders must assure that the state plan should:

- Be long-range and specify all required courses and educational experiences that will help a student prepare for transition from high school to postsecondary status.
- Contain measurable postsecondary goals related to a set of appropriate activities.
- Focus on how it will help the student be successful through the transition.
- Assist the student and family in helping the student design the most successful steps for reaching his or her goals.

In order to meet the first part of this framework, it is necessary to connect the transition plan with the state-required diploma options. For example, in the state of North Carolina, students are required to develop career pathways in the eighth grade. These pathways then affect the type of diploma received at graduation. The pathway, referred to as the Occupational Course of Study (OCS), requires students to take the same core curricular areas as other pathways with flexibility for the IEP team to design appropriate work-study courses (North Carolina Department of Public Instruction, 2001a). The OCS pathway requires detailed planning so that the student will receive the appropriate number of credits, job shadowing opportunities, internships, and apprenticeships in a timely and sequential manner. Transition services align directly with making these choices of a career pathway. There is no reason why the practice currently in place of including transition services in the IEP at age 14 should be discontinued, since eighth-grade students are required to have a career pathway. The law does not preclude a school system from developing plans earlier. Students are better served by developing these plans in coordination with other programs so that general and special education can collaborate on how to assist students with reaching their goals.

Developing appropriate postsecondary goals for students with disabilities will also change the way schools have traditionally considered their role. Through the IEP, the school must develop goals related to training, continuing education, employment, and/or independent living. This will be a challenge for IEP members who are used to writing short-term goals and objectives and who may be unfamiliar with transition assessments, tools, and strategies that may be age appropriate for students older than high school age (O'Leary, 2005; Williams, 2005). Although IDEA (2004) does not include the language of the 1999 IDEA amendments requiring linkages to other agencies, this change will be impossible to implement without interagency dialogue and participation (O'Leary, 2005). These changes will necessitate greater involvement of the vocational rehabilitation system and coordination among agencies in supporting the transition of children to postsecondary activities.

Although only students with IEPs receive these goals, a critical element of high school reform is connecting the high school with the community of work and further education. All children need assistance in understanding their options and in being prepared to take the next step. Working on transition services will require the school system to work internally between the Special Education Department and the Career Technical Programs in order to determine which technical courses are appropriate for transition students. To the benefit of all students, the school district must establish and expand liaisons with business, industry, and community colleges, and develop relationships with the Chamber of Commerce. The state department can also play a role by allocating some of its reserved funds for developing and implementing transition programs (IDEA, 2004). New federal monies through American Recovery and Reinvestment Act of 2009 have indicated transition as a priority item.

Creative Solutions

- Students should be actively involved in their transition planning at younger ages as appropriate. Promoting self-determination has produced positive outcomes related to transition planning.
- Appropriate transition assessment should precede goal planning. Students should receive individual conferences with counselors and teachers prior to IEP team meetings regarding the results of the assessment.
- Courses should be selected early enough so that students can complete their chosen course of study.
- All appropriate agencies should be involved in transition planning so that all options can be explored for students.

RESOLUTIONS AND MEDIATION

From its inception, a critical element of the laws for students with disabilities has been to provide parents with the right to utilize processes to challenge whether the school is meeting its legal obligations. Concerned that the processes in place did not adequately address parental needs, Congress added a new process in the 2004 reauthorization. Parents can now avail themselves of voluntary dispute resolution prior to mediation or hearing (Hazelkorn, Packard, & Douvanis, 2008; Zirkel & Gischlar, 2008).

Context for the Law

Parents have several options for resolving disagreements with a school. The first avenue is within the regular IEP process: Parents can request that the IEP team address any aspect of the IEP, including related services and placement (IDEA, 2004). It is only when this process is not effective that parents usually pursue the other avenues provided to them. One option is to lodge a complaint with the state department and request an investigation (IDEA, 2004). This process may be effective when the school is not complying with the provisions in the IEP. For example, the IEP may specify that physical therapy be provided twice a week and the parent is complaining that it has been two months since the child received any physical therapy. On the other hand, if the parent is complaining that the IEP should provide for physical therapy every day instead of twice of week as currently stated in the IEP, the state department is unlikely to formally intervene through the complaint process to judge the adequacy or appropriateness of the IEP. For this kind of challenge, parents can file a due process complaint and will be afforded the right to a hearing. This "due process complaint" can be used to challenge virtually any matter related to the identification, evaluation, educational placement, or provision of a free appropriate public education (FAPE) to the child (IDEA, 2004).

These hearings can be time consuming, highly adversarial, and expensive due to the cost of legal representation and expert witnesses. Congress established in its findings in the reauthorization that parents and schools "should be given expanded opportunities to resolve their disagreements in positive and constructive ways" (IDEA, 2004). These expanded opportunities are mediation and resolution. The 2004 reauthorization of IDEA requires all states to establish and implement a process by which mediation can be used as an alternative to resolving conflicts. The primary goal of mediation is to resolve the complaint between the two parties by a neutral intermediary. Many of the parameters for the mediation are stipulated by IDEA, with the intention that it is accessible to parents and that the mediator is both neutral and knowledgeable about special education law requirements. The state bears the entire fiscal responsibility for the mediation process so that cost is not a deterrent to either the LEA or parents in pursuing mediation (IDEA, 2004).

What the Law Requires

With the 2004 reauthorization of IDEA, Congress added resolution as another means of avoiding due process hearings. Under this provision, the LEA has 15 days from a parent's filing of the due process complaint to hold a "preliminary meeting." This meeting can be waived only if both the parents and LEA agree in writing to waive the meeting or if they both agree to go to mediation (IDEA, 2004). The meeting must include the parents, an LEA representative with decision-making authority (for finances and/or services, depending on the nature of the dispute), and members of the IEP team with specific knowledge of the facts identified in the complaint. The LEA cannot have an attorney present unless the parents bring an attorney, although there is nothing to preclude the LEA from consulting with its attorney before agreeing to a resolution. If a resolution is reached, the agreement is legally binding in both state and federal courts (IDEA, 2004). However, parties have three days in which to change their minds and nullify the agreement. If this happens, they can pursue mediation or the due process hearing.

Creative Solutions for School and Special Education Leaders

- General education curriculum specialists can provide increased support to special education teachers in order to improve teachers' subject area knowledge and provide them with new resources and methods. Conversely, special education teachers can do the same with various strategies and adaptive methodologies. This proactive approach is consistent with congressional findings that professional development for all personnel who work with children with disabilities should include "the use of scientifically based instructional practices, to the maximum extent possible" (IDEA, 2004).
- Scientifically based instructional practices should be used routinely. The 2004 reauthorization requires that special education and related services identified in the IEP be "based on peer-reviewed research to the extent practicable" (IDEA, 2004). It may be difficult for teachers to always articulate practices based on research, but the curriculum specialist and special education leaders can help make sure teachers are familiar with varied approaches and practices and that appropriate choices are made in preparing the IEP.
- Provide impartial facilitators at IEP team meetings. This kind of support should reduce parental complaints.
- Communicate with parents throughout the entire process. Disputes often arise because of miscommunication. Be sure to identify someone at the central office that parents can contact when they have a dispute with the school staff, principal, or IEP team.

ALTERNATIVE METHODS FOR EVALUATING LEARNING DISABILITIES

The way in which disabilities are defined and labeled has been one of the most controversial aspects of special education law. The definition for *learning disabled* is no exception. After hearing complaints from scholars and practitioners alike, Congress decided not to require LEAs to use the definition that is based on an achievement and ability discrepancy model. Instead, Congress said schools could base identification on the response to scientific, research-based interventions (discussed further in Chapter 8 "Response to Intervention and Inclusion: Facilitating Collaborative Arrangements"). In a local education agency that has embraced participation of all leaders, special education and general, it should be desired and even expected that all leaders contribute to discussions on when the LEA should take advantage of flexibility in the law.

A *specific learning disability* is a disorder in basic psychological processes that results in "the imperfect ability to listen, think, speak, read, write, spell, or do mathematical calculations" (IDEA, 2004). The disorders include conditions such as "perceptual disabilities, brain injury, minimal brain dysfunction, dyslexia, and developmental aphasia. It does not include visual, hearing, or motor disabilities, mental retardation, emotional disturbance or problems resulting from environmental, cultural, or economic disadvantage" (IDEA, 2004). Nearly half of the students considered eligible for special education services under IDEA are considered specific learning disabled (Committee on Education and the Workforce, cited in Boehner & Castle, 2005). The number of students identified as having a specific learning disability has grown more than 300 percent since 1976 and now includes nearly 6 percent of all school-age children (Cortiella, n.d.; Mercer & Pullen, 2009).

The 2004 congressional findings address concerns about the overidentification of minority students, particularly at schools with majority white students and teachers (IDEA, 2004). The congressional findings focus on reducing this identification through scientifically based early reading programs, positive behavioral interventions and supports, and early intervention services. In addition, the law requires that materials and processes used in evaluation and placement not be racially or culturally discriminatory (IDEA, 2004).

For decades, the measurement process used for determining this disability has been operationalization (Mercer & Pullen, 2009; Visser, 2002). *Operationalization* is the discrepancy between a student's achievement level and potential. Achievement level has typically been determined by class work and grades, whereas some form of standardized test score or IQ has determined potential. A student was considered learning disabled if a discrepancy existed of more than one standard deviation. The language in the law did not specify the size of the discrepancy, so states determined their own guidelines. Therefore, a child may have a learning disability in one state but move to another state and not be deemed eligible to have a learning disability in that state.

What the Law Allows

The 2004 reauthorization of IDEA allows LEAs to eliminate the IQ–achievement discrepancy in evaluating whether a child has a learning disability. The new law states, "A local education agency shall not be required to take into consideration whether a child has a severe discrepancy between achievement and intellectual ability." Instead, a local education agency may use the response to a "scientific, research-based intervention" as part of the evaluation process (IDEA, 2004). Rather than reaching a definitive conclusion, the issues facing an LEA can be addressed collectively in order to decide whether to exercise the flexibility. Before exercising this flexibility, school districts should have sound practices consistently throughout the district on implementation of a response to intervention model.

The language in the new law is vague in describing alternative methods of identification. One possibility is to wait until the guidelines to the law provide greater specificity—perhaps with the next reauthorization. Another option is for the state departments to help clarify the alternative identification method they suggest for their state. This would ensure accountability and consistency within a given state but perhaps not across states. Senate report 108–185 states, "In order to prevent radical differences in how local educational agencies determine the presence of specific learning disabilities, the committee encourages States to develop research-based models that can be adopted by local educational agencies" (Klotz & Nealis, 2004; Mellard & Johnson, 2007). For the state to take a leadership role, local leaders should encourage their state to establish a research priority in identifying and validating "response to treatment" or "response to intervention" models.

For example, the state could provide guidance in using the response to intervention (RTI) model, which is considered the most promising at this time (Baily, 2003; Brozo, 2009; Mellard & Johnson, 2007). This model involves students progressing through a multitier intervention process. The regular education classroom instruction serves as the first tier. Those students identified as struggling after Tier I instruction are then moved to a second level of interventions, typically including small-group instruction using an evidence-based practice. Students' responses to these interventions are closely monitored and charted. Those students who continue to struggle are then moved to a Tier-3 model or placed in special education depending on the state recommended system (3- or 4-tier model).

Critics contend that LEAs overidentify children with specific learning disabilities. The new language could exacerbate this problem, allowing schools to identify even more students who are simply low-achievers rather than those who have a neurological condition associated with a specific learning disability. Some requirements in the 2004 reauthorization should reduce this risk: A child cannot be identified as eligible if a determinate factor is lack of appropriate instruction in reading, lack of instruction in math, or limited English proficiency (IDEA, 2004). The essential components of reading instruction are defined in NCLB (2002) as phonemic awareness, phonics, vocabulary development, and reading fluency, including oral reading and reading comprehension. Yet, this is a crucial question for leaders to consider in deciding whether to pursue an alternative method.

If response to an alternative scientific, research-based intervention is pursued, LEAs need to consider steps necessary to minimize the risk of overidentification. For example, LEAs will need to identify key staff members who are affected by these changes, including school psychologists, special education teachers, and instructional leaders. These individuals will need to become experts in the area of appropriate interventions and response-to-treatment documentation. General education classroom teachers will then need specific guidance so that they will know if students have received appropriate instruction, struggling students have been appropriately identified, and research-based interventions have been tried and documented. Leaders must be prepared to provide detailed, meaningful training and in-service training if the LEA chooses to pursue an alternative method of evaluation.

Before a local education agency can embrace an alternative method, there must be adequate funding for developing models, training personnel, and implementation. Federal funding for IDEA continues on an incremental implementation, rather than full-funding. In 2009, with the passage of the Americans Recovery and Reinvestment Act (ARRA), IDEA funding to local educational agencies increased for a two-year period. However, this funding only covered approximately 25 percent of the state expenses for educating students with disabilities. After two years, the ARRA funding created a huge funding cliff for many school districts around the nation. The responsibility of adequate funding then lies in the hands of the state, at a time when many states are struggling with a tight economy. The LEA will want to know whether the state is committed to assisting LEAs with alternative models or whether it will need to identify other funding sources to assist the state with the alternative method.

Creative Solutions for School and Special Education Leaders

- Form a central office response to the intervention team to oversee the rollout of this process.
- Provide systematic training throughout the district on the school assistance team process and key concepts of response to intervention.
- Assign key personnel to assist schools as their school assistance teams implement a problem solving model.
- Design a central office database for all students in the Tier-2 and Tier-3 process. This affords staff an opportunity to analyze student data individually and by school.
- Provide schools with research-based intervention tools and appropriate levels of staffing to provide these interventions.

UNIVERSAL DESIGN OF LEARNING: USING LAWS TO FURTHER INNOVATION

The 1997 reauthorization calls for providing maximum access to the general education curriculum in order to improve educational results for students with disabilities. *Universal design of learning* is a promising concept for achieving access, particularly for students with more significant disabilities (discussed at length in Chapter 10, "Universal Design for Learning").

Context of the Law

The cornerstones for IDEA are providing a free appropriate public education in the least restrictive environment (IDEA, 2004). The seminal court case to discuss the meaning of FAPE, *Board of Education* v. *Rowley*, held that "appropriate" meant that it provides some educational benefit to the child. The *Rowley* opinion also put great emphasis on the individualized education and related services specified in the individualized education plan (IDEA, 2004). Thus, the individualized approach coupled with procedural protections was intended to ensure that a child with disabilities received "some benefit" from the services. The least restrictive environment requires that "to the maximum extent appropriate," students with disabilities will be educated with students without disabilities in regular classes with supplementary aids and services, if needed. The 2004 reauthorization strengthens this requirement by requiring the IEP to provide "an explanation of the extent, if any, to which the child will not participate" with children who do not have disabilities (IDEA, 2004). Added to this individualized approach is an increasing emphasis on achievement in the general curriculum and accountability as measured through the statewide testing program. This is quite evident as NCLB (2002) requires all students be tested and that adequate yearly progress among all groups of students, including those with disabilities, be reported.

What the Law Requires

Under the 1997 IDEA reauthorization, all students, regardless of their abilities, must be given the opportunity to become involved with and progress in the general education curriculum. The congressional findings for the 2004 reauthorization added an emphasis that this access to the general curriculum should occur "in the regular classroom" to the maximum extent possible (IDEA, 2004). The 2004 reauthorization also requires the special education and related services in the IEP be based on scientifically based academic instruction and use of "peer-reviewed research to the extent practicable."

This emphasis on scientifically based practices is consistent with the Assistive Technology Act of 1998 (ATA), which encourages universal design. In this act, *universal design* is defined as "a concept or philosophy for designing and delivering products and services that are usable by people with the widest possible range of functional capabilities, which include products and services that are directly usable (without requiring assistive technologies) and products and services that are made usable with assistive technologies." This definition for universal design is also used by IDEA. Universal design is specifically addressed in the legislation in regard to assessments: The state and district "shall, to the extent feasible, use universal design principles in developing and administering any assessments" (IDEA, 2004).

Although IDEA does not require universal design, LEAs provide access to the general curriculum in the general education classroom, setting in motion the need for differentiated instruction. This teaching theory is based on the premise that instructional approaches should vary and be adapted in relation to individual and diverse students in classrooms: Classroom teaching is a blend of whole-class, group and individual instruction. One way to differentiate instruction is the use of universal design of learning. According to the Center for Universal Design, the intent of universal design is to simplify life for everyone by making products, communications, and the building environment more usable by as many people as possible at little or no extra cost. In contrast to after-the-fact adaptations such as Braille, recorded texts for visually impaired students, or captioned materials for hearing-impaired students, universal design provides a more efficient way to provide access by considering the range of user abilities at the design stage of the curriculum and incorporate accommodations at that point (Hitchcock, Meyer, Rose, & Jackson, 2002; King-Sears, 2009; Meyer & Rose, 2000). This "built-in" access for a wide range of users, those with and without disabilities, is the underlying principle of universal design. And it is consistent with the congressional findings that the need to label children as "disabled" is reduced by use of whole-school approaches (IDEA, 2004).

Creative Solutions for School and Special Education Leaders

There are heavy expenses involved in converting to universal design:

- The LEA will need to convert curriculum materials to digitized form so that it can be manipulated to include captions for all graphic representations and images as well as use powerful video anchors that include descriptions of what is being viewed.
- If LEAs want to be innovative, there are funds to assist them. States can use reserved funds to support technology with universal design "to maximize accessibility to the general education curriculum" (IDEA, 2004). In addition, states can create a "high costs fund" reserve to help LEAs or a consortium of LEAs with the financial impact of a high-need child with a disability (IDEA, 2004).
- Local educational agencies can use up to 15 percent of their funding for coordinated early intervening services for students who are not identified as educationally disabled but who need additional academic and behavioral support (IDEA, 2004). These funds could be used to purchase technology that not only benefits a child with disabilities but also other students with no disabilities. It is a way to use the laws to further innovation.

Summary

In this chapter, a framework is given for leaders to use in addressing key elements of special education law. Box 2.3 can be used as a "quick reference," offering advice regarding situations that are most likely to occur.

The context of the law should always be considered when making decisions affecting local policy and, more important, affecting children. Virtually any element of the special education law can be viewed within a broader context. Viewing a provision within this context is useful for understanding the congressional intent and the importance of the provision. It sets the stage for considering different ways to treat the provision. The congressional findings are one important source for better understanding the purpose of the legislation. The next stage is always to be very clear about what the law requires. Leaders should look directly at the law rather than relying solely on interpretations by others. It is important at this stage to be extremely clear about precisely what the law requires and allows. Leaders can work with the team of educators to identify the challenges. In response to challenges, leaders can look for the most obvious routes to addressing the challenges, and also seek creative opportunities to reach win-win situations.

It is critical to be able to link legislation with education reform at a national, state, or local level. Leaders can always connect an element of the law with other reforms. For example, how does the requirement align with the school or school district's vision and goals? Because federal legislation influences state regulations, it is also important to consider how legislation such as IDEA (2004) links to other federal reforms, such as NCLB (2002), and how is the state implementing these reforms. Although there are attempts at consistency across states, one of the criticisms of NCLB in particular is that there was so much disparity among states in implementation. The clear purpose in making these connections is so that leaders can implement a cohesive vision rather than fragmented requirements. After identifying the potential relationship to other reforms, regular and special education leaders should work together in identifying how to best implement the requirements for a cohesive choice.

Whenever the law *allows* rather than *requires* an approach, leaders have the opportunity to think carefully, deliberately, and creatively about whether to exercise the flexibility. Leaders must consider if exercising flexibility will help the school district meet the particular needs of all students, including those students with disabilities.

Sometimes the legal requirements relate to an outcome rather than a process, or the requirement is relatively broad rather than with detailed specifications. In these instances, strong leaders will seek opportunities for innovation. Being an advocate for all children is the bottom line, in that by moving beyond

---

BOX 2.3

Advice for School and Special Education Leaders

- Understand your state regulations as they relate to interpretation to federal statutes and regulations. Be aware if your state exceeds or differs from federal legislation.
- Develop central office leadership teams that collaborate and are cross-functional across departments. Provide collaborative professional development to both general and special educators.
- When implementing a district policy, form a team consisting of central office, school, and local stakeholders. Design an effective rollout plan with built-in follow-up and monitoring.
- School and district staff should be trained as facilitators at IEP team meetings so that communication disputes can be resolved at that level, thereby reducing the need for further litigation.
- Become knowledgeable about research-based practices that are effective and develop a system for monitoring the fidelity of their implementation.

BOX 2.4

Resolution of the Vignette

Another meting could be scheduled, giving the parent and child time to share their ideas, goals, and hopes for the future. A conference could be held prior to the meeting with the student so that he could participate in his own transition planning. A curriculum could be utilized to assist the student in transition planning.

---

compliance means that schools will better serve students with disabilities and by doing so, will meet the legal, moral, and ethical responsibility to advocate and meet the needs of all children. For some educators, the disposition may already exist and it is only a matter of developing the skills. For those who need to change their beliefs, going through these steps will help them do so until their belief system has changed.

Any aspect of special education law can be taken through this framework by general and special education leaders. It will transform the approach to laws from a compliance mentality to a springboard for even better strategies for improving educational opportunities for all children. In the case of Donny, the vignette in this chapter, the situation leading to the angry parent would never have happened with an innovative team,

and that is because the IEP team would have met the parent's enthusiasm with its own enthusiasm for how transition services can be creatively addressed. The IEP team would have welcomed the parent's information, and, if necessary, rescheduled for an additional meeting in order to have time to consider the information and make any further contacts. Perhaps some education leaders might think that they don't have the time to expend on one child like this. But the innovative leader recognizes that time spent at the leadership level to seek better solutions as a system will pay off when working with individual children, and that challenges with individual children will sometimes help point out problems with the system. Innovative leaders always seek to make the system work better for every child, just as the resolution to the vignette presented in Box 2.4.

Chapter Questions

1. With the goal of accurately identifying and effectively serving students with learning impairments, what are the constraints in using an alternative model for assessing learning disabilities? What would be the advantages?

2. What role should the state have in pursuing alternative models?

3. In an LEA, who should participate in discussions about whether to pursue flexibility allowed by law? Is it only central office staff? Does it rest with only special education leaders or is it a broad mix of general and special education leaders?

4. There are other aspects of IDEA that provide flexibility. For example, the reauthorization relaxes requirements for IEPs and IEP meetings by eliminating the requirement for short-term objectives in the IEP (IDEA, 2004); allowing the parent and LEA to agree to changes in the annual IEP without convening an IEP meeting (IDEA, 2004); and permitting a member of the IEP committee to be excused in writing in advance of the

IEP meeting (IDEA, 2004). How will you make decisions on when and how to use this flexibility so that students are still well served?

5. Universal design for learning offers great promises for enhancing the general curriculum, but faces barriers in funding, professional development, and persuading those in authority to commit to the idea. Is it worth the investment? How would you go about addressing these barriers? Who needs to be involved in making these decisions among general and special education leaders?

6. The concepts of special education laws can be the springboard for all types of reform: parental involvement, differentiation/individualization, equal opportunities, least restrictive environment, free appropriate public education, and procedural protections. How do these concepts relate to your vision? How can you build on these concepts and the accompanying legal requirements to better serve students with disabilities—or even all students?

CHAPTER 3

School Reform and the Standards-Embedded Curriculum

Louise Anderson Allen

INTRODUCTION

The borders that once separated students with disabilities and their curriculum from mainstream education have become increasingly indistinct. These changes began with the Civil Rights Movement of the 1950s and 60s and increased with the waves of educational reform that occurred from the 1980s into the twenty-first century. Public school education has always been buffeted by the shifting morals and values of U.S. society and these changes are reflected in the content of the curriculum and how it is delivered through instructional practices. School reform now sees curriculum as a standardized state function to be written, directed, and assessed through state accountability measures—all of which have great import for the education of children with exceptionalities and the administrators charged with educating them. Just as society has altered its view on the general curriculum, there have also been dramatic changes on the curricular issues for exceptional children.

The first shift in the format of special education was from the developmental models, developed in the 1970s, to the functional models of the 1980s and 90s. The developmental model "was based on the assumption that the educational needs of students with severe disabilities could best be met by focusing on their mental age as derived from a developmental assessment" (Browder et al., 2004, p. 212). In contrast, the functional model was focused on assisting students to develop a set of priority skills that would allow them to function in their daily lives in their communities. By the 1990s, with prompting from federal legislation and by the collective efforts of professionals and parents, the curricular focus shifted away from functional skills to including exceptional children in general education schools and classrooms (Hallahan, Kauffman, & Pullen, 2009).

Probably the greatest difference between schools of the 1960s and those of today is our increased knowledge of human learning that prompted the development of specialization of educational programs. Today's schools label learners according to their needs, and curricula are developed to accommodate these individual differences. Although educators have a long history of working with students with exceptionalities, before 1975, this took place in special rooms within school buildings, in special schools, or in institutions. Called feebleminded, backward, retarded, and different, exceptional children were linked to "bad blood" at the beginning of the twentieth century and were sterilized so that they could not reproduce. Over the course of that century, this attitude has changed dramatically and now children with disabilities are not viewed as less than human and shut away from the world (Kode, 2002). As important as that progress is, services to these students were unfortunately less than uniform. Several federal laws (discussed later) were enacted that sought to organize all the programs and to determine legally what were the rights and obligations of special educators, school districts, and systems to children with exceptionalities.

The passage of the 1975 law, Education for All Handicapped Children Act (Public Law 94-142), began revolutionary changes in the education of exceptional children because it promoted general education practices for children with disabilities at full public expense. This required states to provide "a free, appropriate public education for every child between the ages of 3 and 21 . . . regardless of how seriously, he [or she] may be handicapped." This is known as the "principle of zero reject," meaning that all students must be provided full educational opportunities and additionally, all students with disabilities must have equal educational opportunities with students without disabilities to participate in nonacademic and extracurricular services. Another law passed in 1986, PL 99-457 (Section 619, Part B and H) extended the requirements for a free, appropriate education to *all* children with disabilities, even infants and toddlers from birth to age 5.

These laws, however, were specific to children with exceptionalities. Although certain segments of the population were focused on that group of students during this same time period, politicians and business people were also looking at public education in general and how to reform it to meet new expectations. Their actions would ultimately affect the education of all students, creating an inclusive educational system impacted by federal intervention for students with disabilities, students with exceptionalities, and general education students. Many of the challenges and issues are summarized in Box 3.1.

The Impetus for Reform

On September 27, 1989, a two-day education summit at the University of Virginia in Charlottesville occurred. The group set about the task of establishing national education goals. The well-publicized education summit marked a change in the way the public would view and

---

BOX 3.1

Challenges and Issues for School and Special Education Leaders

- Addressing and integrating reform within the school for students with disabilities
- Understanding how previous reform initiatives have impacted special education
- Understanding how No Child Left Behind, the Individuals with Disabilities Education Act, and reform and standards for school and special education leaders intersect
- Determining the implications and avenues to make curriculum decisions for all students, including children with disabilities
- Determining effective scheduling models to ensure the participation of children with disabilities

talk about curriculum—a slow but steady change that came into the common consciousness throughout the 1980s. The summit represented a shift in the focus of school reform efforts, as politicians from both political parties deliberately turned their attention away from such issues as school funding and equal access and towards educational outcomes and accountability (Marshall, Sears, Allen, Roberts, & Schubert, 2007).

The general feeling at the education summit was that even though *A Nation at Risk* had been published in 1983, little had been accomplished in terms of student achievement, despite an increase in resources to public education. In a final press release, the conference participants stressed the need for creating a "system of accountability," and called for more systematic reporting of school, district, and state performance, as well as increased parental choice, school-based management, and alternative certification for teachers. Thus, the education summit represents a pivotal moment because it links the politically driven but essentially nonmandated *A Nation at Risk* of 1983 to the legal enforcement of policy in the No Child Left Behind Act of 2002 (Marshall et al., 2007).

Striking for its charged rhetoric, *A Nation at Risk* equated the state of education in the United States to an "act of war" and made direct comparisons between the economic competitiveness of the U.S. economy and other countries, particularly Japan, South Korea, and Germany. Additionally, the report cited a number of "indicators of risk" that included declining Scholastic Achievement Scores (SAT) scores; low student achievement in literacy, science, and math; and poor showings on international comparisons of student achievement. In calling for strengthened graduation requirements, the report stressed the "new basics" as a core curriculum and recommended that all students take a minimum of four years of English, three years of mathematics, three years of science, three years of social studies, and one-half year of computer science. The report recommended that "schools, colleges, and universities adopt more rigorous and measurable standards, and higher expectations, for academic performance and student conduct, and that four year colleges and universities raise their requirements for admission" (p. 27). Without question, *A Nation at Risk* focused the public's attention on education reform in a new way and helped shape the public discourse on reform throughout the 1980s and 1990s (Marshall et al., 2007)

In the few years after the publication of *A Nation at Risk*, the National Governors' Association (NGA) in 1985, created seven task forces to study and report on seven "tough questions" concerning education reform. In 1986, the NGA released *Time for Results: The Governors' 1991 Report on Education*, which reported on the recommendations of the seven task forces and looked ahead five years to 1991. The task force on leadership and management recommended that state governments "provide incentives . . . to promote school site management and improvement," "collect statewide information on the process and the outcomes of schooling," and "reward principals and schools for performance and effectiveness" (National Governors' Association Center for Policy Research and Analysis, 1986, pp. 59–60).

Business Leaders Become Educational Policymakers

Another group eager to take part in the national school reform movement was the business community. Corporate America's interest in school reform became quite pronounced in the 1990s, with business leaders gaining unprecedented levels of input into education policy (Weisman, 1991a). With a membership of 200 corporate leaders representing the nation's biggest companies, a nine-point education initiative was crafted with which to lobby state legislatures and monitor state progress on school reform (Weisman, 1991b).

By the time the nation's governors gathered for their education summit, many of the recommendations that would find their way into the school reform legislation of the 1990s had already been made. Now it was time for action. When President George H. W. Bush and the governors concluded their meeting, they decided for the first time to establish national education goals that would "guarantee an internationally competitive standard" in six areas by the year 2000 (Marshall et al., 2007).

This call for national goals did not go unnoticed by professional curriculum organizations such as the Association for Supervision and Curriculum Development (ASCD) that addressed the various aspects of national and state control of curriculum in its *1994 Yearbook* (Marshall et al., 2007). In the foreword, ASCD president Barbara Talbert Jackson wrote: "State and local governments have played only marginal roles in deciding the content of curriculum. But more and more, as student performance overall continues to be lackluster, and as employers and the news media continue to make comparisons with students in other developed nations, there is a growing advocacy for a national voice in the curriculum to provide coherence and a standard of accountability" (p. v). In 1994, Goals 2000 legislation became that national voice, proclaiming eight goals that eventually became law (Olson, 2006).

School Reform

As a result of these actions by government leaders, significant changes were occurring in the public discourse on education and in the political meaning of curriculum. School reform in the 1990s became particularly centered on *standards* and *accountability*. Throughout this time period, those words, along with *excellence* and *reform*, gained popular usage and attention in the media. The public's interest was spurred by alarm over the dramatic increase in the immigrant populations, the federal budget deficit, a changing postindustrial economy, and the pressures of globalization, education reform became a major vehicle for political realignment in the 1980s and 1990s. In some sense, the political debate over what schools should teach had never been more in the public eye. As this debate moved alternatively between local control and school autonomy on the one hand and centralization and accountability on the other, political analyses focused on differences—as defined by race, ethnic, class, gender, and ability. The national question on education seemed focused on coping with these differences, sometimes by denying them and sometimes by celebrating and meeting diversity on its own terms. The initial result was a hodgepodge of various school reform efforts at the local and state levels that were often played out as a tension between control and autonomy (Marshall et al., 2007; Olson, 2006).

Much like the beginning of the twentieth century, when intensified immigration and urbanization sparked changes in public thinking about U.S. education (Kendall, 2010; Tyack, 1974), the 1990s saw many competing reform efforts come into being as a result of national anxiety over diversity and economic uncertainty. As the political landscape shifted in the 1980s and 1990s, talk on the national scene focused on the "achievement gap." This term referred to persistent differences in average standardized test scores among white, black, and Hispanic students.

Eliminating this gap had been a national concern at least since 1965, when the Elementary and Secondary Education Act (ESEA) became law. This act created the largest federal program in U.S. schools at the time and it had a major impact on the policies in K–12 education by dramatically expanding the federal government's financial and political stake in school performance and student achievement. Also, the ESEA contributed to growing professional interest in accountability since Title I of this law was concerned with creating educational equity for low-income students (McLaughlin, & Rhim, 2007; Nolet & McLaughlin, 2005).

In 1969, the federal government established the National Assessment of Educational Progress (NAEP) to measure student achievement and to provide yearly updates on the state of progress of the nation's schools. The establishment by President Nixon of NAEP and the growing political and professional interest in accountability as defined by educational outcomes were parallel developments. In 1971, Ralph Tyler, who served as the director of NAEP, noted that "ten years ago, the word [accountability] rarely appeared in educational publications and was not mentioned on the programs of educational organizations" (Lessinger & Tyler, 1971, p. 1). The rhetoric of accountability eventually seeped into the public consciousness; and it would be that language and the legacy of NAEP and ESEA that would help shape the No Child Left Behind legislation some 30 years later (Marshall et al., 2007).

As noted, the 1990s saw some of the most profound changes in the federal and state involvement in school reform since the national curriculum reform projects of the 1960s. In the 1980s, access to equal educational opportunities *within* schools had increasingly become a focus of political analysis in the curriculum field by several scholars. For example, Jean Anyon (1980) examined the link between social class and the kind of curriculum one experienced in school. The concern with educational opportunity reached a high point in 1985 with the publication of Jeannie Oakes' influential study of tracking. *Keeping Track: How Schools Structure Inequality* helped illuminate a shift in how school reform was being considered in the 1980s and 1990s. In Oakes' view, "Educational reform should concentrate on making schools themselves fair and equitable places for students to be" (p. 205). Oakes' book presents an interesting contrast with the direction of government educational reform. Her recommendation that "schools should cease to sort and select students for future roles in society" (p. 205) ran counter to the developing obsession with excellence. By 1990, "maximizing equality of opportunity" meant establishing tougher content standards and graduation requirements—all of which has and will continue to have great implications for educators who work with children with disabilities.

School Reform and Special Education

At the same time as the National Governors' Association was focusing its work on general education, the federal government began to intervene more closely in the education of children with disabilities and exceptionalities. In 1990, PL 94-142 was amended with the Individuals with Disabilities Education Act (IDEA), which replaced the word *handicapped* with *disabled,* and expanded the services for students with disabilities, and instituted person-first language (i.e., a "person with disabilities" rather than a "disabled person"). Also passed in 1990, the Americans with Disabilities Act (ADA) extended civil rights protection in employment, transportation, public accountability, state and local government, and telecommunications to people with disabilities. Then in 1997, IDEA was reauthorized (Woolfolk-Hoy & Hoy, 2003). Close to 40 years after the passage of the PL 94-142 in 1975, there have been huge changes in the meaning of an *appropriate education* for all children. It is important to understand that the development and expansion of special education to cover all children from birth to age 21 came about due to the passion and perseverance of three groups; parents, educators, and legislators (Crockett & Kauffman, 1999; Crockett, 2007).

There are three major requirements in these laws that are of particular interest to school and special education leaders and other educators: the individualized education program (IEP), the least restrictive placement, and the protection of the rights of students with disabilities and of their parents. The *individualized education plan* is a legally mandated, specially designed program of study for each child that includes learning goals and a schedule for charting progress toward those goals, services to be provided, and how the student will participate in the regular school program. It is written by a team that usually includes the student's teacher or teachers, a school psychologist or a special education supervisor, the parent or guardian, and the student (IDEA, 2004; Latham, Latham,

---

BOX 3.2

Vignette: *"What Gets Measured Gets Done"*

By all accounts Kevin was a delightful student, although he had entered this school, his third in that year, far behind his peers in the first grade. Given the transiency of his family's living pattern, the school principal was concerned about how this would impact Kevin's success so she asked his teacher to work with the curriculum specialist to design learning activities that would help Kevin learn the state-mandated learning objectives. After working with Kevin by providing evidence-based interventions in general education and determining his response to the interventions, all three educators were sure that he needed to be tested for exceptional children services because he demonstrated no improvement. After much discussion with his grandmother, his legal guardian, Kevin was assessed with a battery of tests as a second-grader, which determined he had a learning disability (LD). A meeting was held with his teachers, his guardian, and the school administration where Kevin's individualized education program (IEP) was developed. Each year, Kevin's IEP goals and objectives were measured. As a result, Kevin was able to progress through elementary school with the LD teacher working in concert with each of his grade-level teachers.

1. In what ways does this vignette signify the important concepts of due process, family involvement, and least restrictive environment?
2. How is the role of the school principal central to the decisions made about Kevin's education?
3. What laws that protect the rights of students with special needs and their parents are reflected in this vignette?

& Mandlawitz, 2008). A *least restrictive environment* means that the educational setting is as close to the general education setting as possible. Over time, this concept has shifted from the mainstreaming of children with disabilities in regular education classes to inclusion, which entails restructuring educational settings to promote belonging for all students (IDEA, 2004; Woolfolk-Hoy & Hoy, 2003).

As you will see with Kevin in the vignette in Box 3.2, these laws also *protect the rights of students and parents*. Schools must have in place confidentiality regulations to protect student records. Parents have the right to see all records related to the placement, testing, and teaching of their child. They may bring an advocate or a representative with them to an IEP meeting. Parents or caregivers must also receive written notice (in their native language) before any evaluation or change in a student's placement will occur. Students with exceptionalities and the procedures used for placement are protected by due process and parents have the right to challenge any placement or IEP decision (IDEA, 2004; Latham et al., 2008).

Although the needs of these children and the advocacy of their parents or caregivers and teachers led to much improvement in special education, there were no federal guidelines for any type of standards to be applied to special education curriculum. With the development of the IDEA and the involvement of the NGA in general education taking place in the early 1990s, as noted earlier, at about the same time reform in standards-based education was also taking place at the policy level.

Standards-Based Reform

The debate on national standards was elevated to the policy level through a series of commissions and reports that began to appear following the creation in 1990 of the National Education Goals Panel. The panel consisted of governors, members of Congress, members of President Clinton's administration, and state legislators. Charged with monitoring and reporting on state-by-state progress toward Clinton's new education goals, the National Education Goals Panel quickly recommended that Congress establish the National Council on Education Standards and Testing to study the feasibility of establishing national standards. *Raising Standards for American Education*, the report issued by this group, recommended creating a body to approve national education standards. In November 1993, the National Education Goals Panel followed up with its own report, titled *Promises to Keep: Creating High Standards for American Students*. This report focused on two of the National Education Goals—Goal 3: Student Achievement and Citizenship, and Goal 4: Teacher Education and Professional Development (Marshall et al., 2007). "The National Education Goals Panel strongly supports the development of clear, rigorous content standards," the report noted, "and it believes that voluntary national standards are essential to this effort" (p. 68).

Promises to Keep (National Education Goals Panel, 1993) recommended charging the National Education Standards and Improvement Council (NESIC) with reviewing and certifying national content standards in eight subject areas: English, mathematics, science, history, geography, foreign language, citizenship/civics, and the arts. Professional organizations would develop the standards and submit them to the NESIC, which would certify only one set for each of the eight subject areas. The NESIC-certified national standards would then be available for use and adaptation by state governments as they developed their own content standards. The report was clear in noting that "the panel would oppose any federal effort to require States and local schools to use such national standards" (p. 68). In addition to being voluntary, the standards must be "academic," "world-class," and "useful and adaptable," as well as originating through "bottom-up development" characterized by "a consensus building process that involves educators, parents and community leaders from schools and neighborhoods across the country" (pp. 68–69). Congress passed President Clinton's Goals 2000: Educate America Act in March 1994 and the establishment of the National Education Standards and Improvement Council passed into law (Marshall et al., 2007).

Another aspect of President Clinton's education agenda in 1994 was state accountability. With passage of the Goals 2000 legislation in the spring of 1994, attention turned toward reauthorization of the ESEA, particularly Title I funds for compensatory education programs. On October 20, President Clinton signed into law the Improving America's Schools Act, a bill reauthorizing ESEA that for the first time linked Title I grants to school reform efforts. This new legislation required states to construct school improvement and assessment plans based on state-developed content and performance standards in at least mathematics and reading. Progress toward meeting these standards was to be measured three times over the course of a student's school experience: between grades 3 and 5, grades 6 and 9, and grades 10 and 12 (Summary of the Improving America's Schools Act). States were also authorized to use Title I funds for schoolwide improvement projects, provided a certain percentage of students met low-income criteria (Marshall et al., 2007).

When the National Governors Association began to take the lead in promoting school reform efforts, many state governments had also become active in legislating various kinds of school reform initiatives. Spurred into action by a Kentucky Supreme Court decision that found inequities in school funding that were in violation of the state constitution, that state's legislature passed the landmark 1990 Kentucky Education Reform Act. This act represented the most sweeping statewide reform effort at the time by equalizing state funding, creating a mechanism for school-based decision making, setting performance standards, and instituting a state-directed system of accountability that rewarded schools that were able to reach the standards and sanctioned those that did not. Kentucky modified that act in 1998 by establishing the Commonwealth Accountability Testing System (CATS). The system put in place a national basic skills test, administered in grades 3, 6, and 9, with state core content-area tests administered variously in all other grades (Kentucky Department of Education, 2000).

The refinement of the 1990 Kentucky Education Reform Act illustrates how the focus of school accountability systems in the 1990s evolved from an initial concern with what Darling-Hammond and Ascher (1991) have called *professional* accountability to one that emphasized *bureaucratic* accountability. Bureaucratic accountability rests on procedural, top-down directives, whereas professional accountability requires teachers to make their own decisions concerning students, and therefore assumes a high level of competency and knowledge. Included in Kentucky's original reform legislation was an effort to promote school-based decision making throughout the state, a response to the Carnegie recommendations that posited the balance between more decision-making autonomy on the part of schools in exchange for increased accountability. Yet, as the 1990s wore on, the question of such autonomy seemed to become lost as states enacted increasingly rigid accountability requirements grounded in bureaucratic management and governmental oversight.

In 1998, the Center for Education Reform, the Thomas B. Fordham Foundation, Empower America, and the Heritage Foundation sponsored an update to the original 1983 *Nation at Risk* report. This update, "A Nation Still at Risk," claimed that U.S. schools were continuing to fail because the gap in the quality of schools was based on poverty and race. Citing these as moral reasons for change, the update offered two main renewal strategies—standards, assessments, and accountability, and competition and choice—as the means to providing equal educational opportunity for all students (U.S. Department of Education, 1998).

By 2001, 49 states had developed versions of these strategic renewal strategies. Not only did virtually every state create its own educational standards but 28 implemented state-mandated assessments, with 17 states instituting promotion and retention standards based on these assessments (Fuhrman, 2001; Viadero, 2003). In the view of some, though, this "whips and chains" mentality dependent on standards-based assessment to determine which schools, which teachers, and which students achieve success is one of the major drawbacks of the current federal law of No Child Left Behind (Marshall et al., 2007).

No Child Left Behind Law

The No Child Left Behind Act was signed into law in January 2002 as the first reauthorization of the ESEA. The act disbanded the National Education Goals Panel that reported on national progress toward the 2000 education goals, surviving even as the year 2000 passed into 2001. No Child Left Behind dampened much of the impetus of Goals 2000 and federal involvement in establishing and monitoring voluntary national standards.

The NCLB Act required states to use their own assessments in measuring reading and math achievement in grades 3 through 8 and to use NAEP tests on a sample of fourth- and eighth-graders every other year. States were further required to demonstrate academic proficiency for all students within 12 years. Schools that were unable to make adequate progress for two years would be required to allow students to exercise the option for "school choice" and go elsewhere to attend school, whether public or private.

National standards became a politically expedient way to symbolically address issues of accountability, to shift the public policy debate away from inputs—or the distribution of resources both in and out of schools—toward outputs that are used punitively. With the politics of the standards debate, the national discourse had been slowly but steadily shifting toward systems of accountability that are used to punish schools, teachers, and principals. No Child Left Behind put the public education system on notice to perform or else, just as Ravitch warned in 1992 when she wrote, "If the public schools abandon their historic mission, if they . . . foster racial and ethnic separatism, they will forfeit their claim to public support" (p. 11, as quoted in Marshall et al., 2007).

Standards for School and Special Education Leaders

Programs for school and special education leaders have also been impacted by the changing economic, social, and political landscapes of the American culture. Due to the global economy, there has been heightened interest in providing business solutions to the problems of the nation's public schools (Crockett, 2007; Murphy, 2001), with important implications for school and special leaders. Additionally, as public schools continue to adapt to a growing diverse population (which includes students with disabilities), so must preparation programs continue to teach prospective leaders how to lead schools that reflect this change in the U.S. student population. In the earlier vignette, Kevin's principal is reflective of this new expectation for school leaders.

A key element to this change in preparation programs is a vision of an educational leader who has a deeper understanding about the centrality of teaching and learning (Murphy, 2001; Olson, 2008) to any school improvement program and/or mandated reform. School and special education leaders must also be knowledgeable about the change process, proficient in practicing transformational leadership, capable of utilizing collegiality and collaborative relationships as the foundation of a learning community, and also be ethical and moral leaders (Murphy, 2001; Olson, 2008). This new vision of the educational leader grew out of the work of the Interstate Schools Leaders Licensure Consortium (ISLLC), chaired by Vanderbilt Professor Joseph Murphy. That vision has now been incorporated into the work of the Educational Leadership Constituent Council in the Standards for School Leaders (see Figure 3.1) and the aligned with these principles are the Council for Administrators in Special Education Performance-Based Standards for Special Education Administrators (2008) (see Figure 3.2) and Standards for Education Leaders (2002).

FIGURE 3.1   ELCC Standards for Educational Leaders, 2002

Standard 1:	Candidates who complete the program are educational leaders who have the knowledge and ability to promote the success of all students by facilitating the development, articulation, implementation, and stewardship of a school or district vision of learning supported by the school community.
Standard 2:	Candidates who complete the program are educational leaders who have the knowledge and ability to promote the success of all students by promoting a positive school culture, providing an effective instructional program, applying best practice to student learning, and designing comprehensive professional growth plans.
Standard 3:	Candidates who complete the program are educational leaders who have the knowledge and ability to promote the success of all students by managing the organization, operations, and resources in a way that promotes a safe, efficient, and effective learning environment.
Standard 4:	Candidates who complete the program are educational leaders who have the knowledge and ability to promote the success of all students by collaborating with families and other community members, responding to diverse community interests and needs, and mobilizing community resources.
Standard 5:	Candidates who complete the program are educational leaders who have the knowledge and ability to promote the success of all students by acting with integrity, fairly, and in an ethical manner.
Standard 6:	Candidates who complete the program are educational leaders who have the knowledge and ability to promote the success of all students by understanding, responding to, and influencing the larger political, social, economic, legal, and cultural context.

Source: Authored by NPBEA (National Policy Board for Educational Administration).

FIGURE 3.2   Council for Administrators in Special Education Performance-Based Standards for Special Education Administrators (2008)

Standard 1	Leadership and Policy
Knowledge	
ACC1K1	Needs of different groups in a pluralistic society
ACC1K2	Evidence-based theories of organizational and educational leadership
ACC1K3	Emerging issues and trends that potentially affect the school community and the mission of the school
ACC1K4	National and state education laws and regulations
ACC1K5	Current legal, regulatory, and ethical issues affecting education
ACC1K6	Responsibilities and functions of school committees and boards
SA1K1	Models, theories, and philosophies that provide the foundation for the administration of programs and services for individuals with exceptional learning needs and their families
SA1K2	Historical and social significance of the laws, regulations, and policies as they apply to the administration of programs and the provision of services for individuals with exceptional learning needs and their families
SA1K3	Local, state, and national fiscal policies and funding mechanisms in education, social, and health agencies as they apply to the provision of services for individuals with exceptional learning needs and their families
Skills	
ACC1S1	Promote a free appropriate public education in the least restrictive environment
ACC1S2	Promote high expectations for self, staff, and individuals with exceptional learning needs
ACC1S3	Advocate for educational policy within the context of evidence-based practices
ACC1S4	Mentor teacher candidates, newly certified teachers and other colleagues
SA1S1	Interprets and applies current laws, regulations, and policies as they apply to the administration of services to individuals with exceptional learning needs and their families
SA1S2	Applies leadership, organization, and systems change theory to the provision of services for individuals with exceptional learning needs and their families
SA1S3	Develops a budget in accordance with local, state, and national laws in education, social, and health agencies for the provision of services for individuals with exceptional learning needs and their families
SA1S4	Engages in recruitment, hiring, and retention practices that comply with local, state, and national laws as they apply to personnel serving individuals with exceptional learning needs and their families
SA1S5	Communicates a personal inclusive vision and mission for meeting the needs of individuals with exceptional learning needs and their families

Standard 2	Program Development and Organization
Knowledge	
ACC2K1	Effects of the cultural and environmental milieu of the individual and the family on behavior and learning
ACC2K2	Theories and methodologies of teaching and learning, including adaptation and modification of curriculum
ACC2K3	Continuum of program options and services available to individuals with exceptional learning needs with exceptional learning needs
ACC2K4	Prereferral intervention processes and strategies
ACC2K5	Process of developing individualized education plans
ACC2K6	Developmentally appropriate strategies for modifying instructional methods and the learning environment
SA2K1	Programs and services within the general curriculum to achieve positive school outcomes for individuals with exceptional learning needs
SA2K2	Programs and strategies that promote positive school engagement for individuals with exceptional learning needs
SA2K3	Instruction and services needed to support access to the general curriculum for individuals with exceptional learning needs
Skills	
ACC2S1	Develop programs including the integration of related services for individuals based on a thorough understanding of individual differences
ACC2S2	Connect educational standards to specialized instructional services
ACC2S3	Improve instructional programs using principles of curriculum development and modification, and learning theory
ACC2S4	Incorporate essential components into individualized education plans
SA2S1	Develops and implements a flexible continuum of services based on effective practices for individuals with exceptional learning needs and their families
SA2S2	Develops and implements programs and services that contribute to the prevention of unnecessary referrals
SA2S3	Develops and implements an administrative plan that supports the use of instructional and assistive technologies

Standard 3	Research and Inquiry
Knowledge	
ACC3K1	Evidence-based practices validated for specific characteristics of learners and settings
SA3K1	Research in administrative practices that supports individuals with exceptional learning needs and their families

(Continued)

FIGURE 3.2   (*Continued*)

Skills	
ACC3S1	Identify and use the research literature to resolve issues of professional practice
ACC3S2	Evaluate and modify instructional practices in response to ongoing assessment data
ACC3S3	Use educational research to improve instruction, intervention strategies, and curricular materials
SA3S1	Engages in data-based decision-making for the administration of educational programs and services that supports exceptional individuals with exceptional learning needs and their families
SA3S2	Develops data-based educational expectations and evidence-based programs that account for the impact of diversity on individuals with exceptional learning needs and their families
SA3S3	Joins and participates in professional administrative organizations to guide administrative practices when working with individuals with exceptional learning needs and their families

Standard 4	**Individual and Program Evaluation**
Knowledge	
ACC4K1	Evaluation process and determination of eligibility
ACC4K2	Variety of methods for assessing and evaluating individuals with exceptional learning needs' performance
ACC4K3	Strategies for identifying individuals with exceptional learning needs
ACC4K4	Evaluate a student's success in the general education curriculum
SA4K1	Models, theories, and practices used to evaluate educational programs and personnel serving individuals with exceptional learning needs and their families
Skills	
ACC4S1	Design and use methods for assessing and evaluating programs
ACC4S2	Design and implement research activities to examine the effectiveness of instructional practices
ACC4S3	Advocate for evidence-based practices in assessment
ACC4S4	Report the assessment of individuals with exceptional learning needs' performance and evaluation of instructional programs
SA4S1	Advocates for and implements procedures for the participation of individuals with exceptional learning needs in accountability systems
SA4S2	Develops and implements ongoing evaluations of education programs and personnel
SA4S3	Provides ongoing supervision of personnel working with individuals with exceptional learning needs and their families
SA4S4	Designs and implements evaluation procedures that improve instructional content and practices

Standard 5   **Professional Development and Ethical Practice**

Knowledge	
ACC5K1	Legal rights and responsibilities of individuals with exceptional learning needs, staff, and parents/guardians
ACC5K2	Moral and ethical responsibilities of educators
ACC5K3	Human rights of individuals with exceptional learning needs and their families
SA5K1	Ethical theories and practices as they apply to the administration of programs and services with individuals with exceptional learning needs and their families
SA5K2	Adult learning theories and models as they apply to professional development programs
SA5K3	Professional development theories and practices that improve instruction and instructional content for individuals with exceptional learning needs with exceptional learning needs
SA5K4	Impact of diversity on educational programming expectations for individuals with exceptional learning needs
SA5K5	Principles of representative governance that support the system of special education administration

Skills	
ACC5S1	Model ethical behavior and promote professional standards
ACC5S2	Implement practices that promote success for individuals with exceptional learning needs
ACC5S3	Use ethical and legal discipline strategies
ACC5S4	Disseminate information on effective school and classroom practices
ACC5S5	Create an environment which supports continuous instructional improvement
ACC5S6	Develop and implement a personalized professional development plan
SA5S1	Communicates and demonstrates a high standard of ethical administrative practices when working with staff serving individuals with exceptional learning needs and their families
SA5S2	Develops and implements professional development activities and programs that improve instructional practices and lead to improved outcomes for individuals with exceptional learning needs with exceptional learning needs and their families

Standard 6   **Collaboration**

Knowledge	
ACC6K1	Methods for communicating goals and plans to stakeholders
ACC6K2	Roles of educators in integrated settings
SA6K1	Collaborative theories and practices that support the administration of programs and services for with individuals with exceptional learning needs and their families
SA6K2	Administrative theories and models that facilitate communication among all stakeholders
SA6K3	Importance and relevance of advocacy at the local, state, and national level for individuals with exceptional learning needs and their families

(Continued)

FIGURE 3.2 *(Continued)*

Skills	
ACC6S1	Collaborate to enhance opportunities for learners with exceptional learning needs
ACC6S2	Apply strategies to resolve conflict and build consensus
SA6S1	Utilizes collaborative approaches for involving all stakeholders in educational planning, implementation, and evaluation
SA6S2	Strengthens the role of parent and advocacy organizations as they support individuals with exceptional learning needs and their families
SA6S3	Develops and implements intra- and interagency agreements that create programs with shared responsibility for individuals with exceptional learning needs and their families
SA6S4	Develops seamless transitions of individuals with exceptional learning needs across educational continuum and other programs from birth through adulthood
SA6S5	Implements collaborative administrative procedures and strategies to facilitate communication among all stakeholders
SA6S6	Engages in leadership practices that support shared decision making
SA6S7	Demonstrates the skills necessary to provide ongoing communication, education, and support for families of individuals with exceptional learning needs
SA6S8	Consults and collaborates in administrative and instructional decisions at the school and district levels

Source: Council for Exceptional Children: Professional Standards Website, www2.astate.edu/dotAsset/118756.pdf. Reprinted with permission.

These standards are intended to "reculture the profession of school administration" through the "reconstitution of university leadership preparation programs" that certify and re-certify school administrators. As university programs seek accreditation through the National Council for Accreditation of Teacher Education (NCATE), more and more school administrators are reconfiguring their curriculum to incorporate the standards. The intention is that the graduates will reflect the knowledge, skills, and dispositions to transform schools (Allen, 2006; Crockett, 2007). Both the National Association of Secondary School Principals and the National Association of Elementary School Principals offer workshops and development programs based on these standards (Crockett, 2007; Murphy, 2001; Olson, 2008).

Curriculum Decisions for ALL Students

Given the impact of NCLB (2002) on curriculum practices in general education classrooms and the increasing importance of information gathered from state accountability systems, there has also been a growing interest in the implications of school reform for students with disabilities and exceptionalities. Even though some scholars have documented that students with disabilities have been excluded from participation in assessments, one of the key components of NCLB, these students have been consistently excluded from the tests by not reporting their scores and by not even allowing the students to take the tests (McLaughlin & Rhim, 2007; McGrew, Thurlow, & Spiegel, 1993). States have begun to seriously review such testing practices and are looking for ways to best include the assessment of children with exceptionalities in the accountability measures (Elliott, Erickson, Thurlow & Shriner, 2000; Nagle, Yunker, & Malmgren, 2006).

We do know that states have, however, made great strides in revising or developing guidelines for classroom accommodations for testing purposes, because in 1991, only 30 states had written policies but by 1995, that number had grown to 43. Unfortunately, between 1991 and 1995, few states were able to document the exact number of exceptional children who had participated in statewide tests. This dramatic change can perhaps be attributed to the passage of the IDEA Amendments of 1997. It placed emphasis on access to the general curriculum and participation in statewide assessments and the reporting of the results, exceptional students can no longer be "exempted without documentation or indication of how student learning will be assessed" (Elliott et al., 2000, p. 39).

The Individuals with Disabilities Education Act established several interrelated goals: Children with disabilities have a right to a free appropriate public education (FAPE) and must be provided with the least restrictive environment (LRE) appropriate to that child. The LRE can be viewed as the vehicle for full educational opportunity so long as effective curriculum and instructional practices are employed in the best interests of exceptional learners. The purpose of schooling is to provide a "full educational opportunity—an appropriate public education that is firmly fixed on productive learning for each student, that acknowledges the reciprocity between student and setting and that marshals its resources under the guiding principle of social justice" (Crockett, 2007; Crockett & Kauffman, 1999, p. 202).

Access to the core curriculum for students with disabilities has been a goal of many special education professionals. Federal law no longer limits LRE to physical placement in the general classroom; also, current revisions to the law indicate that students with disabilities must have access to the core general curriculum especially if they are to participate in the current standards-based reform movement (Fisher & Frey, 2001; IDEA, 2004; Suk-Hyang, Wehmeyer, Soukup, & Palmer, 2010). There are several legal issues that leaders need to remember (see Box 3.3).

Curriculum Planning for Special Education

Children with disabilities need a wide range of school and community age-appropriate experiences; they also need a process that individualizes those activities, making them meaningful curricular activities (Fisher, Frey, & Lapp, 2009). Udvari-Solner (1995) developed a process for curriculum adaptation which includes "the identification of goals and objectives, articulation of the expectations for the student's performance, determination of the content to be taught and instructional strategies used, selection of specific adaptations, and evaluation of the effectiveness of the adaptations" (as cited in Fisher & Frey, 2001, p. 2). Fisher and Frey's 2001 study of nine urban special education teachers confirmed that exceptional students should receive their educational services within the general classroom in order to access the curricula and its supports, including peer support and instructional technology. By incorporating the necessary modifications into daily routines, special education students were successful with the general education curriculum (Fisher et al., 2009).

BOX 3.3

Legal Issues

- All students must participate in a standards-embedded curriculum.
- All decisions related to the child should be done in a collaborative team fashion. Scheduling should assure that general and special teachers work together to assure access to the curriculum for all students.
- All students need to be included in the curriculum, even those with severe disabilities.

Administrators will also need to assist teachers in learning how to monitor and adjust the classroom environment for student differences by:

- Making careful observation of the classroom;
- Listening to students when they speak about their needs; and
- Making physical accommodations to the classroom setting that will encourage success and will require educational leaders to help teachers think outside of "desks in rows" mentality. (Crockett, 2007)

As Kevin's principal did, educational leaders will need to:

- Encourage teachers to seek additional training to learn about students with disabilities or exceptionalities.
- Work with experts in learning new instructional strategies.

In general, principals can encourage educators to:

- Plan a curriculum with standards and objectives that are both appropriate and challenging for students in general and special education classes.
- Assess students' needs and interests, and offer the support necessary to facilitate change.

This information will be useful in developing a meaningful curriculum that incorporates a learner's needs and interests. Leaders and teachers build connections between the home and the community by:

- Inviting parents and families to school for a variety of activities
- Establishing contact through newsletters, phone calls and home visits
- Providing learning opportunities for teachers about the different cultures in the school by offering access to relevant professional literature, community tours, and being aware of popular music, toys and television programming
- Using community resources that are valued by students; the school and its educators are seen as honoring the culture of its students

Assessments of students' needs will include:

- Gathering information from students through interviews, informal observations, and conversations. Interest and attitude surveys will also provide information about students, along with journal entries.
- Gathering information from families and caregivers. Parents are also experts about their children.
- Using a start-of-the-year survey along with informal conversations with parents or caregivers will offer information on past experiences, hopes, and goals of students.
- Previous testing results and other information found in the student's records will inform curriculum and instructional planning.

Linked to these assessments is the development of a meaningful curriculum, which is derived from:

- Materials and topics that are of interest to students.
- Using a problem-centered approach, students will be provided with opportunities to make choices about learning based on their own decisions.

The more opportunities that are provided for choices will help students to develop a more intrinsic approach to learning by seeing it as a self-directed activity and not one centered on a teacher, parent, or authority figure. Learning will have more meaning and will become more important when it is student centered.

Administrators should encourage teachers to:

- Connect the life of the learner and to organize instruction in such a way that resonates with student needs and interests. These learning activities should foster teacher–student interactions and student–student interactions.
- Know how to monitor and adjust the classroom environment for student differences, which may include tailoring instructional objectives and/or modifying expectations in specific areas. In their own interactions with teachers and students, leaders will need to model careful listening and their thinking and learning processes. This should help teachers model the same processes for their students.

By being respectful of human dignity and differences, administrators and teachers will set the stage for the classroom environment that is respectful and where learning and learner are valued. By using concrete examples, visual displays, advance organizers of lessons, along with community resources, and in-class and out-of-class opportunities for study, students with exceptionalities can be successful in the general classroom setting.

Implementing Standards across the Curriculum

As discussed earlier, since the 1983 publication of *Nation at Risk*, meaningful curriculum, standards, and accountability have become dominant topics in any conversation about improving education. Increasingly, these discussions have also begun to include how to accomplish equity while implementing standards-based curriculum for all children. Today, there is a two-pronged focus: what is a meaningful curriculum and how to assess the performance and progress of all children on such a course of study (Chappell, 2008; Williams et al., 2009). Advice for implementing standards is suggested in Box 3.4.

With the 2004 amendments to IDEA and the supplementary regulations, the United States Department of Education made comprehensive changes in the curriculum issues that affect students with exceptionalities. Most conspicuous in these new amendments were the new provisions that relate to Response to Intervention (RTI), dealing with how students would have access to and progress in general education along with how students would participate in mandated state and district achievement tests. As we progress through changes in legislation, students with learning challenges will increasingly receive instruction through multitiered instruction using RTI. The approach, implemented in the general education, will serve as a basic decision-making and problem-solving tool before students are referred to special education. As discussed later

---

BOX 3.4

Advice for School and Special Education Leaders

- Provide teachers guidance and support in developing productive classroom environments that foster learning for all students by helping the teachers develop and build a knowledge base and skill set to work with students.
- Assist teachers in considering and planning for students with disabilities.
- Build connections between the home and the school.
- Remember the importance of the child's culture and how it relates instruction.
- Promote inclusive scheduling models to strengthen RTI practices.

in more detail in Chapter 8, "Response to Intervention and Inclusion: Facilitating Collaborative Arrangements," students will travel through the two tiers of general education instruction before they can be determined eligible for special education services. Inherent to these changes were the expectations (and the compliance with regulations) of the government that children with exceptionalities would be provided with the appropriate instruction plans that would meet the specific needs of these children, enabling them to perform on assessments based on the mandated standards of the general curriculum (Chappell, 2008; Pugach & Warger, 2001; Williams et al., 2009). Schools, districts, and states now have to report the academic performance of students with disabilities and are being held much more accountable for the educational outcomes of students with disabilities. More than ever, school districts and individual schools, along with their educational administrators, need to understand how to best provide a standards-based education to students with disabilities and improve their school performance (Leif, 2001; Rice, 2006).

Much of school reform has focused on curriculum with creation of standards in content areas by professional educator organizations. The National Council of Teachers of Mathematics crafted their first set of standards in the late 1990s. Today, the National Council of Teachers of English, the National Council for the Social Studies, and the National Science Teachers Association have all developed content standards in the data and have passed content standards for students in specific subjects (Leif, 2001; Rice, 2006). As professional organizations, each of these groups seeks to improve its profession and education by focusing on the quality of its respective teachers.

Although special educators had not typically participated in the creation of these standards for general education, there is now a shift in the "legislated focus" on curricula that bring educators and students with exceptionalities into the dialogue of what students will know and be able to do when they have completed a course of study. Even though IDEA still requires that each student with exceptionalities has an IEP, NCLB mandates that outcomes linked to the general education program have become the goal. Students with exceptionalities must be provided with modifications and adaptations of instruction that will enhance their participation and progress in the regular curriculum. Consequently, special education teachers are now being held to similar standards as general education teachers.

As Darling-Hammond (2009) reported in her research, a well-prepared teacher has more influence on a child's learning than any other factor under a school's control. Ever cognizant of the importance of teachers, the Council for Exceptional Children (CEC) has worked for over 75 years to create and implement standards for teachers. Developed for use by colleges and universities that prepare teachers, CEC, along with other professional organizations noted earlier, is now at the forefront in educational reform where performance-based standards are the expected norm for all educators involved in public schools, especially since the passage of the NCLB legislation in 2002. The CEC has developed a Code of Ethics and a set of Knowledge and Skills Standards that represent the knowledge and skill base that professionals entering practice or assuming advanced roles should possess to practice safely and effectively.

Of particular interest to educational leaders are the CEC Standards for Professional Educators (Figure 3.3). These are the principles that educators use in implementing their responsibilities to the students, the school, the system, and the profession itself. They are used by educators to measure excellence in all areas of professional practice of special educators.

Scheduling Models of Organization

The dominant model for organizing schools over the past 50 years has been to assign one teacher to 25 or 30 students, but there has been a move (linked to the crisis attached to

FIGURE 3.3   CEC Standards for Professional Educators

Special education personnel are committed to the application of professional expertise to ensure the provision of quality education for all individuals with exceptionalities.

Special education professionals participate with other professionals and with parents in an interdisciplinary effort in the management of behavior.

Professionals seek to develop relationships with parents based on mutual respect for their roles in achieving benefits for the exceptional person.

Special education professionals serve as advocates for exceptional students by speaking, writing, and acting in a variety of situations on their behalf.

Professionals ensure that only persons deemed qualified by having met state/provincial minimum standards are employed as teachers, administrators, and related service providers for individuals with exceptionalities.

Special education professionals function as members of interdisciplinary teams, and the reputation of the profession resides with them.

Source: Council for Exceptional Children. *What Every Special Educator Must Know: Ethics, Standards, and Guidelines for Special Educators,* 5th ed. Arlington, VA: Council for Exceptional Children, 2009. Reprinted with permission.

A Nation at Risk) that prompted educators to look for other scheduling methods that would make better use of school time. Not only have various state and federal programs been mandated as a part of the elementary school day, high schools have also had to respond to increased graduation requirements, which overwhelmed students with subjects, teachers, books, and assignments. In 1994, the National Education Commission on Time and Learning determined that the traditional ways of organizing schools contributed to both disciplinary and achievement issues in schools.

Additionally, federal laws passed in the late 1980s, 90s, and 2000s helped more and more children be identified as students with disabilities. Consequently, schools were prompted to implement other models, such as the inclusion classroom where a regular classroom teacher works in concert with a special education teacher. Parallel block scheduling is another organizational plan for both elementary and high schools developed in the 1960s that has recaptured educators' attention as it promises to address student achievement, class size, and grouping issues.

Parallel block scheduling allows for varying class size, providing students who learn at different rates with more or less time as needed for instruction. It uses the instructional skills of teachers to create optimal learning sessions. This model is flexible in that it can be adapted to meet the needs of schools with unique populations and resources. Research on block scheduling has shown that student achievement has increased, critical thinking skills have improved, more collaborative learning and teaching practices are employed, and there are more opportunities for curriculum enhancement and student-initiated learning (Biesinger, Crippen, & Muis, 2008; Gullatt, 2006; Salvaterra & Adams, 1995).

Studies show that students were learning more, had improved attitudes about school and teachers, and attached reduced stigma to those who receive services (Garber, 1997; Hopkins, 1990; Nilholm, 2006; Roaf, 2008; Wilson, 1993). Research on team teaching, block scheduling, and inclusion in a high school found them to be complimentary and mutually supportive for students with exceptionalities. Researchers determined that longer block classes allowed for more student-centered learning, which resulted in changes in teaching practices that benefited all students, especially less traditional students. They did offer a caution, however, about organizational and communication problems affecting both teachers and special students in a block schedule (Biesinger et al., 2008; Gullatt, 2006; Weller & McLeskey, 2002).

Summary

The purpose of this chapter was to establish the avenues by which twentieth-century school reform led to the development of curricular changes for students with disabilities and what these changes mean for current school and special education leaders and those in preparation programs. Driven initially by the Civil Rights movement, school reform and standardization are now attending to the educational goals for all children. This chapter highlighted the laws that brought about these changes and it also spoke to standards-based reform and its place in special education, culminating in the NCLB Law. Finally, this chapter also addressed how the Council on Exceptional Children's Professional Standards impact curriculum and instructional scheduling models. School and special education leaders are encouraged to understand both standards as they make their schools more inclusive. The resolution to the vignette is shown in Box 3.5.

Chapter Questions

1. What is your philosophy about inclusion? Develop a position statement and action plan that complies with PL 94-142 (and is consistent with your philosophy) in the school or district you hope to lead.

2. What kinds of programs can school and special education leaders utilize that will prepare the parents or guardians of general education students to understand and support the programs for students with exceptionalities?

3. As the special education supervisor or school leader, what will you need to know about the certification status, maturity level, and educational background of your teachers in order to make the best placement for children with disabilities?

4. How can special education leaders become knowledgeable about the laws concerning children with disabilities and exceptionalities?

5. What resources exist in your district that will assist general education classroom teachers in preparing curricula for the inclusion?

6. How can school leaders assure that their school is in compliance with the relevant school and special education laws?

7. How can teachers best conduct family conferences with parents of students with exceptionalities?

8. Outline the steps you should take to prepare a school to make an orderly and productive transition to inclusion.

BOX 3.5

Resolution to the Vignette

The school is in compliance with the law. Kevin was given the required strategies in the general classroom setting with a specialist before he was referred for special services to determine his response to the intervention.

CHAPTER 4

Assessment and the IEP Process

GLORIA D. CAMPBELL-WHATLEY

INTRODUCTION

According to the Individuals with Disabilities Education Act (IDEA), assessments are required before students are able to receive special education services. Assessments determine if a student has special needs, and they verify educational interventions, accommodations, and the related services a student requires.

The purpose of this chapter is to describe special education assessment procedures and the involvement of special and general education leaders in that process. The chapter will provide insight on the steps from referral to eligibility and the individualized education plan (IEP) process. Also, various informal assessment techniques that are used for evaluating academic achievement for students with disabilities are discussed.

Special education leaders who are proficient in working with building-level leaders are better able to develop and plan effective districtwide awareness, screening, assessment, and placement. General education and special education leaders who have developed an understanding of the principles of special education assessment and who regularly evaluate assessment strategies and methods have a better chance of using techniques that are appropriate (Sergiovanni, 2009). A variety of techniques used with these students improve performance and achievement.

The implementation of testing provisions related to the IDEA 2004 have generated a variety of issues that challenge our educational system. Accountability, progress monitoring, and data management pose challenges, especially to our assessment procedures. Although a free appropriate education (FAPE) has been the focus of IDEA, we are now turning our attention to the changing landscape of special education that has a far-reaching effect on public schools and the general education environment. The Individuals with Disabilities Education Act goes into specific details around assessment, placement, and procedural requirements (Bartlett, Etscheidt, & Weisenstein, 2007). Before going further, read the challenges and choices that most leaders will face when dealing with assessment issues in Box 4.1.

BOX 4.1

Challenges and Issues for School and Special Education Leaders

- Implementing the Individuals with Disabilities Education Act to assure the rights of students with disabilities
- Assuring that students with disabilities have access to modifications and accommodations to support their academic progress and participation in testing
- Modifying existing instructional and assessment systems and aligning those systems to general education standards to accommodate all students, regardless of disability status
- Developing avenues for special education and general education leaders and teachers to collaboratively design assessment systems to appropriately measure content
- The development of a collection of various measurement data (formal measures such as standardized tests and/or informal measures such as work samples, observations, and interviews) to increase efforts to make informed decisions about students
- Prereferral strategies, classroom intervention techniques, and other options that limit disproportionality

ASSESSMENT TO PLACEMENT: AN OVERVIEW

The tier process is used to identify students who need special services. In the first tier (the tiers are discussed in detail in Chapter 8 "Response to Intervention and Inclusion: Facilitating Collaborative Arrangements"), school staff, teachers, and administrators are involved in universal screening of academics and behavior. If the students still do not meet classroom expectations, they receive supplemental instruction in Tier 2. If interventions do not work, they are then referred to special education in the third tier. To determine eligibility for special education and related services and accommodations, individualized formal assessments are administered to the student—generally, IQ and achievement tests in conjunction with other measures. The student is then determined eligible for services by a multidisciplinary team based on information derived from formal assessments and measures. The student is then placed into a specific special education category (i.e., learning disabled, mentally impaired, emotionally disturbance, hearing impairment).

After a student is "placed," individualized diagnostic assessments are used to formulate the specific goals and objectives for the IEP, which is written annually. Informal assessments are also used in conjunction with formal diagnostic assessments to evaluate student progress.

Prereferral

The Individuals with Disabilities Education Act (2004) emphasizes the use of prereferral interventions (Tier 1 and Tier 2) to reduce labeling, overidentification, and disproportionality. As soon as data are gathered and the cause for possible academic or behavioral concern is realized, school and special education leaders can then encourage general education teachers to use effective and well researched intervention strategies. After a period of implementation, the student can be assessed to determine his or her response to the intervention (Hilton, 2007). If the student shows improvement, special education services are normally not recommended (Overton, 2009; Turnbull, Huerta, & Stowe, 2009).

School-based prereferral/response to intervention (RTI) teams are also good options for school leaders to initiate to prevent overidentification in special education (e.g., all but 4 states have RTI and RTI teams in the United States [http://state.rti4success.org/index.php?option=com_chart]). The purpose of the school-based team will be to offer appropriate intervention methodologies, monitor implementation, and evaluate changes in the student's behavior or academic skills. The members of the team can consist of a special educator, counselor, school leader, and the general education teacher of the student who is having difficulty. When appropriate, parents or caregivers can be members of the team to provide continuity between the school and the home environment.

Referral

A formal written request to approve a student for special education services is called a *referral*. The referral form usually contains areas of academic or behavioral concern, the prereferral intervention methods, and information provided by the student's family. The multidisciplinary team reviews the complete referral form and any other supplementary material.

Parental Consent

According to IDEA, the parent or legal guardian must be informed of all evaluation procedures. Parental rights must be provided to the legal guardians of the child in their native language. (Parents and families are discussed fully in Chapter 6, "Building Ethos and Interpersonal Relationships with Families and Students.") Typically, notification of these rights is provided by special education administrators. Similarly, parental rights are provided in a suitable form for parents and caregivers with visual or hearing impairments (IDEA, 2004; Overton, 2009).

Parents and caregivers have the right to due process and may file a complaint against the school when they are not pleased with the identification process, evaluations, educational placement, or rights to a free appropriate education. They also have a right to access and can request copies of student records and to amend any existing record. If they have a dispute with the school, IDEA (2004) includes a provision for mediation. In addition, parents have the right to request an individual evaluation when they disagree with test results or procedures, or reject placement of their child in special education. The law assures that parents participate in the decision-making processes. Input from parents is important to the multidisciplinary team. They can provide useful information about the family history as well as knowledge and facts regarding the strengths and weaknesses of their child (Turnbull et al., 2004).

Eligibility

Several procedural safeguards should be followed during eligibility assessment. To decrease the possibility of subjectivity and discriminatory assessment, IDEA (2004) mandates that a multidisciplinary team makes decisions in a collaborative manner. The team may consist of parents, general and special education teachers, a school counselor, a school nurse, the principal, a behaviorist, a speech clinician, an audiologist, a physician, a social worker, and/or other school personnel. Team members must use multiple assessments.

Although other tests accompany the IQ and achievement test, these two are most commonly used for eligibility. The law requires using standardized tests for classifying students as disabled, yet procedures are problematic. A number of controversial issues surround IQ tests—for example (1) they have been identified as culturally biased, (2) they cannot predict behavior outside of the school, (3) students with disabilities are not usually included in the normative sample, and (4) some test items require academic knowledge that the student may not yet have acquired (Edwards, 2006; Overton, 2009; Venn, 2007). Yet, IQ tests are still basically used in many states to determine eligibility. Many times, tests are unable to predict behavior or ability accurately. Therefore, the information obtained from tests should be interpreted cautiously, as they indicate but do not substantiate a student's abilities (Venn, 2007). Consider the following:

- Because of the problems with standardized procedures, both special and general education leaders can be sensitive to parents when they express doubts about the results of tests. Students might need to be reevaluated or school personnel may need to employ varied types of informal assessments to help substantiate results of the assessment.
- Special education leaders can assure that assessors carefully observe standardized procedures. Students should be assessed in all areas of their suspected disability and the instruments are to be psychometrically sufficient (IDEA, 2004; Overton, 2009).
- Leaders can obtain as much information as they can on how to limit overidentification and disproportionality (some suggestions are offered later in this chapter).

Placement

Students may be considered eligible for services in 13 categories as determined by IDEA 2004: (1) Learning Disabilities, (2) Mental Retardation/Intellectual Disabilities, (3) Emotional or Behavior Disorders, (4) Speech or Language Impairment, (5) Deaf/Blindness, (6) Deaf, (7) Other Health Impairment, (8) Autism Spectrum Disorders, (9) Hearing Impairment, (10)Traumatic Brain Injured, (11) Multiple Disabilities, (12) Visual Impairment, and (13) Orthopedic Impairment. A definition of each category is provided in Figure 4.1.

Students with disabilities receive special education services in a variety of educational settings according to the severity and intensity of need. For some students, placement in the general education classroom with academic and behavioral modifications may be the most appropriate educational environment, whereas others require a more restricted or separate setting. The various educational settings within the continuum of services include the following: (1) general education classroom, (2) resource classroom, (3) self-contained/separate classroom, (4) public/private separate facility, (5) public/private residential facility, and (6) homebound/hospital environment (IDEA, 2004). (See Figure 4.2.)

Observing the design of continuum, as you move up the pyramid, the environment becomes more and more restrictive (see Figure 4.3). For example, students with severe mental impairments, behavior disorders or physical impairments may be placed in homebound or residential settings, while students with academic type deficits will be placed at the lower, less restrictive end of the continuum in resource rooms or the general education classroom.

The student should be educated in the "least restrictive environment" (LRE) according to the severity of the disability (IDEA, 2004). The special education and school leader can work together to assure that:

- A variety of service options are available to meet the needs of students.
- Students stay in the general education environment as much as possible and only when the severity of the disability makes that environment in effective.

FIGURE 4.1 Thirteen Disability Categories as Defined by IDEA 2004

Learning Disabilities	A disorder in one or more basic psychological processes involved in understanding or using language, spoken or written, that may manifest itself in the inability to speak, read, write or spell, or do mathematical calculations, including such conditions as perceptual disabilities, brain injury, minimal brain dysfunction, dyslexia, and developmental aphasia.
Mental Retardation/ Intellectual Impairments	Mental retardation/intellectual impairment means "significant sub-average general intellectual functioning, existing concurrently with deficits in adaptive behavior and manifested during the developmental period that adversely affects a child's educational performance." It is important to note that the basis for a classification of mental retardation is the source of a student's learning problem, not the student's actual IQ.
Emotional or Behavior Disorders	Emotional disturbance is a generic term used to describe a disability characterized by a student's inappropriate behavior and emotional disabilities that result in a need for special education and related services. The term is defined in the current IDEA as a condition exhibiting one or more of the following characteristics over a long period of time and to a marked degree that adversely affects a child's educational performance: <ul><li>An inability to learn that cannot be explained by intellectual, sensory, or health factors,</li><li>An inability to build or maintain satisfactory interpersonal relationships with peers and teachers,</li><li>Inappropriate types of behavior or feelings under normal circumstances,</li><li>A general pervasive mood of unhappiness or depression, and</li><li>A tendency to develop physical symptoms or fears associated with personal or school problems.</li></ul> The term includes schizophrenia, but does not apply to children who are socially maladjusted, substance abusers, or adverse behavior in the home unless it is determined that they have an emotional disturbance.
Speech/Language Impairment	Speech/language impairment is a communication disorder, such as stuttering, impaired articulation, a language impairment, or a voice impairment, that adversely affects a child's educational performance.
Deaf/Blindness	Deaf/blindness is regarded as a concomitant of hearing and visual impairments, the combination of which causes such severe communication and other developmental and educational needs that the individual cannot be accommodated in special education programs solely for children with deafness or children with blindness.
Deafness	Deafness is a hearing impairment that is so severe that the child is impaired in processing linguistic information through hearing, with or without amplification, that adversely affects a child's educational performance.

(Continued)

FIGURE 4.1 *(Continued)*

Other Health Impairment	Other health impairments describe a condition that results in limited strength, vitality, or alertness, including a heightened alertness to environmental stimuli, that results in limited alertness with respect to the educational environment, that (1) is due to chronic or acute health problems such as asthma, attention deficit disorder or attention deficit hyperactivity disorder, diabetes, epilepsy, a heart condition, hemophilia, lead poisoning, leukemia, nephritis, rheumatic fever, and sickle cell anemia; and (2) adversely affects a child's educational performance. The category of other health impairments encompasses a wide range of medical conditions. Contagious diseases, such as AIDS, may fall within the definition of "other health impairment."
Autism Spectrum	Autism is a developmental disability that significantly affects verbal and nonverbal communication and social interaction, and therefore impacts a child's educational performance. It is generally evident before age 3. Other characteristics often associated with autism are engagement in repetitive activities and stereotyped movements, resistance to environmental change or change in daily routines, and unusual responses to sensory experiences. The term does not apply if a child's educational performance is adversely affected primarily because the child has an emotional disturbance, as defined in the current IDEA. A child who manifests the characteristics of autism after age 3 could be diagnosed as having autism if these criteria are satisfied.
Hearing Impairment	This is an impairment in hearing, whether permanent or fluctuating, that adversely affects a child's educational performance, but it is not included under the definition of deafness in this section.
Traumatic Brain Injury	A traumatic brain injury is an acquired injury to the brain caused by an external physical force, resulting in total or partial functional disability or psychosocial impairment, or both, that adversely affects a child's educational performance. The term applies to open or closed head injuries resulting in impairments in one or more areas such as cognition; language; memory; attention; reasoning; abstract thinking; judgment; problem-solving; sensory, perceptual, and motor abilities; psychosocial behavior; physical functions; information processing; and speech. The term does not apply to brain injuries that are congenital or degenerative, or to brain occurrences such as strokes or aneurysms. However, the Department of Education has issued policy guidance that these types of brain injuries may meet the criteria for several other IDEA disabilities.
Multiple disabilities	Concomitant impairments (such as mental retardation–blindness, mental retardation–orthopedic impairment, etc.), the combination of which causes such severe educational needs that the person cannot be accommodated in special education programs solely for one of the impairments.
Visual Impairments	A visual impairment, even with correction, adversely affects a child's educational performance. The term includes both partial sight and blindness.
Orthopedic Impairments	A severe orthopedic impairment adversely affects a child's educational performance. The term includes impairments caused by a congenital anomaly (e.g., clubfoot, absence of some member), impairments caused by disease (e.g., poliomyelitis, bone tuberculosis), and impairments from other causes (e.g., cerebral palsy, amputations, and fractures or burns that cause contractures).

Authority: 20 U.S.C. 1401(3); 1401(30).

FIGURE 4.2   Educational Settings and Services

Homebound/Hospital	Services are provided at the student's home [and] in a hospital.
Public/Private Residential	Services in a special school or institution.
Public/Private Separate	A special day school with students with like characteristics.
Self-Contained/Separate Classroom	Educated in a separate special education class.
Resource Room	Academic instruction is in the general education [classroom] and part of their instructional time is spent in a special education class.
General Education	Students spend their time in the general education class and receive consultation services through inclusive arrangements.

Source: Compiled from R. L. Taylor, L R. Smiley, and S. B. Richards, S. B. *Exceptional Students: Preparing Teachers for the 21st Century.* Boston: McGraw-Hill, 2009.

FIGURE 4.3   Continuum of Services

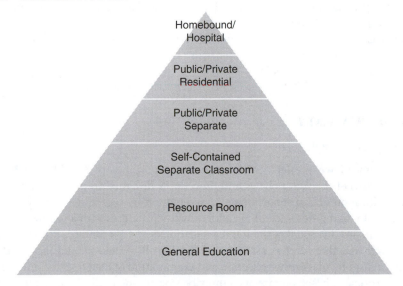

- Nonacademic and extracurricular activities, such as counseling, transportation, health services, recreational activities, special-interest groups, must also be made available to students, no matter the environment (IDEA, 2004).
- Children who have been referred to or placed in a private school or facility is provided a free appropriate education that meets the standards of the LEA and the state education agency (SEA), with no cost to parents, with all the rights of a student at a public facility (IDEA, 2004).
- Be aware of possible alternative placements within the community setting.
- Keep exact records and make data-based decisions as much as possible when considering placement.
- Monitor instruction in private facilities where special education students are attending.

Reevaluation

Each child's program needs to be reviewed, and IDEA (2004) states that the IEP team determines if a reevaluation is necessary. In most cases, students who are severely mentally impaired are not retested every three years. There are cautions if the student is determined not to be reevaluated. The law to reevaluate was originally created because students are sometimes inappropriately labeled. For example, let's say a student is evaluated with a standardized IQ test in third grade. When reevaluated after three years, in sixth grade, the student may not score in the mentally impaired range. If not retested, a student might remain in a class for the mentally impaired indefinitely, and would be denied an appropriate education. In *Hoffman* v. *The Board of Education*, a litigation case regarding reevaluation, a child in kindergarten was tested and placed in a class for the mentally retarded. He was not retested until 12 years later. When he was retested, the test scores did not fall into the mentally retarded range. The court rewarded the parents $750,000 to compensate for the child's lost earnings (Murdick, Gartin, & Crabtree, 2007).

Here are two points to remember:

- School and special education leaders can encourage teachers to recognize those who have been identified as mentally impaired, but whose academic performance and reasoning skills appear much higher.
- Informal assessments may demonstrate that certain students who are not performing in the mentally impaired range. School leaders can persuade teachers to refer these students for reevaluation as soon as possible.

DISPROPORTIONALITY

IDEA(2004) regulations state that:

The State must have in effect, consistent with the purposes of 34 CFR Part 300 and with section 618(d) of the Act, policies and procedures designed to prevent the inappropriate overidentification or disproportionate representation by race and ethnicity of children as children with disabilities, including children with disabilities with a particular impairment described in 34 CFR 300.8 of the IDEA regulations [34 CFR 300. 173] [20 U. S. C. 1412(a) (24)]. Each State that receives assistance under Part B of the Act, and the Secretary of the Interior, must provide for the collection and examination of data to determine if significant disproportionality based on race and ethnicity is occurring in the State and the local educational agencies (LEAs) of the State with respect to:

- The identification of children as children with disabilities, including the identification of children as children with disabilities in accordance with a particular impairment described in section 602(3) of the Act;
- The placement in particular educational settings of these children; and
- The incidence, duration, and type of disciplinary actions, including suspensions and expulsions.

Students with cultural and linguistically diverse backgrounds have historically been disproportionately determined eligible for special education services (Artiles, 1998; Artiles & Bal, 2008; Artiles, Reschly, & Chinn, 2002; Artiles & Trent, 1994; Harry, 2008; Harry, Arnaiz, Klingner, &

Sturges, 2008; Skiba et al. 2008). Statistics show that the percent of diverse students exceeds the percent of majority students in special education, especially African American males. Typically, males are referred more than females for behavioral problems, but African American males are referred more for behavior problems than males from European backgrounds (Coutinho, Oswald, & Best, 2002; Patton, 1998).

African Americans and bilingual students may be referred to the categories of emotional disturbance or behavioral disorders because of cultural differences (Anderson & Webb-Johnson, 1995; Ortiz & Yates, 1983). Students may appear academically deficient or seem to act inappropriately when in actuality it is a language or culture difference. These actions may be misinterpreted as a disability, therefore educators refer these students more often (Coutinho et al., 2002; Turnbull et al., 2010).

There are several reasons why children from culturally and linguistically diverse backgrounds may be at an unfair disadvantage when given standardized test (Artiles, 1998; Artiles & Bal, 2008; Artiles et al., 2002; Artiles & Trent, 1994; Edwards, 2006; Harry, 1995; Harry, 2008; Harry et al., 2008; Harry, Allen, & McLaughlin, 1995; Hilliard, 1995; Ortiz, 1997). Test items might have inappropriate content, because various diverse groups have not been exposed to cultural or geographic specific information, especially when the student's dominant language is not English (Fradd & Hallman, 1983; Overton, 2009; Reynolds, 1992). Also, the predictive validity of an instrument may differ when given to students from diverse backgrounds. Another possible disadvantage of standardized testing is if the examiner is of a different culture than the child, the child may think the examiner is unapproachable and therefore a suitable test rapport may not form (Fuchs, Fuchs, & Hamlett, 1989). Because of these reasons, broader and more comprehensive assessment procedures are encouraged.

Supposedly, IDEA (2004) guarantees nondiscriminatory assessment to assure objectivity in testing. However, despite the language in the federal definition and the major court cases that surround the issue, discriminatory assessment still exists (Russo & Talbert-Johnson, 1997). There are several landmark cases that address discriminatory assessment. One such case is *Larry P* v. *Riles* in 1972. The case was filed as a class action suit for African American elementary students in educable mentally impaired classes in California. Because of the overclassification of African Americans in mentally impaired classes, the plaintiffs believed that the students had been inappropriately labeled. In the San Francisco School District, the student population was only 28.5 percent African American, yet 66 percent represented students receiving services for the educable mentally impaired. At that time, statewide, approximately 10 percent of California's school-aged population was African American, and 25 percent was represented in mentally impaired classrooms (Murdick et al., 2007). Students had been placed chiefly on the basis of the IQ tests. The court decided that standardized intelligence tests could not be used to identify and place African Americans in classes for the mentally impaired. The court ruled that every African American child that had been determined mentally impaired had to be reevaluated with assessments other than standardized test to eliminate disproportionate placement (Rothstein, 2000).

In *Hobson* v. *Hansen* (1967), the federal court in Washington DC examined the use of standardized test for tracking students in public schools in various ability groups. The plaintiffs represented African American and children from low socioeconomic (SES) backgrounds. Because these children were disproportionately placed and overrepresented in low-ability tracks, the court decided that tests were used inappropriately and that African American and children from low SES were denied the right to equal educational opportunities.

Boyle and Weishaar (2001) listed some of the items on the test that might be suspect:

What is the color of rubies?

What does COD mean?

Why is it better to pay bills by check than by cash?

Why is it generally better to give money to an organized charity than a street beggar?

What are you supposed to do if you find someone's wallet or pocketbook in a store?

What is the thing to do if a boy (girl) much smaller than yourself starts to fight with you? (p. 26)

As you can see, according to the child's culture, neighborhood, or environment, the "right" answer may vary greatly.

Disproportionality is addressed by IDEA (2004) as the law states that no one test or procedure should be used to make eligibility decisions about a student. Assessment instruments should be valid and reliable and should evaluate cognitive, behavioral, physical, and developmental factors (Turnbull et al., 2004). There should be a variety of formal and informal assessment tools and strategies to measure the student's ability. Additionally, assessment should regard the teacher's instructional style and the student's educational history, cultural context, and preferences.

Adherence to the federal regulation is questionable since test bias seems to still be an issue. For example, because a child has a Hispanic background does not mean that he or she should be given the test translated into Spanish, but the child's geographic origin needs to be considered. A student who speaks Spanish from Brazil will have language nuances and culture different from one speaks Spanish and is from Mexico or Spain. Consequently, educational leaders can ensure that standardized measures employed to evaluate students for placement in special education does not discriminate against children from culturally and linguistically diverse backgrounds (Russo & Talbert-Johnson, 1997).

The Individuals with Disabilities Education Act (2004) states:

In the case of a determination of significant disproportionality with respect to the identification of children as children with disabilities, or the placement in particular educational settings of these children, in accordance with §300. 646(a) of the IDEA regulations, the State or the Secretary of the Interior must:

- Provide for the review and, if appropriate revision of the policies, procedures, and practices used in the identification or placement to ensure that the policies, procedures, and practices comply with the requirements of the Act.
- Require any LEA identified under §300. 646(a) of IDEA to reserve the maximum amount of funds under section 613(f) of the Act to provide comprehensive coordinated early intervening services to serve children in the LEA, particularly, but not exclusively, children in those groups that were significantly overidentified under §300. 646(a) of the IDEA regulations; and
- Require the LEA to publicly report on the revision of policies, practices, and procedures described under §300. 646(b)(1) of the IDEA regulations.

The State educational agency must examine data, including data disaggregated by race and ethnicity, to determine if significant discrepancies are occurring in the rate of long-term suspensions and expulsions of children with disabilities:

- Among LEA's in the State; or
- Compared to the rates for nondisabled children within those agencies.

The State must monitor the LEA's located in the State, using quantifiable indicators in each of the following priority areas, and using such qualitative indicators as are needed to adequately measure performance in those areas, [including] disproportionate representation of racial and ethnic groups in special education and related services, to the extent the representation is the result of inappropriate identification.

School and special education leaders can:

- Help teachers review data and become aware of the patterns of referrals—that is, the discrepancies in race and gender (Coutinho et al., 2002; Russo & Talbert-Johnson (1997).
- Determine the equity and effectiveness of the process by assessing the validity of the referrals (Skiba et al., 2008; Weinstein, 1977).
- If there are excessive referrals, especially in the prereferral and implementation process, check to see if the reasons are related to problems with curriculum and/or instruction. Examining teacher strategies might provide insight into the trend, as the instruction the student receives may need to be augmented or restructured (Patton, 1998).
- Students may be in need of counseling or other services rather than special academic remediation (Weinstein, 1997).
- In the vignette in Box 4.2, Malik is a typical student who would fit the profile for being disproportionately placed. He is an African American male from a single-parent home with low SES status. School and special education leaders can lessen disproportionate placement by assuring that school personnel and the school district understand various cultures through in-service and guest speakers. Knowledge of strategies and practices that work best with urban and diverse students may help the imbalance in special education

---

BOX 4.2

Vignette: *"What to Do with Malik"*

Mrs. Gray was thinking about her class and the challenges and issues facing her students' achievements. One of the biggest challenges was Malik. She thought, "I really like Malik—he's a bright, energetic African American boy that is liked by his former teachers." Malik experienced academic difficulty in reading since kindergarten. His previous teachers attributed his behavior to a developmental delay and believed he would "catch up." However, he is continuing to have reading difficulties. He is the poorest reader in this second-grade class. Mrs. Gray wants Malik to be tested for special education. She's tried to get help from his home, but Malik's mother is working two minimum-wage jobs and has three other small children. Although she seems concerned about his reading problem, she doesn't seem to have the time and energy to concentrate on helping him.

Mrs. Gray thought, "I am really eager for him to get some extra help. I want to try some different interventions, but I don't know any other methods other than the group methods I usually use. I could talk to the special education teacher but he is here only half day and his time is limited.

"My attempts at finding assistance have been futile. When I talk to Mrs. Redding, the counselor, she has very few suggestions other than referring Malik to special education. Our school-based RTI team is in the primary piloting phase and seems unable to meet the needs of

(Continued)

> *Malik at the present time. I only have planning meetings with the other second-grade teachers once a month. The last time we met, the other second-grade teachers mentioned some of the same problems with nonreaders as I am having. Their suggestions are limited and very similar to what I have already attempted."*
>
> *Mrs. Gray's thoughts continue. "Mr. Harrison, the principal, doesn't seem too interested in students who are having difficulty. He acts like he wants them out of the school. He says they bring our test scores down. He tends to focus on the smarter, more affluent students. When teachers are having academic or behavioral difficulty with a student, he always suggests that we 'go through the counselor and refer the difficult student.' I guess I'll just write down a few adjustments I made to document the evidence-based interventions so Malik can hurry up and get some extra help.*
>
> 1. How can the school leader help students having academic difficulty?
> 2. What is the involvement of the special education leader?
> 3. Do you think Malik should be served in special education or do you think his difficulties can be handled in the general education setting?
> 4. What is the purpose of special education? Should any child who does not fit into the norm be referred?
> 5. Is the collaboration process in the school a good one? Why? How might it be improved? How might the school administrator initiate collaborative procedures and a strong RTI team?
> 6. Are inclusive practices used in the school? How can you tell?
> 7. Is the teacher making an informed decision about Malik? What other information should be obtained?
> 8. Are there any cultural-specific methodologies that might be more effective for Malik?

determination. Teacher expectations, perceptions, and interactions with regard to race and gender can change as they are provided more in-depth information, methodologies, and strategies (Patton, 1998; Townsend, 2002).

- Salend and Duhaney (2005) recommend classroom-based assessments rather than standardized tests. They also suggest a diverse multidisciplinary planning team. The planning team can examine and institute a number of techniques such as curriculum-based approaches, portfolio assessment, rubrics (discussed later in the chapter), and self-evaluation.
- More community and family involvement translates into more cross-cultural competency and communication with diverse families, particularly in the prereferral process (Harry et al., 2008).

HIGH-STAKES TEST VERSUS ALTERNATIVE ASSESSMENT

The No Child Left Behind (NCLB) law has created a stir in the educational community, especially regarding accountability procedures for children with disabilities. The education reform plan included stronger accountability, expanded flexibility and local control, expanded options for parents, and an emphasis on teaching methods that have been proven to work. The law was intended to close the achievement gap for disadvantaged and minority children and their peers. As a result of the law, each state had to create assessment measures and be held accountable for increasing the achievement of all students to the same academically high standards. The law required student progress and achievement to be measured through yearly standardized measures. Because all children are required to learn at the same high levels of achievement, these requirements have proven to be challenging for children with disabilities (Little & Houston, 2003; McGlinchey & Hixson, 2004; Salend, 2008). Under NCLB:

> Each state is to develop and implement measurements for determining whether its schools and local educational agencies (LEAs) are making adequate yearly progress (AYP). AYP is an individual state's measure of progress toward the goal of 100 percent of students achieving to state academic standards in at least reading/language arts and math. It sets the minimum level of proficiency that the state, its school districts, and schools must achieve each year on annual tests and related academic indicators. Each state must develop and implement a statewide accountability system that will be effective in ensuring that all local educational agencies, public elementary schools and public secondary schools make adequate yearly progress. An accountability system should be developed based on academic standards and assessments to include the achievement of all students. Sanctions and rewards will be instituted to hold all public schools accountable for student achievement. Adequate yearly progress requires the same high standards of academic achievement for all students using statistically valid and reliable measures to show continuous and substantial academic improvement for all students. There should be separate measurable annual objectives for achievement for all students including racial/ethnic groups, economically disadvantaged students, students with disabilities (IDEA, Sec. 602) and students with limited English proficiency.

The participation of students with disabilities in the high-stakes tests described in NCLB is controversial. Pressure from varied initiatives such as state standards, charter schools, vouchers, and private schools have established precedence, and accountability and assessment have become the core of academic learning. Competency tests linked to educational standards have been implemented in more than 20 states. Districts have enacted varied rewards and penalties for students' performances on high-stakes test. State requirements and policies have become more specific as federal requirements change. More students are included in assessment systems and accommodations are becoming more prevalent. Incorporating assessment results and research-based approaches into quality instruction has been a challenge (Salend, 2008).

Some research indicates that students with disabilities are showing an improvement in their performances on high-stakes tests. Many systems are merging alternative-type assessments into existing programs to meet the challenges of high-stakes testing by aligning performance standards to alternative assessment tools (Thurlow, 2002). Shared decision making among special and general educators is coming to pass, but there is little connection between general and special education reform. Special education has little representation in team discussions. Schools are faced with developing assessment practices that are meaningful to parents and that adequately measure the progress of students. Leaders should remember to:

- Encourage special education and general education teachers to work together to create a curriculum aligned to general education for students with special needs students, making the two systems compatible (Lynch & Adams, 2008).
- Develop standards-based IEPs that consider the students' needs and state standards that can be used to measure AYP in conjunction with data-driven assessments to support the process.
- Determine if the assessments are working, if adjustments are needed, and how well information taught in the classroom is being measured.

- Make sure that students have access to the general curriculum and support inclusive practices (Hardman & Dawson, 2008).
  — Include content and performance standards will need to be written so that they are broad and inclusive to meet the needs of students with disabilities and they can be measured for AYP.
  — Extend and expand the assessment system and require accommodation to assist with mastery for children with disabilities.
  — Use the results of the assessments to plan instruction.
  — Use criteria-related assessment (such as curriculum-based instruction, discussed in the next section) for AYP measures.
  — Teach students specific items that are similar to those used in high-stakes testing.
- Create diverse multidisciplinary teams (Salend, 2008).
- Be aware of the range of testing accommodations, such as timing and scheduling, settings, and linguistically based accommodations. These make a big difference with students who are from another culture or use another language (Salend, 2008).
- To know testing policies are not one-size-fits-all when it comes to children with disabilities. Make sure intensity, difficulty and duration of the tests are appropriate.

There are a number of alternative assessments, and informal nonstandardized tests that have been proven to be effective options to promote the inclusion of students with disabilities. There are a number of legal decisions that school leaders should consider in Box 4.3.

Alternative Assessments

Various widespread alternative assessment procedures have been used consistently as traditional norm-referenced testing has been criticized, especially for students with disabilities. Standardized, norm-referenced tests require students to depend on rote memory and answer with a single response (Taylor, 2009). Typically, norm-referenced tests represent the information taught in the actual curriculum and there are usually problems with test administration, interpretation, and bias. Additionally, norm-referenced tests typically are not good measures for incremental academic growth from week to week and may not accurately reflect student learning (Deno, 2003).

BOX 4.3

Legal Issues

There are a plethora of legal issues in this chapter; however, to impede due process procedures, the following is advised:

- Make sure all appropriate policies and procedures are closely followed regarding assessment measures.
- All decisions related to the child should be done in a collaborative team fashion. The parent should be notified or included in decision making.
- Placement should be in the least restrictive environment possible.
- Procedures that delay overidentification and disproportionality should be actively in place (i.e., prereferral teams, response to intervention, and other methods suggested) and used efficiently and effectively.
- If due process proceedings occur, attempt to meet with the parent and solve the issues before litigation goes too far.

Students with disabilities especially have difficulty with standardized tests and memory, and thus need multiple formats to present learned information.

General education teachers, however, express concerns with standards and have reservations about accommodations, modifications, and alternative assessment procedures (Yell & Katsiyannis, 2004). Relevant items related to assessment are listed here:

- Teachers who adapt their assessment techniques have a better chance of meeting the needs of students with disabilities.
  — Both special and general education teachers working in a collaborative manner can construct various assessments that assess content while taking into account the child's disability status.
  — The student will benefit because the assessment will be devised from more than one perspective.
- Teachers may need additional guidance through supplemental in-service training related to the use of test scores because perceptions and beliefs about grading will vary.
- Leaders can help facilitate this process by setting guidelines for optional testing and grading procedures and by creating a climate that encourages differences.

To facilitate the adaptations for testing students in the inclusive settings, it is wise to examine effective informal assessment techniques that already exist, such as (1) performance assessment, (2) authentic assessment, (3) criterion-related assessment, (4) curriculum-based assessment, and (5) portfolio assessment. The definition of each informal assessment and a sample item is provided in Table 4.1.

These techniques offer an alternative to standardized multiple-choice formats. They require the student to demonstrate or perform a task rather than use memorization techniques. Techniques such as these are applicable to students like Malik, in this chapter's vignette. For example, Malik may have good comprehension skills but his reading level is low. Alternative assessments tap into what he really knows, as they provide varied ways to assess a student's ability.

PERFORMANCE ASSESSMENT   A performance assessment requires the student to construct, create, demonstrate, or illustrate a task (Taylor, 2009). The objectives and the components of the task are scaled, using a scoring rubric. A student does not just solve a math problem; rather, she or he applies the information in a practical manner. Performance-based tasks can be constructed in reading, language arts, mathematics, and many other subjects.

AUTHENTIC ASSESSMENT   Authentic assessment is similar to performance assessment in that the student demonstrates, creates, or illustrates a task. It differs in that it needs to be performed in a real-life or a real-world setting. Additionally, the task must be worthwhile to the academic or behavioral goals of the student. For example, in social studies, the student may need to construct a map and actually use the map as a reference to find a location within the city (Taylor, 2009).

CRITERION-RELATED ASSESSMENT   Criterion-related assessments compare the performance of a student to criteria rather than the norm group. The criteria may be the objective on an IEP or a standard. Most criterion-related assessments are teacher made; however, there are some published assessments. The Key Math 3 (Connolly, 2007) and the Woodcock Reading Mastery Test Revised (WRMT-R) (Woodcock, 1998) are examples of published criterion-related assessments (Venn, 2007). These tests can also be used to measure adequate yearly progress.

CURRICULUM-BASED ASSESSMENT   Curriculum-based assessment is based on the goals, objectives, and criteria embedded in the curriculum. Research shows that students have strong academic

TABLE 4.1	Alternative and Informal Techniques	
Test	**Definition**	**Example**
Criterion-Referenced Test	These tests compare a student's performance to a specific criteria rather than the performance of another student. The tests are and measures for AYP.	Margie will be able to answer 4 out of 5 single-digit addition problems. $5 + 4 =$ $7 + 3 =$ $2 + 1 =$ $6 + 8 =$
Curriculum-Based Assessment	Measures are developed from the instruction provided in the curriculum according to the academic outcomes in the school and the classroom.	Name all of the characters in the basal reading story, "Malik and His Hat."
Portfolio Assessment	A collection of a student's performance in various subjects that demonstrates a collective view of the student's strengths and weaknesses. It may consist of work samples, test results, pictures, homework assignments, and other artifacts.	A science portfolio might contain: • Samples of homework • Pictures and the results of a science fair project • A classroom lab report
Authentic Assessment	The student applies acquired knowledge in a real-life setting.	Opening and using a savings account to demonstrate knowledge of the combined skills of addition and subtraction.
Performance Assessment	Requires the student to demonstrate his or her knowledge of a particular skill. The format and presentation is flexible.	There will be a concert in the theater. Fifteen students will sell tickets. The seating capacity is 2,000. The VIP section will contain 45 tables. How many people will need to sit at each table? How many tickets will each student need to sell? How did you construct your answer? Can you diagram the theater?

Source: Taylor, Donald L., *Assessment of Exceptional Students,* 8th Edition, © 2009. Reprinted by permission of Pearson Education, Inc., Upper Saddle River, NJ.

gains when using curriculum-based assessment methodologies (Deno, 2003; Fewster & Macmillan, 2002; Fuchs et al., 1989; Madelaine & Wheldall, 2004; Marston, Fuchs, & Deno, 1986; McGlinchey & Hixson, 2004). Teachers determine the skills, concepts, and objectives in the curriculum to be taught and assessed. The method is most useful when using traditional approaches such as basal readers or phonetic instruction. Curriculum-based measures have been proven as a valid, reliable methodology for screening and placement purposes (Deno, 2003; McGlichey & Hixson, 2004).

PORTFOLIO ASSESSMENT   A portfolio assessment is a purposeful collection of artifacts, tasks, activities, or products, performed by the student, over time, that demonstrate the student's achievement and ability (Taylor, 2009). The student chooses the artifacts according to criteria selected by the teacher. The collection should reflect the student's strengths and weaknesses. Classroom tests, video or audio recordings, progress notes, pictures, or projects can be included in the portfolio. The portfolio is a flexible tool and can be integrated within any classroom instruction, intervention, or subject.

Portfolios may also represent certain subject areas. For example, a reading portfolio can contain a recording of the student's oral reading or journal entries. A science portfolio might contain a lab report or pictures of a science fair project. A math portfolio might contain diagrams of problem-solving processes (Poteet, Choat, & Stewart, 1993).

This multidimensional tool reflects the learning goals and objectives of both the instructor and the student as the child has the opportunity to have input. The process encourages not only collaboration between students and teachers but also between general and special education teachers. The information provided in a portfolio assessment can also enhance eligibility decisions and would offer information that is not evident in norm-referenced testing. Because the data in the portfolio are so varied, it has been successfully used in some systemwide assessments. The following list provides tips related to portfolio assessment.

- Special and general education leaders together can implement schoolwide portfolio assessment. Using portfolio assessment districtwide, however, does raise some concerns with reliability, validity, cost, time of administration, and subjectivity in scoring—just as with all alternative assessments (Taylor, 2009).
- It is essential that portfolio assessment procedures be supported in order for the process to be successful. Special education leaders can prepare special and general education teachers through in-service education activities.
- School and special education leaders can encourage teachers to collaboratively decide on the type of alternative assessment tools, goals, objectives, and concepts.
- Special education leaders can assist general education leaders with policies and procedures when developing and using alternative tests.
- Both special and general education leaders can help determine how these assessments fit into the general education curriculum and assure that the tests and procedures mesh into the instructional processes within the current educational constraints, especially if they are to be used for AYP accountability.
- Assessments can be designed to be comprehensive—that is, items can be constructed so they will isolate a particular skill. For example, items that measure mathematics should not require advanced reading skills. School and special education leaders can make certain that special educators are included in item design, as they have had more contact with students with disabilities.

Research shows that when teachers use alternative informal assessments and revise and adapt students' instructional programs, students demonstrate greater academic gains (Deno, 2003; Madelaine & Wheldall, 2004; Stecker & Fuchs, 2000). The use of informal assessments as alternative evaluations for high-stakes testing improves the reliability of the test.

Special education assessment is comprised of the collection of measurement data in order to make informed decisions about students. The compilation of data may include formal and informal test information, work samples, observations, and interviews (Yell, 2006). A variety of decisions are determined from these assessments, including prereferral strategy options, eligibility determinations, IEP goals and objectives, classroom intervention techniques, AYP accountability, as well as accountability information. Here are some things administrators can do:

- Educational leaders can encourage teachers to use informal assessments in conjunction with formal diagnostic assessments to evaluate student progress. Informal assessments are a way to integrate alternate procedures into the current norm-referenced multiple-choice formats.
- Special education leaders can assure that general education leaders understand federal guidelines and implementation procedures in relation to multiple assessments.
- Working collaboratively, general and special education leaders can use methods that best fit the assessment practices within the school system. Students with disabilities can effectively participate in high-stakes testing if accommodations are designed according to student needs during the assessment.

For students with disabilities, assessments are linked to instruction through the IEP process. Components of the assessment and IEP development process is described in the next section.

THE INDIVIDUALIZED EDUCATION PROGRAM

The individualized education program, or IEP, is a legal document that guides and directs the educational and behavioral intervention plan for the student. Diagnostic-based tests are used for assessments in the IEP. The document, developed by a school-based team, is a written statement for each child with a disability, from ages 3 to 21. When it is developed, reviewed, and revised, it must contain the following components (Turnbull, Turnbull, & Wehmeyer, 2009).

- *Identifying Information* includes the name of the child, the parents' names, address, primary and/or secondary exceptionality, evaluations given, date of birth, grade, school, evaluator, and dates tested.
- *Present Level of Educational Performance* summarizes the current academic and behavioral functional level (both strengths and needs) of the student and the impact of the disability. Usually this information is derived from formal high-stakes test, informal classroom-based test, and sometimes observations of the student.
- *Annual Goals* are the perceived expected student academic, physical, social, or/and behavioral gains that are projected usually for the coming academic school year.
- *Objectives* are the benchmarks set for student improvement. These are written in observable and measurable terms.
- *Related Services* are accommodations, supports, personnel, and modifications that the student needs to function in the least restrictive environment.
- *Participation with Nondisabled Peers* is the time and classes the student is to spend in the least restrictive environment in an inclusive general education setting.
- *Participation in State and Districtwide Testing* includes the modifications the student needs and his or her level of participation. If the student is not to participate, an explanation is needed.
- *Dates of Initiation* pinpoints the duration of services and the location and intensity of services that are to be provided.
- *Transition Services*, usually provided at ages 14 to 16, provide the student's postschool goals, objectives, and course of study. Components of the individualized transition plan (ITP) are provided in Chapter 7 of this book.

- *Measures of Progress* indicates the student's progress on the determined goals and objectives.
- *Behavior* sometimes interferes with academic achievements; therefore, it is addressed in the IEP as part of the Behavior Modification Plan.
- *Limited English Proficiency* includes the accommodations a student might need if they speak another language.
- *Assistive Technology* includes devices that students who are blind, visually and hearing impaired, and deaf will need to effectively communicate. The IEP will also consider special instructional needs such as Braille or technological needs.

The IEP team is composed of several individuals such as the parent or caregiver, a special education teacher, a general education teacher, and a representative of the local educational agency (LEA) (i.e., individuals who have knowledge of or can supervise instructional implications, provision of services, the general education curriculum, interpret evaluation results or having other special expertise). The LEA has the responsibility to assure that the family is a member of any group making decisions about the student. The parent, family, or caregiver and the LEA decide whose attendance is necessary at the conference. The team can convene using video conferencing techniques, conference calls, or other ways to confer.

Compliance of the IEP rests with the local educational agency or a state education agency (SEA). Misunderstanding of the issues can sometimes be tricky and cost the district money in unnecessary litigation. School and special education leaders work as a team with teachers and parents to assure that students receive a free appropriate education (FAPE).

Leaders need to determine if mandated procedures and policies have been adhered to. For example, they assure that the parent or guardian has been contacted for participation in the IEP team in a timely manner and they check that the appropriate members are on the IEP team. Leaders can also be aware of the following tips:

- Pertinent issues about the child are addressed during the meeting.
- Service delivery and accommodations are appropriate and timely.
- Collaboration efforts between general and special teachers in the instructional setting, especially observing state high-stakes assessments and other measures, have been effective.
- Accessibility and accommodations for families have been provided, such as offering the team options of the telephone or videoconferencing for the IEP meeting.
- The IEP is transferable. If a child comes from another state or different school district, the IEP can be transferred and comparable services should be offered until a new IEP has been constructed. Schools and school systems should make an effort to make sure the transfer of the IEP is as seamless as possible and to observe the applicable days of transfer according to the state.
- A special education child attending private school can still receive services at no cost to the parent. Through conference calls or meetings, it must be assured that the IEP is followed. Thereafter, meetings to revise the IEP are at the discretion of the public school. For the IEP, most instructional interventions are based on informal teacher tests.
- Be sure to document pertinent information about the child, including useful behavioral and academic strategies, parental interactions, and so on. After all, the documentation will be useful during legal or due process procedures.

Instructional intervention and evaluation of student performance in the classroom is part of the daily routine. For special education teachers, assessment for instructional purposes is essential to develop, evaluate, and change strategies for the student. Teachers are able to identify the strengths and weaknesses of the student and decide on the best intervention. Assessments help teachers determine intervention priorities, develop instructional objectives, and decide on various curricular materials. Examples of teacher measures include classroom tests, worksheets, task analysis, error analysis, observations, and behavior management information (Venn, 2007).

The Individuals with Disabilities Education Act (1997) mandated the increase in participation of general educators in the IEP process. The IEP should be written collaboratively with other professionals as well as the parent. Working together on the development of the IEP increases the relevance of the document and collaboration in inclusive arrangements (Kamens, 2004). General education leaders can assure:

- Teachers use some systematic means to collaborate in order to properly prescribe appropriate educational programming and measure student success.
- Through collaboration, general and special educators develop a program based on the strengths and weaknesses of the student and formulate goals and objectives that are realistic and achievable.

Summary

This chapter has provided suggestions for special and general education leaders to implement appropriate assessment practices for students with disabilities. A general summary of noted advice is listed in Box 4.4. Accountability for student performance was mandated by IDEA (2004). Because of the changes in the law, many more public schools are moving more aggressively toward inclusionary, cooperative, and authentic assessment practices. An important role of educational leaders is to integrate special education assessment into the mainstream of the school, rather than treat it as an appendage. The more knowledge the general education leader has about special education intervention and assessment practices, the greater cooperation and collaborative practices there will be among teachers. Results should yield fewer students referred for special services and a greater awareness of sound assessment methodologies. The resolution to the vignette is given in Box 4.5.

BOX 4.4

Advice for School and Special Education Leaders

- Assessment, placement, and the IEP in special education is a collaborative process. Make sure that a team, rather than an individual, decides all steps in the process.
- Nondiscriminatory testing, open-ended referral forms, prereferral teams, assessing the validity of referrals, classroom-based assessments, multidisciplinary planning teams, and response to intervention techniques are effective in reducing overidentification and disproportionality.
- Alternatives to formal assessments produce helpful data that may improve the evaluation process and can improve the reliability of formal test. General and special education leaders can collaboratively devise varied informal testing procedures (portfolio, authentic, criterion referenced, curriculum based, performance based), goals, concepts, and tools in order to adequately assess the achievement of students operating and how these test mesh with the general curriculum and instructional process.

BOX 4.5

Resolution to the Vignette

A prereferral/RTI team could suggest a number of strategies to be used in the general education setting. It is the intention of IDEA to stop the overidentification of cultural and linguistically diverse groups in special education.

Chapter Questions

1. Name and describe two alternative assessments.
2. Why is it important for the curriculum and the IEP to be aligned?
3. How many steps are there in the assessment process? List and describe each.

4. Why are preferral/RTI teams important?
5. Do standardized tests have more value than informal measures? Explain.
6. What are the two IQ tests most often used?

CHAPTER 5

Discipline

Functional Behavior Assessment and Behavior Intervention Plans

GLORIA D. CAMPBELL-WHATLEY

YA-YU LO

RICHARD B. WHITE

INTRODUCTION

Issues surrounding students who are at risk of or exhibit behavioral problems are addressed increasingly in the professional literature. Students' inappropriate behaviors include bullying, physical and verbal outbursts, fights, and alcohol and drug abuse, just to name a few (Houchins, Puckett-Patterson, Crosby, Shippen, & Jolivette, 2009; O'Shea & Drayden, 2008). Administrators struggle to stay within the framework of the law to address the needs of students with and without disabilities alike as discipline referrals increase (Rose & Gallup, 2006). Students' problem behaviors in the school settings not only demand significant amounts of administrator and teacher time and effort but also create a chasm in the teachers' abilities to provide effective instruction to the students while responding to the discipline issues (Chitiyo & Wheeler, 2009).

Students who present behavior challenges in schools often times need intensive and extensive supports and strategies that are inherently different from other students. This chapter guides special and general educational leaders to positive, appropriate decision-making related to law, procedures, and alternatives to maintain and sustain a safe and orderly environment for all students in schools. Major disciplinary laws and litigation governing students with disabilities, such as Manifestation Determination, as well as litigation addressing suspension and expulsion, will be discussed. Examples of a proactive behavioral approach—namely, positive behavioral interventions and supports (PBIS)—which is useful in special and general education settings, will be outlined. Dimensions of a classroom climate that encourages appropriate behavior and functional behavior assessment for students with challenging behaviors will also be discussed.

The No Child Left Behind Act of 2001 (NCLB) and the Individuals with Disabilities Education Act of 1997 and 2004 (IDEA) mandated that schools (1) ensure positive and safe environments for all students and (2) address the behaviors that impede the learning of self or others for students with disabilities, respectively. Several legal concerns may result from these mandates as administrators and teachers interpret discipline application and the laws. In conjunction with safety, avoiding unnecessary legal dilemmas will be at the forefront of decisions about disciplinary issues and resulting consequences.

Most local and state education agencies have existing policies regarding behavior violations as schools have to deal with a range of severe to moderate problem behaviors and consequences. Behaviors such as tardiness, absences, truancy, skipping school or classes, and failure to complete assignments are often considered minor behavioral infractions, whereas noncompliance, disrespect, cheating, profanity, vandalism, verbal threats, or fighting without injury may be considered as having the potential to result in a more significant disruption to the educational environment. Violations such as physical assaults, possession of weapons and illegal drugs, use of fire, gang activity, robbery, sexual harassment, or acts that constitute threats to others or result in injuries are often classified as violent and aggression that possibly can result in either temporary or permanent expulsion. Although the more serious crimes are less frequent than minor infractions, they are the ones that receive more attention because of the nature of their severity.

Despite schools' efforts to reduce violence in schools, the most recent national statistics on school crime and safety (Robers, Zhang, & Truman, 2010) continue to present pressing concerns to administrators and school leaders. For example, consider these circumstances of the 2007–2008 school year:

- There were 1,701 homicides among school-age youth ages 5 to 18.
- Eighty-five percent of public schools reported incidents of crime taken place at school, totaling approximately 2 million crimes.
- One-fourth of public schools reported that bullying occurred among students on a daily or weekly basis.
- Thirty-two percent of students ages 12 to 18 reported that they have been bullied at school.
- Ten percent of teachers in city schools reported being threatened with injury and five percent were actually physically attacked.
- One-third of teachers agreed or strongly agreed that students' behavior violations interfered with their teaching or the learning of others. (Robers et al., 2010).

To improve the overall school safety and school climate, and to promote all students' positive learning, what is needed is not for schools to be more strict, to use more punitive consequences, or to establish more of the "safety watch" systems. Such practices have failed to reduce the very problems being targeted for reduction (Anderson & Kincaid, 2005). What is needed is a school discipline practice that will allow administrators and school leaders to focus on creating a social context that promote all students' success through a positive, proactive, and effective teaching environment (Sugai & Horner, 2008).

In the following sections, we first discuss and explain laws and litigation related to discipline and student behavior. We then introduce a schoolwide, multitiered prevention practice—namely, schoolwide positive behavior support (SWPBS)—as a preferred practice in U.S. schools, followed by the discussion of functional behavioral assessment and individual behavior intervention plan, most relevant for cases like Bobby (see vignette later in this chapter). A summary of challenges and issues are listed in Box 5.1.

BOX 5.1

Challenges and Issues for School and Special Education Leaders

- Legal issues related to discipline of students with disabilities
- Creating and sustaining a safe and orderly school climate for all students
- Providing support to students with varying levels of behavioral and social needs
- Maximizing time for leadership activities while minimizing time for managing behavior
- Supporting teachers and staff related to student discipline

---

LAWS GOVERNING DISCIPLINE IN SPECIAL EDUCATION

The Individuals with Disabilities Education Improvement Act of 2004 provides protection to students with disabilities who exhibit discipline-related actions in school as well other students and staff members. Specifically, school personnel may do the following:

- Suspend or remove a child with a disability with a code of student conduct violation from his or her current placement for no more than 10 school days consecutively or cumulatively (as long as the series of removals does not constitute a pattern) to the extent those alternatives are applied to children without disabilities [34 CFR 300.530(b)(1) & 34 CFR 300.536(a)(2)(i)-(iii)] [20 U.S.C. 1415(k)].
- Remove a student to an interim alternative education setting for no more than 45 school days, regardless if the child's conduct is a manifestation of his or her disability, if the child possesses or carries a weapon on school premises; knowingly possesses, uses, sells, or solicits sale of illegal drugs at school; or has inflicted serious bodily injury on another person while at school [34 CFR 300.530(g)(1)-(3)] [20 U.S.C. 1415(k)(1)(G)(i)-(iii)].
- Apply the same disciplinary procedures to children with disabilities in the same manner and for the same duration as those for students without disabilities, if the behavior is found not to be a manifestation of the child's disability [34 CFR 300.530(c)] [20 U.S.C. 1415(k)(1)(C)].

However, school personnel must also do the following:

- Conduct a manifestation determination within 10 school days of any decision to remove a child with a disability that leads to a change of placement, to determine if the conduct in question had a *direct and substantial relationship* to the child's disability, and review all relevant information, including the child's IEP to determine if the IEP has been implemented appropriately [34 CFR 300.530(e)(1) and (2)] [20 U.S.C. 1415(k)(1)(E)].
- Conduct a functional behavioral assessment (if not already done previously on the same behavior) and implement a behavioral intervention plan (with modification if a plan already exists) to address the behavior under question, if the child's conduct was determined to be a manifestation of his or her disability [34 CFR 300.530(f)] [20 U.S.C. 1415(k)(1)(F)].
- Continue to provide educational services to the child in the alternative setting to allow the child to continue his or her participation in the general education curriculum and to progress toward meeting his or her IEP goals and objectives [34 CFR 300.530(d)(1)] [20 U.S.C. 1415(k)(1)(D)].

Table 5.1 lists several issues and concerns related to students with disabilities on discipline-related behavior, as well as school's rights according to IDEA (2004). Let's examine the case of Bobby in the vignette in Box 5.2 and relate it to several of the inquiries on Table 5.1.

TABLE 5.1 IDEA 2004 Regulations Related to Discipline of Students with Disabilities

Inquiry	The Agency's Rights	Statute
1. A student with a disability violates a code of the student conduct.	The school personnel may remove the student in violation from his or her current placement to an appropriate interim alternative education setting (IAES), another setting, or suspension for not more than 10 school days consecutively.	§300.530(b)(1)
2. A student with a disability violates a code of the student conduct again.	Additionally, the school personnel may remove the student for not more than 10 consecutive school days in that same school year for separate incidents of misconduct (as long as those removals do not constitute a change in placement).	§300.530(b)(1) and §300.536(a)(2) (i)–(iii)
3. What happens to a child with a disability on the 11th cumulative day of removal?	Provide services to the child to the extent required under Sec. 300.101 (i.e., free appropriate public education, FAPE), which clarifies the child must continue to receive educational services in order to participate in the general education curriculum and progress toward meeting the child's annual IEP goals.	§300.530(d)(1)
4. What constitutes a day of removal?	In-school suspensions would not be considered a part of the days of suspension as long as the child continues to participate in the general curriculum and receive services in the school, unless the school personnel determine such suspension as a unique circumstance on individual case basis. Bus suspensions would be considered as a suspension if transportation were part of the IEP, unless the public agency provides some other way of transportation.	§300.530(a) and (d)
5. What constitutes a change in placement?	The removal is for more than 10 consecutive days or if the child has been subjected to a series of removals that constitute a pattern, including situations when (a) the series of removals total more than 10 days in a school year, (b) behaviors are substantially similar, and/or (c) additional factors like length of removal, total amount of time removed, and proximity of removals present a pattern.	§300.536
6. Consideration of case-by-case circumstances in determining if change of placement is appropriate.	School personnel may consider any unique circumstances on a case-by-case basis when determining whether a change in placement is appropriate. Possible factors for considerations may include disciplinary history, ability to understand, expression of remorse, and supports provided prior to the violation.	§300.530(a)

(Continued)

TABLE 5.1 IDEA 2004 Regulations Related to Discipline of Students with Disabilities		
Inquiry	**The Agency's Rights**	**Statute**
7. What should be done if the violation involves drugs, weapons, or serious bodily injury?	The school personnel may remove a child with a disability for no more than 45 school days whether or not the behavior is determined to be a manifestation of the child's disability under three special circumstances: • carries a weapon or possesses a weapon at school; • knowingly possesses or uses illegal drugs or sells or solicits the sale of a controlled substance at school; and • has inflicted serious bodily injury upon another person while at school.	§300.530(g)
8. When is a school required to perform a manifestation determination?	• There is no requirement for a manifestation determination for removals of less than 10 consecutive school days that do not constitute a change of placement. • A manifestation determination must occur within 10 days of any decision to change the child's placement because of a violation of a code of student conduct.	§300.530(e)

9. What happens if the violation was a manifestation of the disability or failure to implement the IEP?	• If it was failure of the school to implement the IEP, there is an obligation to take immediate steps to ensure all services are provided according to the IEP.
	• If the violation was a manifestation of the disability, then the IEP team must either:
	
	  • Conduct a functional behavioral assessment (FBA) and implement a behavioral intervention plan (BIP); or
	  • Review the existing BIP and modify as needed; and
	  • Return the child to the placement from which he or she was removed.
		§300.530(e)(2)-(3) and (f)

10. What happens if the violation was NOT a manifestation of the disability or failure to implement the IEP?	A child with disabilities may be disciplined in the same manner and for the same length of time as a child without disabilities would be disciplined except that the child continues to receive services.	§300.530(c)
11. When must services be provided and what is the nature of this obligation?	• If the total number of removal days is 10 school days or less, a public agency is only required to provide services if it provides services to children without disabilities who are similarly removed. • When a child is removed for a violation that is not a manifestation of the child's disability and involves drugs, weapons, or bodily harm, the child must continue to receive educational services as provided for in IDEA's FAPE provisions.	§300.530(d)(1), (3), and (5)

TABLE 5.1 (Continued)		
Inquiry	**The Agency's Rights**	**Statute**
12. Who has the right to request a due process hearing to appeal decisions?	• Parents may appeal decisions regarding placement or manifestation determination by filing a complaint pursuant. • LEA may appeal a decision to maintain the current placement of the child, if maintaining the current placement is likely to result in injury to the child or others.	§300.532(a), §300.530(e), And §300.531
13. What are the procedures for filing a Due Process complaint?	• The hearing requested must allege a violation that occurred not more than two years before the date the parent or local education agency (LEA) knew. • The parent must be informed of any free or low cost legal services. • The due process complaint must remain confidential. • Filing party must forward a copy to the state education agency (SEA). • Complaint must include available contact information for child and school of attendance if homeless.	§300.507, §300.508(a) and (b)
14. What specific information should be included in the complaint?	• Contact information for child and school. • Description of the nature of the problem. • Proposed resolution of the problem to the extent that it is known to the filing party.	§300.508(a) and (b)
15. What happens if there is a request for an expedited hearing?	The LEA or SEA is responsible for arranging the expedited due process hearing that must occur within 20 school days of the date the complaint is filed, and that the hearing officer must make a determination within 10 school days after the hearing.	§300.532(c)(2)
16. What is the authority of the hearing officer?	A hearing officer hears and makes a determination regarding an appeal, in which he or she may • return the child to the placement if it is determined that the removal was a violation or that the child's behavior was a manifestation of the child's disability; or • order a change of placement to an appropriate IAES if it is determined that placement could result in injury.	§300.532(b)

Source: U.S. Department of Education. *Building the Legacy: IDEA 2004* (2004). Part 300—Assistance to states for the education of children with disabilities, Subpart E Procedural safeguard. Retrieved from http://idea.ed.gov/.

BOX 5.2

Vignette: "Bobby Slapped Somebody Again, but You Can't Expel Him Because He Is in Special Education"

Principal Monroe sat at his desk with his head in his hand. He had already left a message for the special education director, Dr. Unique. He wanted to know what to do with Bobby. Bobby, an African American male middle school student who has learning disabilities as his primary disability category and emotional and behavioral disability as his secondary disability category, had slapped another student again. Bobby's parents were at the school all the time trying to make sure his rights were not violated. They threaten to hire a lawyer, but they forget about the other children. Other parents were beginning to complain and there have been rumors of legal assistance. Bobby has instigated fights before. His individualized education plan (IEP) and his behavior intervention plan (BIP) had been updated twice this year after manifestation determination, but nothing had changed.

"What can I do?," Principal Monroe thought to himself. "Why are there laws protecting these students with disabilities? Why can't I just expel him, like I have done before with everyone else, especially with all the trouble he has caused? I've got to figure a way to get this student out of my school. He has caused a lot of trouble. What about the laws protecting other students? When Dr. Unique calls me back, I am going to tell her that I want this student gone. It seems that I will be facing a lawsuit no matter what, so I might as well do what I am going to do. I know that Dr. Unique is a strong advocate for something called positive behavioral interventions and supports (PBIS). I know Bobby has had a functional behavior assessment (FBA), but I am not sure the BIP is working. There is a lot to consider here."

As you read through the chapter, think of these questions.

1. Can Bobby be suspended again? What must be considered before he is suspended?
2. Do the other parents have a right to sue because of Bobby's behavior? What about the rights of the other students?
3. What does manifestation determination mean and how is it observed? How does the result of the manifestation determination affect Principal Monroe's selection of disciplinary actions for Bobby? Can Bobby not be suspended again?
4. What can we do with Bobby's BIP? Does he need another FBA? What could Principal Monroe do differently to prevent this problem?

Bobby has committed a serious infraction of the school's *Code of Student Conduct* repeatedly and has been suspended (Inquiry1). He now has reached his total of 10 days for being removed/suspended (Inquiry 2). An emotional and behavioral disability is part of his disability for which he receives special education services and he is protected under manifestation determination (Inquiry 8). If he is suspended again, as Principal Monroe wishes to do, the suspension will constitute a change in placement (Inquiry 5). Principal Monroe has the option of using in-school suspensions, as Bobby could continue to receive appropriate educational services at school to meet his IEP goals and objectives (Inquiry 4). In-school suspension may remove Bobby from the classroom setting temporarily, but it does not address the change in his behavior. Bobby's IEP team has updated his individualized education plan and behavioral intervention plan (BIP) on two occasions after manifestation determination in one year with limited success (Inquiry 9). It is within the law to examine students with disabilities on a case-by-case basis (Inquiry 6). Suggesting a change in special education placement might be a viable approach for Principal Monroe. After all, if Bobby remains in in-school suspension, the setting will still be very limited to his educational improvement. Reconvening an IEP meeting with the parents and suggesting extended time in the special education class might be a feasible solution. Instead of Bobby being in the general education class, where he is now placed for the majority of his day, he can spend increased time in a resource setting and can still be included in the general education classes where he is least likely to get into an altercation with another student. Additionally, it will still be important for the IEP team to revisit Bobby's IEP and BIP to make sure all the interventions and educational services are implemented appropriately. Bobby's parents may be more amenable to this suggestion. The parents have the right to due process at any time regarding the placement (Inquiry 12). With visible positive behavioral changes after a period of time, Bobby may still be transitioned back to the general education classroom for the majority of his school day. Essentially, Bobby should receive interventions that will allow him to learn and practice appropriate ways to resolve problems or conflicts and exercise socially interactive behaviors with peers. The next section offers explicit suggestions regarding Bobby's functional behavior assessment (FBA) and behavioral intervention plan (BIP), preceded by discussion of a schoolwide behavior support approach that will be beneficial to Principal Monroe in reducing and preventing future infractions from all of his students and in maximizing the BIP effectiveness for Bobby.

When responding to cases like Bobby, school administrators and leaders should remember to:

- Always check the legalities of any decision before talking to the parents.
- Actively listen to the parents and make suggestions that are amenable to them if possible.
- Include the student in decision making if he or she is old enough.
- Use proactive rather than punitive approaches to solve problems.
- Find other avenues other than suspensions and expulsion.

Special education administrators should:

- Be available to offer feasible suggestions other than suspensions or other punitive approaches.
- Assure the parents that they are advocates for the child's best interest.
- Make sure that parents understand all of their rights.

POSITIVE BEHAVIORAL INTERVENTIONS AND SUPPORTS AS A PREFERRED APPROACH

Positive behavioral interventions and supports (PBIS) has a long history of establishment with research support. It was originated as an alternative-to-aversive approach by providing person-centered planning and overall lifestyle improvements to individuals with severe disabilities who exhibit extremely dangerous behavior (Carr et al., 2002; Horner et al., 1990; Meyer & Evans, 1993). With decades of expansion, PBIS is now broadly referred to the application of positive behavioral interventions and supports resulting in socially important behavior changes of students with a wide range of severity and intensity levels of challenging behaviors across various educational settings (Sugai & Horner, 2002; Sugai et al., 2000). Within the school context, schoolwide positive behavior support (SWPBS) offers a much needed level of consistency and support to the entire school and allows school leaders to establish a more positive school climate and pupil performance for *all* students, including students with disabilities like Bobby.

Schoolwide Positive Behavior Supports (SWPBS)

Schoolwide positive behavior support is best characterized as a whole-school systemic approach emphasizing effective behavioral interventions at all levels for achieving social and learning outcomes while preventing problem behaviors (Sugai & Horner, 2008). Schoolwide positive behavior support is a preventive approach that emphasizes teaching of positive behavior in contrast to zero tolerance or punitive approaches that are often ineffective and counterproductive (Skiba & Peterson, 1999, 2000). Instead of improving school climate, punitive approaches are associated with higher frequencies of inappropriate social behavior, lower academic outcomes, and higher frequencies of negative teacher–student interactions (Skiba & Peterson, 2000). In some cases, punitive actions such as out-of-school suspension may actually reinforce student misbehavior by enabling the student to escape school demands. An aversive approach to schoolwide discipline is also associated with discriminatory outcomes that exacerbate disproportionality (e.g., Cartledge & Dukes, 2008; Shaw & Braden, 1990). Studies of suspension rates have consistently demonstrated that African American males are suspended at higher rates even for mild rule violations (Gregory & Mosely, 2004; Skiba, Michael, Nardo, & Peterson, 2002; Skiba, Poloni-Staudinger, Simmons, Feggins-Azziz, & Chung, 2005), and that the school approach to discipline is a stronger predictor of suspension rates than student behavior (Skiba et al., 2008). Classroom-based punitive approaches are also related to higher levels of problem behavior. For example, high levels of teacher verbal reprimands are associated with higher frequencies of inappropriate behaviors (Beyda, Fentall, & Zerco, 2002).

The SWPBS system provides a more positive and effective alternative. Schools that implement SWPBS usually experience fewer inappropriate student behaviors; fewer office discipline referrals, suspensions, and expulsions; less administrative time allocated to disciplinary issues; and more administrative time for instructional leadership (Simonson, Sugai, & Negron, 2008). The key features of SWPBS include: "(a) a prevention focused continuum of support, (b) proactive instructional approaches to teaching and improving instructional behaviors, (c) conceptually sound and empirically validated practices, (d) systems change to support effective practices, and (e) data-based decision making" (Sugai & Horner, 2002, p. 2).

The prevention-focused continuum of support entails a three-tiered framework for intervention and is perhaps the most known feature of SWPBS (Sugai & Horner, 2002). Primary-level intervention is also commonly referred to as *universal or schoolwide intervention* and is instituted to support positive behavior for *all* students. All students are served at this level and the interventions include the efforts from *all* school personnel throughout the school day across *all* settings. Secondary intervention is commonly referred to as *targeted intervention* and is directed at selected groups of students or individual students. Tertiary intervention is commonly termed *intensive individual intervention* and is directed at students with significant behavioral challenges. The tertiary-level intervention often involves the implementation of a functional behavior assessment. The intensive intervention plans are more effective when delivered within a continuum of behavior support. When positive, consistent, and proactive practices are in place for all students, the improved school climate has an ameliorative effect on students with more intense needs and the capacity of school personnel to deliver more intensive interventions for individual students is strengthened (Walker, Ramsey, & Gresham, 2004). (The tier approach is further delineated in Chapter 8, "Response to Intervention and Inclusion: Facilitating Collaborative Arrangements.")

The role of both the school and special education administrators within SWPBS is to lead in the effort to:

- Identify meaningful schoolwide outcomes related to implementation.
- Establish and invest in schoolwide systems.
- Select and implement effective practices.
- Collect and use data to make decisions. (Simenson et al., 2008)

Meaningful outcomes could include meaningful decreases in office disciplinary referrals and behavioral incident reports, reduced use of exclusionary time-out, improved attendance and student performance, increased instructional time, and improved staff and family survey results regarding school safety (Bohanon et al., 2006; Ervin, Schaughency, Matthews, Goodman, & McGlinchey, 2007; Miller, George, & Fogt, 2005; Muscott, Mann, & LeBrun, 2008; Nelson, Martella, & Marchand-Martella, 2002).

The school administrator must delineate and identify outcomes and put into place systems that support the SWPBS effort such as a school PBIS team. Current literature suggests a number of steps for effective practice of SWPBS (e.g., Lo, Algozzine, Algozzine, Horner, & Sugai, 2010; Miller et al., 2005; Public Schools of North Carolina, 2008):

- The PBIS team should be a representative team of faculty and specialists with a commitment to effective SWPBS implementation.
- A school administrator with leadership responsibility for SWPBS implementation must be a member of the team.
- The PBIS team's responsibility is to make decisions regarding needed supports such as a SWPBS data system and professional development needs.
- Once a data system is obtained and employed, the team monitors schoolwide behavioral outcomes, such as office disciplinary referral data, to identify and makes data-based decisions to ameliorate problems.
- The team might identify problematic locations or instructional times of the day and devise new school procedures that will address the concern.
- The team also uses data to identify children having behavioral difficulty and in need of more intensive help.
- The team should share data outcomes and celebrate improvements regularly with all school personnel, parents, and community members.
- The school administrator must be centrally involved and supportive of these efforts.
- In addition to implementing systems of support and data-based decision making, the team must promote effective schoolwide practices.
- The school administrator must be involved in encouraging consensus on a set of three to five positively stated schoolwide expectations and making those expectations a central feature of the school's identity.
- Schools must identify explicit routines and procedures in positive terms (e.g., "raise your hand to share ideas") that are aligned with the expectations for all major settings within the school, so that students have a clear understanding of how they should behave.
- Faculty must develop shared lessons that explicitly teach established routines and procedures through clear description, modeling, and student opportunities to practice and practice again.
- Faculty must commit to "catching the students doing it right" much more than catching the students' behavioral errors. The SWPBS system accentuates reinforcement, including high

frequency of teacher praise for students behaving appropriately. The school administrator should educate faculty about the importance of encouraging students to develop socially appropriate behavior and not depending on punitive consequences to suppress problem behaviors.

- When students make behavioral errors, there should be a consistent response from faculty to errors that is free from anger, encourages student self-correction, and reinforces students when they self-correct.
- The school administrator has a critical role in encouraging and reinforcing faculty when they demonstrate fidelity to the positive and effective practices.

Effective Classroom Practices within SWPBS

After the school has established schoolwide expectations, classroom teachers must establish classroom rules that are aligned with the school expectations. The teacher should define three to five positively stated classroom rules that are publicly posted and explain for students how to behave in the classroom (Sugai & Horner, 2002). For example, if the school expectation is "Be Respectful," the classroom rule might be "Raise your hand to receive permission to speak." In some schools implementing SWPBS, teachers are choosing to unify classroom rules within grade levels or even cross-grade levels, or by team or department. The role of the school administrator is to assure that classroom rules are aligned with and support school expectations. Just as routines and procedures are set and explicitly taught for all school settings, routines and expectations for classrooms also need to be set and explicitly taught. There are a myriad of procedures that require behavioral rehearsal such as how to enter the room, how to store personal belongings, where to obtain instructional materials, where and how to turn in written work, how to line up, and how to obtain permission to use the restroom. Teachers who have clearly described and taught these and other procedures have better organization and more predictable structure. Often if a teacher is experiencing a general management problem specific to a common task, a revised and strengthened procedure is needed. School administrators can support teachers by encouraging faculty to share ideas for improved classroom procedures and encouraging adoption of more effective procedures.

Catching students doing right and being good is important in the school and classrooms. For some time, research has indicated that teachers who praise appropriate behavior frequently, specifically, and contingently promote more positive behavioral outcomes (Conroy, Sutherland, Snyder, Al-Hendawi, & Vo, 2009; Conroy, Sutherland, Snyder, & Marsh, 2008; Sutherland, Wehby, & Copeland, 2000). This type of praise, often termed *effective praise*, entails the teacher specifically naming the student's appropriate behavior and praising that behavior immediately after the behavior occurred. A simple way for school administrators to assist a teacher with this necessary skill is simply to record the ratio of specific praise statements to corrections of student misbehavior during a brief observation and discuss the results with the teacher. The use of devices such as MotivAider® (2011), where a teacher can clip the device on his or her belt or place it in a pocket as a prompt (through a silent vibration) to deliver praises to students every certain period of time (e.g., 1 minute, 2 minutes), is also a useful self-management tool for behavioral changes. The goal is to achieve more frequent and correctly delivered praise statements.

Effective correction of misbehavior is as important as effective correction of academic errors. Corrective feedback or corrective teaching always emphasizes direction to the student for correct performance, providing opportunity for the student to self-correct, and reinforcing self-correction. Effective practices within SWPBS entails a continuum of strategies to respond to misbehavior (Sugai & Horner, 2002), but the emphasis should always be on corrective feedback in all cases. A simple example of corrective teaching would be to:

- Name the misbehavior (e.g., "Jason, you are out of seat").
- Provide direction to correct the misbehavior (e.g., "Please take your seat").
- Follow with praise for the specific self-correction (e.g., "All right, good job following our rule: Stay in Your Assigned Seat").

Research has also supported the conclusion that effective teaching supports effective classroom management and vice versa (Heward, 1994). Teachers who employ active teaching techniques such as choral responding and response cards that provide students with many opportunities to respond and a high level of active student responding have higher rates of student engagement and reduced classroom disruptive behaviors (Christle & Schuster, 2003; Hayden, Borders, Embury, & Clark, 2009; Lambert, Cartledge, Heward, & Lo, 2006). Highly engaged students simply have less opportunity to misbehave. In addition, when students are responding frequently and correctly to academic prompting, teachers have more opportunity to specifically praise collective or individual student responses. For this reason, school administrators should emphasize to faculty the importance of effective instructional strategies as a preventive means to addressing misbehaviors in the classrooms. Additionally, administrators should assure that teachers understand the difference in punishment versus the use of positive consequences, which encourage students to be responsible for their behavior and learn to make good choices.

Functional Behavior Assessment (FBA) and Behavioral Intervention Plan (BIP)

As mentioned previously, IDEA (1997, 2004) mandated that schools must conduct an FBA and develop a BIP for students with disabilities who are suspended for more than 10 days in a school year due to their challenging behavior. In addition, if such plans already exist, modifications must take place as appropriate to address the students' needs. Although mandated for students with disabilities who exhibit discipline problems, researchers have highlighted the importance of FBA implementation by demonstrating that the FBA procedures should be applicable to all students (e.g., both students at risk for and with disabilities) for a variety of observable problem behaviors (e.g., both low-incidence and high-incidence behaviors) in multiple contexts (e.g., classrooms, playgrounds) (Sugai & Horner, 1999–2000).

An important defining feature of a functional behavior assessment is to determine the cause or purpose (i.e., to escape an aversive situation/task or to obtain something desirable) of a student's problem behavior and to use the obtained information for intervention development (Scott & Nelson, 1999). Generally speaking, FBA is a process of assessing and identifying the relationships between environmental events (antecedents and consequences) and the occurrence or nonoccurrence of a problem behavior (Dunlap et al., 1993; O'Neill et al., 1997; Sugai, Lewis-Palmer, & Hagan-Burke, 1999–2000). Failure to address the behavioral function may inadvertently strengthen a problem behavior by reinforcing its occurrence (Vollmer & Northup, 1996). For example, contingent adult attention such as reprimands (e.g., "Stop talking") or disapprovals (e.g., "Pay attention to your work") following the occurrence of disruptive behavior can actually produce a consistent and higher level of such problem behavior than has been maintained by adult attention. Similarly, the use of timeout procedures (e.g., requesting students to stand in the hallway outside of the class) may increase the rate of a student's off-task behavior when escaping from instructional activities serves as the purpose of the off-task behavior. Additionally, an intervention that is functionally unrelated to the specific nature of the problem behavior will produce ineffective results because the student's behavioral need is not addressed and it fails to provide appropriate reinforcement for more desirable behavior (Vollmer & Northup, 1996). A common example of such intervention is punitive procedures (e.g., suspension and detention), which rarely provide reinforcement for desirable behavior nor do they involve the provision of instruction for skill acquisition.

In short, FBA is a procedure that can help teachers and administrators find out why the child behaves in a certain way and use the information to develop interventions that can directly address the behavior purpose. Functional behavior assessment can also help school personnel predict a child's behavior and be proactive in making the behavior less likely to happen in the future (O'Neill et al., 1997). Current literature has documented a plethora of research demonstrating the effectiveness of FBA-based interventions on a wide range of students' challenging behaviors in school settings (e.g., Blair, Umbreit, Dunlap, & Jung, 2007; Ellingson, Miltenberger, Stricker, Galensky, & Garlinghouse, 2000; Filter & Horner, 2009; Ingram, Lewis-Palmer, & Sugai, 2005; Lo & Cartledge, 2006; Payne, Scott, & Conroy, 2007; Reid & Nelson, 2002). Considering the usefulness of FBA, administrators should encourage teachers to use FBA whenever a child's problem behavior seems to persist or deteriorate with existing classroom management practice or interventions (Sugai & Horner, 1999–2000).

When conducting an FBA, administrators should assist teachers or other school personnel in completing a four-phase process (O'Neill et al., 1997; Sterling-Turner, Robinson, & Wilczynski, 2001):

1. *The description and problem-identification phase:* Information regarding the target problem behavior is collected through a variety of indirect measures (e.g., record reviews, interviews, rating scales) and direct observations (e.g., antecedent-behavior-consequence recording).
2. *The interpretation and hypothesis-developing phase:* Preliminary data are interpreted and hypotheses or summary statements are generated with regard to the target problem behavior and its associated variables (antecedents and consequences).
3. *The hypothesis verification phase:* Hypotheses are tested systematically to confirm the accuracy of the hypotheses generated from the data.
4. *The intervention phase:* A BIP is developed based on the FBA results and consequently is implemented with ongoing evaluation and modified where appropriate.

Now, let's return to Bobby's case to see how modifications may be made to his existing BIP for more positive outcomes. Although Bobby's behavioral intervention plan has been updated twice, his poor behavior persists. It is likely that Bobby's current BIP did not (or no longer) address(es) his behavioral purpose appropriately. It is probable that either the former BIP had misalignment with the previous FBA results or Bobby's behavior has changed its function/purpose. In either case, it is well advised that a new FBA is conducted.

In order to determine why Bobby continued to slap his classmates in school, the IEP team will first identify the pattern of Bobby's "slapping" behavior (e.g., What does the behavior look like? When and under what situations did the behavior occur? Who were involved in these repeated incidents? What happened to Bobby as a consequence? What did Bobby get or avoid out of his own behavior? Were there any events that seemed to trigger Bobby's behavior?). The IEP team may conduct interviews with teachers or staff members who observed Bobby's slapping incidents, contact Bobby's parents regarding any unusual events that might have had an effect on Bobby's behavior, and/or talk with student victims and Bobby.

The team may also conduct classroom observations to record how Bobby interacts with his teacher and peers, and how he responds to instruction or teacher directives (phase 1). Based on the descriptive data obtained from phase 1, the IEP team will then generate a hypothesis about Bobby's behavior (e.g., "When asked to complete a reading task that is challenging, Bobby fidgets, makes noises, gets out of his seat, engages in verbal conflicts with peers, and slaps peers to avoid instruction and peers' teasing") (phase 2). Essentially, the hypothesis should include the relationship between the target problem behavior and the associated antecedent(s) and consequence(s). To test the hypothesis, the IEP team may observe Bobby during instruction and collect data on Bobby's misbehavior to confirm or disconfirm this hypothesis (phase 3). In the last phase of FBA, the IEP team will develop a BIP that involves (1) removing or neutralizing problematic triggers/antecedents, (2) teaching prosocial behavior and appropriate replacement behavior, and (3) encouraging appropriate behavior, and correcting and discouraging misbehavior (O'Neill et al., 1997). The IEP team will then implement the BIP across classroom settings and continue to observe Bobby's behavior while the intervention is in place to determine whether the intervention is effective and accordingly make data-based decisions (phase 4).

To increase the effectiveness of a BIP, the IEP team should ensure a direct alignment of interventions to the FBA results. Literature has well documented that interventions that are not aligned with the FBA results do not produce effective behavioral changes and may even deteriorate the students' problem behavior (e.g., Ellingson et al., 2000; Ingram et al., 2005). In addition to the alignment of interventions to the FBA results, the IEP team also must monitor the fidelity (i.e., the degree to which the intervention plans are implemented accurately) of the BIP implementation. Interventions with good fidelity have been associated with larger effects, whereas incorrectly implemented interventions produced little change in students' behavior (Stage et al., 2008; Wood, Umbreit, Liaupsin, & Gresham, 2007). Monitoring of the intervention fidelity will be a critical task for the IEP team to ensure Bobby's needs are appropriately addressed. Also, remember the legal issues summarized in Box 5.3.

BOX 5.3

Legal Issues

- Special education leaders are a primary point of contact when rules and regulations involving discipline and the students with disabilities needs to be further defined.
- A change in placement may be warranted rather than continually suspending a student without considering the manifestation determination. Remember the 10-day (consecutive or cumulative) rule.
- Before speaking to families, determine the legalities of the situation as it relates to students with disabilities.
- Make sure the discipline approach "fits" the level of the behavior infraction that the student has committed.

Summary

Schools and special educators have major responsibility for adopting legal and evidenced-based practices that promote safe and orderly schools and avoiding illegal or counterproductive strategies that threaten school order. School administrators cannot effectively address the behavioral problems of students like Bobby by taking a case-by-case and scattershot approach without data-based decision making. See Box 5.4 for specific advice for leaders.

There must be a comprehensive plan in place for promoting positive behavior that includes schoolwide accountability outcomes for behavior, systems for promoting those outcomes, effective academic and behavioral instruction practices throughout the school, and valid schoolwide data for driving decisions. The resolution to the vignette is shown in Box 5.5.

BOX 5.4

Advice for School and Special Education Leaders

- Schoolwide positive behavior support is a proactive, positive, and effective alternative to more punitive approaches.
- Adopting preventive and proactive approaches and deemphasizing reactive practices enable school leaders to create more positive school climate where all students can learn and all teachers can teach.
- Students with more chronic or persistent problem behaviors may require more intensive behavioral support with a well implemented "system" support from the schoolwide and classroom levels.
- Finding the function or determining the cause of an inappropriate behavior leads to interventions that attend to the connected events that caused the behavior.
- Behavior intervention plans are to be adapted if the chosen intervention is not effective.

BOX 5.5

Resolution of the Vignette

After meeting with Dr. Unique, it became clear to Principal Monroe that the FBA and BIP for Bobby needed much revision. There were conflicting opinions on the IEP team regarding the antecedents or triggers that were setting off Bobby's slapping behavior and differing opinions on the consequences that were sustaining the behavior. There were no data to justify any individual's opinion. The team had no defensible hypothesis regarding the function that was being met by the slapping behavior. The team decided to conduct a worthy functional behavioral observation to try to get better understanding of the relationship between antecedents, behavior, and consequences (i.e., function). The observations that were conducted indicated that Bobby would often wander into other students' space and inappropriately touch others when he was not engaged in or able to follow the instruction. Other students would then tell him to go away, get his hands off them, or get back to his seat. Bobby would then talk back to them and then peers would talk back and sometimes tease Bobby. Then Bobby would slap. Once he would slap, the teacher would remove Bobby from the room. The team hypothesized that Bobby was slapping to escape from instruction that bored or frustrated him and to escape other students' reprimands and ridicules. In addressing Bobby's behavior, Bobby's classroom teacher taught him to ask for help appropriately when feeling frustrated by displaying a "Help!" flag signal on his desk and waiting for his teacher to come over. Bobby's teacher also practices with him the correct way to respond to peers' teasing.

Principal Monroe was also starting to see some very real instructional differences across the classrooms of the school since they had begun implementation of the schoolwide positive behavior approach (SWPBS). In Bobby's classroom, the teacher had started to use strategies that gave Bobby more opportunities to respond and he was doing so at a much more successful rate. Since he was more engaged in instruction, he wandered much less. In addition, the teacher had spent much more time teaching students the school rule, "Be responsible," and the related classroom rule, "Stay in your assigned seat unless given permission to leave." She did the same for the school rule, "Be safe," and the related classroom rule, "Keep hands, feet, and objects to yourself." Bobby was given much higher frequencies of specific and contingent praise for following the rules. Importantly, the classroom teacher stopped sending Bobby to the office (i.e., removing Bobby from the instruction). The number of corrective teaching episodes for out-of-seat behavior was decreasing steadily. She also had revised procedures for classroom transitions so there was much less "down" time. Since the other students had learned to "Be respectful," they teased or reprimanded Bobby negatively much less often. As a result, the office disciplinary referrals for physical assault had also ceased. Bobby, Bobby's parents, the teacher, and the other students celebrated their classroom data charts that showed no physical assaults last month by anyone at any time. Principal Monroe was certainly spending fewer hours with Bobby in the office. In addition, he had the satisfaction of moving away from knee-jerk suspensions that never solved any child's problems and seeing real instructional successes.

Chapter Questions

1. Verbal and physical aggression is a prevalent problem in schools. As an administrator, what proactive steps would you take to lessen incidents in your school district?

2. You are devising a schoolwide positive behavior support for your school that is in an urban neighborhood. What do you need to consider when collecting office disciplinary referral data? What types of PBIS teams would be appropriate?

3. You are observing a teacher who has a problem with a student with a learning disability who gets angry, shouts, and corners students. You go to the classroom to observe. What will you note about the teacher? What will you note about the student? What particular laws or inquiries in Table 5.1 relate to the student, if any?

CHAPTER 6

Building Ethos and Interpersonal Relationships with Families and Students

JAMES E. LYONS

INTRODUCTION

If special education and school leaders, teachers, and other staff are to work effectively with families, parents, and students, they will need to build and sustain a school and district ethos that fosters mutual collaboration and cooperation. As defined in Chapter 1, *ethos* is an organization's distinguishing characteristics, values, ideology, or guiding beliefs. In essence, it is the sum total of an organization's key elements, including its structure, personnel, management practices, decision-making system, communication patterns, beliefs, values, history, traditions, and customs. Together, these factors make up both the psychological and sociological dimensions of an organization and combine to become how the organization is generally perceived by those who have contact with individuals who represent it. When the ethos of any organization is positive and healthy, usually a mutually beneficial symbiotic relationship will exist between the organization and its key stakeholders. When such a mutually beneficial symbiotic relationship exists in school and district settings, school leaders, teachers, families, and students are usually able to resolve conflicts, solve problems, and productively work together for school improvement and student success. Moreover, when school and district staff members and families are able to establish positive interpersonal relationships characterized by mutual trust and respect, they will likely be able to establish and maintain two-way communication.

To effectively perform the roles and responsibilities expected of school personnel at the building level, principals, assistant principals, and other school-based professional staff need to be able to work in concert with families and parents to help students succeed in school. This is true of students in general, but it is particularly important in cases when students have learning problems, disabilities, or need special education services. Institutionalized legal requirements and regulations that mandate family involvement increase the roles and responsibilities of special education leaders. Family and parent involvement in special education was formalized in the original language of the Education of the Handicapped Act (PL 94-142, 1975), extended in the early childhood education amendments, and greatly strengthened in the 1997 reauthorization of the Individuals with Disabilities Education Act (IDEA; Gersten, Irvine, & Keating, 2002) Similarly, in the latest reauthorization of the IDEA in 2004, families of special education children were explicitly given the right to play an active role and participate in making decisions regarding their children's educational programs and learning goals. This requirement empowers families and caregivers to actively participate in the process and to serve as supporters and advocates for their children. When a spirit of collaboration and cooperation prevails, there is less likely to be conflicts and misunderstandings. However, when they do occur, it is likely that they will be more easily resolved when school staff members, families, and students share positive relationships.

The No Child Left Behind (NCLB) Act of 2001 (2002) was a reauthorization of the federal Title I program intended to provide enhanced educational assistance to poor and disadvantaged students. It also included a requirement in Section 1118 that mandated that schools organize programs of parental involvement and to communicate with families about students' achievement and the quality of schools. Specifically, NCLB repeatedly specifies that all schools that receive Title I funds must develop a parental involvement component and that communications with families must be clear, useful, and in languages that all families can understand (Epstein, 2005). Although NCLB is normally thought of in terms of its requirements for annual achievement tests, assessing the progress of major subgroups of students, and having highly qualified teachers, like IDEA, it too explicitly and strongly mandates parental involvement in their children's education. Thus, in public schools today, the letter and spirit of the law clearly indicate that parental and family involvement is a key component in the educational system. At the same time, however, most professional educators, particularly school leaders, recognize and appreciate the many benefits that ensue from involving families in their children's education in spite of and not because it is mandated. For some specifically stated challenges and issues for schools and special education leaders, see Box 6.1.

BOX 6.1

Challenges and Issues for School and Special Education Learners

- How to develop and maintain positive and cooperative working relationships with families of students who are exceptional and/or who have disabilities or special needs
- How to resolve conflicts, solve problems, and productively work with parents
- How to legally and effectively provide parents their appropriate and mandated rights to be involved in making decisions affecting their children's education
- How to eliminate or minimize those school-related barriers that frequently serve to thwart or prohibit family and parent involvement
- How to effectively employ the strategies and practices that foster and increase family and parent involvement
- Learning the features of effective family involvement programs in schools

THE SCHOOL–FAMILY–STUDENT ETHOS

When a family has a student who needs or is receiving special education services, the relationship between the family and the school is a very crucial one. Some researchers contend that cultivating good relationships with families of students with disabilities is an essential part of effective special education services (Barbour, Barbour, & Scully, 2010; Bateman & Bateman, 2001; Gersten, Keating, Yovanoff, & Harness, 2001). First, when it is initially suspected that a child may need to be assessed to determine if he or she might need some type of special education, school staff members must be sensitive to how family members are likely to react when they are approached about this. This is because when families learn or are told that their child has a learning problem, they often experience feelings of anger, blame, frustration, and a sense of loss and grief (Evans, 2003; Runswick-Cole, 2007). Other researchers have also addressed the many feelings that families experience when learning that their children need special education services and the kinds of support they need (Ferguson, 2002; Fox, Vaughn, Wyatte, & Dunlap, 2002; Russell, 2008) to establish a positive relationship between school and family. For example, consider the following suggestions:

- *Get to know the family and establish a level of trust with them.* This trust can best be established and sustained by developing a caring school and district ethos (Noddings, 2005; Ramirez & Soto-Hinman, 2009). This will greatly facilitate subsequent interaction between members of the educators and the family. Moreover, by establishing a caring, considerate relationship with the family very early, the stage will often be set for cooperative working relationships throughout the process of serving the student who has special education needs. If a healthy ethos is to be perceived by families and students, all facets of the district should be assessed to determine if they contribute to the desired end result—which is a welcoming, collaborative, supportive, and service-oriented district—to foster the type of ethos needed to effectively serve families.
- *Hold face-to-face meetings.* Face-to-face meetings with families and education personnel are encouraged to assure that they are receiving messages via the families' body language. If possible, meetings should be held with all caregivers together so that the message from educators does not get changed or misinterpreted as it is passed on, leading to more stress at home (Evans, 2003; Runswick-Cole, 2007). For example, in the vignette on Tyler, who has been diagnosed with attention deficit hyperactivity disorder (ADHD), it seems that his relationship with his father may be affecting his behavior at school, but the teacher is dealing only with his mother (see Box 6.2). Educators must be patient and willing to meet with families several times if needed because they often must go through many emotions when caregivers are reaching acceptance of their child's disability.
- *Encourage questions.* Additionally, families and caregivers need to be encouraged to ask questions and school representatives must answer them frankly (Evans, 2003; Turnbull, Taylor, Ervwin, & Soodak, 2011).

Establishing and Sustaining Positive Relationships

From what we have come to know, the opportune time to begin establishing a relationship with families of children is when their children first enter any school, regardless of whether it is an elementary school, a middle school, a high school, or a school with some other organizational structure. This is to assure that new students and their families are immediately

---

BOX 6.2

Vignette: *"Conference Agenda: A Flexible or Inflexible Tool"*

Tyler was assessed and subsequently diagnosed with attention deficit hyperactivity disorder (ADHD). He is a fourth-grader who is served in special education under the "other health impaired" category of IDEA. At his school, Tyler is usually fidgeting and is frequently disruptive in class. His teacher has tried many interventions and approaches to encourage him to improve his behavior. His disruptive behavior prevents him from achieving up to his potential, prohibits other students from doing their work, and requires a disproportionate amount of time from his teacher and her assistant. Tyler's teacher, Ms. Green, has held three conferences with Tyler's mother during the last two months regarding her son's behavior. During each of these conferences, the mother has said that Thler's disruptive behavior is caused by her recent separation from her husband, and she always wants to focus on this during the conferences. She contends that Bobby was close to his father, and he has been getting increasingly more disruptive and defiant since his father moved out. Although Ms. Green can empathize with the situation, she believes that Tyler's mother is using this as a reason for not collaborating with her to help Tyler improve his classroom behavior. Therefore, Ms. Green has scheduled yet another conference and this time she has written up a parent conference agenda form so that she and Tyler's mom can focus only on Tyler's behavior problems, suggestions for cooperatively managing the problem with his mother's assistance, and how and when his mother will be informed of his progress toward improving his behavior.

1. How would you assess the situation with Bobby in terms of what relationship the school should try to establish and maintain with his mother and father?
2. What advice should the principal offer Ms. Green to hold a more effective conference with Bobby's mother?
3. What type of relationship should this teacher seek to establish with Bobby's parents?
4. Should the conference be inflexible or flexible?

---

made to perceive that they are welcome and invited to become an integral part of the school, its programs, and activities. If schools are to be successful in this endeavor, this attitude needs to be pervasive throughout the school staff and embraced in theory and demonstrated in practice.

Joyce Epstein, director of the Center on School, Family, and Community Partnerships at Johns Hopkins University and a well-known authority on home–school–family involvement, contends that schools that are true learning communities welcome and appreciate families of *all* students and recognize that families care about their children's success and wish to see their children succeed (Epstein, 2001; Epstein & Salinas, 2004). However, she notes that most families need more and better information from schools to become more productively involved in their children's education (Epstein, 2001). Further, Epstein states that families can remain connected to their children's schools only if they exchange useful information every year about school programs, children's progress, academic decisions, and other school matters (Epstein, 2001, p. 163). A comprehensive overview of six types of family involvement in schools has been provided by Epstein and her collaborators (Epstein, 1995; Epstein et al., 2002). The six types of involvement they advocate are listed in Figure 6.1.

FIGURE 6.1 Six Types of Family Involvement

Families	Assisting families with parenting skills, family support, understanding child and adolescent development, and setting home conditions to support learning at each age and grade level.
Communicating	Communicating with families about school programs and student progress.
Volunteering	Improving recruitment, training, activities, and schedules to involve families as volunteers and as audiences at the school or in other locations.
Learning at Home	Involving families with their children in academic learning at home, including homework, goal setting, and other curriculum-related activities.
Decision-making	Including families as participants in school decisions, governance, and advocacy activities through school councils or improvement teams, committees, and parent organizations.
Collaborating with the Community	Coordinating resources and services for families, students, and the school with community groups, including businesses, agencies, cultural and civic organizations, and colleges or universities.

Source: Compiled from J. L. Epstein. School/family/community partnerships. *Phi Delta Kappan, 76*(9) (1995): 701–712. Printed with permission of Phi Delta Kappa International, www.pdkintl.org.

Relationships with Families

In education today, the vast majority of scholars and professional educators recognize the benefits for establishing and sustaining positive relationships with families. Gonzales-Dehass, Willems, and Doan-Holbein (2005) found that students from elementary to high school show a beneficial relationship between parental involvement and the following (student) motivational constructs: school engagement, intrinsic/extrinsic motivation, perceived competence, perceived control, self-regulation, mastery goal orientation, and motivation to read. Moreover, two of the major, most well-known federally supported education programs in the public schools mandate parental involvement—namely, NCLB and IDEA. The Individuals with Disabilities Education Act requires that families, parents, and caregivers who have children who need special education or related services be provided specific rights to actively participate in decisions affecting the assessment, placement, and educational and related services provided to those children. Thus, it is incumbent on special educators as well as school-based professional educators, principals, and teachers to get to know and establish relationships with families of children who have special learning or behavior needs.

Several authors (Applequist, 2009; Kozik, 2005; Murray et al., 2007; Pogoloff, 2004) have provided sound, useful advice for professional educators to establish relationships with families. They note that educators should seek to develop a personal relationship with families, characterized by trust. If the family members are going to candidly discuss personal family issues, problems, challenges, and more that might be affecting their children, they must to know that their confidentiality will be observed, respected, and protected. When the families are not of the same background, culture, or class of the professional educators, the school professionals must be sensitive to this and perhaps make a special effort to help these families perceive that they and their children are valued members of the school family. The authors support that administrators practice the concept of servant leadership when working with families. By that, they mean that administrators should by word and deed convey that their role is to serve, assist, and support

FIGURE 6.2   20 Thoughtful Practical Suggestions for School Professionals

Developing a personal relationship with families so they will feel comfortable in sharing crucial, relevant information about their child and the family.

Soliciting information from families using multiple formats (i.e., in writing, by phone, face to face meetings, etc.).

Starting every conversation with something positive about the student and/or family member.

Demonstrating interest, respect, and caring about the student as a whole person who also participates in family activities and other activities and has some interests outside of school.

Telling families that you want to know what they think their child's strength and needs are.

Developing a plan to communicate something positive about the student on a regular basis.

Interacting with students and families in multiple environments.

Conducting informal meeting with families and students prior to Individualized Education Program (IEP) meetings.

Planning meetings with the student and family's schedule as the first priority.

Writing down parent/family and student input and using it when developing the IEP.

Not sending formal notices without consulting with families and informing them of the purpose of the notice.

Being sensitive to the emotions of families.

Listening to families.

Not doing other tasks while caregivers and families are talking.

Providing specific, detailed information to families related to goals, objectives, expectations, strategies, teaching methods, or ongoing progress of students.

Not hesitating to provide information more than once.

Communicating honestly with families.

Respecting and guarding confidentiality at all times.

Being available when needed.

Not giving up.

Source: Compiled from S. M. Pogoloff. Facilitate positive relationships between parents and professionals. *Intervention in School and Clinic, 40* (2004): 116–119. Printed with permission of the author.

families and caregivers in a collaborative manner to help students achieve success. Moreover, the authors contend that knowing students and their families is the foundation to engaging them successfully, regardless of their class, race, gender, or disability. Pogoloff (2004) has provided 20 thoughtful, practical suggestions for school professionals to facilitate positive relationships with families/parents of special education children (see Figure 6.2).

INVOLVING FAMILIES AS PARTNERS

Family involvement is considered essential in improving the educational achievement of students with educational disabilities or behaviors that inhibit their learning. Family involvement was an original component of IDEA, and the role of families has been expanded in each reauthorization of the law, both in Part B of IDEA (2004), which covers all special education children served in public schools, and in Part C of IDEA (2004), which addresses parental involvement for infants and toddlers. Consequently, school leaders, particularly principals, have been charged with and expected to incorporate family involvement in the administration of special education programs for over 30 years. However, because most administrator preparation programs ordinarily require little, if any, study in how to cultivate and sustain family involvement in schools in general and in special education in particular (Crockett, 2002; Crockett, Becker, & Quinn, 2009), most principals have had to engage in on-the-job training to hone their knowledge and skills in this area. Similarly, for the most part, teacher education programs have also given scant attention to family involvement in general or special education preservice programs. Accordingly, most practicing principals and students in preservice administrator preparation programs would be better equipped to lead schools if they were more familiar with the principles and practices for involving *all* families and parents in their children's education—particularly those families who have children with special learning needs or challenges.

Fortunately, there are a number of resources and individuals with knowledge and expertise in this area to consult to enhance one's knowledge of family involvement practices. Several of a few well-respected individuals with expertise in this area include:

1. Joyce L. Epstein (Epstein et al., 2002), who directs the Center on School, Family, and Community Partnerships at Johns Hopkins University
2. Eugenia Hepworth Berger, author of *Parents as Partners in Education* (2008)
3. Maxine B. Zinn, Stanley Eitzen, and Barbara Wells (2011), authors of *Diversity in Families*
4. Patricia Ruggiano Schmidt (2005), editor of *Preparing Educators to Communicate and Connect with Families and Communities*
5. Ann P. Turnbull, Rutherford Turnbull, Elizabeth J. Erwin, and Leslie C. Soodak (2011), authors of *Families, Professionals, and Exceptionality: Positive Outcomes Through Partnerships and Trust* (6th ed.)
6. Gerardo R. López (2001a, 2001b), who has argued that educators should redefine how they view parental involvement

Concepts gleaned from scholars in this area are addressed in subsequent sections of this chapter.

BARRIERS TO FAMILY INVOLVEMENT

There are a number of barriers that serve to prevent or limit family involvement in their children's schooling. Scholars have studied these barriers from both a parental perspective and the perspective of school professional staff members (Lynch & Stein, 1987; Rusnswick-Cole, 2007). Reasons given by families identified as barriers to participation included work schedules, time constraints/conflicts, communication problems, feelings of inferiority, and uncertainty about their child's unique problems. School professionals identified barriers to family involvement to issues such as parental apathy, lack of released time for teachers to contact or meet with families, lack of expertise, and feeling overburdened and devalued. Some authors identified reasons for lack of parental involvement as the inability to attend meetings, communication problems, lack of time, and feelings of inferiority when interacting with teachers and other helping professionals (Mostert, 1998; Ramirez & Soto-Hinman, 2009). When examined as a whole, families tend not to be active in the children's schooling tend to center around several reasons, which are discussed next.

Bureaucratization of Processes and Procedures

Today, due primarily to school consolidation to achieve economies of scale, the U.S. public educational system has become a large, bureaucratized enterprise. As a result, the educational system is more institutional and impersonal. Hence, the schooling process has become more akin to mass

---

BOX 6.3

Legal Issues

Specifically, major laws, mandates, and initiatives have been enacted to improve educational opportunities and programs for children who are poor, have disadvantages and disabilities, and have learning challenges.

- Federal mandates that provide a free and appropriate education to children with disabilities or special needs and their families has been one of the most challenging of the many responsibilities held by school leaders.
- Leaders should recognize and anticipate that, given the complex mandates and regulations that govern special education, inevitably there will be some conflicts with families as they seek to assure that their children receive an appropriate education in the least restrictive environment.
- Families and parents in pursuit of programs, accommodations, and services that school leaders are not able to provide in a timely manner, if at all, may result in stressful, emotionally charged meetings for both families and school personnel. Leaders must learn to empathize with families and stay mindful that the families are only seeking what they perceive to be best for their children.
- Regarding legal issues, school and special education leaders, who most frequently are the ultimate recipients of families' anger, should be able to stay calm, remain professional in demeanor, and be able to take frustrations and anger in stride while continuing to work through the conflict and eventually do what is in the child's best interest.

---

production, factory-like enterprises, and is seen by some parents and students as disinterested institutions to families and students as unique individuals. As a consequence, many families find that it is difficult and sometimes intimidating to access and establish personal relationships with professionals. Moreover, due to the large size of many schools, elaborate processes and procedures are encountered when families wish to interact with personnel to resolve an issue or problem with their child. To minimize this problem, educational professionals should:

- Examine their policies, procedures, and practices and take steps to create a more user-friendly, welcoming, and less bureaucratic environment.
- Simplify and publicize their policies, regulations, and procedures, and develop programs and practices to see that families and parents understand these.
- Create a full- or part-time parent advocate position to assist families and parents in accessing personnel, understanding policies and procedures, and resolving issues and problems.
- Refer to Box 6.3 for several legal issues that that leaders need to remember.

Professionalization of Education

The contemporary public educational system is a very complicated one with many different programs, requirements, regulations, and standards to be met by students, including achievement test expectations. As complex organizations, schools operate under an elaborate set of formal and informal rules, most of which are fully understood only by the school professionals. As a result, the vast majority of noneducator, lay families and parents are ill-equipped to understand all of these programs, regulations, requirements, and so on. Family members who do not understand these rules and regulations will often be confused and will get lost in the bureaucracy while trying to figure them out (Johnson, Pugach, & Hawkins, 2004; Turnbull et al., 2011). Accordingly, even when they are motivated to be involved in their children's education and meet with professionals, parents frequently find it difficult to fully comprehend the programs and requirements in the school system or district. Thus, the educational process is now elaborate and complicated; few other than the professional educators are really intimately familiar with the educational programs and requirements. Since special education programs and their many accompanying regulations and requirements are generally deemed to be the most complicated of all programs offered in public education, it is little wonder that families who have children needing or receiving special education often find it challenging, frustrating, and stressful when they have to interact with professional educators. This suggests that special education and school leaders should take extraordinary efforts to help families understand the many intricacies of special education programs, services, and practices with which they should be familiar.

Communication Problems

Developing and sustaining communication with the various publics, patrons, and parents served by the schools is an ongoing challenge for public school personnel. In particular, school principals, teachers, counselors, and other school-based professionals employ many strategies to inform and communicate with families regarding school activities, and the academic progress of their children. However, when it comes to maintaining communication with families and parents, the vast majority of schools encounter problems (Johnson et al., 2004; Mostert, 1998; Ramirez, & Soto-Hinman, 2009). Section B of IDEA (2004) mandates that families will be actively involved in the assessment process, the development of the individualized education plan (IEP) for the child, the child's learning placement, and the substantive decisions regarding the child. Therefore, it is essential that school personnel develop and maintain ongoing communication with families.

Various authors (Johnson et al., 2004; Russell, 2008; Turnbull et al., 2011; Zinn et al., 2011) cite several of the key reasons why families and parents of special education students encounter problems in communicating with professional educators. First, it is important to note that families often come from cultural or socioeconomic backgrounds different from school personnel—which can make communication difficult. Moreover, parents contend that when educational jargon and abbreviations (acronyms) enter into the process, teachers and families and caregivers may be speaking two related but different languages with different vocabularies and styles. The result is often an argument—the teacher and the parent think they understand each other but actually having a very different understanding of the same conversation.

Second, the problem of different cultural and socioeconomic backgrounds is compounded by the different communication styles families employ that may be far different from the styles normally used by professional educators. For example, some families are loud and emotional to one another, whereas other families are more reserved and restrained. Parents and families also note that a teacher might interpret a mother's loud and emotional response as aggression when that style of communication is the family's communication norm. This suggests that educational personnel might try to determine the normal communication styles of families as they get to know them.

Third, to facilitate effective communication with families, the ability to read and interpret nonverbal communication is important. Nonverbal communication includes facial expressions, body language, eye contact, amount of personal space required, and the way one listens. If the school staff members are unable to read and understand the nonverbal communication of family members, they will likely not be able to communicate effectively with them because it is an important aspect of communication, particularly when individuals are from different cultural and socioeconomic backgrounds.

Family/Parent Time Constraints

Although school professionals sometimes attribute lack of parental involvement to apathy or indifference, it may often be due to family/parent time constraints or related issues. Many families, particularly those from lower social economic backgrounds, have time constraints and/or competing demands on their time. Research shows that lower-income, minority, and non-English speaking families are often not involved in school activities in the traditional ways expected by educators (Finders & Lewis, 1991; Zinn et al., 2011). Often these family members have inflexible work schedules that preclude taking time off to visit the school and/or participate in decision making relating to their children. If meetings to discuss their child's educational program, learning or behavior problems, placement, or IEP are scheduled during the school day, it may be difficult or impossible for the appropriate family members to attend. To minimize family time constraint problems, school personnel should determine what the constraints and relevant factors are and plan strategies to accommodate and work around them.

Techniques for Involving Families

The most important technique for getting families involved in their children's education is to establish relationships and contact with them as soon as the school year begins (Johnson et al., 2004; Murray et al., 2007; Russell, 2008). Ideally administrators should make sure that the following procedures are in place:

- Teachers should contact families/parents before school opens by meeting with them, calling them, or sending them a letter or postcard. The advantage of a phone call or face-to-face meeting is that both of these options provide an opportunity for the teacher to ask if there is anything that the parent wishes to share about the child as the new school year begins.
- Teachers should contact families before or at the beginning of the school year to establish a relationship with the child's family and it communicates the teacher's level of commitment and caring right at the beginning of school. It conveys the message to families that the school in general and the teacher in particular wishes to involve them in the child's education. Moreover, it eliminates the possibility for the first contact with the family to be precipitated by a problem, which will likely create negative feelings (Johnson et al., 2004).
- Techniques such as a parent handbooks, newsletters, regular progress reports, occasional notes, and telephone conferences should be implemented (Turnbull et al., 2011).
- Frequent face-to-face conferences are held with school professionals, usually the child's teacher(s). The purposes of conferences are listed in Figure 6.3.

FIGURE 6.3 Conference Purpose

To share information about the home and school environment.
To work together to help the child develop and share information on the child's progress.
To develop rapport and mutual commitment to the child's optimal development.
To cooperate in alleviating problems or concerns.

Source: Compiled from A. P. Turnbull, R. L. Taylor, E. J. Erwin, & L. C. Soodak. *Families, Professionals, and Exceptionality: Positive Outcomes through Partnerships and Trust* (6th ed.). Upper Saddle River, NJ: Pearson/Merrill-Prentice Hall, 2011.

Communicating with Families

It has been said that trust is the glue that holds relationships together and that communication is the vehicle that builds and sustains trust and those relationships. This is applicable both to personal, informal relationships as well as more formal business, professional, and organizational relationships, including the schools. Thus, to effectively serve families and students, school professionals need to foster and sustain ongoing two-way communication. School personnel interact with families on two levels: institutional and individual (Epstein, 1995). An organization operates at the institutional level when it invites all families to an event or sends all families the same communications such as letters, newsletters, and so on. Conversely, the organization is operating at the individual level when an administrator or teacher communicates with a specific family or meets individually with families to discuss an issue involving a child. Thus, to develop and maintain a strong communication program, professionals need to strike the appropriate balance between institutional and individual communication with families and they should know which one is most suitable in a given situation.

Given the nature of the contact and communication that normally occurs between school professionals and families of special education students, individual communication is usually more appropriate and, in most cases, is the type of communication required. Since much of the communication between families and professionals will be private and confidential, channels for individual communication should be selected and employed. For example, at the beginning of the year, teachers of students with disabilities or special needs should consult with families and determine their preferred method(s) of communication regarding the child's educational program and progress during the year. It has also been noted that one of the most important communication skills needed in working with families of students receiving special education services is the ability to listen (Davern, 1996; Hornby, 2000; Kozleski et al., 2008; O'Shea, Algozzine, Hammitte, & O'Shea, 2001). Consequently, active listening to what is said (and what is not said) when conferring with families may reveal much relative to what is occurring in a family that may be impacting the child's education or behavior at school.

Creating Family Education Initiatives

Given the demographics of most public school systems, and the complexity of the process, coupled with the other competing obligations on families' time, administrators find it necessary to employ various and sundry strategies to educate families on policies, programs, regulations, and practices. Therefore, they find that they must develop and carry out various types of family education initiatives. Although this is true for families in general, it is even more crucial for families who have children who need special education services. The research on family involvement in schools indicates that all families want what is in the best interest of their children, but they often do not always know what it is or how to get it. Accordingly, the responsibility for helping families learn techniques and strategies for getting involved in their children's schools rest with professional educators, particularly school principals, as they are the school leaders who have the most direct and ongoing contact with families. In order to adequately foster family involvement, administrators must:

- Have the requisite knowledge and skills needed to develop and manage these programs.
- Provide families and students the assistance, support, and rights they deserve when they are properly equipped to do so.

- Encourage families to cooperatively participate in their children's education. To be active and full partners with education personnel in implementing the level of collaboration expected and required in implementing IDEA, families of students who require special education must have the basic information needed to fulfill the designated role specified for families in the law.
- To be sure that families understand their rights specified in the latest reauthorization of IDEA (further delineated in Chapter 2 "Laws and Policy Affecting Schools: Going Beyond Compliance"); Section 504 of the Rehabilitation Act of 1973; information on the child's suspected disability, behavior, or learning problem; the process for assessing the child; educational placement option(s); procedure for developing the IEP; plan for monitoring/assessing the child's progress; the role of the school personnel; and expectations of the family in helping the child with his or her development, learning, behavior, or disability.
- Involve school personnel who are most familiar with the child in helping to educate families. This should be done in their primary language of the parents/families; in terms that they clearly understand; on an individual basis with families so they will feel comfortable in discussing the school, the child, the family/family situation; and any issues or problems they wish to address concerning the child or family (IDEA, 2004).

In some cases, information may be discovered in these meetings that indicate that a child's problem(s) may stem from the family, home environment, or parenting practices. Researchers note that five parenting practices of families with children with behavior problems are (1) lack of family problem-solving skills, (2) noncontingent positive reinforcement, (3) physical or harsh punishment practices, (4) minimal supervision, and (5) inconsistent discipline (O'Shea et al., 2001).

The school staff may conclude that they will need to work with the family to address parenting practices, since they often impact why some students with behavior problems act out at school. The vignette about Tyler is illustrative of a case where the student is presenting behavior problems both at home and at school.

The special education administrator can schedule annual meetings with families of students with special needs to help them better understand special education issues. A good overview of the focus, structure, content, and activities that might be addressed in these meetings, including length of time, usually short, running from 7:00 to 9:00 pm, with a 30- to 45-minute presentation (Evans, 2003). The program can include a talk, or video on such topics as the special education identification process, advocacy practices, understanding various disabilities, child aggression, the development of speech and language, team work in special education, and resources for special needs children outside the school system. A question-and-answer session may follow the presentation during which families receive a short handout that covers the main points of the presentation and a phone number to call.

Special education administrators can also provide a parent-to-parent support group. This is simply a group made up of families and caregivers of students who participate in special education programs and services who meet to share information, resources, techniques for working with their children, and to serve as a source of support for each other. These parent-to-parent support groups also serve the valuable function of helping members realize that there are others who are experiencing many of the same challenges and issues they face so they feel less isolated and alone. Moreover, these families and caregivers are often able, through sharing their experiences, to establish support networks that enable them to provide tangible support to each other such as carpooling, supervising each other's child, working jointly on advocacy issues, and in some cases establishing personal friendships.

Resolving Conflicts

Dealing with conflict is part and parcel of the every leader's responsibility. The special education or the principal's office is usually the collection place for major conflicts in the school, regardless of whether the parties involved are students, families, teachers, or other staff. The conflicts that involve exceptional students are often more complicated, protracted, and difficult to resolve in comparison to the problems of general education students. In great part, this is because there are more regulations, guidelines, and requirements that govern special education, particularly disciplining students who have been classified as exceptional and/or who have disabilities. Mitchell Yell, Joseph B. Ryan, Antonis Katsiyannis, among others, offer legal, sound, and practical advice regarding disciplining students with disabilities (Ryan, Katsiyannis, Peterson, & Chemler, 2007a; Yell, 2006). Moreover, because families of students with disabilities often perceive that they must assume a greater role in monitoring their child's education and school experiences, they are more likely to play an advocacy role in supporting their child's education. In many cases, their advocacy efforts result in conflicts with school officials over determination of the exceptionality of the students and the most appropriate services to be provided. These conflicts, many times, can be resolved with the assistance of the special administrator. Nevertheless, it is crucial that school leaders take a proactive role to resolve these conflicts at the school level if possible or they will invariably become more difficult to solve when they are elevated to a higher level, often leaving ill-will in their wake. In some cases, failure to resolve these problems at the school level results in protracted litigation in the courts.

A second factor that contributes to conflict between families of students with disabilities and school personnel is IDEA (2004) and the rights and responsibilities that it places on families to actively participate in a series of crucial decisions affecting their children's education. Indeed, a fundamental component of IDEA is parental involvement. In comparison, no such requirements are placed on families of students in general education. While they may, if they choose, be actively involved, there is no federal mandate that they be actively involved in making key decisions regarding their children. However, there are provisions throughout IDEA that require parental involvement. The most specific and important provisions in which families must be involved include assessment, IEP meetings, and placement. Given the specific requirement that families be involved in these three decision-making phases, if parents/families refuse to participate, they will engender conflict. If and when they refuse to participate, it places the school personnel and the parent(s) in an adversarial position, thus guaranteeing conflict. On the other hand, the parent(s) might agree to meet, but might refuse to concur or support a decision that school personnel deem to be in the best interest of the child. Here, again, this places the parent(s) and school personnel in an adversarial position.

What can school leaders do to minimize the number and intensity of conflicts with families of children with special needs?

- First, we recommend that they seek to establish and maintain a positive relationship with and display a caring attitude toward all students and families. This will increase the level of trust between families and school staff members, which will serve to improve the capacity to resolve conflicts.
- Second, leaders and other staff should provide families information and educate them on their child's learning, behavior, or disability challenges.
- Third, the positive attributes and areas in which the families' child has shown progress, if possible.

Accommodating Family Rights

To effectively and efficiently provide leadership in special education, administrators should be prepared to honor and meet both the spirit and letter of the law in accommodating family rights. This ranges from being flexible in planning meetings at times that will accommodate families' schedules to conducting informal meetings with families to holding IEP meetings to explain their roles and prepare them to fully and intelligently participate to scheduling meetings with special education administrators. It also means taking steps to ensure that families are fully aware of what their rights are vis-à-vis to their child who may need or is served by any type of special education. At a minimum, this means informing families that:

- Their child is entitled, through IDEA (2004) Part B in the public schools, to receive a free and appropriate education from ages 3 to 21.
- Parental consent is required before a child is evaluated for special education the first time (IDEA, 2004).
- Families have a right to inspect and review all records relating to their child that a public agency, including the school, collects, maintains, and uses regarding the identification, evaluation, or educational placement of the child or the provision of a free and appropriate education to the child. (IDEA, 2004)
- Families have a right to obtain an independent evaluation of their child (IDEA, 2004).
- Parental consent is required for a child's initial placement in special education (IDEA, 2004).
- Families have a right to challenge or appeal any decision related to the identification, evaluation, or educational placement of their child or the provision of a free and appropriate education to their child (IDEA, 2004; Yell, 2006).

FEATURES OF EFFECTIVE FAMILY INVOLVEMENT PROGRAMS

Research indicates that family involvement increases student academic achievement. The benefits of family involvement includes higher test scores, better grades, better attendance, higher levels of completion of homework, and more positive student motivation and attitudes about schoolwork (Turnbull et al., 2011; Walker, Colvin, & Ramsey, 1995). An examination of successful family involvement programs indicates that they have common characteristics; these are addressed in the following sections.

Proactive Focus and Ongoing Involvement

Some researchers note that teachers often wait for families to take the first steps in getting involved in their children's education (Walther-Thomas, Korinek, McLaughlin, & Williams, 2000). The exceptions are when school administrators and teachers first solicit the involvement of families when their children are causing problems at school, most frequently learning or behavior problems. Obviously, when the first contact with families or parents is precipitated by a perceived problem with their children, it does not bode well or set the stage for a positive relationship. Moreover, since these initial contacts often place the families in a defensive posture vis-à-vis school personnel, both families and school representatives are sometimes trying to address students' needs and problems under stressful conditions. Such contacts, which sometimes become adversarial, do not provide ideal conditions for wholesome family involvement and effective school–home relations. For these reasons, it is recommended that personnel take a proactive stance to involve families in their children's education very early in the school year before problems necessitate contact. Successful parental involvement programs, then, are proactive; they reach out to families to establish positive relationships and to make the families an integral part of the school.

Clearly Explained Goals

Another characteristic of effective family involvement programs is that they have clearly explained goals, objectives, and expectations for family and parental involvement. They develop programs and employ practices to clearly and regularly inform families about programs, operational procedures, and how and when families may contact school personnel. Also, leaders in these schools carefully study the demographics of their families and students and they develop outreach programs and techniques that are geared specifically for the family and student populations they serve. The leaders anticipate questions that families will have and information that they need to assist their children in the learning process. When working with families of students with disabilities, it is crucial that school personnel collaborate with the appropriate family representatives to determine the developmental, learning, and behavior goals for their children.

Accommodation of Diverse Families

Far too frequently educators incorrectly believe that families are not involved in their children's education if their behavior does not fit their definition of parent involvement. This is because many educators often have a "one-size-fits-all" mentality relative to parental involvement, which does not apply to the diverse families represented in most schools today (Zinn et al., 2011). Principals and teachers usually view parental involvement as parental participation in school-initiated, school-based, time-limited activities. This includes attending Open House, "Back to School" night, Parent–Teacher Association meetings, parent conferences, book fairs, fund raisers, and so on, or serving as a chaperone for field trips, school volunteer, grade parent, or school advisory/planning/governance team member. This tends to reflect the suburban middle-class, "parental-presence-at-the-school" view of parental participation because it often requires flexible work schedules, transportation, frequent parent–school communication, and the like. When the type of involvement does not fit this definition, educators often perceive that the families are not involved, which perpetuates a stereotype.

Some researchers argue for a broader, more encompassing definition of parental involvement (López, 2001a, 2001b; Anderson & Minke, 2007). Their premise is that families are so diverse that the traditional view of parental involvement does not fit many families of the current generation of students. The researchers contend that many families, particularly those who are marginalized, will not or cannot engage in the traditional school-based, time-specific activities planned for families. Factors such as family structure, economic status, employment status, competing demands on their time, cultural values, beliefs, linguistic background, and past experiences with schooling all affect if, how, and to what extent families are involved in their childrens' schooling. Gerardo R. López has strongly advanced the case that parental involvement needs to be redefined to recognize that marginalized families can be highly involved and supportive of their children's education without visiting the campus to participate in traditional "parental-presence-at-the-school" activities. By examining the behavior of Latino migrant families, López (2001b) found that it is possible for families to strongly support and be deeply involved by instilling in their children the value of education, encouraging upward mobility, regularly sending them to school, and teaching them the value of hard work. One of the most salient points that López makes is that it is absolutely crucial that principals and teachers develop a relational bond with students and their families to establish and maintain a supportive, collaborative relationship and meet the needs of migrant families on an ongoing basis (López, 2001a, p. 281). Although his research primarily examined Latino families, his findings are very insightful, particularly for diverse parent groups.

Other researchers have, however, noted that some families—particularly those from minority groups, from lower socioeconomic levels, and families of children with behavior problems—have limited traditional involvement with the schools (Dodd, 1996; Kozleski et al., 2008; Ramirez & Soto-Hinman, 2009). Therefore, it is crucial that school leaders and other school personnel make a special effort to involve families from these categories—even if it means in nontraditional ways. To aid educators in working with diverse families, Zinn and colleagues (2011) and Parette and Petch-Hogan (2000) developed some very helpful suggestions. These include assessing family interests, learning techniques for collaborating with diverse families, assessing one's own attitudes about diverse students, and becoming familiar with general family–school issues.

It is especially important that families of students with special needs be identified and encouraged to be involved in the school and in their children's education. Moreover, Davern (1996) recommends that these families be informed about the general education program and activities as well as special education programs available in or through the school. The reason is that these families usually want to know the opportunities that are available for their children to be involved in schoolwide activities in a similar manner as students in the general education program. This is important because families of students with disabilities usually wish for their children to participate in as many activities as possible with other students in the general school population. Moreover, this is a fundamental premise of the "least restrictive environment" guideline that undergirds special education programs, services, and activities, particularly student placements. At the same time, these families need to and are mandated by IDEA to be actively involved in the decisions relating to the special education services in which their children are involved.

Summary

School and special education leaders today must practice their craft in an environment that is increasingly more challenging and turbulent. In addition to the array of responsibilities that must be carried out to lead school districts and individual schools, the heightened accountability movement that has been foisted on public education during the last 30 years has engendered the expectation that leaders perform their roles ethically, legally, effectively, and efficiently, usually under close public scrutiny. The expectations have been increased for improved student academic performance of students in general, but they have particularly been increased for targeted groups of students who formerly were not served well in far too many cases. Box 6.4 offers advice for leaders.

Leaders should also work to eliminate or reduce the barriers that prohibit families of students receiving special education services from getting involved in schools and participating in their children's education. Some of the major barriers include bureaucratization of processes and procedures, professionalization of schooling, communication problems, and family/parent time constraints. In contrast, some features of successful family involvement programs

---

BOX 6.4

Advice for School and Special Education Leaders

Research indicates that there are a number of other things that both special and school leaders can and should do to effectively provide the leadership needed to manage special education programs and related services.

- Leaders should develop, foster, and sustain the ethos that communicates to both families and children with special needs that the spirit and letter of the law will be honored, respected, and adhered to in practice.
- It is extremely crucial that principals, teachers, and school-based staff members establish a positive relationship and establish trust with families and children who may need special education services.
- Every effort should be made to assure that these students and their families are an integral part of the school and school system, as well as its programs and activities.
- Programs and strategies should be developed and employed to involve, educate, and communicate with these families in the ongoing activities of the school, and particularly in the programs and activities for children who have learning or behavior problems and/or disabilities.
- Programs and strategies recommended by recognized authorities on family involvement in schools such as Epstein and colleagues (2002), Berger (2004), Schmidt (2005), López (2001a), and Turnbull and colleagues (2011) should be studied and, when deemed feasible, implemented.

---

include a proactive focus and ongoing family–school involvement/communication, clearly explained goals, and accommodation of diverse families.

School and special education leaders should develop initiatives and strategies to engage in ongoing two-way communication with families of students who are participating in special education program or services. Since these families often perceive that they must actively advocate for and monitor their children's education, they should be strongly encouraged and supported in their efforts to participate. This can best be done by providing unfettered opportunities for them to communicate with the appropriate school or system staff members at times and places that accommodate the parents' schedules. In particular, school principals and special education leaders should arrange for families of students with special needs to have face-to-face meetings with teachers and other school personnel on a regularly scheduled and on an as-needed basis. Box 6.5 has the resolution to the vignette.

BOX 6.5

Resolution of the Vignette

The child's caregiver may have more insight on the child's difficulty than the school. The parent's claim could be quite legitimate and should not be ignored. It seems that counseling is in order for Tyler.

Chapter Questions

1. What strategies should school principals and special education leaders employ to establish and maintain positive relationships with families of special education students? Which strategies would likely be most successful in schools in which you have worked or are working?

2. What are some features of effective family involvement programs? What steps would you follow in developing a coherent family involvement program for families of children with disabilities or special needs?

3. What are the most important rights of families mandated in the most recent reauthorization of IDEA?

4. What are some of the barriers to family involvement in schools in general and with families of children receiving special education or related services in particular? What might be done to reduce these barriers?

5. What are the most important things leaders should keep in mind as they develop and plan family involvement activities for children with disabilities and/or special needs?

6. How should school leaders today define *parental involvement*?

CHAPTER 7

Transitioning from Early Intervention to Adulthood

Dawn A. Rowe

Lee Sherry

INTRODUCTION

Transition to adulthood is an important stage in life for students with disabilities and their parents. Planning for transition provides parents with links to teachers, counselors, related service personnel, and community agency support services. Over the years, parent and family involvement and interagency collaboration have been found to be consistent predictors of postsecondary success of young adults with disabilities (Kortering, Braziel, & McClannon, 2010; Kraemer, McIntyre, & Blancher, 2003; Repetto, Webb, Garvan, & Washington, 2002; Williamson, Robertson, & Casey, 2010). Kochhar-Bryant, Shaw, and Izzo (2007) emphasize the importance of collaboration between agencies and families to organize appropriate resources for students to increase the chance for appropriate services and positive postsecondary education, employment, and independent living goals outcomes. Kraemer and colleagues (2003) specifically found that parent knowledge of community agency support services and their involvement in transition planning was significantly related to students' overall quality of life.

This chapter will address the principles and practices of interagency collaboration and coordination of services for infants, toddlers, children, and youth with disabilities and their families. The key roles of school personnel and service providers in community agencies providing comprehensive services will be discussed. In addition, techniques that build and facilitate effective interagency collaboration, teamwork, and networking will be delineated. This chapter addresses many of the challenges and issues that leaders face regarding transition (outlined in Box 7.1).

BOX 7.1

Challenges and Issues for School and Special Education Leaders

- Implementing the Individuals with Disabilities Education Act to assure the rights of students with disabilities pertaining to transition planning and the transition components of the individualized transition plan (ITP) and individualized family services plan (IFSP).
- Providing family and community outreach and support.
- Empowering parents with the information and knowledge necessary to advocate for their children and be active partners in the collaboration process.
- Designing planning strategies and procedures based on student population, available resources, personnel, and cultural diversity.
- Developing a proactive approach to communicating with agency partners.
- Defining goals and establishing roles within in school and community level transition teams.
- Encouraging teambuilding and teamwork.

The amendments of the Education for All Handicapped Children Act of 1975 in 1986 (PL 99-457) has been called the most important legislation ever enacted for young children with disabilities (Follari, 2011; Meisels & Shonkoff, 2000; Richards & Leafstedt, 2010). Before this law, Congress estimated that states served about 70 percent of preschool children with special needs. Early intervention services for infants and toddlers with disabilities, aged birth through 2 years old, did not exist in many states. The law called for "statewide, comprehensive, coordinated, multidisciplinary, interagency programs of early intervention services for all handicapped infants ant their families" (Individuals with Disabilities Education Act, 1986). The law did not mandate universal services for all children younger than 6 years of age, but it strengthened incentives for states to serve 3- to 6-year-olds and established a program (Part C) to provide services for children from birth to age 3. Although passed in 1986, the full implementation of the law did not take place until the early 1990s (Follari, 2011; Richards & Leafstedt, 2010; Meisels & Shonkoff, 2000). In the reauthorization of Individuals with Disabilities Education Act (IDEA) in 1997, the law contained two main provisions for providing services. The first part established a requirement for states to develop a comprehensive system of early intervention services for infants and toddlers with developmental delays or disabilities. All children from birth through 2 years of age who were experiencing developmental delays, as measured by appropriate assessments, were entitled to services. The second part required states to provide free and appropriate public education and related services for all eligible children with disabilities from the age of 3 to 5 (Follari, 2011; Meisels & Shonkoff, 2000).

Today, all states participate in IDEA's early interventions provisions and receive funds under the law. The Individuals with Disabilities Education Act (2004) requires early intervention services for any child with disabilities under the age of 3 who:

(a) is experiencing developmental delays, as measured by appropriate diagnostic instruments and procedures in one or more of the areas of cognitive development, physical development, communication development, social or emotional development, and adaptive development; or

(b) has a diagnosed physical or mental condition that has a high probability of resulting in developmental delay. (IDEA, 2004)

Each state may also serve at-risk infants and toddlers; and "(ii) children with disabilities who are eligible for services under Section 619 and who previously received services under this part until such children enter, or are eligible under State law to enter, kindergarten or elementary school, as appropriate, provided that any programs under this part serving such children" (IDEA, 2004). The statute recognizes that effective early intervention services required the contributions of professionals from many different disciplines. Multiple perspectives are woven throughout the planning and implementation of the law, and the activities prescribed under Part C must be guided by a State Interagency Coordinating Council (SICC).

To receive federal funds, each state is required to select a lead agency to administer its service system and must appoint the SICC to assist in its planning, development, and implementation. The intent of this requirement was to overcome the typically fragmented systems of services found within many states. Part C is administered by the federal Department of Education; however, each state is given authority to designate its own lead agency. At the onset of the implementation of the law, about one-third of the states chose departments of education as their lead agency, slightly fewer selected departments of health, and the remainder designated other agencies, such as departments of mental health or human services (Garwood, Fewell, & Neisworth, 1988; Morrison, 2011).

Collaboration between health care and education agencies at the local, state, and federal levels is particularly critical to the successful implementation of early intervention services (Reedy & McGrath, 2010). The IDEA (2004) requires that early intervention services for infants and toddlers be delivered according to an individualized family service plan (IFSP) developed by a multidisciplinary team that includes the child's parents and other family members. Review the vignette in Box 7.2 and answer the questions. Think about how the vignette relates to transition. What needs to be done for Raoul?

BOX 7.2

Vignette: "Raoul's Transition Plan"

Raoul is an 18-year-old Hispanic student diagnosed with a moderate intellectual disability and autism. He primarily communicates through adapted sign language, gestures, words, and vocalizations that his family and teachers understand. He was provided with the services of an interpreter and training in sign language in elementary and middle school. The school discontinued his interpreter services because they thought that Raoul was not benefitting and could effectively communicate using adapted sign language, word gestures, and vocalizations. His parents disagreed.

Raoul's family has been actively involved in his education and transition planning process. They attend all IEP/ITP meetings and contribute to the development of a plan for their son. They also help reinforce his goals at home and are concerned about supports needed once Raoul leaves high school to support his independence and employment ambitions. They have phoned the school many times asked that the interpreter be reinstated; however, the principal believes it is not necessary and so time-consuming for such a low-functioning student. The principal has talked to the special education director and asked her to attend the IEP/ ITP meeting.

1. Does Raul need an interpreter? Who should decide?
2. Who should be invited to Raoul's transition planning meeting?

THE INDIVIDUAL FAMILY SERVICE PLAN (IFSP)

The IFSP is the planning tool used for infants and toddlers and their families. The family and the school jointly identify resources and priorities related to the development of the child. At the conference, the child's strengths, weaknesses, and future goals are discussed. Additionally, the required related services, accommodations, and modifications are determined. The IFSP is a written statement for each infant and toddler and the child's family. When it is developed, reviewed, and revised, it must contain the following components (Turnbull, Turnbull, & Wehmeyer, 2009).

- *Indentifying Information* contains the student's and parents' names, address, primary and/or secondary exceptionality, evaluations given, date of birth, grade, school, evaluator, and dates evaluated.
- *Family's Strengths and Preferred Resources* are given by the caregiver. They identify the family's strengths, needs, resources, and priorities related to enhancing the child's development.
- *Family's Concerns and Priorities* are the concerns for the child with special needs as they relate to the whole family.
- *Child's Strengths and Present Level of Development* is the infant or toddler's current functioning level, cognitively and physically. Development also includes speech, language, psychosocial, motor, and self-help development, based on objective criteria.
- *Outcomes* is the expectations for the family and child. It also includes the expected date for the beginning and ending of services and duration of services, and the responsible agency is provided.
- *Service Coordinator* or case manager is the person who coordinates the plan.
- *Transition* includes the procedures for entering preschool or other services.
- *Statement of Eligibility* determines if the family and child will receive services. Eligibility is determined by a team.

The IFSP differs from the IEP. First, this document greatly involves outcomes related to the family. The focus is more on the child's home and natural environment, such as the community and parks, rather than the school. Second, activities such as everyday routines and activities are included. Third, multiple agencies are usually involved in the IFSP plan, as the child typically needs occupational therapy, physical therapy, speech therapy, and a number of other related services. The IFSP generally integrates all these services into one plan. As IDEA indicates, a coordinator is assessable to the family to help with IFSP development and implementation.

When developing the IFSP, the family's resources, concerns, and priorities are considered. The IFSP is developed to provide support and augment the ability of the family to care for the child with disabilities. Usually the development of the IEP is seen as a partnership between the family or caregiver and the intervention team.

At the beginning of the IFSP process, a formal assessment and evaluation (play-based assessment) is provided. A functional assessment is conducted in order to obtain the family's concerns and priorities, in conjunction with the team, which is developing goals, objectives, outcomes, and resources to increase the success of implementation. The team then assigns responsibilities to assure that the goals are met. For example, a physical therapist may observe the child climbing steps and can suggest to the parent how to assist the child at home to improve physical functioning (http://ericec.org/).

School and special leaders can:

- Monitor services that are offered and provided.
- Assure a smooth transition between the IFSP and the IEP process.

- Assure that students with disabilities receive FAPE.
- Encourage parents and assist them in reaching their goals and accessing services (Zhang, Fowler, & Bennett, 2004).
- Help families feel comfortable by using relationship building and partnerships techniques.
- Know the family expectations.

The IDEA requires states and local districts to provide special education services to all children with disabilities, ages 3 to 5 years old. The regulations for these programs are similar to those regulations for school-age children except (Marion, 2010; Odom, 2000):

- Preschool children do not have to be diagnosed and labeled under one of the traditional disability categories (e.g., mental retardation/cognitive disabilities, emotional/behavioral disorders, physical impairments) to receive services. They may receive services under the eligibility category development delay. This provision of IDEA allows states to serve at-risk students from ages 3 to 9.
- Each state may also serve children who are:
  a. Experiencing developmental delay as defined by the state and as measured by appropriate diagnostic instruments and procedures and
  b. By reason, thereof, need special education and related services (IDEA, 2004).
- Individual education plans must include a section with suggestions and information for parents.
- Local schools may choose to use a variety of service-delivery options (home-based, center-based, of combination programs), and the length of the school day may vary.
- Preschool special education programs must be administered by the state education agency but services from other agencies may be contracted to meet the requirement of a full range of services for young children with disabilities.

Service Delivery Options for Early Intervention Programs

Heward (2009) provides a summary of service delivery alternatives for early intervention programs. As previously noted, IDEA (2004) requires that early intervention services be provided in natural environments to the greatest extent possible. Natural environments are defined as the same home, school, and community settings in which typically developing children participate (Kramer, Caldarella, Christensen, & Shatzer, 2010; Noonan & McCormick, 2006). The setting or early intervention varies, depending on the age of the child and the intensity of special supports that the child and the family may need. There are four settings that are frequently used to provide services to young children with disabilities. Hospitals are often used to deliver early intervention services for infants and newborns with significant disabilities. Most early intervention services are provided in the child's home, in a center-based program outside of the home, or in a school facility. Young children with less significant developmental delays often receive services by an itinerant professional—perhaps a special education in a general education preschool.

Hospital-based early intervention services are provided to newborns and their families when they require specialized health care and are placed in neonatal intensive care units (NICUs). Many NICUs employ a variety of professionals such as neonatologists who provide intensive medical care of infants in need of special medical assistance. Social workers or psychologists are available to assist parents and families address emotional stressors and financial concerns. Infant education specialists may also be available to assist parents establish interactions with their infants.

In home-based programs, parents typically assume the primary responsibility of the caregiver and teacher for their child with special needs. Early intervention specialists visit the home regularly to support families by modeling intervention procedures and teaching strategies. Home early interventionists may visit as frequently as several times per week. They monitor the progress the child in making and recommend changes in the program plan. Home-based early intervention programs are natural environments where parents can provide more time and attention than professionals may be able to offer in a professionally staffed center or school.

Center-based programs provide early intervention services in a special setting outside of the home. The programs may be offered as part of a hospital, a day-care center, or a preschool program. Some children may attend a specially designed development center of a training program that offers a range of services for children with disabilities. Centers may employ a team of specialists from different fields such as education, physical or occupational therapy, speech–language pathology, or medicine to coordinate multiple aspects of the intervention program. A center-based program may be an effective service option for children with severe disabilities where a variety of services are provided in a single location. Frequently, center-based programs are designed for typically developing children, as well. This arrangement allows students with disabilities to interact with their nondisabled peers.

Combined home-center programs bring together both home visitation opportunities and center-based activities. Some children with disabilities require a more intensive approach than a few hours a day or week. Home-center programs combine the availability of a variety of professionals in a single location with the continuous attention and sensitive care provided by parents at home. Frequently, home visits focus on the ongoing individualized consultation and collaboration with parents and families and address a review of progress as well as planning the next steps.

Transition from early intervention (Part C) services to school district programs is a transition across service systems and presents potential problems to assure a smooth delivery of service from one system to the next. The IFSP requires that there be a plan to support the transfer of service responsibility from the early intervention system to a preschool program. A case manager is responsible for the development of the plan. Disputes over the determination of appropriate education plans, delays in initiating services, and disagreements about whether children enrolled in early intervention programs qualify for special education classes are not uncommon.

Early Intervention Program Requirements

The early intervention program has policies and procedures that describe how families will be involved in transition planning (IDEA, 2004). School and special education leaders can assure the following:

- Local early intervention program personnel notify the school district of children who will shortly reach the age of eligibility for preschool services under Part B (IDEA, 2004).
- Initial planning for transition of the child at age 3 begins six months to one year prior to the child's third birthday.
- Local early intervention program (with consent of the family) must convene a transition conference to include early intervention personnel, the family, and the school district (if the child is potentially eligible for Part B preschool) not less than 90 days or more than 9 months before the child's third birthday to discuss possible services the child may receive (IDEA, 2004).
- The child who may not be eligible for school district preschool services are privy to reasonable efforts to convene a transition conference among early intervention providers, the

family, and providers of other appropriate services that the child may receive not less than 90 days or more than 9 months before the child's third birthday to discuss possible services that the child may receive (IDEA, 2004).

- The local early intervention program must develop a transition plan as a part of the IFSP. This transition plan must include the steps to be taken to support the transition from early intervention to preschool or other community services (IDEA, 2004).
- Interagency agreements for transition are required between local early intervention programs and each school district.
- Families are informed of the provisions in the law that state that they may request the participation of the early intervention service coordinator or other representatives of the Part C system to be in attendance at the initial individual education plan team meeting. If requested, an invitation to the initial IEP meeting must be sent to the early intervention service coordinator or other representatives of the Part C system to assist with the smooth transition of services (IDEA, 2004),
- The state's Department of Education has policies and procedures ensuring that children who participate in early intervention programs and who will be participating in preschool programs under Part B experience a smooth and effective transition (IDEA, 2004).
- The child's school district will participate in the transition conference arranged by the local early intervention program for those children who are potentially eligible for the school district prekindergarten program for children with disabilities (IDEA, 2004).
- "By the third birthday of a child participating in the early intervention program for infants and toddlers with disabilities, an IEP or an IFSP must be developed and implemented" (IDEA, 2004).
- "Each school district will participate in transition planning conferences arranged by the state lead agency for the infants and toddlers with disabilities early intervention program" (IDEA, 2004).
- "If the child's third birthday occurs during the summer, the child's IEP team determines the date when service under the IEP or IFSP will begin" (IDEA, 2004).

The National Early Childhood Transition Center has completed a series of studies to identify the recommended practices for early childhood transition. These nationally validated transition practices are categorized into two major areas (1) interagency service system practices and (2) child and family preparation and adjustment. School and special education leaders should assure that:

- A primary contact person for transition is identified within each agency or program.
- Community—and programwide transition activities and timelines are identified.
- Referral processes and timelines are clearly specified.
- Enrollment processes and timelines are clearly specified.
- Agencies develop formal mechanism to minimize disruptions in services before, during, and after the transition of the child and family.
- Staff and family members are actively involved in design of transition processes and systems.
- Staff roles and responsibilities for transition activities are clearly delineated.
- Conscious and transparent connections are made between curricula and child expectations across programs/environments.
- Methods are in place to support staff-to-staff communication within and across programs.
- Families meaningfully participate as partners with staff in program—and communitywide transition efforts.

- Individual child and family transition meetings are conducted.
- Staff follow-up on children after the transition to support their adjustment.
- Team members share appropriate information about each child making a transition.
- Transition plans are developed that include individual activities for each child and family.
- Staff know key information about a broad array of agencies and services available within the community.
- Children have opportunities to develop and practice skills they need in order to be successful in the next environment.
- Families are aware of the importance of transition planning and have information they need to actively participate in transition planning with their child.
- Families' needs related to transition are assessed and addressed.
- Families have information about and are linked with resources and services to help them meet their specific child and family needs.
- Families actively participate in gathering information about their child's growth and development.

As young children enter preschool or kindergarten programs in the school, IEP meetings must be scheduled so that school district plans can be made. These IEP meetings should be designed to address the type of services the child and family received in early intervention, early intervention strategies that were successful for the child and family, the settings in which IFSP outcomes have been successfully met, goals necessary to facilitate the transition between service systems, and priorities and recommendations for IEP goals.

INTERAGENCY COLLABORATION FOR TRANSITION FOR SCHOOL TO THE COMMUNITY: MOVING FROM ENTITLEMENT PROGRAMS TO ELIGIBILITY SERVICES

The K–12 educational system is a system of entitlement. State and local education agencies are required by law (IDEA, 2004) to provide students with disabilities a free appropriate public education (FAPE) where special education and related services are designed to meet an individual's unique needs and prepare them for further education, employment, and independent living. Adult service agencies operate in a totally opposite manner. Adult service is a system of eligibility where individuals must meet certain requirements deemed appropriate by a particular agency in order to receive services. Many individuals with disabilities fail to receive services once they leave high school due to their lack of knowledge about particular agencies and the requirements and process for getting services. Because of the difference in service delivery (i.e., school, adult agencies), it seems imperative that schools and agencies work collaboratively in order to assist students with disabilities in a smooth transition from school to the adult world.

For schools to provide effective transition services, it is necessary to use "best practices" when implementing secondary transition programs to promote success for students with disabilities (Baugher & Nichols, 2008; Kochhar-Bryant, 2009; Kohler & Field, 2003). Kohler (1996) developed *A Taxonomy for Transition Programming* that identifies five primary components of effective secondary transition practices, including (1) student-focused planning (e.g., student participation in transition planning, planning strategies); (2) student development (e.g., life skills instruction), (3) interagency collaboration (e.g., collaborative service delivery); (4) family involvement (e.g., family participation in transition planning, family empowerment); and (5) program structure (e.g., program evaluation). *A Taxonomy for Transition Programming* has been

---

BOX 7.3

Advice for School and Special Education Leaders

- Involve parents as early as possible in ITP and IFSP planning and consider their expectations.
- There are a number of service delivery models for students. Be sure to be aware of them and how they fit various populations.
- Coordinate services for students so there is little overlap.

---

widely supported in the transition literature and provides a detailed framework for implementing and delivering secondary transition programs and practices that lead to improved outcomes for students with disabilities (Kohler & Field 2003; Test et al., 2008). The individualized transition plan (ITP) contains all of those structures. See Box 7.3 for additional advice.

The Individualized Transition Plan (ITP)

The ITP is required for students at the age of 16 (IDEA, 2004). It is developed to guide individual career-related skills. The curriculum facilitates the development of work-related skills as determined through vocational assessments that focus on the needs, skills, and interest of the individual within the context of future work environments. The individualized transition plan includes transition services needed, annual transition goals and objectives, related services, and interagency linkages and responsibilities (Turnbull, Turnbull, & Wehmeyer, 2009). It structures educational experiences to prepare students to make the transition to adult life. The ITP should include the following components:

- *Postschool Outcomes* includes the transition services needed, such as career planning, social skills, community participation, postsecondary education, daily living skills, physical care, and self-advocacy.
- *Transition Activities and Services* are activities needed to achieve postschool outcomes.
- *Annual Goals and Objectives* define the purpose and aspirations in each prescribed area.
- *Related Services* are needed to meet the student's objectives, such as vocational guidance, counseling, assessments, job placement, and follow-up services.

The individualized transition plan is designed to be an outcome-oriented process that considers a student's needs related to preferences and interest that involves instruction, related services, community experience, and other postschool and adult living objectives (IDEA, 2004). Usually, secondary teachers, in conjunction with the student's family and the ITP team, identify the goals, objectives, and plausible outcomes. The student is provided activities that enhance career education choices, on-the-job training, vocational classes, community-based activities and vocational interest and ability inventories. Information gleaned from these processes help with decision making toward the student's instructional goals and objectives and a suitable career path.

Although encouraged in middle school or early years, families are generally informed of the transition process in the ninth grade. At that time, career expectations are gathered from the student and family and matched to vocational aptitude, ability, and interest assessments and profiles.

Postsecondary options—such as support services, independent living, case management services, and self-advocacy techniques—are then suggested to the student and family. Agencies that match with the student's developing profile are then introduced. It is important to address social skills and self-advocacy techniques, as they are necessary job-seeking and community-living skills.

A cohesive transition team substitutes effective collaboration. After exploring postsecondary options, evaluations, and assessments, the ITP meeting should consist of all entities (school and outside agencies) that are applicable to the student's instructional goals and outcomes and community-living paths.

School and special education leaders can:

- Assist with supporting the linkages to outside agency support.
- Pursue outside funding.
- Attend transition team meetings.
- Create cooperative arrangements with local vendors as possible placement sites.
- Have teachers who involved with transition to work cooperatively with other schools or districts.
- Monitor implementation of the ITP.
- Make sure that students are registered with mental health agencies as needed.
- Assure that documentation is appropriate.
- Assure that follow-up with adult agencies is consistent.

Collaboration and Effective Interagency Agreements

A Taxonomy for Transition Programming promotes interagency collaboration as a key component of "best practices" in secondary transition to promote positive postschool outcomes for students with disabilities (Kohler, 1993; Kohler, 1996; Test, 2000). In other words, key people, businesses, and agencies should work together to support a student's pursuit of successful postschool outcomes (Test, 2004). Additionally, IDEA (2004) mandates the "development and implementation of transition programs" and promotes interagency collaboration as a means of supporting the transition of students with disabilities. Since the 1980s, *interagency collaboration* has been identified as a key component in the transition planning process in order for youth with disabilities to achieve successful adult outcomes (Test, Fowler, White, Richter, & Walker, 2009). It can be defined as a relationship entered into by two or more individuals and organizations that is mutually beneficial and well defined to achieve common goals (i.e., between families and schools, and between schools and outside agencies). Interagency collaboration includes a commitment to the team, jointly developing the structure and sharing responsibility of authority and accountability for success and sharing resources and rewards. In short, it is multiple agencies working together to improve the life of a student with a disability (Test et al., 2009).

Collaboration among agencies is important because services are generally administered by dozens of inflexible and diverse separate agencies and programs, which usually have their own individual funding, guidelines, requirements, and rules governing expenditure of funds. Without collaboration, it is difficult to align services in order to maximize benefits for the student. Most importantly, unlike public education, there is no legal mandate for students after they graduate from high school to receive services. It is crucial to begin this process early to receive the best possible assistance with transitioning.

Effective interagency agreements involve all key stakeholders who are committed to change. This commitment to change must incorporate not only those individuals who have the power and authority to negotiate change, but also the individuals and family members whose lives will be affected. Stakeholders should choose a realistic strategy that reflects the priorities of the individuals and organizations involved along with available resources. When developing the agreement, stakeholders must develop a shared vision of better outcomes for students with disabilities.

School and special education leaders can create an open communication system that allows them to disagree and use conflict resolution as a constructive means of moving forward by:

- Setting attainable goals that will promote success of their mission. Blalock (1996) proposes that interagency teams and activities are "critical for real change in transition programs and occur most meaningfully at the local level" (p. 149)
- Further emphasizing that these teams have the potential to considerably enhance the secondary preparation and postschool options for students with disabilities
- Assuring that interagency agreements occur at several levels (i.e., individual transition planning committees, school-based transition committees, community-based transition teams, regional transition teams, and state transition teams)
- Positioning the individual transition planning committee or the multidisciplinary team (MDT) so that each individual student is prepared for postsecondary goals in education and independent living (if appropriate); these teams need to confer at least annually
- Charging the school-based transition teams with making curricular changes, developing individualized transition planning tools and procedures, integrating vocational assessment into transition planning, developing instructional delivery, integrating vocational assessment, and developing instructional delivery through teacher staff developments
- Requiring community-based planning teams to identify common goals; develop action plans; problem solve in order to facilitate collaboration among schools, parents, adult agencies and services; create employment opportunities for students; and seek additional sources of support when necessary (Cameto, 2005; IDEA, 2004; Test et al., 2006; Test et al., 2009)

Strategies for Building and Facilitating Effective Teams

The initial stage in building an effective team includes identifying initial members, selecting a team leader, establishing rapport among members, and agreeing on a goal (Blalock, 1996). Five fundamental characteristics must exist: trust, goals and objectives that are beneficial to all stakeholders, long-term relationships, service competence, and a customer service orientation (Fabian, Luecking, & Tilson, 1994; Kortering, 2009). The foundation of an effective team is based on mutual understanding.

Special and general education leaders can assure:

- Coordinated and planned communication between the school and agencies.
- That services do not overlap.
- That services are not interrupted when students are transferring from school to a secondary source or agency. Schools and adult agencies will need to combine resources during transfer.

AGENCIES, ORGANIZATIONS, AND COMMUNITY RESOURCES   The school district is the organization with which most school leaders are familiar. In accordance with IDEA (2004), schools and special education leaders are to assure the following:

- Starting at age 14, or earlier if needed, a student's postsecondary goals in the area of education, employment and training, and independent living are identified.
- Personnel who can assist the student develop and achieve postsecondary goals are identified.
- The student applies for needed services.
- The student's annual progress is reviewed by all stakeholders.
- A summary of performance is created to help describe a student's present and future educational and functional needs prior to exiting high school.

Other organizations that could be involved in an interagency agreement with the schools to improve postschool outcomes for students include but are not limited to (1) the Department of Mental Health, (2) postsecondary education institutions, (3) vocational rehabilitation, (4) the Social Security Administration, (5) One-Stop Career Centers, (6) Job Corps, and (7) Goodwill Industries (Steere, Rose, & Cavaiuolo, 2007).

The Department of Mental Health provides a comprehensive system of services responsive to the needs of individuals with mental illness. Services through this agency could include supported and sheltered employment, competitive employment support, case management services, therapeutic recreation, respite, and/or residential services. If this is a service that may benefit a student, parents should be encouraged to call the local mental health office to begin the referral process.

There are many postsecondary educational opportunities for students with disabilities in the United States. Along with the multitude of four-year institutions that provide various educational programs aimed at preparing students to earn an undergraduate or graduate degree in their career of choice, there are also many community colleges that offer a variety of certificate and associate degree programs for students. Programs at technical schools provide students with relevant technological skills needed to meet the demands of current industries. Through these programs, students will develop real-world skills and advance their careers. It is important for students to meet with the Admissions office to discuss the requirements for entry and also contact the Disability Services department to discuss student rights and responsibilities, accommodations, and other needs in order to be successful. School guidance counselors are valuable resources to help students connect to the correct people at their chosen academic institution.

Vocational rehabilitation (VR) is a major service provider for individuals with disabilities and an important agency to include in transition planning. This provider assists persons with cognitive, sensory, physical, or emotional disabilities to attain employment and increased independence. While students are enrolled in high school, they are afforded services such as vocational guidance and counseling; medical, psychological, vocational, and other types of assessments to determine vocational potential; and/or job development, placement, and follow-up services. Postsecondary services offered through VR include apprenticeship programs, vocational training, and/or college training designed to achieve a particular vocational goal. Individuals with disabilities who have service providers through VR could receive housing supports or transportation services, interpreter services, and/or orientation and mobility services.

A student should begin the referral process during the close of her or his eleventh-grade year. In order to be eligible for services, the student must have a documented disability. The referral process may be completed through a school's transition specialist or other resource teacher or guidance counselor assigned to assist with this process. Referral in high school is preferable because it allows a student to connect with the VR counselor prior to exiting high school, which lends itself to a smoother transition.

The Social Security Administration (SSA) provides benefits to people of any age who are unable to do substantial work and have severe physical or mental disabilities. The programs offered through the SSA include Social Security Disability Insurance (SSDI), Supplemental Security Income (SSI), Plans to Achieve Self-Support (PASS), Medicaid, and Medicare. Work incentive programs may include cash benefits and insurance while working; help with extra work expenses because of a disability, and/or assistance to start a new line of work. Financial incentives for further education and training are also available. Due to the number of different programs that SSA provides, it is suggested that a student and his or her family call their local SSA office to talk with a counselor who can explain eligibility requirements in more detail.

One-Stop Career Centers are located all over the country. A multitude of services and resources can be accessed through this agency, which provides a variety of services to help employers and job seekers meet their workforce development needs. Most services offered through One-Stop Career Centers are free. Staff is available to help individuals with job searching and placement, resume writing, job service registration, unemployment insurance claim filing, in addition to providing information on other community resources and programs. There are also a range of different assessments available through a One-Stop Career Center as well as career counseling, job skills classes, and assistance in developing an individual employment plan. Also available are multiple levels of job training.

Job Corps is a no-cost alternative to traditional education. It is a program funded through the U.S. Department of Labor that offers an education and vocational training program for people ages 16 to 24. Through Job Corps, individuals are able to earn a high school diploma or GED, learn a trade, and/or get help finding employment. Career counseling and transition support is available for up to 12 months after someone graduates from his or her program. Specific job skills are focused on while enrolled in Job Corps. To enroll in Job Corps, applicants must meet all of the following eligibility criteria: (1) be between the age of 16 and 25 (for otherwise eligible individuals with disabilities, the maximum age limit may be waived, but the minimum age is still 16); (2) have a signed consent form for automatic Selective Service registration (for male applicants); (3) be a U.S. citizen, a U.S. national, a lawfully admitted permanent resident alien, refugee, asylum seeker, or parolee, or other alien who has been authorized by the Attorney General to work in the United States; (4) be a low-income individual; (5) be an individual who is one of the following: a high school dropout, an individual who requires additional education, vocational training, or intensive career counseling and related assistance in order to participate successfully in regular schoolwork or to secure and hold employment, basic skills deficient, homeless, runaway, foster child, or a parent.

And finally, Goodwill Industries is North America's leading nonprofit provider of education, training, and career services for people with disadvantages, such as welfare dependency, homelessness, and lack of education or work experience, as well as those with physical, mental, and emotional disabilities. At Goodwill, professionals are available to help people find help for the problems that are keeping them from being successful at work. This may include child care, transportation, counseling, life skills programs for people with disabilities, and any number of other services. If the local Goodwill doesn't provide the service, they can connect job seekers with other community organizations that do.

Summary

Don't forget the important legal issues listed in Box 7.4. Additionally, school leaders should remember the following:

- Choose a curriculum that suits the population of your school. One curriculum does not fit all, however; you must base educational decisions on individual needs, preferences, and interests. Ensure that the teachers and staff at your school have a multitude of resources at their side to assist them with meeting each student's unique needs.
- Develop a team. Ensure that your team possesses the qualities that will allow the team to sustain over time. Keep the team focused on meeting the goal of improving early childhood or postschool outcomes for students with disabilities. Be a leader and a facilitator, and keep an open mind and a positive attitude.
- Remember that serving students with disabilities is a major component of Annually Yearly Progress (AYP) and should not be overlooked. There are certain indicators in all state performance plans that your district uses to assess the effectiveness of educating students with disabilities, monitoring their progress, and assisting them in reaching their future goal. Data collected yearly by state and local education agencies on performance plan indicators should help drive decision-making and help to improve programming—whether it be for children entering the school from early intervention programs or for students leaving schools for postsecondary programs.

While we are considering transition services for students who are moving from school to the community in either postsecondary education and training, employment, or independent living, it is also important to examine the transition that occurs for children with disabilities who enter the public schools at the opposite end of the age range. It is essential to assure that young children who enter school districts from preschool programs or early intervention programs or child-serving agencies make a successful transition from the community to school programs. The resolution to the vignette is provided in Box 7.5.

BOX 7.4

Legal Issues

- In transition, students with disabilities or who have developmental delays need to have an IFSP and ITP. These documents are formed in collaboration with a team.
- Initial planning for transition of the child at age 3 begins six months to one year prior to the child's third birthday. With consent of the family, a transition conference must convene and include early intervention personnel, the family, and school district personnel not less than 90 days or more than 9 months before the child's third birthday to discuss possible services that the child may receive (IDEA, 2004).
- The child who may not be eligible for school district preschool services should receive reasonable efforts to convene a transition conference among early intervention providers to discuss possible services that the child may receive (IDEA, 2004).
- Families must be informed of the provisions in the law and they may request the participation of the early intervention service coordinator or other representatives of the system to be in attendance at the initial individualized educational plan team meeting.
- Starting at age 14, or earlier if needed, the student's postsecondary goals are identified and annual progress is reviewed by all stakeholders. The student applies for needed services. A summary of performance is created to help describe the student's present and future educational and functional needs prior to exiting high school.

> ### BOX 7.5
>
> ### Resolution of the Vignette
>
> Parents have important input and serve as essential members of the team. If they are concerned about the reinstatement of the interpreter, some arrangement should be given to services, even if they are minimal.

Chapter Questions

1. What is the purpose of transition planning?
2. What is the role of the special or general education leader in the transition planning process?
3. How can the school leader help students transition from early intervention programs to school or from school to adulthood?
4. What are the roles of the postsecondary agencies during the transition process?
5. Why is it imperative that the school, the family, and the postsecondary agencies collaborate?
6. How can the school leader facilitate partnerships between the early intervention programs and the school and among and post-secondary agencies and the families?
7. Why are goals, roles, and processes so important in effective teamwork?

Response to Intervention and Inclusion

Facilitating Collaborative Arrangements

Gloria D. Campbell-Whatley

Loury Ollison Floyd

Khalilah S. O'Farrow

Cheryl T. Smith

INTRODUCTION

Collaboration is an interactive process. Working collaboratively is the best option for special and general education leaders to make combined behavioral and academic decisions about students. According to the 2004 amendments to the Individuals with Disabilities Education Act (IDEA), states must use a process to determine if a child responds to scientific, research-based intervention and data-based documentation of repeated assessments to determine the response to intervention (RTI) before the child is placed in special education. Special and general educational leaders can assist these processes by allowing teacher teams to make joint decisions by changing traditional time constraints, organizational structures, and professional responsibilities. This chapter outlines the benefits of integrating services in inclusive settings and promoting the current venues of RTI. The pros and cons of inclusive practices and the RTI process and their relation to problem solving will be explained. Various coteaching models and team formats are discussed. The chapter also offers special and general education leaders various strategies to

---

BOX 8.1

Challenges and Issues for School and Special Education Leaders

- Implementing and using various coteaching models to increase inclusive practices
- Using prereferral intervention strategies, classroom differentiated instructional techniques, and other options that limit disproportionality
- Developing avenues for special education and general education teachers to collaboratively design assessment systems and evidenced-based interventions for students with learning challenges, as needed in the tiered approach of RTI.
- Developing positive behavior supports and functional behavior assessment while using a collection of various measurement data (formal measures such as standardized test and/or informal measures such as work samples, curriculum-based measures) to make informed decisions about students' interventions
- Involving families in RTI and other inclusive practices
- Understanding IDEA and NCLB and how they relate to inclusion and RTI

---

encourage collaboration and the implementation of the multitiered approaches of RTI. Box 8.1 outlines the challenges and issues in this chapter.

One of the many educational challenges for the twenty-first century is preparing educators not only to meet the needs of all students with disabilities but also to comply with federal legislation, such as the Individuals with Disabilities Education Act (IDEA). The IDEA (2004) mandates educators to provide students with disabilities appropriate services within the least restrictive environment. The term, *least restrictive environment,* requires that students with disabilities receive free and appropriate public education designed to meet their educational needs alongside their peers without disabilities in general education settings to the maximum extent appropriate. Federal legislation requires that in determining the student's least restrictive environment, the first consideration should be the general education classroom with provision of supplementary aids and services. More restrictive settings, such as special education classrooms, may only be considered when education in the general education classroom with the use of supplementary aids and services cannot be achieved. It would be difficult for this to occur, unless teachers work collaboratively.

The least restrictive environment and options have progressively developed from mainstreaming since their beginnings in PL 94-142, the Education of All Handicapped Children Act (EHA, 1975) to inclusion in the last amendment of the law, the Individuals with Disabilities Improvement Act (IDEIA, 2004). Generally, mainstreaming was used when students with disabilities were placed in general education settings alongside their peers without disabilities for specific academic subjects, electives, or extracurricular activities in order to provide more opportunities for social interaction. The overall goal of inclusive settings is to promote the academic success of students with disabilities by addressing their needs in the least restrictive environment to the maximum extent possible (Dettermer, Thurston, Knackendoffel, & Dyck, 2009; Vaughn, Bos, & Schumm, 2003).

Trends in the 1970s and 1980s indicated that most children with disabilities, especially the mild mentally impaired and the learning disabled, were served in the resource room. As the EHA was amended, schools moved toward providing more inclusive settings in general education for children with disabilities. The role of special educators included a greater dependence on collaboration to meet a range of student needs in the general education setting. Varied knowledge and skills were displayed by special educators—such as differentiated instruction, assessment, monitoring student progress, assessment and communication—to meet student needs through inclusion (Hoover & Patton, 2008; Lembke, Garman, Deno, & Stecker, 2010). Yet, there is still too great a dependence on separate settings. In 2009, 58 percent of children and youth spent most of their school day in regular class, compared to 33 percent in 1990. In 2009, about 86 percent of students with speech or language impairments spent most of their school day in general classes. And 62 percent of students with developmental delay and of students with visual impairments spent most of their school day in general classes. In contrast, 16 percent of students with intellectual disabilities and 13 percent of students with multiple disabilities spent most of their school day in general classes (National Center for Educational Statistics, http://nces.ed.gov/programs/coe/indicator_cwd.asp).

So, there is an increase in the trend that more students with disabilities are integrated within general education classrooms throughout the school day. Response to intervention is showing promising data to affect the phenomenon (Dufrene et al., 2010; Salend, 2008).

Currently, as educators progress through changes in legislation, students with learning challenges will increasingly receive instruction through multitiered instruction using RTI. The approach, implemented in the general education sector, will serve as a basic decision-making and problem-solving tool before students are referred to special education. The vignette in Box 8.2 explores a school that is planning to have a pilot program to begin the training for RTI.

BOX 8.2

Vignette: *"Uh-Oh, Here Comes Ms. Greiner"*

Ms. Ransom was standing in the hall getting ready to enter the teacher's workroom. She thought, "Here comes Ms. Greiner and I bet she wants to discuss those two special education students in my room. She is always trying to 'catch me' on my planning periods to discuss them. I admire her as a dedicated teacher and she seems to have good ideas, but come on, there has got to be a better way to discuss students with disabilities. I don't want to use all my planning period talking to her. I have other work I want to address. There has got to be some formal way we can plan, other than seventh-grade planning time each month. I think she might be meeting with some other grades at the seventh-grade planning time. She is always hinting around about teaching together, but I'm not sure about her skills to teach English—after all, she has special education training and I am not really sure what that entails. I am concerned about Mrs. Greiner, but something else is coming down the wire as I speak. We have been selected as a pilot school for RTI for next year. I'm not sure if the kids who need special education will even be able to get it. As I understand it, they will be served in my classroom. Maybe I need to find time to speak to her 'cause I think I may really need her then.

1. Identify some strategies that would encourage Ms. Greiner and Ms. Ransom to have productive collaboration sessions.
2. Should the principal be involved, and if so, to what degree?
3. Should families of children with disabilities be involved, and if so, to what degree?
4. What is response to intervention? Does it mean that students with behavior challenges will be served in general education classrooms?

General and special education administrators and teachers continue to evolve to meet new multitiered instructional programming demands and to collaborate on inclusive strategies as they support the concept that addresses the demands of all students' needs (NCLB, 2002). Research supports the notion that educating students in a separate setting decreases interactions with peers, reduces opportunities for equal access to the general curriculum, and increases dispro-portionality (Barton, 2010; Friend & Bursuck, 2009; Friend & Cook, 2007; Salend, 2008; Zirkel & Krohn, 2008). As students with disabilities are immersed, and opportunities are presented for students to remain in the general education setting without labeling, higher academic expecta-tions are set in motion as these students are prepared to interact effectively with peers.

UNDERSTANDING THE RTI PROCESS

The NCLB (2002) and IDEA (2004) intersect and set the stage for RTI, as both require im-proved outcomes for all students using scientifically based instructional practices. No Child Left Behind requires accountability through adequate yearly progress (AYP), and the Individuals with Disabilities Education Act mentions "a process that determines if the child responds to a scien-tific research-based intervention as part of the intervention procedure" (IDEA, 2004). Response to Intervention addresses students with challenges as well as assists schools with meeting yearly progress goals (Cummings, Atkins, Allison, & Cole, 2008). Implemented in the general class-room, RTI is a process in which students are provided quality instruction while their progress is monitored. If there is no measured improvement (a response to the instruction), they are then considered for special education (Bradley, Danielson, & Doolittle, 2005; Hoover & Patton, 2008; Mellard & Johnson, 2008; Tuckwiller, Pullen, & Coyne, 2010). The use of evidence-based inter-ventions is key to RTI, and documentation of these interventions is required before a student is referred to special education by IDEA and NCLB. Through general education, the student's response to education is the basis for making decisions. Since RTI is a process that uses all re-sources within a school, there needs to be a well-integrated system of instruction, evidence-based interventions, and student outcome data between general and special education teachers.

Response to intervention is proactive because it uses systems that prevent academic failure. The school uses a universal screening method to locate students with behavior and academic challenges in the general education setting. That is, those who are not meeting the academic and behavioral objectives (the 20 percent with challenges) of supplemental instruction (Zirkel & Krohn, 2008). Changes made in the instructional environment are preferred because students' overall performance usually improves best in that setting (Mellard & Johnson, 2008). If there is still no notable improvement, the students are then referred to special education. If less than 80 percent of the students are not meeting benchmarks, the core program is changed. Response to intervention also encourages parental involvement as well as staff development and collabora-tion. There are three tiers that students flow through in the RTI process (Jenkins, 2007; Mellard & Johnson, 2008; National Center for Response to Intervention, www.rti4success.org/). A diagram of the tiers is seen in Figure 8.1; the process is explained in the next sections.

Tier 1

In Tier 1, the student receives high-quality, research-based instruction or behavior interventions in the general/inclusive education classroom. Iin this tier, school staff, teachers, and adminis-trators are involved in a universal screening of academics and behavior. Using specific criteria, collaborating teams examine data to determine students who have challenges. High-quality, research-based instruction via differentiated instruction is provided as the *core* instruction.

FIGURE 8.1 Response to Intervention Framework

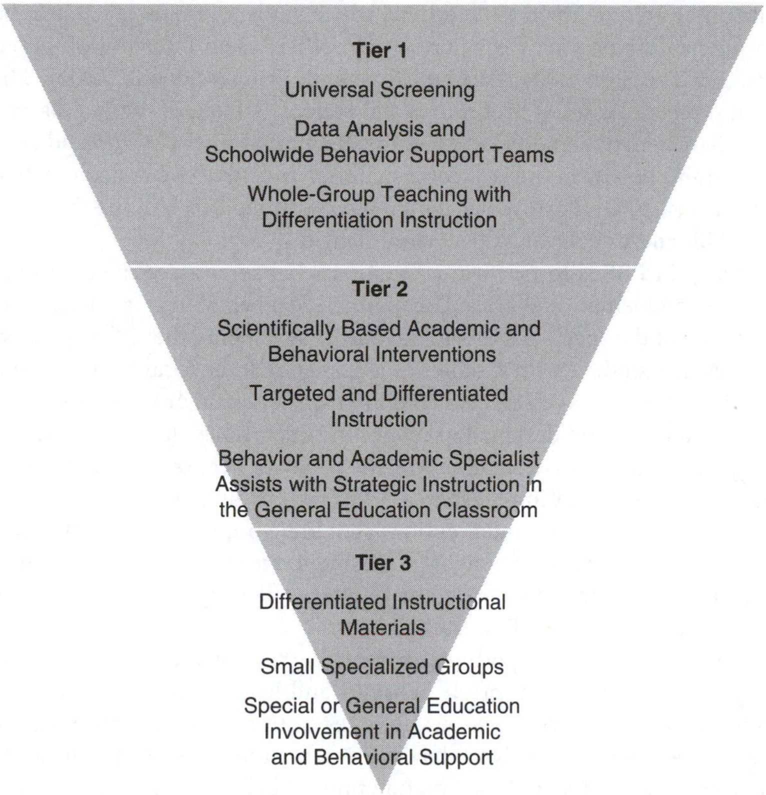

Tier 1

Universal Screening

Data Analysis and
Schoolwide Behavior Support Teams

Whole-Group Teaching with
Differentiation Instruction

Tier 2

Scientifically Based Academic and
Behavioral Interventions

Targeted and Differentiated
Instruction

Behavior and Academic Specialist
Assists with Strategic Instruction in
the General Education Classroom

Tier 3

Differentiated Instructional
Materials

Small Specialized Groups

Special or General Education
Involvement in Academic
and Behavioral Support

Source: Compiled with permission from T. Jenkins. (2007). *When a Child Struggles in School: Everything Parents and Educators Should Know about Getting Children the Help They Need.* Charleston: Advantage, 2007.

PROGRESS MONITORING AND DIFFERENTIATED INSTRUCTION   The informal measures mentioned in Chapter 4 are typically used for progress monitoring such as curriculum-based measures or alternative assessments. These measures determine the skills acquired in the curriculum. If they are administered frequently and the results are charted or diagrammed, the percentage, level, or slope can show change at intervals or throughout the school year. Examples of measures include Dynamic Indicators of Basic Early Literacy Skills (Rouse & Fantuzzo, 2006) and CBM Probes Intervention (Reschly, Busch, Deno, & Long, 2009).

Differentiated instruction is teaching students according to their strengths and methods of learning using varied instruction, rather than a standardized approach (Cox, 2008; Tomlinson, 2003). Because each learner comes to school with a different set of learning needs, students are placed at the center of instruction and learning. Varied instruction is determined through flexible grouping or whole-group, small-group, and/or individualized instruction based on student interest and academic level. Teachers can use varied instructional methods that are linked to assessment. For example, the core instruction is content, process, and product according to the student's way of learning. For example, each child may be given the same *content* but it is presented in a different way. *Process* is the way you teach, paying attention to different learning styles and interest. *Product* is the varied ways students can demonstrate what they learn (Rock, Gregg, Ellis, & Gable, 2008).

ADDRESSING BEHAVIOR   In-school and out-of-school suspensions, absentees, and discipline referrals to the office are examined to determine which students are most likely to have problem behaviors. Implementing positive behavior support (PBS) as an intervention is recommended (Dettmer, Dyck, & Thurston, 2004; Turnbull, Turnbull, Erin, & Soodak, 2006). The PBS intervention is a comprehensive set of procedures and support strategies that are based on an individual's needs, characteristics, and preferences that help him or her develop and engage in adaptive, socially desirable behavior and overcome patterns of destructive and stigmatizing behavior (Alberto & Troutman, 2009). Positive behavioral interventions are proactive. They involve teaching alternative skills and/or adapting the environment.

The first step in PBS is to perform a functional behavior assessment (FBA) on students who have the most problematic behavior. Use of functional behavior assessments are required by IDEA (1997) as one of the special factors to include in developing the IEP as positive behavioral support strategies. If a student with disabilities is suspended, the local educational agency must develop a functional behavioral assessment and intervention plan, or review one if it exists.

Before interventions are designed to reduce the occurrence of problem behavior, hypotheses are developed and tested to determine why the behavior occurs. With the help of the school counselor and/or special education teacher, a functional analysis of the assessment can reveal problem areas that suggest certain interventions should be implemented. Pertinent questions to include in the examination are: What might be causing the behavior? What does the person hope to achieve with this behavior? What is an alternative, socially appropriate way to achieve this? What can be done to avoid the need for the behavior?

These questions promote hypothesis-driven interventions that place more emphasis on skill building and supporting appropriate behavior and less on punishing problem behaviors. This focus increases the prospect of a successful intervention, thereby increasing the probability that generalization will occur. Positive behavioral interventions—strategies to teach alternative skills and reduce problem behavior based on functions of behavior—can be implemented. These methods are applicable to RTI as they contribute to the scientific advancement of intervention efforts (Alberto & Troutman, 2009). School leaders can:

- Find a quick, low-cost method of screening that has good validity that can provide outcome data.
- Find appropriate criterion-reference measures—ones that compare student performance to a predetermined performance level.
- Appoint and engage in a school team (i.e., instructional, behavioral) to collect data, enter the information in a database, analyze data, review aggregated data with the teachers, and determine times through the year that progressive measures are administered.
- Use assessment data for other purposes, such as AYP and other ongoing progress monitoring.
- Provide avenues to inform parents of their child's progress and assessment results.
- Provide technology, resources, and other material.
- Make sure students receive appropriate instruction.

Tier 2

If the students still do not meet the classroom expectations, they receive supplemental instruction. Differentiated instruction, modifications, and specialized equipment, or technology to *target* their academic and behavioral needs are provided. Students' responses to intervention are well documented during this stage, as they are essential for prereferral decisions. If classroom expectations are still not met, the duration and frequency of supplemental intensive specialized instruction, varied behavior modification, or special education is required. Instruction can be provided by a reading specialist or other specialist rather than the general education teacher. The intervention is intended as remediation. A problem-solving team (e.g., multidisciplinary, student, instructional) can help plan instruction. The team should work together to (1) identify the problem or need, (2) identify instructional and management goals, (c) make a decision on what intervention(s) to implement, and (4) evaluate the results of the intervention (Aldeman, 1996; Graden, Casey, & Bonstrom, 1985; McKenzie, 2010; Ormsbee, Myles, & Simpson, 1999). If the evaluation process reveals that specific interventions did not solve the problem, then alternative solutions are considered. Remember, problem solving is an ongoing process.

Mellard and Johnson (2008) suggest that school leaders can:

- Provide appropriate reading and math intervention programs for examination.
- Suggest appropriately trained staff to deliver continued and varied progress monitoring techniques.
- Schedule time for collaboration.
- Provide means to monitor instruction and student movement from tier to tier.
- Participate in the problem-solving team.

Tier 3

Students receive intensive instruction in special or general education settings. The student is still provided high-quality, scientifically based, individualized interventions, designed to meet the specific need of the child, such as direct instruction and metacognitive strategies. Progress monitoring is still provided.

Special and general education administrators and leaders work together to:

- Develop a school environment that encourages collaboration through these processes.
- Provide and facilitate schedules to support individualized instruction.
- Provide guidance to parents and school-based teams.
- Monitor progress of students within general and special education.
- Provide consultation for behavioral and academic practices.

BENEFITS AND PRACTICES OF INCLUSION AND COLLABORATION

School and special education administrators can promote inclusive education by providing time for teachers to plan and collaborate. In an effort to promote successful inclusive education, leaders can encourage teachers to partner with one another, accept one another's ideas, and share resources. Through collaboration and inclusion, students with disabilities have greater access to the general curriculum, and general education teachers become more knowledgeable about individualized instruction.

Collaboration is an interactive process characterized by mutual respect, trust, and open communication (Dettmer et al., 2009; Tomlinson, 2003). Increasing collaboration in inclusive education settings serving students with and without disabilities requires structures and processes whereby every member of the group is working together toward a shared, common purpose (Cesar & Santos, 2006; DuFour, 1997; Pinchot, 1998; Wilson, 2008). Collaborative consultation requires strong trust and an effective, organized communication system. Communication enables educators in the collaborative process to resolve any problems or conflicts that may arise.

On the other hand, ineffective communication throughout the collaborative process may lead to misunderstanding and lack of trust.

COTEACHING METHODS AND TEAM FORMATS

Recent research on teaching students with disabilities concluded that most students should spend much of the school day in regular classrooms (Dettmer et al., 2009; McLeskey, Hoppey, Williamson, & Rentz, 2004). Both IDEA (2004) and NCLB (2002) mandate that students with disabilities be served in the least restrictive environment—in most instances the general classroom. In the spirit of the aforementioned law and policy, reform initiatives have been proposed to address serving the increasing number of students with disabilities who receive the vast majority of their education in general education classrooms.

Within the field of special education, professionals are searching for effective methods and strategies to meet the needs of students with disabilities who are receiving services in general education classrooms. Developing practices that will decrease student academic failures and increase successful student learning thrive in school communities where collaboration is being encouraged (Friend & Bursuck, 2009; Friend & Cook, 2007; Walther-Thomas, Korinek, McLaughlin, & Williams, 2000). Collaborative school communities recognize the potential of teamwork to help individuals and groups accomplish their schools.

Coteaching occurs when the licensed teacher and specialist are both in the classroom during the same lesson and both participate in the instruction, delivering substantive instruction to a diverse, blended group of students in a single physical space (Friend & Cook, 2007; Friend & Pope, 2005; Vaughn, Bos, & Schumm, 2000). The professionals should be licensed teachers or specialists (e.g., a general education teacher and a special education teacher, a teacher and a speech/language therapist) (Friend & Cook, 2007; Villa, Thousand, & Nevin, 2008).

Several coteaching approaches have been designed and implemented to meet student needs, the classroom environment, demands of the curriculum, and teachers' comfort level in teaching practices and content knowledge and skills. There are five basic approaches to coteaching: (1) one teach–one assist/observe, (2) station teaching, (3) parallel teaching, (4) alternative teaching, and (5) team teaching. The definition, setting, advantages, and disadvantages of each are listed in Table 8.1.

Coteaching approaches require levels of trust and commitment, ranging from the highly integrated approach of team teaching to the limited approach of observe/assist. The concept of coteaching may be unnerving for those involved because of difference in teaching styles and the interactions in the class. As relationships between the coteachers mature, however, a variety of coteaching approaches can be used to meet the needs of diverse student populations in the general classroom. The higher levels of coteaching approaches involve a high degree of comfort as teachers' roles become more unplanned and natural, but also require more communication (Bouck, 2007). When done correctly, coteaching approaches provide teachers with more confidence about working with a diverse population and allow teachers to see their coworkers and students in new ways while establishing positive relationships.

Coteaching is a way to deliver instruction as part of the philosophy of inclusive practices. Many benefits of the teaching pair are shared. Students receive improved instruction and instructional fragmentation is minimized. Coteaching does not work without a sense of support among the coteaching pair. The coteachers must have mutual and shared respect for one another's philosophical beliefs, personal teaching characteristics, and academic knowledge and skills. The pair must share a professional relationship in which there is parity, respect, communication, and trust.

TABLE 8.1	Advantages and Disadvantages of Coteaching Approaches	
One Teach–One Assist	**Advantages**	**Disadvantages**
(Individualization) Students work in a large group with one teacher and individually with another teacher.	• Excellent for new coteaching situations or when one teacher is considered the expert. • Students are able to receive one-on-one instruction.	• May be the only model implemented in a coteaching situation
Station Teaching		
(Small Group) Students, in groups of three or more, rotate to various teacher-led and independent work stations where new instruction, review, and/ or practice is provided. Students may work at all stations during the rotation.	• Provides active learning format • Increases small group attention encourages cooperation and independence • Allows strategic grouping • Increases response rate	• Requires considerable planning and preparation • Increases noise level • Requires group and independent work skills • Is difficult to monitor
Parallel Teaching		
(Small Group) Students are divided into mixed-ability groups, then each partner teaches a group. The same material is presented in each group.	• Provides effective review format • Encourages student responses • Reduces pupil–teacher ratio for group instruction/review	• Is hard to ensure equal depth of content coverage • May be difficult to coordinate • Requires monitoring of partner pacing • Increases noise level • Encourages some teacher–student competition
Alternative Teaching		
(Big Group; Small Group) One partner teaches an enrichment lesson or re-teaches a concept for the benefit of a small group, while the other partner teaches and/ or monitors the remaining members of the class.	• Facilitates enrichment opportunities • Offers absent students "catch-up" time • Keeps individuals and class on pace • Offers time to develop missing skills	• May be easy to select the same low-achieving students for help • Creates segregated learning environments • Is difficult to coordinate • May single out students
Team Teaching		
(Whole Group) Team members alternate roles presenting new concepts, reviewing, demonstrating, role-playing, and monitoring.	• Provides systematic observation/data collection • Promotes role/content sharing • Facilitates individual assistance • Models appropriate academic, social, and help-seeking behaviors • Teaches question asking • Provides clarification (e.g., concepts, rules, vocabulary)	• May be job sharing, not learning enriching • Requires considerable planning • Requires modeling and role-playing skills • Becomes easy to "typecast" specialist with this role

Source: Compiled with permission from M. Friend and W. Bursuck. *Including Students with Special Needs: A Practical Guide for Classroom Teachers,* 5th ed. © 2009. Printed by permission of Pearson Education, Inc., Upper Saddle River, NJ.

In order for coteaching to flow smoothly, classroom dynamics and the roles and responsibilities of each teacher should be discussed. Important concepts and interactions—such as interpersonal strengths and teaching approaches and strategies—need to be discussed. Leaders should consider the following questions when encouraging coteaching pairs.

- What is the minimum amount of time for coteaching?
- What should happen if someone is late?
- When will they plan?
- How many students with special needs should be in a cotaught class?
- At what stage of development are the teachers in their coteaching?
- Will coteaching occur daily? For certain periods? For a particular grading period?

Administrative support is crucial to the success of coteaching practices. Research shows that administrative attitudes and policies affect the ability and interest of teachers working collaboratively (Hands, 2010; Lehr, 1999; Villa et al., 2008). Villa and colleagues (2008) encouraged special and general leaders to:

- Provide a vision for the school to assure teachers that coteaching is an organizational strategy that adds to instructional strategies that benefit teachers as well as students. Coteaching empowers teachers to meet national and special education competencies and standards.
- Build consensus through respecting and recognizing teachers who promote the practice of coteaching. Incentives can include praise, special training opportunities, mentoring, travel to conferences, off-campus retreats, and so on.
- Promote professional development for coteaching, while encouraging innovation and different teaching styles, instructional skills, and ways to present content. Teachers and staff need to know how to plan collaboratively and be able to use the different approaches to coteaching.
- Schedule time to plan and share, while encouraging teachers to develop a trusting interaction in the coteaching relationship.
- Formulate and lead teachers through an action plan and pilot it for a year,

COLLABORATING WITH OTHERS

Collaborating with Families

A discussion of collaboration and consultation would not be complete without mentioning of families. Families create conditions that support and maximize children's behavior and achievement at school. Because a child's family is usually her or his first and most invested teachers, family input is critical in the education of students (Reedy & McGrath, 2010; Smith, Gartin, Murdurdick, & Hilton, 2006).

A key component of effective inclusive education programs is communication and collaboration with the student's family (Villa et al., 2008). Salend (2008) suggests that special and general education administrators are encouraged to:

- View families as valuable resources and partners in the educational process.
- To increase family collaboration and inclusion:
  a. A variety of strategies are to be used to share information about the student with his or her family.
  b. Families are to engage in curriculum planning and IEP meetings to provide information about the child's strengths, challenges, and progress.
  c. Resources are to be provided to assist students in completing their homework.

Special and general education administrators should remember to include families in home learning activities (Grande, 2004). These activities increase school and home collaboration by:

- Encouraging family/school partnerships that promote children's learning
- Providing some level of continuity between home and school
- Enabling families and teachers to share curriculum-related interactions with the children

Collaborating with Paraeducators

The prefix *para* is defined as "at the side of or beside." A paraeducator is a person who works alongside the administrator, specialist, or teacher. His or her position is sometimes instructional in nature, as the paraeducator delivers direct or indirect services to students. However, they work under the supervision of a teacher or other professional staff member who is responsible for the overall conduct of the class, the design and implementation of individual educational plans, and the assessment of the effect of the programs on student progress (Dettmer et al., 2009).

Paraeducators should be considered as an extension of the teacher. Vigilant planning on the part of the teacher and with the paraeducator will establish a relationship built on respect, which will contribute to increased capacity to meet the needs of all students—both with and without disabilities. Paraeducators should be permitted and encouraged to assist with the instructional process and daily routines (Floyd & Vernon, 2007; Giangreco, Suter, & Doyle, 2010).

In recent years, as more children with special needs are integrated into programs originally designed for students without disabilities, the role of paraeducators has grown. The inclusive service delivery model and RTI has increased the need to support both the students and teachers; thus, paraeducators have been hired to assist with behavioral and physical challenges of children with special needs. The success of paraeducators' services depends on professional abilities of these assistants. It also greatly depends on the ability of the administrators and teachers—both general and special educators—to collaborate and communicate with the paraeducators. In a classroom with one to four students with disabilities, paraeducators are able to check student progress, provide individual or small-group tutoring assistance, directly assist the classroom teacher, and report back to the special education teacher (Carnahan, Williamson, Clarke, & Sorensen, 2009; Elliott & McKenney, 1998). Remember Ms. Greiner and Ms. Ransom from the earily vignette? They might want to discuss with their administrator the possibility of having a paraeducator to assist in the general education classroom during the pilot implementation year.

There are challenges for school and special education leaders to appropriately educate and train paraprofessionals because their roles have developed over time. Paraprofessionals can join coteaching teams and work well within some approaches, such as station teaching. There is also a need for paraprofessionals as instructional assistants in inclusive settings and when implementing RTI, especially delivering differentiated instruction. Because paraprofessionals are now so involved in instruction, leaders must assure that they receive adequate training (IDEA, 2004).

Collaborating with Colleges/Universities

School/university partnerships offer a new perspective to professional development by providing opportunities for administrators to understand inclusive education. Such opportunities will also provide opportunities for teachers to interact and collaborate with colleagues, evaluate and reflect on their instructional practices, and expand their existing knowledge so that they are able to brainstorm new ideas to use in their classrooms with their students. According to Warren and Peel (2005), "Teachers receive a greater sense of unity, [a] greater sense of empowerment, a higher sense of responsibility for their school's destiny and an increased level of pride" as a result of successful partnerships between schools and universities (p. 351). Accordingly, these partnerships have become prominent in school reform efforts. University personnel from schools of education not only work with teachers and school administrators in the area of professional development and program implementation but also to assist with other tasks such as grant writing, technical assistance, and mentoring.

IMPLEMENTING RTI AND INCLUSION

How can schools and districts implement RTI and other inclusive practices smoothly and effectively? As emphasized throughout this text, effective school-level leadership is an essential component in the development and implementation of any program (Dettmer et al., 2009; Friend & Bursuck, 2009; Jenkins, 2007; Mellard & Johnson, 2008; Villa et al., 2008; Walther-Thomas et al., 2000). Several legal issues shown in Box 8.3 should be considered.

Professional development is heavily utilized for both the preparation and in-service of teachers and staff. Consider the following:

- Structured professional development should include consensus building early on.
- Begin with examining and understanding the rationale for change.
- Share theoretical, ethical, and data-based rationales to encourage participation and present information within the context of improving the school and school district.
- Develop a shared mission statement to use toward consensus building and share with teachers, staff, parents, and the community.

Implementing a successful pilot program is an important element to consider. Planning pilot programs should include both general and special education administrators. Creating successful examples of the desired program to emulate is essential (Bouck, 2007; Villa et al., 2008; Walther-Thomas et al., 2000; Wilson, 2008). Here are some pointers to consider:

- Allow for consideration of all the supports and resources needed. Once plans are in place, schools can move toward a successful implementation. Plans should be flexible.
- It is important for those not involved in the pilot to see positive changes. Observing reflective implementation supports confidence and promotes participation.
- Be sure to provide a complete description of the program as well as comprehensive documentation about both summative and formative measures during and after implementation.

BOX 8.3

Legal Issues

There are a plethora of legal issues in this chapter; however, to impede due process procedures, the following is advised:

- Both general and special administrators need to be aware of the regulations related to RTI, as it now being used to determine classification for learning disabilities (Zirkel & Krohn, 2008). According to 2006 IDEA regulations (§300. 307), (1) each state will choose eligibility criteria using the severe discrepancy, (2) RTI, or (3) some other research-based procedure. Even if RTI is not chosen as a means to determine eligibility, data-based documentation—including repeated assessments—is still required.
- Procedures that delay overidentification and disproportionality should be actively in place (i.e., prereferral teams, RTI, and other methods suggested) and used efficiently and effectively.

- Once the pilot program has begun, its success and the receptivity of the specific environment will determine how quickly the program can be expanded. Ongoing professional development should be present.
- The stronger the framework, design, and communicated expectations, the more successful the program.
- Remember before change occurs, teachers are likely to discard innovations before they have had adequate time to see the success of the intervention. Give teachers time to see the effect of the intervention.
- Teams provide coordinated support, therefore administrators can prepare staff to expect fluctuations in successful implementation. However, continuous work on program goals are encouraged, as expansion depends on success (Fullan, 1993).

Summary

Box 8.4 list three important things for leaders to remember.

Options have steadily developed through the years as laws were created and amended. Because of new developments in IDEA and the passing of NCLB, special and general teachers are expected to work collaboratively to help students remain in the general education classrooms. Response to intervention is now being implemented in many schools and has changed the way schools determine eligibility for special education. Students are now receiving evidence-based interventions in the classroom and are being positively affected. It is imperative that general education and special education leaders work collaboratively with teachers to establish common goals and serve as catalysts for creating a climate for these new developments (Friend & Bursuck, 2009). Training teachers to use coteaching models and providing in-service to increase collaboration with families, paraeducators, and universities widens the scope of inclusion by proactively involving appropriate people to the process of inclusive education. As administrators accept the challenge of implementing these programs, the school will experience the positive aspects of growth and development, and will see the value in moving toward more inclusive leadership. The resolution to the vignette is shown in Box 8.5.

BOX 8.4

Advice for School Leaders

- Be sure to provide in-service training for RTI and inclusion.
- Pilot programs for at least a year before trying full-scale implementation.
- Collaborate with special education administrators to assure appropriate program administration.

BOX 8.5

Resolution to the Vignette

Administrators should be involved in scheduling time for special and general education teachers to collaborate, especially if inclusion and RTI are to be implemented appropriately. Additionally, teachers need in-service to understand RTI.

Chapter Questions

1. What are some potential variables inside and outside of schools that can either facilitate or hinder local efforts to become more inclusive?

2. Think about the perspectives of administrators, teachers, and/or specialists involved in implementing RTI. Create a list of what you think would be their greatest accomplishments and concerns.

3. How can an administrator shape the collaborative process by requiring special educators, general educators, and other personnel to work together? Should this collaborative process be voluntary?

4. How can you create a plan to work with Ms. Greiner and Ms. Ransom toward implementing inclusion?

5. How can school leaders foster communication and collaboration with others (i.e., families, universities, paraprofessionals)?

CHAPTER 9

Leadership in a Multicultural Setting

Gloria D. Campbell-Whatley

Khalilah S. O'Farrow

Ozalle M. Toms

INTRODUCTION

In today's schools, teachers are not only faced with the challenge of utilizing various multicultural strategies to help prepare students for academic success, but they must also help students develop the skills necessary to interact within a culturally pluralistic and democratic society. As more students from diverse ethnic, cultural, and social backgrounds enter public schools, teachers must provide an enriching learning environment that encourages academic equality and achievement. Such a learning environment would acknowledge the importance of integrating cultural and personal experiences that students bring with them to the classroom structure. The promise of effective integration of multicultural education within special education classrooms provides students with diverse experiences and greater chances for academic success; however, the challenge is to actually make it happen.

Multicultural education, a reform movement designed to promote cultural pluralism, brings about educational and social equity for all students. It also places variables such as ethnicity, race, gender, social class, and language at the center of the teaching and learning process (Grant & Sleeter, 2011a; Grant & Tate, 1995). The integration of multicultural education within special education provides culturally diverse students with exceptionalities various opportunities to maximize their academic potential by making instruction more relevant to their cultural heritages, experiences, and perspectives (Gay, 2002a; Grant & Sleeter, 2011b; Green, 2010). The outcomes of multicultural special education include improvement of academic performance, acceptance of diversity, and changes in the attitudes and behaviors for teachers and students Nieto, 1998; Ramsey, Williams, & Vold, 2003; Yellin & Mokhtari, 2010). The overall goal of multicultural education is to enhance the school and classroom environment to encourage academic performance and improve social interaction among diverse students. Several challenges and issues in Box 9.1 will be discussed throughout the chapter.

BOX 9.1

Challenges and Issues for School and Special Education Leaders

- Helping teachers learn stronger positive attitudes toward diverse students
- Finding in-service to assist teachers to learn how to infuse diversity into the curriculum
- Locating strategies and approaches to facilitate diversity in the schools
- Locating materials to facilitate the infusion of diversity into the curriculum

---

Multicultural Special Education

Multicultural education within the context of special education shares the same goal of multicultural education in any other setting. In other words, there is generally no difference between multicultural special education and multicultural education. As demonstrated in the vignette in Box 9.2, there is a need to address culture as well as special education.

Multicultural special education intends to modify the school environment by changing the curriculum, instruction, and social interactions within classrooms to ensure equity among students (Cartledge, Gardner, & Ford, 2009; Nieto, 1998; Ramsey et al., 2003; Winzer & Mazurek, 1998). In addition, through multicultural special education, teachers encourage students to have equal respect for one another by providing them with the skills to develop cross-cultural sensitivity, and the competencies necessary to function in a pluralistic society (Winzer & Mazurek, 1998).

BOX 9.2

Vignette: *"Does Culture Make a Difference?"*

Mrs. Tompkins was sitting with her head in her hands wondering what to do. She was thinking about the hodge-podge of diverse children in her sixth-grade classroom. They were all having academic difficulty. Marcia moved here from Spain one year ago. Although she speaks Spanish and English, Spanish is the primary language spoken in the home. The language and cultural differences have been a challenge since her family moved here. Her parents, however, have been very supportive. They were concerned with the strategies and approaches used in the general education classroom. Although Marcia spoke fluent English and was a scholar in Spain, she was having great difficulty in class.

Mrs. Tompkins also thought about Xiong, whose Hmong family has been in the United States for less than a year. He lives with his parents, paternal grandparents, and several extended family members. His family does not speak English at home; Xiong speaks English fluently yet he is already talking about dropping out of school.

Then there is Dominick, who seems to be African American and is registered as an African American—"But I detect an accent," Mrs. Tompkins thought to herself. "He seems to be so unmotivated. What kinds of activities could I devise to get him interested in class?

"How can I work with all of these variations in culture? Should I start them on Tier 1? Maybe they are eligible for special education?"

1. How can special education leaders address these concerns?
2. What can school administrators do to address issues of cultural diversity?
3. What can special education administrators do to address issues of cultural diversity?

TABLE 9.1	Links between Multicultural Education and Multicultural Special Education
Multicultural Education	**Multicultural Special Education**
Provides equal access to educational services for all students	Provides equal access to educational services for all students
Assumes that all students have full and equal opportunity to learn in school and to be respected	Assumes that all students have full and equal opportunity to learn in school and to be respected
Transforms the curriculum	Individualizes the curriculum
Makes modifications in classroom climate, teacher's attitudes and expectations, teaching strategies, curriculum content, and materials	Makes some degree of modification in educational programs; includes curricular materials, teaching techniques, behavior management strategies, and specially designed equipment or facilities
Teach[es] students to accept and appreciate individual differences	Teach[es] students to accept and appreciate individual differences

Source: Compiled from M. A. Winzer and K. Mazurek, *Special Education in Multicultural Contexts.* Upper Saddle River, NJ: Merrill, 1998.

Winzer and Mazurek (1998) described various similarities between multicultural education and multicultural special education. Table 9.1 displays various links between multicultural education and multicultural special education.

As the diverse student population increases in general and special education settings, the integration of multicultural education becomes a necessity. General education and special education teachers' ability to address multicultural education helps to strengthen and support learning experiences among all students. This increase in student diversity within the classrooms and decrease in teacher diversity contributes to the need for all teachers to provide enriching and engaging environments that encourage academic success among students from traditionally underrepresented populations.

Multicultural education, as well as multicultural special education, provides students with greater opportunities to excel academically and socially by structuring the classroom environment and instruction to incorporate beliefs, values, and practices relevant to their cultural and personal experiences. Many teachers who express their concerns about multicultural education have shown resistance to integrating culturally diverse perspectives within the academic environment, or feel they are minimally prepared to teach diverse students. Teachers who resist the practice of integrating multicultural education within the academic environment often fail to honor diverse cultural heritages by not acknowledging multiple perspectives, and seek to prepare students to merely assimilate or "fit" into mainstream American culture (Artiles, 2009; Ladson-Billings, 1992; Lynn, 1999; Teel, Debruin-Parecki, & Covington, 1998; Villegas & Lucas, 2002a). Teachers who feel minimally prepared express their concern about lack of knowledge regarding resources, materials, and instructional strategies that integrate multicultural content and positively influence learning outcomes for diverse students (Barry & Lechner, 1995; Cirino et al., 2009; Dee & Henkin, 2002; Kitano & Pedersen, 2002; Marshall, 1996). Prominent scholars and theorists have proposed various approaches to multicultural education to support diverse students' academic, social, and emotional development by incorporating cultural resources within the learning environment (Gay, 2002a; Grant & Sleeter, 2011a; Ladson-Billings, 1992; Morey & Kitano, 1997; Sleeter & Grant, 1987; Villegas & Lucas, 2002b).

Integration of Multicultural Education

Many scholars and theorists suggest that multicultural education literature provides various approaches to incorporating cultural diversity within academic settings based on the theoretical frameworks of the assimilation paradigm and the cultural pluralism paradigm (Grant & Sleeter, 2011a; Ramsey et al., 2003; Winzer & Mazurek, 1998). Teachers who are influenced by the *assimilation paradigm* tend to resist integrating multicultural education within classroom practices by neglecting diverse perspectives and failing to support students' cultural diversity, or limiting multicultural education primarily to particular cultural events and celebrations. On the other hand, teachers who are influenced by the *cultural pluralism paradigm* seek to improve students' learning experiences and prepare them for appreciating cultural diversity within a democratic society by integrating multicultural education within classroom practices. Major goals of multicultural education include modifying the learning environment to motivate academic achievement and support students' diverse learning styles by strengthening the value of cultural diversity, equality, social justice, and democracy (Gay, 2002a; Grant & Sleeter, 2011a; Ladson-Billings, 1994; Nieto, 1998; Villegas & Lucas, 2002b). To address the major goals of multicultural education, prominent scholars and researchers have developed approaches to integrate multicultural education within the academic environment.

Grant and Sleeter (2011b), for example, suggested the following five approaches to multicultural practices that emerged from a comprehensive literature review on multicultural education: (1) teaching the exceptional and the culturally different, which seeks to adapt instruction to student differences in order to help them succeed more effectively in mainstream environments; (2) strengthening human relations, which teaches students about cultural differences to promote better cross-cultural understandings; (3) incorporating single group studies, which seeks to raise awareness regarding oppression experienced by specific cultural groups in order to mobilize for social action; (4) integrating multicultural education, which seeks to celebrate human diversity and equal opportunity by integrating race, language, culture, gender, disability, and social class within the academic environment; and (5) providing education that is multicultural and social reconstructionist, which seeks to promote social action and focus more on challenging social inequality (see Table 9.2). To clarify the use of the term *multicultural education*, Sleeter and Grant (1999b) distinguished between multicultural education identified as an approach and as an ideology. As an *approach*, multicultural education signifies creating or modifying educational policies and practices to recognize, accept, and affirm cultural diversity; whereas multicultural education as an *ideology* signifies the need to acknowledge culturally marginalized groups' integration into U.S. society (Sleeter & Grant, 1999b). The researchers

TABLE 9.2	Conceptions of Multicultural Education Integration				
Source	**Context**	**Level 1**	**Level 2**	**Level 3**	**Level 4**
Banks (1993)	*K–12 Courses*	*Contributions*	*Additive*	*Transformation*	*Social Action*
		Emphasis on discrete cultural elements such as foods or holidays	Adds content without changing the curriculum	Changes the curriculum to incorporate diverse perspectives	Encourages decision-making on social issues and action to solve them

also used the term *cultural democracy* interchangeably with the term *multicultural education* as an approach. According to Sleeter (1991), the multicultural education approach, or cultural democracy, attempts to redesign classrooms and schools to model a democratic, equal society, which is also culturally diverse.

Grant and Sleeter (2011b) conducted the literature review to bring conceptual clarity to multicultural education approaches, as well as evaluate the literature for its contributions to both theory and practice. The researchers indicated that multicultural education literature during the 1970s and 1980s failed to provide clear connections among multicultural approaches, theory, and recommended practices. Grant and Sleeter (2011b) expressed that other prominent scholars, such as Banks, have developed a considerable body of literature on multicultural education approaches that provides practical illustrations for teachers.

Banks (1994) identified the following five dimensions of multicultural education: (1) content integration, which deals with the extent to which teachers use examples and content from various cultures to illustrate key concepts; (2) knowledge construction, which consists of methods, activities, and questions teachers use to help students to understand, investigate, and determine how implicit cultural assumptions and biases influence the ways in which knowledge is constructed; (3) prejudice reduction, which incorporates strategies that can be used to help students develop more democratic attitudes and values; (4) equity pedagogy, which seeks to modify teaching styles in ways that facilitate academic achievement among culturally diverse students; and (5) empowering school culture and social structure, which involves restructuring the culture and organization of a school to promote academic and social equality among culturally diverse students. Banks (1994) suggested that the dimensions typology helps practitioners understand and implement multicultural education in thoughtful, creative, and effective ways. In addition, the five dimensions of multicultural education serve as benchmark criteria for conceptualizing, developing, and assessing theory, research, and practice.

Multicultural education literature also provides various conceptions of multicultural integration within higher education and K–12 school settings (Morey & Kitano, 1997). For example, Banks (1993) described four levels of K–12 course curriculum change to integrate multicultural education. Schoem, Frankel, Zúñiga, and Lewis (1993) identified five stages to restructure higher education courses for the integration of multicultural education. Green (1989) described five phases of campuswide curriculum change to incorporate ethnic and women's students. Ognibene (1989) applied a two-dimensional typology that consisted of three ways to include ethnic and women's studies content within the curriculum.

CONSCIOUS LEADERSHIP

The National Council for Accreditation of Teacher Education (NCATE) has established one unit standard that addresses cultural diversity. The unit standard, *diversity,* refers to the design, implementation, and evaluation of instructional curricula and materials to promote teachers' acquisition and application of the knowledge and skills necessary to help all students learn (National Council for Accreditation of Teacher Education, 2001). The diversity standard also addresses experiences working with diverse faculty, teacher candidates, and students in P–12 schools (National Council for Accreditation of Teacher Education, 2001). The various national diversity teaching standards have been established to prepare all teachers to exhibit knowledge of culturally based learning and behavioral styles, teaching styles, and culturally responsive educational practices (Obiakor & Utley, 2001). These standards provide guidance for teachers to effectively promote and integrate multicultural education within the academic environment.

When integrated appropriately, multicultural education enhances quality teacher education by capitalizing on the cultural resources of all students. In addition, multicultural education exposes students to maximum learning through critical thinking and problem solving, and acquaints students with diverse viewpoints and multiple voices to societal discourse (Banks, 1993; Ladson-Billings, 1994; Obiakor, 2001). Multicultural education values diversity and uses diversity in the development of effective instruction for students within the classroom (Gollnick & Chin, 2002). Although national organizations have made progress in identifying standards in competencies for professional practice related to cultural diversity, research findings suggest that in many instances teachers and teacher candidates do not possess sufficient knowledge of cultural issues that influence the teaching/learning process (Capella-Santana, 2003; King, 1991; Ladson-Billings, 1994; Obiakor & Utley, 2001).

There is a dire need for schools to offer many and varied cross-cultural experiences. Educational leaders will need to offer opportunities for teachers to learn to adapt content of instruction and teaching styles. Curriculum, methodology, and instructional materials should be responsive to students' values and cultural norms, therefore special and general education leaders will need to prepare teachers to do the following:

- Develop cohesive and comprehensive multicultural curricula in general and special education.
- Prepare teachers to infuse multicultural principles, strategies and approaches throughout curriculum and lesson plans.
- Respond to the diverse needs of the families of diverse learners.
- Train teachers in essential best practices for diverse students to assure that they teach using culturally responsive practices.

Examining the Characteristics of Culturally Responsive Teachers

Culturally diverse students often enter academic settings that ignore the mobilization of national teaching standards that address cultural diversity. The lack of teachers' awareness of cultural differences can foster inappropriate attitudes and behaviors toward cultural diversity (Gay, 2002b; Rosas & West, 2009; Seidl & Pugach, 2009; Webb-Johnson, 2002). Gay (2002b) suggests that teachers' knowledge about and attitudes toward cultural diversity serve as powerful determinants of students' learning opportunities and outcomes. Recognition of how these important concepts shape culturally diverse students' learning experiences influences the manner in which teachers effectively conduct instruction to encourage active engagement in learning. Teachers often have the belief that all students are the same regardless of their cultural background and that the traditional curriculum, based on mainstream cultural perspectives, is equally effective for all students (Nieto, 1998). Rather than build on students' cultural repertoire of behaviors, teachers typically aim to extinguish and replace these behaviors with conduct more acceptable to mainstream cultural norms and to move quickly to find the deficit in those children who prove less malleable to conformity (Harry & Anderson, 1994). Most special education teachers ignore how culture and language contribute to the learning process of culturally diverse learners and fail to consider integrating culture and language within lesson planning and instruction (Harry & Anderson, 1994). Gay (2002b) believes that an educator who knows and uses students' cultural socialization and experiences in teaching improves the quality of educational opportunities and outcomes. Teachers must understand how their perceptions, behaviors, and affirmations toward culturally diverse students contribute to students' engagement in learning.

Teachers who exhibit cultural competence understand that culture serves as a vehicle for learning. Students' ways of thinking, behaving, and being are deeply influenced by factors such as race, ethnicity, social class, and language (Villegas & Lucas, 2002a). According to Edgar, Patton, and Day-Vines (2002), the following five basic principles establish the foundation for strengthening cultural competence: (1) acknowledging diverse values and viewpoints; (2) conducting a self-assessment of one's own identity, attitudes, values, and beliefs; (3) discussing stereotypes in an effort to bridge cultural biases that impede mutual acceptance and understanding among culturally diverse students; (4) acquiring a knowledge of culture to enhance interaction within the classroom; and (5) including, analyzing, and infusing cultural artifacts and differences in the process of teaching and learning. Teachers who lack cultural competence often misperceive cultural differences as deficiencies, which often result from lack of understanding that cultural differences are directly influenced by social contexts. Duesterberg (1998) argues that teachers fail to realize that students enter classrooms with their own set of beliefs, dispositions, and ways of thinking and acting—all of which have been formed through multiple social and cultural contexts. Teachers who set low expectations for culturally diverse students teach them accordingly, which contributes to lower student motivation toward achievement in school. Culturally competent teachers structure learning environments to encourage students' sense of belonging and to motivate academic excellence (Villegas & Lucas, 2002b).

Teachers have the essential responsibility of providing quality instruction and educational opportunities to promote academic success among all students. Yet, students from culturally diverse backgrounds often become disengaged from school, experience academic failure, or drop out of school as a result of teachers' inability to provide an academic environment that values and encourages diverse participation. Students often lack motivation to succeed in school because their cultural, social, or linguistic characteristics are unrecognized, misunderstood, or devalued. The successful integration of multicultural education within the academic environment rests in how teachers support students' construction of knowledge by providing instruction that is culturally relevant, engaging, and meaningful to produce significant positive outcomes for all students (Utley & Obiakor, 2001; Villegas & Lucas, 2002a). Villegas and Lucas (2002b) emphasize six characteristics of culturally responsive teachers in Figure 9.1.

FIGURE 9.1 Characteristics of Responsive Teaching

Sociocultural consciousness	Self-analysis/reflection that examines one's own identity and the inequalities of society
An affirming attitude toward students from culturally diverse backgrounds	Respect for cultural differences and believing in the positive academic performance of students
Commitment and skills to act as agents of change	Increases collaboration so that school can become equitable over time
Constructivist views of learning	Differentiated techniques that link prior knowledge and skills to learning
Learning about students' past experiences	Environment and community included in teaching
Culturally responsive teaching strategies	A cultural perspective to the curriculum and lessons

Source: Compiled from *Educating Culturally Responsive Teachers: A Coherent Approach* edited by Ana Maria Villegas and Tamara Lucas, the State University of New York Press.

Designing a culturally relevant curriculum is a developmental process. After special and general education leaders examine their existing curricula, they can determine the needed level of cultural connection. Leaders can help teachers acquire cultural competence in many ways:

- Help teachers develop multicultural competence in assignments, projects, lessons and unit plans, and instructional delivery.
- Invite culturally competent or urban teachers as guest speakers or workshop providers to help teachers infuse diversity into the curriculum and lessons.
- Require and consider issues of diversity as an integrate part of lesson and unit conceptualization. The objectives should reflect how the class will contribute to skills related to diversity.
- Help teachers locate additional readings and materials that include the interests and contributions of diverse populations and that reflect multiple perspectives. Where feasible, encourage teachers to use multiple ways to teach the class through varied modalities, especially technology. (See Chapter 10 related to the universal design for learning and response to intervention in Chapter 8.)
- Require that classroom projects and activities, as well as curriculum, have evidence of diversity and are infused throughout, as opposed to isolated single lessons.
- Consider the format in which course content is presented (e.g., lecture, large-group discussion, small-group activity, reading assignment, simulation, performance activity, etc.). Use strategies and lessons that require hands-on activities and group work. Activities that are more diversity related include reflective writing, simulations, games, exploring family histories, and examining personal histories.

Other suggestions are listed in Figure 9.2.

FIGURE 9.2 Culturally Diverse Methodologies

Presentation of Instruction	Incorporating student interests
Addressing Diverse Learning Styles	Collaborative learning group Use of graphic organizers Use of manipulatives Incorporating student suggestion Teacher demonstration/modeling Center activities
Assessing Student Understanding	Oral review sessions Written assignments
Encouraging Student Participation	Affirming student responses Verbal praise Student prompts/signals Building self-confidence Building relationships Promoting respect Working with parents

Source: Compiled from G. Carteledge and Ya-yu Lo. *Teaching urban learners: Culturally responsive strategies for developing academic and behavioral competence.* Thousand Oaks, CA: Corwin Press, 2004.

By affirming cultural differences, teachers help raise students' self-esteem and motivation, which increases their active involvement in learning. The knowledge children bring to school, derived from cultural experiences, is central to their learning (Villegas & Lucas, 2002b). Using students' cultural orientations, background experiences, and ethnic identities as conduits to facilitate their teaching and learning increases the quality of education the student receives (Gay, 2002a). Teachers' ability to integrate multicultural education within the learning environment assists in meeting the challenge of motivating academic achievement among all students (Gay, 2002a; Udvari-Solner & Thousand, 1996). It is imperative for all special education teachers to construct and design culturally relevant instruction that bridges the gap between what students already know and appreciate and what they are to learn. Culturally responsive education includes effective teaching methods and strategies that empower students to grow intellectually, socially, and emotionally by integrating factors that contribute to students' cultural identity within teaching knowledge and skills (Ladson-Billings, 1994; Sullivan et al., 2009; Wlodkowski & Ginsberg, 1995). Remember the advice provided in Box 9.3. The last section of this chapter is devoted to culturally diverse resources that school and special education leaders might find useful.

CULTURAL DIVERSITY INTERNET RESOURCES

The Center for Culturally Responsive Teaching and Learning (CCRTL)

The CCRTL's institutes, workshops, seminars, school site-based training, and individual coaching activities are intended to help schools and districts in reaching their professional development and student achievement goals. The site promotes culturally appropriate instructional strategies for all students but particularly African Americans and Latinos (see www.culturallyresponsive.org/).

Everything English Second Language (ESL)

- Forty-one content-based ESL lesson plans for beginning through intermediate students
- Access to 56 in-service ideas and strategies for both ESL and mainstream educators
- Recommendations on materials and resources for the classroom (see www.everythingesl .net/resources/).

Multicultural Math

The Math Forum's Internet Math Library is a comprehensive catalog of websites and webpages (see www.wfu.edu/~mccoy/multmath.html).

Culturally Responsive Classrooms

This website is a resource for health educators interested in establishing culturally responsive classrooms and in using instruction and assessment strategies that provide all students with the opportunity to develop the knowledge and skills necessary to choose health-promoting behaviors. Materials include a self-assessment, information, resources, and tools to help educators enhance their health education instruction, assessment, and classroom environments to meet the diverse needs of all of their students (see www.rmc.org/allguide/).

World Affairs Council of Oregon

The Council's K–12 program provides people and material resources to schools to enhance international education and multicultural awareness (see www.worldoregon.org/more/education/index.php).

Multicultural Lesson Plans

These lesson plans on this website are designed for students who are learning English as a second language (see www.csun.edu/~hcedu013/plans.html).

CULTURAL DIVERSITY BOOK RESOURCES

Math Resources

Numerous math resource books are available to aid teachers in creating a more culturally diverse classroom. Claudia Zaslavsky has authored several of these books. One book, entitled *Math Games and Activities from Around the World* (Zaslavsky, 1998), is packed with more than 70 new ideas, including board games; puzzles with dots, string, and paper strips; symmetry and similarity of designs; and repeated patterns. For each activity, Zaslavsky provides a bit of historical background (including country or countries of origin), explains how to create the necessary materials, gives directions for doing a play (or making a craft), and offers suggestions for further thought. There is a mixture of puzzles to solve, realistic applications of math principles, and projects to help visualize math concepts.

A second book by Claudia Zaslavsky is titled *The Multicultural Math Classroom: Bringing in the World* (Zaslavsky, 1996) is an excellent resource for potential math teachers. It includes examples of mathematical games from other cultures, ideas for projects, and a list of references. *Multicultural Mathematics: Interdisciplinary Cooperative-Learning Activities* (Zaslavsky, 1993) is set up as a series of exercise sheets, dealing with ancient Egyptian, Chinese, African, American Indian, and other math systems. The suggested age is grades 5 or 6.

There are several culturally diverse resource books that include hands-on activities: *Multicultural Science and Math Connections: Middle School Projects and Activities* (Lumpkin, Strong, & Earle, 1995); *Hands-On Math Projects With Real-Life Applications* (Muschla & Muschla, 2006); and *Math Stories for Problem Solving Success: Ready-to-Use Activities Based on Real-Life Situations, Grades 6–12* (Overholt, Aaberg, & Lindsey, 2008).

English

There are resource books available to help readers understand and adapt to American culture and to cultural differences affecting their communication with American English speakers. *The Multicultural Workshop: A Reading and Writing Program* (Blanton & Lee, 1995) and *Beyond Languages: Cross Cultural Communication* (Levine & Adelman, 1993) are two resource books that provide insight into cross-cultural reactions to assist with expected U.S. behaviors and they both offer practical information for immigrants, refugees, international students, and business people in the United States.

Summary

Multicultural education within the context of special education provides diverse students with exceptionalities greater opportunities to excel academically and socially by integrating variables such as culture, social class, language, and diverse learning styles within the academic environment (Cummins, 2009; Gay, 2002b; Grant & Sleeter, 2011a; Grant & Tate, 1995; Ramsey et al., 2003; Sleeter & Grant, 1999). In order to limit due process, heed the legal advice provided in Box 9.4.

As more diverse students enter public schools, teachers are often faced with the challenge of modifying the academic environment to help prepare students for success, as well as develop the skills necessary to interact within a culturally pluralistic and democratic society. Teachers can provide an enriching academic environment that encourages equality and achievement by integrating students' cultural and personal experiences within the classroom structure. Major goals of multicultural education include modifying the academic environment to strengthen the value of cultural diversity, equality, social justice, and democracy (Gay, 2002a; Gollnick & Chinn, 2002; Grant & Sleeter, 2011b; Ladson-Billings, 1994; Nieto, 1998; Sleeter & Grant, 1999; Villegas & Lucas, 2002b).

Teachers who resist the practice of multicultural education integration within the academic environment often fail to acknowledge diverse perspectives; rather, they seek to prepare students to assimilate into mainstream Western culture (Cockrell, Placier, Cockrell, & Middleton, 1999; Green, 2010; Ladson-Billings, 1992; Lynn, 1999; Teel et al., 1998; Villegas & Lucas, 2002b). Prominent multicultural education scholars have proposed various approaches to integrating multicultural education within the academic environment to support diverse students' academic and social development (Banks, 1994; Gay, 2002a; Grant, & Sleeter, 2011b; Ladson-Billings, 1992; Morey & Kitano, 1997; Sleeter & Grant, 1987; Villegas & Lucas, 2002a). Research on multicultural education integration within classroom practices provides empirical data on factors that influence teachers' ability to support the learning of diverse students with exceptionalities toward academic achievement. The resolution to the vignette is listed in Box 9.5.

BOX 9.4

Legal Issues

- Many times, diverse students who are having academic difficulty need strategies and approaches that lend themselves to diverse populations.
- The Individuals with Disabilities Education Act (2004) emphasizes the use of prereferral interventions (response to intervention [see Chapter 8]—Tier 1 and Tier 2) to reduce the labeling, overidentification, and disproportionality.
- School-based prereferral/RTI teams are also good options for school leaders to initiate diversity-infused approaches and methodologies to prevent overidentification in special education.

BOX 9.5

Resolution to the Vignette

The principal can implement a team-based approach and the premises of RTI to implement and test some strategies for the three students. The applicable interventions should be implemented in the regular classroom environment. If these research-based strategies do not help the students, then infuse diversity into lessons using the suggestions in this chapter.

Chapter Questions

1. What are some suggestions for infusing a reading lesson on the content level? The additive level?
2. How are diversity-infused lessons related to response to intervention and universal design for learning?
3. What types of varied in-service training methodologies could you choose?
4. In what ways could you positively affect teacher attitudes toward diversity?
5. How might you advance diversity initiatives that promote more inclusiveness than add-on approaches?

CHAPTER 10

Universal Design for Learning

Accessing the General Curriculum with Effective Teaching and Digital Technologies

CHRISTOPHER O'BRIEN

NANCY AGUINAGA

VICTORIA KNIGHT

INTRODUCTION

Leaders of contemporary public schools must be prepared to address the needs of an increasingly diverse population. Evident from recent federal legislation for institutions of higher education, school leaders will need to develop action plans and successfully implement programs based on the principles of Universal Design for Learning (UDL). Current legislation is now dictating how teacher education programs across the nation must include the principles of UDL in existing curricula and instruction. The reauthorization of the No Child Left Behind Act (NCLB), also known as the Elementary Secondary Education Act (ESEA), and the Individuals with Disabilities Education Act (IDEA) are likely to follow suit.

The accountability provisions in NCLB have increased expectations for students with disabilities, calling for (1) progress in grade-level, general education content; (2) standards-based individualized education plans (IEPs); and (3) inclusion in statewide assessments. Universal Design for Learning offers a framework for providing a curriculum accessible to all students, including individuals with diverse needs (Rose, Meyer, & Hitchcock, 2005; Spooner, Baker, Harris, Ahlgrim-Delzell, & Browder, 2007). It enhances accessibility of classroom goals, methods, technologies, and materials in the classroom, so that all students have opportunities for meaningful engagement in grade-level content. The challenges and issues discussed in this chapter are outline in Box 10.1.

BOX 10.1

Challenges and Issues for School and Special Education

- Laws surrounding universal design and how they integrate into IDEA and NCLB
- Familiarity with the types of materials, methods, and approaches used in Universal Design for Learning
- Providing teachers support, materials, and resources to appropriately use Universal Design for Learning

---

BOX 10.2

Legal Issues

- NCLB and IDEA both dictate how teacher programs across the nation must include principles of UDL in existing curricula and instruction.
- IDEA ensures students equal opportunity or access to what is being taught.
- IDEA and the Assistive Technology Act of 1990 are synonymous in purpose and language—designing and delivering products that are usable and services that are directly accessible.

The chapter will describe the convergence of general and special education to address diverse learning needs in contemporary U.S. schools in the form of Universal Design for Learning. Trends toward inclusion and increased accountability in schools in recent years have presented enormous challenges to public schools seeking to teach rigorous curricula to a population of students with incredibly diverse backgrounds and abilities. The instructional framework of UDL is gaining in notoriety across the nation. It is premised on the notion that schools will be more successful when they *proactively* design curricula with the assumption of student diversity by integrating specialized instruction and accessible materials into general teaching practice. Technological developments tend to be the driving force in this area and increasingly the call for the UDL framework has become established in federal legislation (O'Brien, Aguinaga, & Mundorf, 2009). Certain legal requirements in Box 10.2 should be remembered as you read the chapter.

OVERVIEW OF UDL

The term *universal design* derives from a movement in architecture, which has as its major premise, that we should design buildings and public spaces so that they will be accessible to all citizens. According to Ron Mace, at North Carolina State University, universal design is the design of products and environments to be usable by all people, to the greatest extent possible, without the need for adaptation or specialized design (Messinger-Willman & Marino, 2010). Further, the intent of universal design is to simplify life for everyone by making products, communications, and the built environment more usable by as many people as possible, as universal design benefits people of all ages and abilities (Bouck, 2010).

Essentially, UDL assumes that learning experiences will be designed such that instruction benefits students of all abilities, interests, and backgrounds (Blue, 2010; Rose & Meyer, 2002; Salazar, 2010). Although the origin of UDL derives, conceptually, from universal design in architecture, the application to learning and educational settings is strongly rooted in special education intervention work. For example, many in the field of special education who specialize in assistive technology have come to realize the benefits of scaling up individualized assistive technologies to a broader use to support academic performance. Some have questioned whether UDL is just about teaching with technology. Others have asked how assistive technology differs from UDL. Edyburn (2003) defines UDL with a clear emphasis on the use of technology. He describes assistive technologies as interventions premised on compensation for lack of function on the part of the student, whereas Universal Design is an instructional approach involving proactive instructional design that would "anticipate and support differences that may interfere with performance" (p. 1).

This instructional design concept is an overarching framework for teaching that aligns well with the current diversity of students in public schools (i.e., very diverse backgrounds, learning needs, learning preferences, and academic abilities/disabilities). School and special education administrators will act as leaders to promote universal design while finding ways to circumvent the barriers in the process. Leaders will need to be instrumental in providing resources to design instructional experiences in schools that will be accessible to all students. This is difficult to do, but technology, in particular, makes it more likely. Currently, this framework is being added to federal educational legislation and is likely to have a substantial impact on the way we think about teaching in the coming years (O'Brien, Aguinaga, & Mundorf, 2009).

As school and special education leaders continue to implement the Individuals with Disabilities Education Improvement Act of 2004 (IDEIA), they will ensure students equality of opportunity or access to what is being taught. The IDEA of 2004 defines *universal design* using the same definition as used in the Assistive Technology Act of 1998:

> The term *universal design* means a concept or philosophy for designing and delivering products and services that are usable by people with the widest possible range of functional capabilities, which include products and services that are directly accessible (without requiring assistive technologies) and products and services that are interoperable with assistive technologies.

Universal Design for Learning provides students an increased opportunity to have access to learning. The Individuals with Disabilities Education Act also includes support for students with *print disabilities* to access instructional materials in a timely manner by mandating digital media regulations related to the National Instructional Materials Accessibility Standard (NIMAS). Supports consist of providing alternate formats such as electronic text, audio, large print, or Braille (Stahl, 2003).

The National Universal Design for Learning Task Force (Sabia, 2008; www.advocacy-institute.org/UDL/organizations.shtml), made up of 28 national organizations representing teachers, school boards, administrators, parents, and advocates representing children with disabilities, recommended legislative language for the Higher Education Opportunities Act (HEOA). The Higher Education Opportunity Act of 2008 was signed into law in August 2008. The legislation overhauls the nation's higher education laws, including reforms making college more accessible to all and enhancing teacher education programs. The principles of Universal Design for Learning have a strong presence in the HEOA legislation, including the following policy language:

- Integrate technology effectively into curricula and instruction, including technology consistent with the principles of Universal Design for Learning.
- Assess the effectiveness of departments, schools, and colleges of education at institutions of higher education in preparing teacher candidates for successful implementation

of technology-rich teaching and learning environments. These should include environments consistent with the principles of Universal Design for Learning that enable K–12 students to develop learning skills to succeed in higher education and to enter the workforce.

- Transform the way departments, schools, and colleges of education teach classroom technology integration, including the principles of universal design, to teacher candidates.
- Build the skills of teacher candidates to support technology-rich instruction, assessment and learning management in content areas, technology literacy, and understanding the principles of universal design.

The No Child Left Behind Act holds schools and local education agencies accountable for the improved achievement of all students. The National Universal Design for Learning Task Force has also recommended the following legislative language for the upcoming NCLB Reauthorization in accordance with providing high-quality education to today's diverse learners. School and special education leaders can help districts in the following ways:

- Develop a comprehensive plan to address the implementation of Universal Design for Learning. The plan must be sufficiently detailed to develop and apply Universal Design for Learning to standards, curriculum, teaching methods, instructional materials, and assessments.
- Support teachers in developing subject matter knowledge and teaching skills consistent with the principles of Universal Design for Learning and move toward the use of universally designed assessments.

ASSUMPTIONS ABOUT STUDENT DIVERSITY

Students can differ from each other in infinite ways. Classrooms today include students with various disabilities, background experiences, levels of motivation, as well as cultural/linguistic differences. Complicating society's preconceived notion of children with disabilities is the fact that the overwhelming majority of children served by special education have what could be described as *academic* disabilities. These include learning, behavioral, attention, speech/language development, and mild cognitive disabilities. These children account for as large a proportion—90 percent of the children served by special education in U.S. public schools (U.S. Department of Education, 2004). Those who need more time or support are frequently left behind and spend the rest of their education trying to catch up. Those who were quick to master the skill have to wait for others, often getting bored and leading to behavioral problems or dropping out. Personalized learning is needed and made possible for many through Universal Design for Learning. The curriculum must be flexible enough to allow all students, including those *in the margins*, to access needed support or added challenge (Rose, Meyer, & Hitchcock, 2005). Box 10.3 presents an example related to student diversity.

A goal of UDL is to identify and remove barriers in the curriculum. The intent of a lesson needs to be considered, and multiple ways to acquire the content and demonstrate knowledge must be allowed. By creating a flexible learning environment, limitations of the curriculum for the greatest number of learners can be diminished, thus providing access to all. A one-size-fits-all teaching approach does *not* fit all students, nor do the traditional practices used in many classrooms fit many learners (Bashan & Gardner, 2010).

BOX 10.3

Vignette: *"Diverse Classrooms in the Digital Era"*

In the last two years, Principal Rodriguez has pushed technology and inclusion. Mrs. Jacobs is beginning to feel that her teaching routines become harder and harder with each passing year, as her classes become more diverse in terms of students' abilities and background and fascination with technology. With inclusion being such a strong trend for children with disabilities, Mrs. Jacobs's eighth-grade social studies classes have increasingly become enrolled with students in special education with limited consultation support from the special education teacher. She now has 9 students with learning and attention disabilities and one student with Asperger's Syndrome in her last period "inclusion" class—as well as the numerous "non-labeled" students who struggle with high-level content, written expression, and reading comprehension.

In addition to meeting the unique learning needs of her students while teaching a rigorous curriculum, Mrs. Jacobs must ensure that her students are prepared for end-of-grade accountability practices. She realizes that her traditional approach to teaching social studies doesn't seem to be reaching the students and she spends more and more time making accommodations for individual students and trying to figure out how she'll ever make it through the textbook. Mrs. Jacobs has come to realize that she needs a new approach to teaching that assumes her students will have extensive needs for building background knowledge and completing challenging class work. This approach will need to build on her knowledge and passion for her content, along with the models of teaching students with special needs. Of course, given the era of digital natives in the classroom, there will undoubtedly be a role for technology to provide in increasing the accessibility of her challenging content. "Where am I going to get the help I need?" she thinks to herself.

1. Can a digital approach really help the students with disabilities in Mrs. Jacobs's class?
2. Can all the students be assisted using technology or is it specifically for the students with disabilities?
3. What is UDL and how does it differ from differentiated instruction?
4. How can technology improve a rigorous curriculum?
5. Provide specific suggestions of how collaboration could help solve Mrs. Jacobs's dilemma.
6. What could Principal Rodriguez do to assist Mrs. Jacobs?
7. Describe how UDL could support each one of Mrs. Jacobs's challenges.

Barriers in the Curriculum for Students with Disabilities

Physical, visual, and learning disabilities can all contribute to interfering with reading or comprehending text on a printed page. A student with a learning disability may not have any difficulty seeing text clearly, but may need prompts to aid in comprehension. Highlighting critical features can also help with vocabulary and background knowledge. Synchronized highlighting and text-to-speech software could help a student with dyslexia recognize a word and pair it with pronunciation. Special and general education leaders can assure that:

- The current focus is on the limitations of the student, not the curriculum. In the process, a rigid curriculum is often the barrier for many students.
- A flexible curriculum could remove the barriers that prohibit students from excelling.
- Students with and without disabilities can benefit from options, choosing what works best for them.

There are several other barriers school and special education leaders will need to consider that would impede instruction (Messinger-Willman, & Marino, 2010):

- Funding sources
- Deficits in teacher knowledge and curricula strategies related to technology and other related UDL information
- Lack of teacher time, training, and teamwork related to UDL
- Availability of workshops and training sessions
- Adjustment of teacher attitude and dispositions regarding new technological features and varied methodologies.

Suggestions to facilitate the removal of these barriers are discussed throughout the chapter.

HOW STUDENTS LEARN: RECOGNITION, STRATEGIC, AND AFFECTIVE NETWORKS

Founders of the UDL framework at the Center for Applied Special Technology (CAST), David Rose and Anne Meyer (Meyer & Rose, 2000; Rose & Meyer, 2002; Rose & Meyer, 2000) apply evidence from neuroscience to the school-based understanding of learner differences, explaining that learning tasks can be divided into activity in the strategic, recognition, and affective networks. The principles of UDL derived from brain research offer tremendous implications for understanding how individuals learn. In basic terms, there are three interconnected yet specialized networks in the brain that correlate with essential learning tasks (Rose & Meyer, 2002).

This conceptualization of recognition, strategic, and affective networks in the learning brain correspond with learning elements suggested by Russian psychologist Lev Vygotsky (1896–1934): (1) recognition of the information to be learned, (2) application of strategies to process that information, and (3) engagement with the learning task (Vygotsky, 1962). Recognition networks enable individuals to acquire and synthesize information, and to determine patterns, concepts, and relationships (e.g., understanding the concept of convection). Strategic networks enable students to develop patterns and strategies for expression (e.g., producing multiple examples of convection). The affective network is significant in that it assigns emotional relevance to learning tasks. Affective networks can provide individuals with motivation and help to establish priorities, guide attention, and make decisions (e.g., choosing whether or not to study convection).

Ultimately, what is most significant in analyzing the neuroscientific evidence on learning and the conceptualization of learning networks is the notion that everyone has natural variance in the function of each of these networks. This translates to a universal commonality in human learning. Schools are not attended by normal and abnormal students nor regular and special education students. Rather, there are typical, expected ranges of variance in learning preferences and abilities (Rose & Meyer, 2002). All students benefit from an instructional design that presumes an inherent diversity of students in the general education classroom.

UDL FRAMEWORK: REPRESENTATION, EXPRESSION, AND ENGAGEMENT

The three specialized networks correspond to the three overarching principles of UDL: multiple means of representation, multiple means of expression, and multiple means of engagement (see Figure 10.1).

FIGURE 10.1   UDL Principles and Teaching Methods

To support diverse recognition networks:
Provide multiple examples.
Highlight critical features.
Provide multiple media and formats.
Support background context.
To support diverse strategic networks:
Provide flexible models of skilled performance.
Provide opportunities to practice with supports.
Provide ongoing, relevant feedback.
Offer flexible opportunities for demonstrating skill.
To support diverse affective networks:
Offer choices of content and tools.
Offer adjustable levels of challenge.
Offer choices of learning context.
Offer choices of rewards.

Source: United States Office of Special Education Programs, Tool Kit on Universal Design for Learning.

- The presence of *diverse recognition networks* corresponds to the need to provide multiple, flexible methods of presentation.
- The presence of *diverse strategic networks* correspond to the need to provide multiple, flexible methods of expression.
- The presence of *diverse affective networks* correspond to the need to provide multiple, flexible options for engagement.

The framework of UDL ensures that students with diverse learning needs can progress in the general education curriculum, instruction, and assessments regardless of their disability, past experience, or ability level. For example, differences in the activity of the recognition network suggest that students need *multiple means of representation* related to academic concepts, or multiple ways to access new information. Differences in the functioning of the strategic networks imply the need for *multiple means of expression* in academic experiences. This translates to multiple ways for students to demonstrate their understanding. Finally, differences in functioning of the affective network suggest a need for *multiple means of engagement*. Academic experiences are enhanced if they are individualized to student interest. Students should be challenged, engaged, and motivated in order to reach their greatest potential in their educational experiences.

Providing Multiple Means of Representation

Teachers using a UDL framework to provide multiple means of representation offer students a wide range of options for accessing academic content. In a UDL classroom, students experience content with varying levels of readiness or background knowledge, varying ability to complete reading tasks, and varying ability to conceptualize abstract concepts. To address these learner differences, teachers can begin by offering options for perception, language and symbols, and comprehension. For example, if students need assistance in order to access textbooks independently, teachers can take advantage of the emergence of digitized textbooks:

- See www.nimac.us, in which text size, background contrast, and color is flexible. In addition, instructional materials should promote alternatives to auditory information and visual information, offering captioning, text-to-speech software (see free download at www.naturalreaders.com), and various graphics, animations, and videos to further explain a concept.
- Strong content resources on the web (from Wikipedia www.wikipedia.org to the digital history website www.digitalhistory.uh.edu) are perfectly designed for text-to-speech (TTS) access, given their digital presentation.
- Other free, public sites even offer reading materials as audio files so that students can download and listen to them on an iPod or on a computer in the classroom (see Librivox for public domain literature in an audio format; www.librivox.com).

Although teachers would like all their students to independently decode text, the goal of content classes is content acquisition, regardless of how students attain the material (O'Brien, 2007). In order to acquire content and learn concepts, students may need alternatives for language and symbols.

- Students who are learning symbols or who are nonverbal might access text with picture and speech output support using software such as Boardmaker with Speaking Dynamically Pro (see www.mayer-johnson.com).
- Digital text can also be supported with video, a logical aid in providing multiple representations of content.
- Teachers can use short clips from movies or documentaries, classroom-ready footage on TeacherTube (www.teachertube.com), web collections of multimedia teacher resources such as Annenberg Media at www.learner.org or Discovery Education Streaming (http://streaming.discoveryeducation.com).

In recent years, studies of instruction in various content areas for students with LD and autism have shown promising results integrating multimedia-anchored instruction (Gersten, 1998) or video modeling (Delano, 2007; O'Brien & Dieker, 2008). Exemplifying a model UDL classroom, recent studies of history instruction for students with LD have shown promising results integrating multimedia-anchored instruction—short video segments (e.g., *To Kill a Mockingbird, Eyes on the Prize)* combined with cooperative learning strategies, various learning strategies for text analysis, and use of primary sources and other expository texts (see Gersten, Baker, Smith-Johnson, Dimino, & Peterson, 2006).

In addition to providing content alternatives using visual and auditory support, teachers can promote comprehension of the content by activating prior knowledge, explicitly highlighting connections, and supporting recall of information. For example, a core element of the University of Kansas Strategic Instruction Model (www.ku-crl.org) is the Content Enhancement series, which includes SMARTER planning and the Course and Unit Organizer Routines. These strategies all have incredible relevance for instruction by focusing on what *big ideas* are most relevant in the content and by helping students see abstract concepts and connections using explicit instruction and graphic organizers (Lenz, Deshler, & Kissam, 2004). Graphic organizers are critical in UDL, helping students to grasp abstract concepts and making critical information conspicuous (Hall, Meyer, & Strangman, 2005). Teachers and students can also create their own graphic organizers using free web resources, such as the brainstorming website www.bubbl.us, and can transform graphic organizers instantly into outlines using free trials found at www.inspiration.com.

Of course, reading comprehension strategies are critical in content-area reading experiences (even when listening), and instruction should emphasize the use of strategies for enhancing the learning process—strategies for enhancing conceptual understanding (i.e., Unit Organizer Routine; Lenz et al., 2004), retention of new vocabulary (see LINCS strategy; Ellis, 2000), and metacognitive strategies to aid in self-monitoring of comprehension (e.g., Paraphrasing strategy; Lenz et al., 2004). Various learning strategies in the University of Kansas Strategic Instruction Model (www.ku-crl.org) offer excellent tools for students, and many of these strategies can be easily embedded in whole-class instruction.

Providing Multiple Means of Expression

When students are provided with multiple means of expression, they are given appropriate scaffolding (i.e., supports, prompts) for demonstrating what they know. To prepare students for the future and promote students' highest potential, teachers must provide all students with appropriately designed instructional materials to allow navigation, composition, and planning. In an increasingly technologically literate world, students need to be able to compose using multimedia (e.g., web designs, storyboards, comic strips). If the focus of instruction is on content relevance (e.g., presentation), rather than prerequisite skills (e.g., handwriting), students should have multiple options for composing and problem solving. Perhaps, in a thematic lesson, students would have options of creating multimedia presentations with relevant images and audio narration across content areas. Students with physical or motor disabilities can interact and navigate text digitally using a single switch, through voice-activated switches, custom overlays for touch screens, or adapted keyboards.

- Assistive technologies (e.g., voice recognition software such as Dragon Naturally Speaking, www.nuance.com/naturallyspeaking/), as well as computer-aided-design (CAD), graphing calculators, and concept mapping tools can be implemented in a universal fashion such that all students will see these skills as valuable and logical ways to express themselves.
- Differentiated instruction can offer a means for scaffolding instruction at appropriate levels for practice and performance (e.g., templates, physical and mnemonic scaffolds, procedural checklists). Teachers could support students in learning strategies for writing (e.g., PENS Sentence-writing strategy) and test-taking (e.g., PIRATES test-taking strategy), but also allow other meaningful expressions of understanding when the goal of the lesson is not *limited* to writing or test-taking (Lenz et al., 2004).

Providing Multiple Means of Engagement

In addition to a means to provide expression, a technique called *differentiated instruction* can also be used as a tool for engaging students in the curriculum by offering students choices in the process (e.g., how students learn) and providing autonomy in the product (e.g., how students demonstrate learned knowledge (Tomlinson, 2001). At times, the teacher needs to select the learning objective; however, it may be appropriate for students to have a voice in various activities related to the objective, such as the level of perceived challenge of the task (e.g., the lexile level of the book), the type of reward or recognition available, the context/content applicable to the skill, and the tools for obtaining the information and/or producing the product (e.g., write an essay independently or present to the class with a group). Interest in the academic content is more likely to occur when students feel a sense of ownership in the process through participation in the design of classroom activities and academic tasks. When students feel materials and activities are personally relevant, they are likely to be engaged in the materials. For example, culturally responsive teaching provides students with authentic learning experiences appropriate for culturally and linguistically diverse learners connecting to students' cultural identities and personal experiences (Villegas & Lucas, 2002).

UDL: WHAT SCHOOL AND SPECIAL EDUCATION LEADERS CAN DO

Potential solutions for special and general education leaders is to provide workshop and training experiences to increase teachers' resources, collaboration, and knowledge about Universal Design for Learning (Messinger-Willman & Marino, 2010):

- Allow time for collaboration of strategies during teacher planning time.
- Provide assistive technology training (online sources include www.atto.buffalo.edu and www.lburkhart.com/links.htm).
- Provide time for teachers to attend workshops and trainings in the district.
- Work collaboratively with universities and colleges in the area to provide resources, workshops, and seminars related to UDL.
- Get family members involved to get support from home networks.
- Urge teachers to value and expect diversity. Individual and group diversity contributes positively to classroom climate, learning outcomes, and community quality. Human commonalities cut across socially constructed categories of race, class, gender, sexual orientation, and disability. It is in the interest of everyone to be in socially inclusive learning environments in which all individuals are valued. Teachers with different expertise can coteach in inclusive settings while providing optimal social and academic results for all students.

Beyond the rhetoric and ethical grounding of the inclusion movement, the myriad challenges associated with inclusive *instruction* amplify the need to bring "what is special about special education" (B. G. Cook & Schirmer, 2003) to the general education classroom (King-Sears, 1997). Unfortunately, the literature on teaching students with disabilities can sometimes appear disjointed, rooted in practices of micro-objective intervention research (Skrtic, 1995), only providing insights into the effectiveness of individual strategies in specific, isolated contexts. By implementing an integrated framework for teaching students in inclusive accountability-driven classrooms effective strategies for the broadest possible range of learners can be realized. Effective inclusion may be best served by a "systems thinking" approach to school change (Betts, 1992), requiring educators to determine the *multiple tactics* that could support inclusion and the ultimate impact of these efforts when implemented in an integrated, coordinated manner.

School and special education leaders must emphasize that using cooperative learning will not solve all the problems of teaching an academically diverse classroom, but that does not rule out its usefulness as a foundation for other effective and inclusive teaching strategies. Cooperative learning is effective in developing interdependence in learning experiences and improves academic achievement when students have individual accountability (McMaster & Fuchs, 2002). It is more likely, however, to operate efficiently with a diverse group, when the class is being cotaught with a learning and behavior specialist (special education teacher). It is even more likely to be effective when teachers use a Positive Behavior Support approach to classroom management, teach students learning strategies, incorporate opportunities for students to be actively engaged and responding, and provide numerous forms of content enhancement. Ultimately, special education research has established a substantial body of intervention and support models to promote inclusion and achievement among students with diverse learning needs. But these models may be most effective when they are integrated into one universal instructional framework that offers an extensive repertoire of methods and points of access (Hall et al., 2005; Jackson & Harper, 2005; King-Sears & Mooney, 2004).

In a UDL environment, it is essential that school and special education leaders promote a proactively embedded multitude of content enhancements and learning strategies into the instructional plan, in order to meet the learning needs of a broad spectrum of students. The UDL classroom sets students up for success rather than reactively responding to common differences in academic potential that are exacerbated by the limited accessibility inherent in textbook-driven instruction (Rose et al., 2005). An important consideration in UDL is the proactive use of multiple teaching and learning strategies in an integrated fashion.

To increase teacher contact time to share instructional methodologies, special and general education leaders can work together to (Messinger-Willman & Marino, 2010):

- Develop a website that provides districtwide resources.
- Hire or develop technology staff to become a specialist that will be a resource for teachers.
- Allow teachers to share ideas (especially those in rural locations) through threaded discussions on the districtwide website, SKYPE, and other on-line tools.
- Develop school-to-school connection learning about UDL through the mentoring process.
- Provide district on-line training and classes.
- Create school and districtwide technology teams.

EFFECTIVE TEACHING PRACTICES TO PROMOTE ACCESS TO THE GENERAL CURRICULUM

Several authors summarized *best academic practices* for inclusion, noting that such practices are not necessarily limited to achievement in content areas but must extend to management of behavior and enhancement of social skills, which underlie the potential for academic success (King-Sears, 1997). Best practices include but are not limited to the following: (1) cooperative learning; (2) strategy instruction, using the explicit, intensive model of instruction; (3) differentiated instruction; (4) self-determination; (5) explicit or direct instruction, particularly for more structured content; (6) curriculum-based assessment; (7) generalization techniques; (8) collaboration between general and special education; (9) Positive Behavior Intervention and Supports (PBIS; Horner & Sugai, 2005); and (10) peer support/social interaction. Authors emphasize the need to integrate these approaches in teacher planning for diversity. From a nontechnological perspective, one could recognize the need to use multiple strategies in a coordinated fashion to address unique learning needs and academic profiles over time.

Many established practices in special education service delivery (see Figure 10.2) reflect the nontechnological potential for high-quality instruction to provide multiple means of recognition, expression, and engagement. Notable in each of these approaches are processes that overlap in activity of the different learning networks. In essence, a strategy that provides multiple access points and multiple means of recognition may also provide students with support in expression

FIGURE 10.2 Effective Teaching Strategies

Differentiated Instruction	Edyburn (2008) suggests that the models of differentiated instruction and UDL are highly consistent, with the emphasis being the proactive design of materials and learning environments anticipating learner differences. Unique to differentiated instruction is a strong emphasis on tiered lessons and the differentiation of content, process, and product (Hall, Strangman, & Meyer, 2003; Tomlinson, 2001).
Collaborative Instruction and Coteaching	This instructional practice is typically referred to as cooperative teaching or coteaching and involves the collaborative partnership between a general educator acting as a content specialist and a special educator acting as a specialist in instruction for students with disabilities (Bauwens & Hourcade, 1991; Cook & Friend, 1995). (This was discussed in Chapter 8.)
Strategic Instruction	The strategic instruction model (see www.ku-crl.org) is an approach that assists students in overcoming areas of deficit in their skill repertoire and improving their metacognitive practices to improve performance in academic content. The larger collection of these learning strategies is referred to as the *learning strategies curriculum* and includes a continuum of strategies to address skills in acquisition of knowledge, storage or maintenance of knowledge, and expression or demonstration of knowledge. Strategies in this curriculum include strategies for reading comprehension (e.g., the word identification strategy, the paraphrasing strategy); memorization of information (e.g., the FIRST-letter mnemonic strategy, the LINCS vocabulary strategy); expression of information (e.g., the sentence writing strategy, the paragraph writing strategy); and demonstration of competence (e.g., the test-taking strategy), which have been shown to be effective in improving student learning and performance (Lenz, Deshler, & Kissam, 2004).
Content Enhancements	These routines are meant to enhance whole-group instruction, typically the instruction provided by general education teachers in inclusive classrooms. Two common examples of content enhancements are use of graphic organizers and mnemonic instruction, both strongly established in the special education literature.
Active Student Response	The term *active student response (ASR)* refers to observable, measurable, curriculum-related responses to teacher-posed questions or instructions. An extensive research base demonstrates the relationship between increased ASR and student achievement. Three easy-to-implement strategies that promote ASR include (1) guided notes, (2) response cards, and (3) peer tutoring (Heward, 2006).
Peer Support	*Peer support* is a general term for a collection of inclusive practices to support students with disabilities in the general education classroom (Maheady, Harper, & Mallette, 2001) such as peer-mediated instruction (PMI) (Fuchs, Fuchs, Mathes, & Simmons, 1997; Greenwood & Delquadri, 1995; Greenwood & Terry, 1993; Maheady, 1988; Maheady et al., 2001); classwide peer tutoring (CWPT); peer-assisted learning strategies (PALS); and reciprocal teaching, which refers to a collection of instructional strategies that require class members to work in reciprocal tutoring pairs as they compete with other teams (Greenwood & Delquadri, 1995).

and thereby lead to higher levels of engagement. Universal Design of Learning, however, is not just traditional teaching. The methods discussed in Figure 10.2 suggest an anticipated repertoire of instructional strategies and service delivery options necessary to proactively design curricula with the assumption of a broad a range of learning abilities, preferences, and needs.

SELECTION OF WEB-BASED RESOURCES THAT SUPPORT UDL

Funding will be a problem for most districts; however, general and special education leaders can use the free resources listed in this section of the chapter to subsidize other efforts such as (Messinger-Willman & Marino, 2010):

- Using state and federal subsidized funding
- Utilizing funding attached to each categorical disability, especially funds linked to physical and related disabilities
- Working with surrounding universities to obtain funding

The list of assistive technologies used in special education services is quite long and many of these devices are highly specialized. Given the utility of digital materials and the ubiquitous nature of web-based resources in education, the following resources are offered as a few promising tools to promote UDL.

On-Line Concept Maps

For teachers interested in developing graphic organizers or more clearly expressing the "big ideas" of their lessons, www.bubbl.us is a free web application. The site allows users to create online concept maps specific to their daily content and to share them with students.

Mathematics Resources

The National Library of Virtual Manipulatives (NLVM), a web-based resource supported by National Science Foundation funding, provides students and teachers with interactive activities or tutorials representing varied mathematical concepts. The premise of the NLVM is the need for students to engage in mathematical concepts rather than simply be a recipient of passive learning. The work also builds on the use of manipulatives in mathematics instruction providing for explicit, visual representation of complex concepts (see nlvm.usu.edu/).

History Resources

Developed by partners including the University of Houston and the Chicago History Society, the Digital History Online Textbook provides a "digital materials" alternative version of a U.S. history textbook including digital text, embedded graphic organizers, and various multimedia representations of significant historical content (see www.digitalhistory.uh.edu/).

The American Rhetoric site is a publicly accessible database of audio archives of significant content from American history. Included in the site's archives are the Top 100 American political speeches in American history and over 5,000 audio clips of notable debates, interviews, and legal proceedings. The site offers a unique opportunity to provide multiple representations of historic events using multimedia from the appropriate period (see www.americanrhetoric.com/newtop100speeches.htm).

Science Resources

An exceptional resource for any biology lesson, the Encyclopedia of Life is a fascinating web-based resource in which individual sites (similar in appearance to wikipedia) are being developed for each of the approximately 1.8 million species of life on the planet Earth. These sites include images of the different species, videos, and digital text summaries (see www.eol.org/). Other similar resources include Encyclopedia of Earth (www.eoearth.org); Digital Universe (www.digitaluniverse.net); and Windows to the Universe (www.windows2universe.org).

English Language Arts Resources

LibriVoxis is a web-based resource with the mission of making every book in the public domain available to the public in an audio format. The site uses volunteers to record readings of books (novels and poetry, etc.) available in the public domain and provide them in digital audio formats (i.e., mp3 format). An English teacher giving homework to read a poem by Edgar Allen Poe can refer students to the text or to LibriVox where they'll find an audio version they can download to their iPod (see librivox.org/short-poetry-collection-003/).

Project Gutenberg is a free, on-line collection of digital texts or ebooks for numerous classic works of literature. Similar to LibriVox, the site also emphasizes the use of audio alternatives read by human volunteers and computer software (see www.gutenberg.org/browse/scores/top).

For teachers who want to create their own books, particularly at the elementary level, CAST developed Book Builder. The site allows teachers to create their own engaging digital texts for their students. Those books created on the site using the built-in digital text components can also be "published" and shared with other teachers around the world who might want to use them. The design process for building the digital books includes embedded reading strategies to support learners with diverse needs in developing the reading skills while providing accessible materials (see bookbuilder.cast.org/).

Video Clips in Various Disciplines

The Learner.org site is supported by Annenberg Media and provides educational videos in multiple academic disciplines. Teachers seeking to use a multimedia-anchored instruction approach might benefit from the freely available resource on this site, particularly when district technology administrators block more prevalent resources such as YouTube (see www.learner.org/index.html).

Resources for English Language Learners

The extremely successful web-based collaborative encyclopedia, Wikipedia, has an alternative version called Simple English Wikipedia, developed for an audience that includes children in the early stages of literacy and others who are still learning English. The site offers all the same advantages of digital text in addition to the use of embedded hyperlinks that aid in vocabulary comprehension and depth of conceptual understanding (see http://simple.wikipedia.org/wiki/Main_Page).

Digital Materials and Electronic Books

In contrast to traditional classroom materials, essentially hardcopy text, there are numerous contemporary alternatives including audio books in cassette tape, CD, or mp3 format (see audible.com, Recordings for the Blind and Dyslexic). More recently, digital texts have moved to the forefront as they allow for use of text-to-speech software. Text-to-speech involves the use of computerized voices that read aloud any sections of digital text selected by a user, thus allowing for students to learn by listening (Rose & Dalton, 2007). The "spoken" text produced by the computer can closely resemble a human voice, with some software developers in recent years creating newer and more accurate representations of the natural timbre and resonance in human voice; prosody is still somewhat lacking. Some software also allows for synchronized on-screen text highlighting parallel to the text-to-speech reader (Pisha & Coyne, 2001).

Text-to-speech is effective for students who struggle with fluency, but there are further benefits as well. Digital texts can also include hyperlinks to key terms, thereby assisting students with limited background knowledge or limited vocabulary knowledge. Hypertext glossaries allow the definition simply to "pop up" on the screen when students don't know the term. This might even include an image of the term in addition to the option to add supplemental graphic organizers or illustrative video clips, as has been included in digital materials developed by CAST (Pisha & Coyne, 2001). In the area of reading comprehension development—a difficult skill set to impact—digital materials can be designed to include embedded comprehension prompts, as seen in the use of reciprocal teaching strategies (Palincsar & Brown, 1984) in the "Thinking Reader" program (digital versions of classic works of adolescent fiction originally developed by CAST (Dalton, Pisha, Eagleton, Coyne, & Deysher, 2001). Another advantage of digital materials for students with limited vision relates to the use of visual images. Unlike static images in traditional texts, digital materials can include links to a description of the image. This description can also be read aloud to the user. Ultimately, digital materials allow for books to be customized to the user, relocating the consideration of limitations away from the student to the book itself.

Summary

Universal Design for Learning requires a paradigm shift from traditional models of both general and special education program delivery. It represents a convergence of general and special education and an instructional design response to the contemporary emphasis on diverse, inclusive classrooms. Conventional models of special education delivery have tried to force students to adapt to curriculum and instruction. Contrary to this view, one of the primary principles of UDL is that flaws or limitations within the curriculum lead to barriers in participation (versus flaws in students leading to barriers in learning). Advice for leaders is summarized in Box 10.4.

BOX 10.4

Advice for School and Special Education Leaders

- Encourage and provide avenues for the use of UDL in classrooms to enhance academic, social, and behavior outcomes for students with disabilities.
- Professional development enhances a teacher's abilities to effectively use UDL in classrooms.
- Beware of barriers to using UDL and provide solutions to promote educational opportunities for all children.
- Promote inclusive education in elementary and special education settings.

Also, UDL supports the idea that teachers should plan collaboratively for supports in the beginning of the lesson to meet needs of all students, rather than trying to make modifications to existing lessons for individual students. Finally, all students—including students with disabilities (e.g., physical, intellectual, multiple), students who are English language learners, students who have various learning preferences, as well as students who are culturally and linguistically diverse—benefit from removing barriers in the typical curriculum by enhancing multiple means of representation, expression, and engagement (Jackson & Harper, 2005; Spooner et al., 2007). Resolution to the vignette is shown in Box 10.5.

BOX 10.5

Resolution to the Vignette

Teaching in a manner consistent with Universal Design for Learning, Mrs. Jacobs recognizes that there is not such a clear line drawn between her "regular students" and her students in special education. The UDL approach creates an inclusive classroom where all students are learning and prepared with the enduring understanding of critical content by focusing on what students need and how they will best learn the content. All her students would benefit from this focus on ways to maximize learning opportunities.

Chapter Questions

1. How does UDL represent a paradigm shift in teaching diverse learners?
2. What are the principles of Universal Design for Learning?
3. How does technology support teaching in a UDL manner?

4. What are digital materials and electronic books?
5. What current teaching strategies support the UDL framework and inclusive instruction?

CHAPTER 11

Program Evaluation Methods for Educational Leaders

Richard G. Lambert

Heather Britt

INTRODUCTION

There are many programs available to school administrators and too little high-quality effectiveness evidence to guide decisions about how to invest limited resources (Gorard, 2010; Kaestle, 1993; Sroufe, 1997). When credible evidence of the effectiveness of an intervention does exist, it is often limited to specific contexts, and programs demonstrated to be effective in one context may not withstand the test of exportability to applications in new settings (Berliner, 2002; Van de Pol, Volman, & Beishuizen, 2010). Many evaluation models are available; regardless of the model, it must be understood that evaluation is an intervention in itself. In other words, evaluators can and do have an impact on the program under investigation. Program evaluations have various functions depending on the desired goals stated by those requesting the evaluation. In each case, the purpose of an evaluation is to:

- Assist in reaching the stated objectives of the program, and thereby improve the quality of its services, and not to serve as an end onto itself.
- Define the purpose of the program, identify the target audience of stakeholders for the results, and propose reasonable methods that fit the identified purpose and target audience.

This chapter will outline effective avenues for special and general educators to use in program evaluation. Read the vignette in Box 11.1 and keep the questions in mind as you go through the chapter.

Diane Rehm, as host of the show on National Public Radio that bears her name, in her typically insightful way, asked Ruth Reichl, author, former restaurant critic for both the *Los Angeles Times* and the *New York Times,* and current editor-in-chief of *Gourmet Magazine,* "Where do the

BOX 11.1

Vignette: "Finding the Optimal Classroom Concentration Levels of Children with Special Needs"

Linda Young, special education coordinator for Platte Valley School System, has started to hear anecdotal evidence from teachers and administrators that the inclusion policies in their elementary schools need to be reviewed and reformed. Specifically, some teachers are unhappy with the concentration of children with special needs in their classrooms and particularly with the unequal distribution of these children within classrooms in the same grade level. Linda decides to appoint a committee to study the issues and recommend several evaluation study options.
    As you read through the chapter, think of these questions.

1. Should inclusion policies in a school system be uniform across the district?
2. Can classroom concentration levels of children with special needs be too high for optimal development and learning?
3. How can school system administrators evaluate educational interventions and their potential applicability to the unique needs of their local school system?
4. How can school and special education leaders determine the effectiveness of local policy initiatives?
5. How can school and special education leaders determine the effectiveness of new instructional strategies in their schools?

standards that you judge a restaurant by come from? Do you decide in your own mind, or is there some set of rules somewhere?" Reichl replied, "There isn't a set of rules, but you judge a restaurant by its own pretentions. I mean, is a restaurant living up to what it wants to be? . . . You obviously can't hold a hotdog stand to the same standard as a restaurant that spends $200,000 a year on flowers. But what you can say is, What is it that they are trying to do, and are they delivering that as well as it can be delivered. And judging that way, you are able to judge a little Vietnamese noodle shop and a hotdog stand and a grand French restaurant." This brief exchange captures much of the essence of program evaluation. Educational interventions for children attempt to meet a wide range of needs, in community and school contexts that have greatly disparate resources, and are implemented with varying fidelity and effectiveness. Yet, an evaluator can still attempt to determine the merit or value of an educational intervention by gathering evidence to determine if its unique goals and objectives are being met. The challenges and issues discussed in the chapter are shown in Box 11.2.

BOX 11.2

Challenges and Issues for School and Special Education Leaders

- Assessing the resource needs of teachers.
- Determining the utility and applicability of educational interventions for use in their local school systems.
- Determining the effectiveness of local policy initiatives.
- Determining the effectiveness of new instructional strategies.

PROGRAM EVALUATION METHODS
FOR EDUCATIONAL ADMINISTRATORS

Program evaluation has become an essential part of the education profession, particularly in the age of accountability in which we currently practice our profession as educators. It is a set of methods that can be used to determine the worth or value of a program (*program,* as used here, may refer to an agency, organization, or intervention) based on specified goals and objectives that have been translated into measurable outcomes. Evaluators conduct context-specific interpretations of what is happening with a program in a real-world setting and attempt to make causal attributions about the effects of that program.

Effective interventions for children with special needs can represent substantial investments of school resources at the micro level and expensive allocations of state and or federal resources at the macro level. Rigorous evaluations of the effectiveness of educational interventions can offer program administrators and policymakers specific feedback regarding the return on their investments. Therefore, rigorous evaluations of educational programs and approaches are worthy of investment whenever such systems are implemented on a large scale in field settings.

To do so, evaluators of programs recognize the importance of setting specific, measurable objectives by which programs can be evaluated, and how specific indicators can be tied to each objective. School and special education leaders obtaining external evaluation can help in these ways:

- Outline realistic indicators that are closely tied to the actual program or intervention, rather than target overly lofty or unrealistic expectations of broad program impact.
- Understand how to fully specify the desired outcomes of programs in terms of how the outcomes can be measured.
- Determine if program administrators are measuring intended program outcomes in a meaningful and useful way.

Evaluators can bring measurement expertise to a program and provide a review of the reliability, validity, and cultural sensitivity of existing outcome measures in the context of the specific target population served. For example, it may not be reasonable to assume that commonly used outcome measures provide information that is equally reliable and valid in a particular context as it is with a broadly based national norm sample. In so doing, evaluators help those involved to understand the importance of multiple data sources and indicators, ideally more than just state test scores. For example, portfolio assessments, work samples, locally developed scoring rubrics, surveys, focus groups, and classroom observational measures can help supplement and compliment the information provided by test scores.

Program evaluation can assist special and school leaders by:

- Documenting the amount of services delivered to the target population, as well as the implementation fidelity to a specific model or approach with which those services are delivered
- Helping program administrators recognize the usefulness of evaluation as a source of feedback and guidance for program improvement and development purposes, including making program implementers aware of national quality standards
- Providing an external and objective voice to help identify the stage of development of a program, its organizational maturity, and the overall effectiveness of its management

---

BOX 11.3

Advice for School and Special Education Leaders

- Translate your school system's mission into practical and achievable goals for instructional improvement.
- Define the outcomes that can help you determine if you are achieving your goals.
- Think beyond the test scores alone to include the intermediate outcomes that will lead to increases in test scores.
- Translate your goals into measurable objectives.
- Develop strategies for measuring the accomplishment of objectives that yield reliable, valid, culturally sensitive, and useful information.
- Nurture a culture of data-driven decision making in your school system.

- Helping to implement appropriate use of experimental and comparative strategies such as random assignment, multiple measures over time, and control or comparison conditions with administrators who may not have considered such rigorous methods or considered them unworkable
- Guiding administrators through the evaluation process to ensure that the role of evaluation in measuring program effects, documenting successes, and selling program impact

Other advice is listed in Box 11.3.

Overview of a Model to Guide Program Evaluation

Throughout this chapter, we will examine one particular model of evaluation. The CIPPI model, an extension of the CIPP model (Stufflebeam & Shinkfield, 2007; Stufflebeam, Madaus, & Kellaghan, 2000), includes the following stages of inquiry: Context, Input, Process, Product, and Impact. Although this model is far from the only model of evaluation available, it has particular advantages as an illustration and teaching tool because it outlines the goals, tasks, and activities that match what evaluators actually do in the field and therefore is well suited to an overview chapter such as this one. The CIPPI model has several advantages as an evaluation approach as well. Such an approach lends itself to program improvement, which is an overall benefit to stakeholders. Using the model also helps build alliances with program management. The CIPPI model is a comprehensive tool adaptable to all types of evaluations. It is also a template onto which other models and activities can be imposed.

Here is an example to illustrate the basic model. Imagine an evaluation of home-cooked meals. The meals would be the *Program*. What factors would be considered when evaluating the *Program*? Let's begin with Context. *Context is the setting or situation in which the Program is delivered.* Considerations would be family traditions, routines and schedules, family composition, family income, any special dietary considerations, cultural factors, and practical considerations such as available sources of food. The next step is to explore Input. *Input is the Program's service delivery plan, from the origins of the interventions to the plans for implementation.* Consider the following: how the meals are planned, the sources of the recipes, how the meals are scheduled, how the shopping is done, by whom and when, and the quality of ingredients. Next, the model looks at Process. *Process is how the Program is implemented or put into action.* Considerations might be who prepares the meals, when they are prepared and how, the cooking process, the kitchen set up and equipment, and how many meals are actually served and how fully they are actually eaten. Next in the evaluation would be the Product. *Product is the Program's achievements or accomplishments. In this phase, informed judgments about the Program's merit or value are made.* Consider the following: the finished product (the meal), the meals as they are served, as well as quality, taste, nutrition, presentation, and satisfaction. The last step in this model is Impact. *Impact moves beyond accomplishment of specific goals (Product) and focuses on the long-term impact of the Program.* Considerations include the following questions: How does eating together impact the family in the long run? What are the long-term health consequences of the meals? How responsive are family eating habits to changes in family dynamics, needs, and composition?

The model therefore facilitates summary judgments about the entire process of planning, preparing, and eating the meals, as well as the long-term consequences of sustaining a diet consisting of these meals. These judgments are based in a comprehensive understanding of family context, culture, and resources. Ongoing close contact with the family is required to collect, analyze, and synthesize all the evidence to arrive at credible and useful judgments, and will result in direct benefits to the family at each stage. Naturally, this process would be expensive, time consuming, and longitudinal in nature if carried to completion. If we think about the meals as analogous to the services delivered by a particular program, this simple example illustrates the flexibility and breadth of the model, how the evidences gathered at each stage facilitate valid interpretations for the subsequent stages, and how each stage could be conducted on its own if specific rather than comprehensive evaluation questions were proposed.

We intentionally did not begin this example with evaluation goals or questions, as would have been appropriate, to illustrate the flexibility of the model. We could use the model to answer the global question: What is the long-term impact of the meals on the health of this family? We could also have answered narrower, more stage-specific questions focused on the adequacy of the cooking facilities and equipment, nutrition, cost-effectiveness, taste, fidelity to cultural traditions, or the impact of the meals on family cohesion. Later in the chapter, each section of the model will be discussed in detail with a set of guiding questions provided. Before we do so, take some time to think through how each of these potential evaluation topics could be analogous to evaluation goals about a special education program in your district.

Step 1: Context Evaluation

To review, the goal of program evaluation is to make judgments about program merit or value. Since making judgments requires good interpretation skills, context is essential. Consider, for example, how different one school can be from another. Everything from the administration, to the community context, to the families and children served, to the experience and education levels of the teaching staff, and to the resources available can combine to make each school context unique. In evaluating a particular program within a school, many factors may become important to understand in order to make the most valid and informed judgments about the extent to which a program's goals are being met: student/family population, linguistics/cultural diversity, the type and concentration of children with special needs, socioeconomic status and poverty levels, parental and community support, funding/resources/facilities, management/climate/support and the nature and quality of the teaching staff.

The central task in a Context evaluation is the development of a thorough understanding of the setting within which the program operates and the conditions under which the treatment or services are delivered. Therefore, effective evaluations take into consideration all aspects of the program beginning with the context. The methods used for educational evaluation of program context can differ depending on the mission of the program, the stakeholders, the money available to perform the evaluation, the purpose of the evaluation, and the target audience for the report.

CONTEXT EVALUATION METHODS AND SUMMARY TASK   Context evaluations focus on the setting for the program, the needs of the program, and the audience for and consequences for the evaluation. This information is usually obtained through the following evaluation strategies: key informant interviews, site visits, and records review. Once an assessment of the context is complete, the summary task is to answer the following question: Based on the initial findings, does the program have a reasonable chance to succeed in this particular context?

SAMPLE CONTEXT EVALUATION QUESTIONS   See Figure 11.1 for questions that will be helpful to general and special education leaders in gathering information during key informant interviews, site visits, and records reviews about the Context of the program.

FIGURE 11.1   Sample Context Evaluation Questions

Population Served

Who are the intended beneficiaries, or target population, of the program?	What are their needs?

The Program

What is the history of the program? What ambient conditions have influenced the program in the past?	What are the attitudes and expectations of stakeholders toward both the program and the evaluation of it?
Describe the funding, governance, and management structure of the program.	Describe the context within which the program operates. Specifically, what are the current ambient social, political, and economic conditions and circumstances that influence the program?
What needs does the program have?	Are there policies within which the program must operate that impact the success of the program?
What barriers does the program face in attempting to meet (1) its objectives and (2) the needs of the target population?	Describe the relationship between the program and the stakeholders. Describe any other relevant facets of the program's external relations and reputation in the community.

Stakeholders

Who has an interest in the success of the program?	What decisions will be based on the results of the evaluation?

The Evaluation Process

What are the attitudes and expectations of the stakeholders toward both the program and the evaluation of it?	Who has an interest in the evaluation? What is the purpose of the evaluation?
What form will the Final Report take? Who will review it? What decisions will be made based on the report, and by whom?	Evaluate the cooperation of the program participants throughout the evaluation process (i.e., access to documents, stakeholders, data sources, etc.).

Step 2: Input Evaluation

Schools and educators are often inundated with marketing for *"magic bullet"* programs that promise to address pertinent issues, and often in record time. Where do these magic bullets originate, and even if they are research-based, are they appropriate for the context of a particular school environment? In other words, what factors do you consider when judging new educational programs and their potential fit for your school? After a solid understanding of school *Context*, evaluators can help administrators consider the research/theoretical base of the program, the credibility of the developers, the past experiences that similar schools had with the program, and the program's cultural sensitivity/match to school and community needs, all in the course of determining whether the program has the potential to meet the needs of the school.

Again, the goal of program evaluation is to make informed judgments about program merit or value. Making informed judgments requires a thorough understanding of the context in which the program will be implemented, and an understanding of the program or treatment itself, including its origins, assumptions, the claims of its developers, and the optimal conditions for implementation and delivery of services. In this step, the evaluator starts with the origins and main features of the intervention, and moves to the site-specific plans for implementation. The evaluator is tasked with investigating why the program administration believes that its particular intervention approach will meet the needs of the target population. In so doing, the evaluator may find that the current program administration does not know the entire history of the choices made regarding the particular local approach to intervention, and may never have considered alternative models for delivering the services it provides.

Many social programs, particularly those based in schools or small nonprofit organizations, have strong cultural traditions that include a generally accepted understanding of their overall purposes and approach. However, organizational cultural norms, even when they are successfully transmitted to new staff within an organization, may not be codified or specified in enough detail to facilitate useful interactions with evaluators or the most helpful evaluation results. Often, the most helpful intervention an evaluator can make when working with a program is to help those involved outline their mission statement, set goals, and translate those goals into specific measureable objectives. To do so, program educators need to understand the fundamental components of what is sometimes called a *logic model* or *theory of change*. There are many resources available to facilitate this discussion (Bagley, 2010; W. K. Kellogg Foundation, 2004) including a variety of forms and templates. These forms can help make unfamiliar and intimidating territory more accessible and friendly for program administrators, as can examples from similar organizations.

The process of creating a mission statement, and the goals and objectives that stem from it, helps those who implement the program work through what they are trying to accomplish. The specification of a logic model can help an organization outline the processes that define the unique way the organization delivers services. The logic model requires one to think about their assumptions; the processes they believe are required to impact the target population, and the unique way they hope to put their organizational fingerprints on the targeted effects. The model includes all the links in the causal chain from the basic program inputs and needs of the population, to intermediate outcomes necessary for the services to reach those in need, to the ultimate desired outcomes.

After the evaluator has outlined the mission statement and logic model process, and program staff has completed the hard work of specifying their key goals and the processes to reach them, then the evaluator can turn the discussion to measurable objectives. In order to facilitate the most meaningful evaluation results, the program participants need to determine objectives that are detailed-specific and measurable. Evaluators can be very helpful at this stage by working with program staff to complete Measurable Objectives Worksheets. The particular example in Figure 11.1 is only one style for documenting objectives. There are many resources available for this process (see United Way of America, 1996). The worksheet is designed to facilitate a rich discussion with program staff about how to operationally define each program outcome in the context of specific program objectives. For each goal the program has set, evaluators and program staff can discuss whether the goal truly matches the organizational mission and is realistic, given resource constraints and the needs of the target population. Then attention can turn to identifying specific objectives and their corresponding indicators and measurement methods. An indicator in this context is a tangible piece of evidence (behavior, knowledge, product, or any other artifact) that can be used to demonstrate that the objective has been met. A measurement method is the way the indicator is collected and can be a survey, test, observational protocol, or even a scoring rubric that is used to judge performance or products.

This particular version of the form also requires the program to set target results for each measurable objective. A program could specify, for example, that students would make 20 percent gain on some particular test, presumably as a result of the intervention that is being evaluated. This whole process can be very cumbersome and daunting for program administrators unaccustomed to evaluation. However, in the current policy climate of accountability, it is very likely that if a program plans to seek additional sources of funding in the future, administrators will encounter demands for evaluation and may even be required to include some evidence of program effectiveness in the application process. Therefore, evaluators can help school and special education leaders become more motivated to participate in this process by facilitating an investigation of the kinds of evaluation and effectiveness evidence that funding agencies in their particular field tend to require and value. Developing a culture of ongoing evidence gathering can fit right into a program's plans for quality improvement, particularly as leaders plan for expansion and the fund raising that may be needed.

INPUT EVALUATION METHODS AND SUMMARY TASK   Key evaluation strategies for Input evaluation are key informant interviews, background research on the origins of the program and its treatment approach, and records review. In addition, the evaluator interacts with and supports program staff at this stage as much as is needed as they formulate their objectives. Specifically, the evaluator reviews any documentation of the program that can be provided, or that has been created during the evaluation, regarding measurable objectives, program logic model or theory of change, and the service delivery plan. The focus is on a comprehensive evaluation of the entire service delivery plan for the program. Building on the summary conclusions from the Context Evaluation phase, and based on all the information gathered from the Input Evaluation phase, does the program have a reasonable chance to deliver the proposed services to the target population? (See Figure 11.2.)

Step 3: Process Evaluation

Let's assume the so-called *magic bullet* has been introduced in your school. What next? If it is an educational intervention, how do you know when teachers have implemented the program? How do you know if the intended services reached those in need? Is it advisable to implement the new program in phases, learning from a pilot phase to facilitate local adaptations? The goal of Process Evaluation is to document and understand the amount of exposure to the intervention that the target population actually received. Before making summary judgments about the impact of a

FIGURE 11.2   Sample Input Evaluation Questions

Mission

What is the mission of the program? What are the goals, midterm and long-term, set by the program?	What specific objectives is the program trying to meet?
Has the program translated its mission and goals and objectives into specific, well-defined measurable objectives?	Does the program have a logic model/theory of change?

Origins of the Treatment or Intervention Approach

Where did the treatment come from, and who developed the treatment?	What is the existing evidence to support the effectiveness of the program?
What evidence exists that indicates that the treatment is appropriate for the population served?	How was the decision made to implement the particular intervention approach?

Service Delivery

How are services typically delivered? What is a typical service delivery cycle?	Does the program have a plan for implementation of the services the program will be providing?
Does the plan contain phases of implementation?	Are there specific checkpoints, milestones, benchmarks, or indicators that signify the end of one phase and the beginning of another?

Plans for Quality Improvement

Does the program engage in any existing and ongoing evaluation of the quality of service delivery?	What program quality standards, specific to the field in which the program operates, are available to the program?
Which programs would be considered the model programs in the field?	Have the personnel of the program visited or consulted with these model programs?
Does the program have an Advisory Board, or other source of ongoing external input from stakeholders?	Does the program have a plan for quality improvement?

program, it is important to first address the more fundamental questions regarding the delivery of services. We are interested in knowing if the program was actually implemented, were services delivered, and did the target audience receive the services that the program is designed to deliver.

In this step, evaluators examine the fidelity with which the program has been implemented by gathering evidence to address these basic questions: (2) Has the target population been served? (2) Were the treatment or intervention services delivered? and (3) At what dosage levels? The essential concern is whether the most basic expectations of the stakeholders have been met. The specific strategies for evaluation in this phase are directly tied to the Service Delivery plan that was acquired during the Input phase. The evaluator's central responsibility is to design a data collection strategy that will document whether the plan was put into action as reported in the Input evaluation. In terms of stakeholder expectations:

- What do the stakeholders (especially funding agencies) expect to happen?
- What level of accountability for program implementation do they expect?

- Look at Standards: Do program implementation standards exist?
- Is there an Implementation Fidelity Checklist available? If not, one may need to be developed with the input of stakeholders, the developers or publishers of the intervention, and program personnel.

Evaluators must create a plan for documenting the implementation of the program. Use attendance data, activity logs, contacts records, descriptions of the activities or interactions, descriptions of the content of the services delivered, and materials disseminated. Make a timeline for data collection and responsibilities. In order to examine a "Dose-Response" relationship, it may be helpful to develop an Intensity of Intervention Scale, and assist the program participants in developing an evaluation information system that will support the steps outlined in the plan. It can often be extremely helpful to intentionally plan a limited initial phase to implementation so that these evaluation methods can be applied to both a pilot phase and a full-scale implementation phase. A preliminary report can be useful at the end of the pilot phase to offer recommendations for context-specific adaptations to the program.

When it comes to direct observation of program implementation, there is no substitute for site visits with a structured agenda, including observations of specific program activities and facilities, and requests for data. It is important that each observer is provided with a detailed site visit protocol, including observational checklists, interview instructions, and daily schedules. It can be very helpful to conduct training exercises and pilot visits prior to sending the observers to the field. If control or comparison conditions are used, it is important to keep the observers blinded, to the extent it is possible, as to whether they are observing treatment or control conditions.

PROCESS EVALUATION SUMMARY TASKS AND METHODS   The goal is to make informed judgments about program merit or value, and making such judgments requires a thorough understanding of the implementation of the treatment. The main function of a process evaluation, or the process evaluation phase of a comprehensive evaluation, is to monitor the implementation of the program. The final evaluation report should contain a detailed description of the services delivered to the target audience, ideally including measures of both quantity and quality. How much service was actually delivered, to whom, and with what quality? An evaluation cannot provide valid judgments of program merit before it includes a detailed explanation of whether the program reached the target audience. The final conclusions from this phase can be both formative and summative. The overall summary judgment involves summarizing conclusions about the implementation of the program. The formative conclusion answers the following question: Based on all the information gathered, can improvements be made to the service delivery system while the program is operating? The summative conclusion answers this question: Based on all of the information gained from the Process Evaluation Phase, was the treatment delivered as intended?

Key evaluation strategies for Process evaluation are observations, interviews, implementation fidelity checklists, contact/activity logs, and records review. Evaluators use attendance data, documentation about contacts between service providers and the target population, descriptions of the program activities, and descriptions of the content of the services delivered and the materials disseminated. When programs do not have existing systems to document this type of information, evaluators can help create them.

When an educational intervention is successfully implemented, it is most often the result of teachers putting into practice a set of new methods in their classrooms. The process by which teachers change their usual practice and adopt new methods can be a very challenging one for them and for those who are attempting to train them in the proper use of new pedagogical techniques. Therefore, the effectiveness of teacher training is often one of the most important elements of an educational program, and evaluators need to examine in detail the teacher professional development strategies that support the implementation of the intervention.

Kirkpatrick's (1998) model for evaluating training programs focuses on systemic change and contains the following stages: (1) Reaction, (2) Learning, (3) Behavior, and (4) Results. This model is based on a theory of practitioner growth that culminates in organizational change. As the cumulative effect of individual teacher growth and development impacts the culture of the organization, its willingness to incorporate, embrace, and sustain systems of teacher support can be impacted (Praslova, 2010). The theory suggests that teachers must first react positively to the system of support in order to engage fully with its services. It is assumed that if teachers do not like and give credibility to the system of support, they will not benefit from it. Next, teachers need to gain knowledge or learn content as a result of participation in the system of support. These two stages are considered necessary but not sufficient indicators of the success of a system of support and function as precursors to application and change of practice in the classroom. Behavior change comes as teachers apply what they have allowed themselves to receive and have learned. Results in this model encompass both ultimate end-points, such as child outcomes, and organizational change that supports the sustainability of the changes made by teachers.

Once evaluators have understood *where* training is taking place (Context), *what* is intended to be delivered to teachers (Input), and *how* the new teaching methods are intended to be actually put into practice in classrooms, the focus can turn to the reactions of the teachers to the training. This is accomplished by using questionnaires, interviewing teachers, conducting focus groups, and reviewing professional development logs. The basic evaluation questions are: How well did the teachers like the training? and Did they fully engage in the process?

Since the main evaluation strategy here is the posttest questionnaire, evaluators need to apply the same general principles of survey research that would apply in any study: (1) maintain the anonymity and confidentiality of the teachers; (2) use qualitative methods to support the item development process to gain an understanding of the language that the teachers use to describe the issues addressed by the survey; (3) pilot-test the survey with teachers, including the use of cognitive interviewing strategies; (4) structure the survey form so it is easy to complete; and (5) include open-ended questions and an appeal for other comments so that teachers can give a complete picture of their experience with the system of support. It can also be helpful to determine the survey content based on the needs of multiple stakeholders, not just the teachers. For example, policymakers and administrators may be interested in specific reactions and opinions from the teachers. The following is a list of standard item types that can serve as a general guideline for discussing with stakeholders the kind of feedback they desire and a starting point for constructing a survey.

- Did the training meet your needs/expectations?
- Did the content of the training apply to your classroom setting?
- Rate the mix of delivery strategies and activities used by the trainer.
- How well did the trainer make you aware of specific objectives for your interactions?
- Were your interactions with the trainer and the other participants interesting and stimulating?
- Did the trainer make effective use of alternative delivery methods (phone, web, video, etc.)?
- Did the trainer provide effective illustrations/practical examples?
- Did the trainer interact with you in a friendly and helpful manner?

- Did the trainer summarize for you key points effectively?
- What specific benefits did you receive from the training?
- Provide an overall rating of the training, including areas for improvement.

A favorable reaction to training on the part of teachers can be one of the preconditions for changes in practice in the classroom, and can certainly help facilitate openness to change. The focus of the evaluation next turns to learning. The following steps can help school and special education leaders/evaluators determine what the teachers have learned through training.

- Initially, the instructional objectives of the system of support have to be determined. This can include both overall instructional objectives for training and specific objectives associated with individual training events.
- It is helpful to identify the primary focus of training activities (acquisition of knowledge, skill development, attitude or beliefs, etc.).
- Skill development can be assessed in the classroom by observation and can be addressed by measures of teacher practice that will be used as part of the summative evaluation strategies.
- Performance assessment can even be built into ongoing mentoring or teacher support activities.
- Attitudes and beliefs that can be addressed through the use of surveys and questions can be added to reaction surveys if needed.
- If the focus is on knowledge acquisition, pretests and posttests may be necessary to measure gains in the knowledge areas involved. If so, do measures of knowledge already exist for the given content area? And how closely are they tied to the specific instructional objectives of the training? Is quite likely that such measures will have to be developed or substantially modified (see Figure 11.3).

FIGURE 11.3 Sample Process Evaluation Questions

Training and Communication

Were frontline service delivery staff trained in a thorough enough manner to lead to complete implementation?	What kind of follow-up mentoring was provided to monitor and support service delivery after training?
Were staff able to visit model demonstration sites prior to implementation? Has the implementation plan been successfully communicated to the frontline service delivery staff in a thorough manner?	Were any changes made to the service delivery plan during implementation, and were those changes communicated to staff?

Implementation

To what extent did the activities of the service delivery staff match the service delivery plan? Were there any problems with frontline staff compliance with the implementation plan?	Were members of the target population cooperating with the implementation of the program?
Does the Implementation Fidelity Checklist data demonstrate any problems with poor execution of the service delivery plan, and is implementation on schedule?	Has program implementation of the program been incorporated into administrative expectations and performance evaluations of staff?
What dosage level (amount of the treatment or program) was actually received by the participants?	Are there any subgroup differences in dosage level?

Step 4: Product Evaluation

Once questions about context, service delivery planning, and implementation have been addressed, it is time to decide whether or not the program has met its objectives and produced the intended effects.

- How do you know when an educational program "works"? What do you look at?
- What kinds of evidence are needed to judge that something "worked" in education?
- Were the immediate and long-term needs of the target audience met?

Evaluators begin to answer these questions by examining the accomplishment of measureable objectives.

The Product Evaluation phase requires the evaluator to develop and implement a plan to collect the outcome information called for on the Measurable Objectives Worksheets. The first task in this process is defining a typical service delivery cycle. In education, this is usually an academic year. Next, the evaluator decides when the first "fair test" service delivery cycle will take place and when pilot testing of processes and procedures has ended. The product evaluation plan should include multiple measures of success collected at multiple points in time using multiple methods of data collection. It is useful to include both quantitative and qualitative outcome measures in this phase. *Quantitative methods* are well suited to gauge the overall or average effect across the target population as a whole and necessary for outcomes that can be easily counted. *Qualitative methods* can be very useful for taking a more in-depth look at the subjective experience of selected program participants.

The role of the evaluator in the Product Evaluation phase is to demonstrate, with the most statistically valid evidence, that program implementation is both associated with specific outcomes and, to the extent possible, causally linked with those same outcomes. In educational evaluation projects, the most common method is the analysis of gain scores based on pre- and postmeasures. Quantitative indicators of student achievement through the use of educational or psychological tests are analyzed and groups that have been randomly assigned to different treatment conditions are compared. It is important to note that if causal inferences are required by stakeholders, experimental methods must be employed.

Research design considerations determine whether causal inferences can be made about the effects of the program from the Product Evaluation evidence. Can the results of the Product Evaluation be attributed to the program and only the program? Have the results been replicated across service delivery cycles? A controlled, experimental, comparative study is necessary if the stakeholders are interested in causality and the answers to these questions. Cost quickly becomes a consideration. Such studies, although necessary if difficult conclusions about cause and effect are to be made, are expensive and require the use of control groups and random assignment.

A complete treatment of experimental methods as applied in field settings is beyond the scope of this chapter. The reader is referred to several specialized sources for a more complete treatment of this topic (Isomursu, Tähti, Väinämö, & Kuutti, 2007; Schneider, Carnoy, Kilpatrick, Schmidt, & Shavelson, 2007). Well-designed field experiments can break down due to factors outside the control of the evaluators. In some situations, random assignment is not possible, although evaluators still want to make use of comparison conditions that do not receive the treatment. These designs are referred to as *quasi-experiments* and the reader is referred to the following sources for a complete treatment of field evaluation strategies under quasi-experimental conditions (Gall & Borg, 2010; McMillan & Wergin, 2010; Shadish, Cook, & Campbell, 2002; Shadish, Cook, & Leviton, 1991).

When the focus is on continuous improvement or patterns of growth, rather than simple gains over the academic year, then three or more measurements are built into the design. This facilitates an examination of trends in improvement and allows for a closer look at periods of time when the program may have worked better than others. It is important for evaluators to note any unintended side effects and to document both the positive and negative outcomes of participation in the program. If sample size permits, it can be useful to examine both the intended and unintended consequences of program participation subgroups of participants. If the program works better for some subgroups in the target population, modifications or adaptations for those in the groups for whom the program was less successful may be suggested.

As part of the Measurable Objectives Worksheets, the program may have set target results. The evaluator needs to interpret the evidence not only in terms of statistical significance testing but also against these targeted goals. In addition, the results can be interpreted relative to any existing standards of growth and improvement, either from previous evaluation studies or generated by the program and its stakeholders. This can be particularly relevant if there are existing studies that previously demonstrated positive effects of program participation in different contexts. Some funding agencies may be interested in determining whether the gains made by program participants were large enough to justify continuing the program. A formal cost-benefit or cost-effectiveness analysis may be a useful part of a product evaluation if needed by the stakeholders and may require consultation with financial professionals.

PRODUCT EVALUATION METHODS AND SUMMARY TASK The central focus of a Product Evaluation is the documentation of program achievements or accomplishments. The evaluator needs to make a summary judgment about whether the program is worth repeating for another service delivery cycle and what outcomes can be attributed to the program. Attributions of cause and effect need to be made with the proper qualifications, as the establishment of cause-and-effect relationships is very difficult in field research and evaluation studies. Furthermore, any interpretations made as a result of the product evaluation should be grounded in the results of the Context, Input, and Process phases of the evaluation. The most valid conclusions can also be the most nuanced, and an objective and external recounting of the practical realities, challenges, and barriers to complete implementation that were faced by the program staff can be the most valuable results of a program evaluation. If appropriate, the evaluator can include recommendations about program modification and extension, or export to other settings. Key evaluation strategies for this Product Evaluation include standardized tests and objective measurements; measures designed to assess knowledge gains, attitude changes, or behavior changes; performance assessment data; observations, collections of program products and other artifacts of the program; and case studies of individual program participants or subgroups.

Sample Product Evaluation Questions for School and Special Education

Program Outcomes:
- Overall, has the product produced the results that were intended?
- Did the test scores improve, and can any observed changes in test scores be connected to program participation?
- Did the program meet all its target results as indicated by the Measurable Objective Worksheets?
- Have other indirect measures of program impact indicated a positive outcome? For example, has teacher morale improved during program implementation?

Cost Considerations:
- Was all the funding spent properly in accordance with the objectives?
- Did the program follow all the financial guidelines from the funding agency?
- Could the same benefits be achieved for less expense?

Step 5: Impact Evaluation

The purpose of Impact Evaluation is to extend beyond product evaluation and its emphasis on the accomplishment of specific, short-term objectives, to a focus on the long-term impact of the program. If the Product Evaluation demonstrated that the program is meeting its objectives, then the Impact Evaluation may focus on higher-order questions such as changes that have taken place that can be attributed to specific aspects of the program. Remember, the goal of Program Evaluation is to make informed judgments about program merit or value. Making judgments requires a thorough understanding of how long the effects last, what caused the effects in the first place, and how long can the program continue.

Lasting impact addresses whether it's reasonable that the program effects will persist beyond participation. Impact can also imply the depth and breadth of the program results. Evaluation can be used to examine whether participants are able to show the benefits of participation in multiple settings, or across various aspects of their lives. For example, if children who have participated in the program exhibit more positive social behaviors at school, do they do so at home as well? Even if an innovative educational program—that *magic bullet*—has "worked," there is no guarantee it will continue to "work," or remain as effective with new groups of participants, or produce similar results in other settings, or even be used in the future at all. So what kinds of evidence are needed to know that a program makes a long-term impact? To establish impact, evaluators need to consider long-term follow-up with the participants—a process that can be very expensive. Simply locating and assessing program participants years after their contact with the program has ended can be extremely difficult. In addition, making valid causal attributions back to program participation, given that other experiences and influences have intervened in the interim, can be quite complex.

Impact Evaluation can also focus on the long-term impact of a program on its community. For example, evaluators can examine whether or not the program has been effective in communicating with the targeted population about the program successes and effects as well as the opportunities to participate. Successful programs make extensive connections with related community agencies and with community organizations that represent stakeholder groups, and have a systematic strategy for recruiting new participants.

IMPACT EVALUATION SUMMARY TASKS AND METHODS The central task in an Impact Evaluation is making an informed summary judgment about the program outcomes that can be expected to last beyond participation and for how long. This process can help a program revisit its core mission, goals, and objectives. At this stage, the evaluator examines the long-range goals of the program in light of the cumulative weight of the evaluation evidence gathered across all stages of the evaluation. The final report can then include suggestions to program administrators regarding revisions that will increase the likelihood of long-term impact. Evaluation strategies can also involve longitudinal follow-up assessment of participants and control group members, community impact surveys, and interviews and focus groups with former participants.

Sample Impact Evaluation Questions

Sustainability:
- Are there resources available to include follow-up in the evaluation plan?
- Has enough evidence of short-term impact accumulated to justify the investment of resources needed to conduct long-term follow-up?
- Has the administration remained stable, and if not, has turnover changed administrative support for the program?
- What resources will be needed to continue, expand, and strengthen the program?
- Can the program be replicated in another service delivery cycle?
- Can the program be transported to other settings?

Longitudinal Follow-Up:
- Does the program have a system for tracking or locating former participants?
- Have the participants ever been followed after completion of the program?
- How long do the effects of the program last?
- What does the program expect/believe/claim will happen to participants in the long run?

Community Impact:
- How effective are the recruitment strategies of the program in reaching all the members of the target population that could benefit from the program?
- Does the program collaborate with community agencies that can help make referrals to and sustain the program?
- What marketing and external communication strategies does the program use and how widely to they reach into the community?

INVESTIGATION AND RESEARCH ISSUES IN PROGRAM EVALUATION   Most educational evaluation situations involve research with human participants. Some contact with human subjects through surveys, interviews, observations, and analysis of test scores is central to the data collection process for almost all educational evaluation projects. Therefore, both evaluators and the educational administrators who collaborate with them need to be aware of and adhere to all applicable ethical principles for research with human participants. Several major professional organizations have set the standard for acceptable professional conduct in an educational evaluation study. The American Psychological Association (Sales & Folkman, 2000), the American Educational Research Association (2009), and the American Evaluation Association (2009) each include in their guiding ethical principles standards specific to the conduct of research with human participants. In addition, the Program Evaluation Standards (Sanders, 1994) includes guidelines regarding the rights of human subjects in an educational evaluation study (see Standard P3).

The basic principles of research with human participants can be summarized as follows: (1) Do no harm, (2) Obtain informed consent, and (3) Guard participant anonymity and confidentiality. Therefore the evaluator must ensure that all reasonable steps are taken to avoid unnecessary risk or hardship for participants. The evaluator must also take steps to inform all participants, or their legal guardians if they are minors, of all they will experience during the study. In addition, the evaluator must store all information and evidences in such a manner that the identity of all participants is protected at all times. No personal or sensitive information about any participant can be disclosed or reported in any way that would facilitate the identification of

---

BOX 11.4

Legal Issues

Thurston (1984) has outlined four areas of legal concern for evaluators: (1) defamation, (2) contracts, (3) evaluation malpractice, and (4) confidentiality. Defamation can become an important issue if negative evaluation results need to be reported. Although simply presenting the truth in an objective and professional manner is the best defense against claims of defamation, evaluators and educational administrators are encouraged to become aware of the legal issues involved with defamation (Fitzpatrick, Sanders, & Worthen, 2010). The Program Evaluation Standards (Fitzpatrick et al., 2010; Sanders, 1994) include guidelines regarding formal agreements between evaluators and educational agencies (see Standard P2). Evaluators are encouraged to establish formal agreements that outline the roles and responsibilities of each party.

  The externality and objectivity of the evaluator, and the validity of the information gathered, are both considered crucial to the usefulness of an evaluation study. Therefore, the evaluator should disclose any potential conflicts of interest as well as any relationships that might compromise the credibility of the evaluation. The Program Evaluation Standards (Fitzpatrick et al.; Sanders, 1994) include guidelines regarding complete and fair assessments and the need for reliable and valid information (see Standards P5, A5, and A6). Evaluators are responsible for ensuring that all their data sources are not just reliable and valid but also culturally sensitive and appropriate for all subgroups in the study.

---

any individual. Only group summaries are to be provided to stakeholders. In advanced evaluation designs, where random assignment to treatment conditions is used to facilitate causal inferences, participants must be informed about the assignment process. They must be aware of the possibility of assignment to treatment conditions along with information about what to expect if they are assigned to any of the groups.

  Since the passage of the Family Educational Rights and Privacy Act (U.S. Department of Education, 2009) and all of the subsequent legislation regarding the rights and protections for research participants, federal law has governed the conduct of researchers and evaluators. Every research or evaluation plan must be approved by a local institutional review board (IRB). The IRB is charged with protecting the rights of human participants and ensuring adherence with all applicable legal and ethical standards. Large school systems often have their own IRB. The IRB for the home institution for the evaluator, often a university, can also be consulted if needed.

  Freedom of information is an essential element of our democratic society. Evaluators need to honor any reasonable requests for information from stakeholders throughout the evaluation process. However, disclosure of information should remain with legal limits. For example, what is reported and at what level of granularity is still subject to the principles of confidentiality and anonymity, and informed consent. Furthermore, there may be specific legal constraints in place prior to and independent of the evaluation regarding the release of school records about families, children, and school system employees. In addition, the use of information obtained from the evaluation of teacher performance falls into a special category. Teacher performance appraisal should be standards based, be obtained from reliable observers, relate to measures of student achievement, be based on multiple indicators, and conform to the existing procedures for performance evaluation already in place in the local school system (Kimball & Milanowski, 2009). Legal issues involved with program evaluation are shown in Box 11.4.

Summary

The earlier vignette from Platte Valley School System only begins to illustrate the range of evaluation questions, goals, and methods that can be applied to educational programs. Given the emphasis on assessing and increasing student achievement for all subgroups of children, and the competing demands for limited resources that are unavoidable components of the work of educational administrators in today's accountability-focused policy climate, educational evaluation methods can facilitate and enhance informed and data-driven decision making.

If school and special education leaders are going to make the most informed policy decisions, they need locally contextualized and up-to-date results from educational evaluation studies.

Educational interventions that promise improvements in test scores rarely deliver on those promises immediately. The real-world challenges of selecting an appropriate program for your local school system, fighting through the struggles of piloting and implementation, making local adaptations in response to the pilot results, and taking the new instructional strategy to scale throughout the school system, can all be enhanced by the methods discussed in this chapter. Furthermore, developing a standardized evaluation protocol that fits your school system will greatly enhance administrative decision making and facilitate the comparison of evaluation results across studies and interventions. The resolution of the vignette is shown in Box 11.5.

BOX 11.5

Resolution of the Vignette

The committee appointed by Linda Young to study the inclusion policies and practices for Platte Valley School System elementary schools developed a set of three proposed studies. The committee recommended that the three proposed studies be implemented in a sequence with sufficient time between each study to consider all the findings of each stage and their implications for school system policy.

Study #1
Context Evaluation Questions:
- How variable are the classroom concentration levels of children in special needs across the system?
- Do concentration levels vary by school, grade level, or type of special need?
- What procedures do elementary principals in the district use to assign children to classrooms?

Context Evaluation Methods:
The committee recommends that a thorough review of school system records be conducted in order to create a database of the classroom concentration levels, and proposes that these data be analyzed for between-school differences. The data are to be further tabulated by grade level and type of special need. A survey of principals is proposed to gather data about classroom assignment methods. The committee also recommends follow-up interviews with principals from school with different concentration levels.

Study # 2
Input Evaluation Questions:
- What is this system's history of classroom assignment policies for elementary schools?
- Have principals ever received training in recommended strategies for creating the optimal classroom concentration levels of children with special needs?

- Have general education teachers in the system received training on how to create the optimal inclusive classroom?

Input Evaluation Methods:

The committee recommends a set of key informant interviews with system administrators who have worked in the school systems for a long period of time. The committee also recommends a thorough review of the research literature on inclusive practices and a phone survey of special education coordinators in neighboring school systems to discuss their inclusion and classroom assignment methods. Site visits to neighboring school systems are also suggested if the survey information identifies particular sites that have unique and innovative approaches to inclusion services.

Study # 3

Process, Product, and Impact Evaluation Questions:

- Will elementary school classroom concentrations of children with special needs become less variable following training for elementary principals regarding how to create more optimal and equitable classroom concentration levels?
- Will teacher morale increase and stress levels decrease following training the training?
- Is academic achievement for children with special needs higher in classroom with lower concentration levels?

Process, Product, and Impact Evaluation Methods:

The committee recommends a series of evaluation studies to address these questions. First, they recommend randomly assigning elementary principals to one of three groups: (1) training prior to year one of the study, (2) training prior to year two of the study, and (3) a holdout condition that will participate in a separate study. The first group will serve as the treatment group during the first year, and the second group will serve as the control group during the second year. By the second year, leaders from all schools in the first two groups will have been exposed to the training. At the end of each year of the study, classroom concentration levels will be monitored, and teacher moral and stress levels will be assessed using surveys. Student achievement for all children will be compared between the groups as well. The training will be thoroughly evaluated using the Kirkpatrick model and recommendations for improving the training will be offered at the end of each year of the study. Administrators in the third group will be trained prior to the third year.

Principals in the third group will be instructed in a method for randomly assigning classrooms to one of two different concentration levels. The concentration levels will be selected to fit within recognized limits for optimal classroom inclusive practices, but will vary to allow for comparisons between classrooms at the lower and upper ends of the acceptable range. Student achievement, teacher stress, and teacher morale levels will be assessed at the end of years one and two in these schools.

Chapter Questions

1. Select a particular grade level or subject area in your school system. Design a needs assessment study to help determine the most appropriate area for setting goals related to instructional improvement.
2. Outline a process for selecting new instructional resources to meet the challenges and needs identified in Question 1. Be sure to consider how appropriate and applicable the intervention is to local context.
3. Develop a plan for the phased implementation of the new instructional intervention. Include a plan for piloting, adapting, and then evaluating the effectiveness of the new instructional intervention.

CHAPTER 12

Human Resources

GLORIA D. CAMPBELL-WHATLEY

JAMES E. LYON

INTRODUCTION

School and special education leaders spend a great deal of time performing personnel-related duties. Comprehensive procedures and policies are vital in order to assure that schools and the school districts hire appropriate professionals to teach children with special needs. A proactive situation encourages both special and school leaders to jointly establish procedures to identify and hire special education teachers.

The basic function of human resources or the personnel department is to recruit, hire, induct, supervise, evaluate, and retain teachers. Special education teachers are usually unsure as to who might hire, supervise, or evaluate them. Typically, special education teachers' answer to special education leaders regarding specialized issues related to children with disabilities but on a daily basis, and for situations that require immediate attention, they answer to the principal. For these reasons, it is important that both special education and general education school leaders understand their role with special education teachers (Capper, Frattura, & Keys, 2000; Leko & Brownell, 2009; McLaughlin & Nolet, 2008; Razik & Swanson, 2010). This chapter will offer suggestions and guidelines for recruiting, screening, retaining, supervising, and evaluating special education teachers.

Each school district usually has a system in place for hiring and evaluating general education teachers and staff, but special education administrators and school leaders need measures to hire and evaluate special education teachers. Although most school systems screen, interview, and hire special education teachers through special education leaders in the central office in concert with building principals, principals are normally responsible for evaluating all personnel in the building. This chapter provides suggestions for principals and school leaders to be more involved in the hiring and evaluation of special education teachers, including (1) recruitment and hiring, (2) interview questions and appropriate answers, (3) orientation activities, and (4) evaluation techniques. The chapter also includes information on teacher retention as the "burn-out" rate is high among special education teachers. Knowing how to support them can help with teacher retention. Challenges and issues in the chapter are listed in Box 12.1.

BOX 12.1

Challenges and Issues for Special Education and School Leaders

- Hiring and recruiting processes for special education teachers
- Interviewing special education teachers
- Information to include in special education teacher orientation
- Providing mentoring to special education teachers
- Legal issues and teacher termination

HIRING PROCESSES

In a number of school systems, hiring is a joint decision between school leaders and the human resources director. In the case of hiring special education teachers, special education coordinators and directors are often actively involved. In an ideal situation, the special education leader works collaboratively with the human resources director and school principal to devise a system to adapt conventional hiring procedures for special education teachers. If there had been a connected system of hiring in the vignette in Box 12.2, more than likely the Office of Civil Rights complaint could have been avoided. School systems that have a more inclusive approach to special education are more apt to have an integrated and connected system of hiring (Bartlett, Weisenstein, & Etscheidt, 2002; McLaughlin & Nolet, 2008; Rebore, 2011).

BOX 12.2

Vignette: *"The Office of Civil Rights (OCR) Complaint"*

Bill, who has multiple dystrophy, was hired as an adaptive behavior teacher even though that was not his area of training. He expressed his concern, but it did not appear to be important during the interview with the principal. The school system's orientation covered logistics but not classroom information. During the school year, Bill's condition deteriorated even though he consorted with Libby, a co-worker who offered him assistance in his classroom. He had no support, even though he wrote a memo to the principal, the director of special education, and the superintendent. He finally called the Office of Civil Rights.

(Adapted from Inclusive Educational Administration: A Case Study Approach *(Weishaar & Borsa 2001).*

As you read through the chapter, think of these questions.

1. Should Bill have been recruited and hired for this position? Was he qualified? Should a teacher with a specific area of special education licensure be placed in a job position with students different from the licensure area?
2. What interview questions should Bill have been asked?
3. What should an orientation program contain related to special education?
4. If Bill qualified for assistance, because of his disability, what should the district have offered him?
5. Was the human resources department proactive in its treatment of a teacher with a disability?
6. Does the treatment that Bill received warrant an OCR complaint?
   In whose favor would the OCR rule? Why?

Recruitment

The objective of any search for school personnel is to recruit and hire the most qualified, knowledgeable, effective, and cooperative professionals possible. The special education director is usually directly involved in recruitment activities for special education teachers. Generally, each district has policies and procedures to recruit and hire teachers. The recruitment policy usually serves as a guideline to specify each vacancy. There is a need, however, to have policies or adapt policies to fit special education teachers because their role differs in relation to the type of students they teach. The special education director can denote the specific competencies the applicant will need. However, school leaders can also have input on desirable teacher competencies and characteristics since special education teachers work in inclusive settings.

The logistics of recruitment include the review of hiring policies and procedures, preparation of the vacancy notice, and a variety of recruitment strategies according to the characteristics and needs of the school district.

- First, a budget for the search that will cover advertising and travel expenses is prepared (Castetter & Young, 2000; Glickman, Gordon, & Ross-Gordon, 2010).
- Second, using the specified guidelines, a vacancy notice is approved. Announcements usually include expected job-related behaviors, competencies, and responsibilities that are specific to the job and the school's needs and characteristics. Listed on the vacancy notice is salary, benefits, and the application deadline.
- Also, the candidate's portfolio, resume, and references can be required with the submission of the application. After the applications are received, a systematic and predetermined time to review, screen, and notify candidates is determined.

A sufficient number of qualified candidates increase the chances for finding good teachers. In order to recruit and select qualified special education teachers, usually an adequate to large number of candidates from which to choose is preferred. If there is not an adequate pool of candidates, the district may assist by appropriating funding for targeted recruitment-related activities.

Funds may be allocated for the special education director to attend job fairs and conferences to actively recruit teachers or the district may want to recruit from a wider area.

- In larger school systems the district may want to consider internal recruitment to increase the candidate pool. There are usually teachers with certification who are not teaching in this area. Internal recruitment usually seeks to identify teachers who are already familiar with the school system's policies and procedures and who are willing consider a position in another teaching area such as special education.
- Nearby universities may suggest preservice teachers who are qualified to fill the position (Billingsley, 2005).

Screening and Interviewing

Although the special education director recruits, collaboration with school leaders to screen the candidate for selection is suggested; after all, the teacher will be working daily at the school. The applications are to be reviewed according to a set of selection criteria that fit the vacancy announcement and are in compliance with district criteria. Resumes are read and various qualifications, credentials, and relevant experiences are determined and listed in an organized format. A system to rate the candidates using a scale—for example, from five (high) to one (low)—according to the criteria is recommended (Miros, 2001). The candidates with the highest ratings are chosen to interview.

Although the resume will reveal the initial qualifications of a candidate, the interview will disclose information about problem-solving abilities, attitude, communication skills, and disposition. If the candidate has teaching experience, interviewers should explore it with the candidate.

- To facilitate a better inclusive environment, a team of educators from the school might interview the teacher. In the vignette, for example, Bill's qualifications and preferences would possibly have been disclosed if a school team had interviewed him.
- A representative composition—including a general educator, counselor, parent, and other special education personnel such as the occupational therapist, speech therapist, or physical therapist—is recommended.
- To ensure that the teacher has experience in an inclusive environment, application or resume items that identify inclusive or collaborate experiences, as well as generic special education qualifications, are desired (Billingsley, 2005; Castetter & Young, 2000; McLaughlin & Nolet, 2008; Young, 2008).

Usually, special education leaders generate a list of appropriate interview questions. However, it is recommended that school and special education leaders, possibly parents of children with disabilities and the entire search committee formulate or choose questions from a list that can be used in a structured, interview format (Lunenburg & Ornstein, 1991; McLaughlin & Nolet, 2008 Miros, 2001; Webb & Norton, 2009). Specific questions allow the team to seek the same point of reference for various answers. Other than general areas of basic qualifications, the following themes are suggested as fundamental to special education: (1) general qualifications, (2) classroom management, (3) the IEP, (4) parent communication, (5) teacher collaboration, and (6) the ability to work with other professionals and paraprofessionals. Some suggested questions may be found in Bateman and Bateman's (2001) *A Principal's Guide to Special Education* and in McLaughlin and Nolet's (2008) *What Every Principal Needs to Know about Special Education* (see Figure 12.1). The expected response is provided.

The interview is not the only source to gather information about the candidate.

- The team can and should also contact the references and previous employers of the candidate. Sometimes, candidates are asked to chose a topic or issue from a list (e.g., philosophy of education, collaboration, or discipline) and asked to write a short essay. Activities such as these also reveal the decision-making ability of the applicant, as well as their writing ability.
- The candidate may also be asked to bring a portfolio or a lesson plan (Miros, 2001). Since technology is at the forefront of education and instruction, a demonstration of their use of technology may also be helpful (Rebore, 2011; Skylar, Higgins, & Boone, 2007).

Actually, in the vignette, Bill did not meet the qualifications for teaching the students in the classroom he was assigned. After the interview and discussion of the candidates, the special education leader, school principal, and the committee can jointly choose the candidate based on the criteria. The specifics of the job—such as working conditions, salary, and assignment—can be explained after the applicant is offered the contract that has been approved by the superintendent and the school board (Billingsley, 2005; Podemski, Marsh, Smith, & Price, 1995; Razik & Swanson, 2010; Sergiovanni, Kelleher, McCarthy, & Wirt, 2004; Uben, Hughes, & Norris, 2004).

FIGURE 12.1 Interview Questions

Question Focus	Expected Response
	General Qualifications
Coursework	Some type of coursework relative to methods in teaching in the area of special education, to which they are applying, is appropriate.
Future classroom arrangement	A room arrangement that facilitates small group and individualized instruction are key indicators.
Lesson elements	Lesson elements that include goals, objectives, materials, procedures, and evaluation are fundamental.
Technological equipment, methodologies, coursework, and software	Prerequisite is the use of basic software programs such as word processing, presentations, and spreadsheets. Discuss a minimum of two fundamental programs that are devised and appropriate for children with disabilities (e.g., Distar, the Kansas Mnemonics Strategies, Touch Math).
Mathematical and language arts methods	Although a preferred method might be mentioned, a strong response would consist of the use of multiple methodologies according to the needs and learning style of the student.
Instructional organization and individualization	Varied instructional arrangements that identify working with students on their independent, instructional, and frustration level are of value. Also, grouping students according to their weaknesses and strengths, and varied types of co-teaching arrangements are strong responses.
Formal and informal assessments	There are several formal individualized achievement assessments applicants may mention, such as the Key Math Diagnostic Test, the Peabody Individual Achievement Test, the Brigance, the Woodcock Reading Mastery Test, and others. Informal assessments will include curriculum-based assessment, performance assessment, authentic assessment, DIBELS, and so on.
Cultural pedagogy and urban experiences	Applicants indicating diverse experiences are possibly more aware of methodologies related to varied teacher styles and individual differences.
	Classroom Management
Discipline procedures	Behavioral-related programs (e.g., token economies, timeout) or cognitively based problem solving programs (e.g., Skillstreaming, Assets) should most likely be mentioned. Problem-solving approaches are strong indicators of well-rounded discipline procedures. Interventions should be research-based strategies.
Functional behavior assessments, positive behavior supports, and behavior evaluation plans	Practice and implementation of a functional behavior assessment and behavior evaluation plans is essential. Prior use and the design of positive behavior supports are desirable. Applicant should be able to use research-based behavioral strategies and know how to use measurements to evaluate the success of the intervention.
Manifestation determination	The behavior as part of the child's disability is the foundation of the explanation.

FIGURE 12.1   *(Continued)*

Question Focus	Expected Response
IEP	
Accommodations in general education setting	Varied instructional strategies and adaptations are indicative of the knowledge needed.
Statewide testing, modifications, and accommodations	Participation and accommodations are dependent on the student's exceptionality category. For example, a student with severe or profound mental retardation may not participate in testing, whereas a student with mild mental impairments might participate because intellectual and academic abilities are higher.
Reconvene IEP teams	Recovering the IEP team focuses on changes in placement, major discipline procedures, or specified instructional outcomes.
Parent Communication	
Communication with parents	Email, telephone, or writing communication systems that would increase contact with parents on a weekly basis are favored suggestions.
Accommodations or concessions to increase parent participation	The possibility of varied conference times, transportation, and child-care arrangements are satisfactory explanations.
Parent conferences	Before the conference, the appointment with parents should be confirmed. Information on the student, such as work samples or data from the cumulative file, is gathered. An agenda is prepared. During the conference, the focus is the child. Both positive as well as challenging behaviors and issues are discussed. Communication techniques and listening strategies strengthen the candidate's response. After the conference, a follow-up to examine relevant strategies and methodologies are a necessity.
Collaboration	
Inclusive instruction in social studies and science	Modifying instruction through task analysis, scaffolding, story webbing, or other step-by-step or simplified procedures to explain material in a simple form is central.
Conflicts/noncompliance with general educators	First, a nonaccusatory conversation with the teacher is paramount. For legal reasons, school leaders should be aware of intense conflict and disagreement among professionals.
Response to Intervention (RTI)	Must be familiar with the Tiers in RTI.
Relationships with general educators	A systematic communication methodology and techniques to establish parity, relationship, ownership, and trust with the general education teacher is key.

Orientation

Orientation should provide a thorough explanation of policies, procedures, and job responsibilities. Districts usually have procedures and services to induct new teachers. For example, the teacher is provided a handbook, attends a workshop, or views a DVD containing information regarding benefits, evaluation procedures, and instructional resources. The induction process serves the crucial function of helping staff members new to a school to get off to the best start possible. Norton (2008) contends that staff induction begins with the job application and then moves through job candidacy and continues on an ongoing basis so long as the organization or the individual views it as necessary. Moreover, he observes that a good induction program has been shown to be instrumental in fostering staff morale and reducing staff turnover. At the building level, the new teacher will more than likely attend an in-service activity to understand school schedules, school routines, attendance procedures, methods to requisition materials, and all other pertinent issues. If there are specific procedures for students with disabilities in a specific special education category, these can be reviewed by the special education director or coordinator. In the vignette, Bill never had the opportunity to understand what he needed to know to instruct the students he was assigned to teach.

Because of the laws that govern special education programs, orientation materials specific to children with disabilities would better prepare new special education teachers. Special education laws and legislation change often and may vary from state to state and from district to district.

- Special education leaders can prepare a manual for new special education teachers. The manual usually contains procedures and forms used in that district—such as the referral process, permission to evaluate, parent procedural safeguards, letters of invitation, placement notices, IEP formats, extended school year timelines, and testing accommodations, modifications, or exemptions. The manual can also contain the sections of the federal and state law pertinent to the areas that teachers are most likely to have questions and concerns (i.e., discipline, confidentiality information, due process, placement) (Glickman et al., 2010; McLaughlin & Nolet, 2008; Miros, 2001).
- A recommended text for first-year special education teachers is *The Exceptional Teacher's Handbook: The First Year Teachers Guide for Success* by Shelton and Pollingue (2000). The text is comprehensive and will help first-year teachers become familiar with the required paperwork.

PERSONNEL SUPERVISION AND EVALUATION

Supervision determines the degree to which the curriculum is being appropriately implemented and the level of achievement of instructional goals, as well as a teacher's knowledge, competence, and commitment to professional growth (Sergiovanni, 2009; Sergiovanni et al., 2004). For special education, supervision also determines the degree to which the IEP is implemented and if the goals of the special education program are achieved. As expected, special education leaders have more expertise in supervising special education teachers. In any event, they have a greater knowledge of the specific areas of exceptionality. However, special education leaders can only periodically evaluate special education teachers, because they are not in the building enough to supervise them on a day-to-day basis.

Many times special education teachers receive minimal supervision because school leaders may be unsure of what instruction they should see during a teacher observation (Bateman & Bateman, 2001). A conscientious school leader can supervise any teacher in the building. Appropriate special education techniques are identified by the ability of the teacher to adequately (1) diagnose learning needs, (2) write an individualized education plan, (3) administer and interpret a number of informal and formal individualized assessments, (4) collaborate with general educators, and (5) mentor (Bartlett et al., 2002; Nolet & McLaughlin, 2005; Podemski et al., 1995; Weishaar & Borsa, 2001; Young, 2008).

Observation

Clinical supervision is the most common structure for performing effective evaluations (Cogan, 1973; Goldhammer, 1969; Webb & Norton, 2009). When the first set of observations is announced to the new special education teachers, a climate of support should be developed because there are so many new challenges for new teachers. After all, most new teachers are overwhelmed and it will take time for them to acclimate to the environment. These first observations can also provide an excellent opportunity for building leaders to positively reinforce the teacher and offer strong encouragement as well as guidance. Observations should never be used as a weapon (as it was in the vignette).

Varied methods, measures, and tools can be used for observation purposes, including but not limited to questionnaires, open-ended narratives, checklists, and district observation forms. Both quantitative and qualitative measures may use matrices, codes, and performance indicators. Combinations of these can be devised by the observer to meet the needs of the school district, school, or teacher (Glickman, Gordon, & Ross-Gordon, 2010).

The observation process is time consuming and includes a great deal of paperwork, but nevertheless, it is an effective source of guidance because it provides more evaluative information to the teacher and school leader.

- It is suggested that the process begin with a preobservation conference between the special education and/or school leader and the teacher to determine the area or areas of instructional focus and finalize the goals and objectives of the lesson. The teacher may choose any instructional area for the observation such as reading instruction, behavior management, and the like.
- For appropriate monitoring, the teacher should provide an outline of the lesson and procedures before the observation. Additionally, it might be helpful to give a brief sketch of the characteristics of the students that have behavioral challenges in the class (Billingsley, 2005; Burello & Greenburg, 1988; Keller, 2004; Odden, 2004; Podemski et al., 1995).
- The reason and the purpose for the observation are determined during the preconference. The time for the observation and the postconference is set (Bateman, Bright, O'Shea, O'Shea, & Algozzine, 2007).

It is important to view the entire lesson, as the teacher may use a variety of strategies to attempt to appropriately engage the students throughout the lesson. Miros (2001) and Billingsley (2005) suggest that leaders observe the suitability of (1) discipline procedures, (2) the use of media and technology, (3) questioning techniques, (4) grouping strategies, (5) accommodations, (6) instructional time, (7) demonstration, and (8) practice techniques.

- The school leader collects observational data for the purpose of supervising as well as evaluation.
- Within a 24-hour period, it is important to reflect on and analyze the observation information before the data gets "cold" and important points are forgotten. Listing effective and

ineffective methodologies, as well as the strengths and weaknesses of teaching strategies are suggested (Glickman et al., 2010).

- A well-written outline or narrative containing these comments is a best practice (Bateman et al., 2007).
- To assure objectivity, the observer can ask a second observer to confirm the techniques and strategies observed during the session.
- The observation is discussed with the teacher at the proposed time. While conferencing, both negative and positive portions of the lesson can be examined. If need be, leaders can provide additional assistance by encouraging the teacher to try specific strategies, texts, websites, or consultation with a mentor teacher (Bateman & Bateman, 2001; Billingsley, 2005; Podemski et al., 1995).
- The teacher is then allowed adequate time to incorporate the suggestions before a second observation and evaluation is done. The goal is to improve the teacher's instruction while promoting evaluation as a collaborative endeavor that is performed with teachers rather than against them (Bateman & Bateman, 2001; Hoy & Miskel, 2007; Osborne, DiMattia, & Curran, 1993; Osborne & Russo, 2006; Podemski et al., 1995).
- The teacher is allowed to make comments at this time. If needed, an improvement plan can be offered to the teacher, including demonstration lessons, class visitations, or the employment of co-teaching methods, among other things (Bateman et al., 2007).

Although the clinical supervision model is widely employed in evaluating teachers, there are some other models that are frequently used to evaluate teachers. Danielson (2007), among others, has advocated other models that may be equally as effective and sometimes more appropriate to use to evaluate teachers. Some of the other models involve analysis of classroom artifacts (i.e., lesson plans, teacher assignments, and student work), teaching portfolios, teachers' self-reports of their practices, student ratings of teacher performance, and student achievement on standardized tests, which may incorporate a performance-for-pay component—to name a few. The latter model, usually called the *value-added model,* determines the performance level of the teachers based on how much their students gain on standardized tests during their time under the teacher's tutelage. Teachers frequently dislike this model due to factors beyond their control that affect student learning.

Danielson (2007) has proposed a framework for professional practice that identifies the aspects of a teacher's responsibilities that promote improved student learning. Her model includes the following four domains:

- *Domain 1: Planning & Preparation* addresses how the teacher designs the lesson.
- *Domain 2: The Classroom Environment* addresses factors in the classroom that are not instruction, such as classroom rapport, student behavior, how the classroom is organized, and so on.
- *Domain 3: Instruction* addresses factors that represent the core of teaching and relate to engaging students in learning such as communication practices, classroom discussion, feedback to students, and so on.
- *Domain 4: Professional Responsibilities* addresses the myriad responsibilities of the teacher outside the classroom such as reflecting on teaching, communicating with parents, demonstrating professionalism, and the like.

Using Danielson's framework, school leaders and principals can employ these four domains to examine how teachers are handling these crucial factors that together contribute to student learning. However, when evaluating special education teachers, the evaluators need to recognize that these teachers frequently employ special strategies and practices to meet the needs of students with special learning needs. Regardless of the teacher evaluation model employed in a school or school system, Norton (2008) notes that performance evaluation requires four basic components: (1) a qualified evaluator, (2) valid and reliable assessment instruments (or other artifacts), (3) timely observations, and (4) appropriate follow-up conferencing and feedback.

TEACHER RETENTION

Currently in special education, we do not have enough teachers to fill existing positions. Although there are a number of general educators seeking employment, there is such a shortage of special education teachers that a large number are hired on limited or alternative licenses. Finding, developing, and keeping qualified teachers is a challenge. Forty percent of special education teachers leave the field before their fifth year of teaching (Irinaga-Bistolas, Schalock, Marvin, & Beck, 2007; Murawski & Dieker, 2008). Due to the growing number of special education students, the shortage of teachers is expected to increase (Bureau of Labor Statistics, 2004).

The first year of teaching is especially critical to teacher retention because of the emotional demands of the job (Billingsley & Tomchin, 1992; Cloud & Fastenberg, 2010; Schlichte, Yssel, & Merbler, 2005). To retain teachers, it is desirable to utilize volunteers or paraprofessionals to assist. Effective techniques that leaders might also want to employ is to encourage the use of team teaching methodologies, promote the use of team decision making, and establish shared responsibilities among general and special educators regarding students receiving special education (Useem & Neild, 2005; Weishaar & Borsa, 2001). The special education teacher can no longer be on a separate wing of the building separated from general education teachers. Collaborative efforts provide teachers time to problem solve and cooperate with each other, interact collectively, review intervention strategies, study laws and regulations, and provide input on professional development (Cox, 2001; Spencer, 2005). Empowered teams that consist of school leaders, guidance counselors, and other specialists will be able to respond to an array of special education programmatic concerns. Arrangements such as these will also assure that general education teachers effectively integrate special education teachers into the general education classroom (Goor, Schwenn, & Boyer, 1997; McLaughlin & Nolet, 2008; Young, 2008).

Leaders with positive demeanors toward special education are more supportive, and usually develop a close working relationship with special education teachers (Cox, 2001; Spencer, 2005). School leaders can attend special education workshops or seminars, on occasion, to gather an understanding of the magnitude of the job. Moreover, they should serve as role models for all staff, encouraging them to become life-long learners and demonstrating this through their own behavior. If teachers receive strong administrative support and are satisfied, they are less likely to experience dissatisfaction and are more apt to remain in special education (Otto & Arnold, 2005; Useem & Neild, 2005).

Special education teachers feel valued when they are provided a suitable workspace just the same as the general education teachers. School and special education leaders can assure that special education teachers have a pleasant environment. Far too many classrooms serving children receiving special education are located in the hall, closet, or under the steps. Leaders can provide appropriate materials for the special education teacher, as well as verbal praise and encouragement (Littrell, Billingsley, & Cross, 1994; Otto & Arnold, 2005; Webb & Norton,

2009). Teachers have a need to know that leaders appreciate their efforts. This appreciation can be demonstrated by the principal encouraging and supporting novice teachers to observe more senior teachers, hiring substitutes to allow teachers to attend and participate in workshops and conferences, and being available to assist with a difficult student or behavior problems that teachers may encounter.

Mentoring

Effective mentoring is associated with teacher retention (Billingsley, 2005; Duffy & Forgan, 2005; Whitaker, 2000). Mentoring for new teachers during the first year of instruction has become a common practice. New teachers usually spend the first year getting to know other faculty and staff and familiarizing themselves with school procedures. In the vignette, Bill received some informal mentoring from Libby, but the teaching assignment may have gone smoother if he had a formal mentoring teacher assigned to him. Most mentor teachers have expertise in teaching techniques, laws, strategies, and interventions. A mentor teacher can assist a new teacher with developing collaborative patterns, teaching and discipline strategies, and organizing the curriculum and classroom (Duffy & Forgan, 2005; Lloyd, Wood, & Moreno, 2000; Young, 2008). Additionally, mentor teachers often have strong work ethics, appropriate attitudes toward students with disabilities, and can function collaboratively and productively with general educators. A teacher like this may have helped Bill adapt easier to a difficult situation.

Special education and school leaders can develop some guidelines for choosing effective mentors. Providing the mentors specific knowledge of their roles and the skills needed to successfully mentor can foster effective partnerships. The mentor and mentee can collaboratively build individual professional development goals that can guide the new teacher throughout the first year. The pair should meet often with the school leader to review progress, reflect, and adjust the goals as needed (Iringa-Bistolas et al., 2007).

According to the size of the school, or geographic location, a new special education teacher may not have a mentor teacher in the building. Williams and Warren (2007) suggest E-mentoring as a way to form a community of novice and veteran teachers. Through email and teleconferencing, the teachers form a virtual network of professionals that produce a flexible outlet for sharing effective strategies and methodologies. E-mentoring forms a learning community that provides support through networking research trends and can enhance teacher rejuvenation. This method does not provide just one person to consult with new teachers but rather a pool of teachers with expertise that crosses over geographical boundaries. New teachers are more apt to connect to a teacher with the same roles and responsibilities, as well as specific areas of expertise. Mentors and mentees can connect in a cost-effective manner that supports group convenience for performing special projects and initiatives. E-mentoring can also support teachers in rural areas.

Lee and colleagues (2006) suggest several strategies that create effective mentoring relationships. School leaders and administrators can meet with and assist the veteran teacher and the new teacher in many ways:

- Share their professional visions related to school and specific roles as a professional and teacher.
- Explore ways to cultivate professional expectations by examining gaps in professional goals.
- Write a philosophy and scrutinize challenges and attitudes that encourage or block the attainment and implementation of success.

BOX 12.3

Advice for School and Special Education Leaders

- Recruiting, hiring, screening, and interviewing are collaborative, joint processes between the special education leaders, the principal, and other school leaders.
- Interview questions applicable to special education teachers, related to the IEP, classroom management, and parent communication, allow educators to have the same point of reference.
- An orientation manual or handbook and in-service training especially related to special education concerns provide teachers information related to laws, legislation, policies, and procedures that affect students with exceptional needs.
- During an observation, special education techniques are identified by the teacher's ability to teach and reach the appropriate goals and objectives of the lesson.
- Emotional support, professional development, and mentoring assist in special education teacher retention.

- Find other avenues to communicate and support each other while strengthening interpersonal skills.
- Plan for classroom management and daily lessons.
- Balance the relationship between the administrator, the veteran teacher, and the new teacher by listening, providing empowerment, and support.

Peer mentoring and peer coaching is another mentoring and professional development approach that is gaining momentum in PK–12 education. The primary model involves using experienced teachers who are deemed to be effective teachers to observe and support new teachers—and in some cases other veteran teachers—by assisting with lesson planning, modeling teaching strategies, evaluating lessons, assessing student work, and managing student behavior. Peer mentoring and coaching can promote collegiality and support, teacher leadership, and professional development in a nonthreatening manner, since these peer coaches are usually not a part of the formal evaluation system. Box 12.3 lists advice for school and special education leaders.

Summary

The legal issues in this chapter are summarized in Box 12.4. The inclusion movement has changed the face of special education and its relation to school leadership structures. The current trend leans toward the collaboration of school and special education leaders. School and special education leaders can collaborate in order to have a more involved role in special education hiring, supervision, and evaluation processes. Teacher shortages continue to present a problem as more and more children are identified as disabled. Teacher support and mentoring can improve and support special education retention. The resolution to the vignette is shown in Box 12.5.

BOX 12.4

Legal Issues

Termination of teachers is a most difficult task, even for the toughest of leaders. However, a task of this sort usually happens at least once during a person's career. The leader can follow basic due process procedures suggested by the school system for the termination of any teacher. It is best practice for leaders to evaluate frequently to see if the teacher's performance is less than adequate. If so, the leader can do everything possible to assist the teacher. If the teacher cannot alter faulty practices, then termination may be the only answer (Hoy & Hoy, 2006; Osborne et al., 1993; Osborne & Russo, 2006).

The major issue to consider in termination is tenure. Many states have different termination policies for nontenured and tenured teachers and specific laws governing tenure and due process procedures (Bingham, 2005; Hoy & Hoy, 2006; Osborne et al., 1993; Osborne & Russo, 2006). Due process procedures are then determined by the specifics of the contract. Additionally, state procedures and board policy must be observed (Podemski et al., 1995). The Office of Civil Rights, the Equal Employment Opportunity Commission, and the U.S. Office of Education are federal and state agencies that offer protection for employees. Also, there are provisions within the Constitution that protect employees regarding fair practice and termination. According to the Constitution, teachers have personal contract rights, due process rights, and protection from discrimination on the basis of race, sex, and disability. Special and school leaders can make sure that they are aware and follow proper procedures to avoid unnecessary litigation (Cooper, Ehrensal & Bromme, 2005; Lucas, 2004; Times Educational Supplement, 2004).

In the vignette, there are two major legal concerns. First, it appears that Bill may be terminated because of the concerns he presented to the administration. He needed assistance because of his physical disability and he was hired in a classroom in which he was not prepared to teach. He, however, very well may have a case with ORC because his physical disability was ignored and could have very well affected his performance in the classroom. Second, Bill has written proof that he continually asked for assistance beginning with his immediate supervisor, then the principal, and ending with the superintendent.

BOX 12.5

Resolution of the Vignette

During hiring, collaborative efforts between the principal and the special education director may have eliminated the mistake of hiring a teacher who did not fit the needs of the classroom. After the teacher continued to send written complaints, concerns, and issues about the classroom related to his physical condition, the administrators may have avoided the ORC complaint by attending to the needs of the teacher.

Chapter Questions

1. Should Bill have updated his certification or license to teach students with adaptive disabilities? Why or why not?
2. When interviewing, what are key characteristics and indicators of "good" teachers?
3. How should school and special education leaders cope with teachers who assure that their "civil rights" are not violated?
4. What are the aspects and characteristics of a good mentoring match?
5. What can be done to assist with teacher retention?

CHAPTER 13

School Finance

James J. Bird

INTRODUCTION

A great deal of specific content knowledge exists in the real world of public education. This content knowledge emerges from several unconnected sources, evolves sporadically over time, and reflects the politics of the possible rather than the science of certainty. School and special education leaders must draw from the literature of instructional pedagogy for best practices in the delivery of special education services. These must be placed within the legislative guidelines of the Individuals with Disabilities Education Act (IDEA). Resources must be used within compliance of auditing practices originating from federal, state, and local levels. Individual case decisions mesh with past practices at the classroom, school site, and district levels. Each of these sources of information contains knowledge that the school leader must assimilate and bring to bear in formulating problem-solving and decision-making strategies.

If there is one constant in this complicated array of realities, it is that all of it is both dynamic and constantly changing. This change dynamic is not coordinated across the various sources, nor is it always compatible, one with another, but rather it proceeds asynchronously and presents quite a challenge for the school leader to simply "keep up" with it all.

At any given time, the "current state of affairs" has many authors. University research informs practice. Advocacy groups induce legislative action. Judicial procedures prescribe corrections or new directions. Because there is lack of clarity over preferred outcomes and little agreement over cause/effect relationships, these activities occur in the political arena and therefore reflect all the trappings of the political process, including power, compromise, bureaucracy, constituencies, and complexity.

Just as in the vignette in Box 13.1, it is on this stage that the daily workings of children with disabilities getting appropriate services are played out. It is at once both global and local. There are only two titles in the organizational chart that have the positional authority to orchestrate the necessary coordination of staff, program, and resources: the superintendent at the district level and the principal at the school building level. These leaders have the daunting tasks of absorbing the knowledge needed to be compliant and innovative; communicating that knowledge to others so that they can also exercise leadership across the schools; and acting in such a way so as to instill confidence and trust through competency, integrity, and authenticity.

This chapter will focus on the school and special education leaders' roles and responsibilities in the areas of resource management, including finance and budgeting. Highlighted areas will include challenges, IDEA 2004, funding formulas, legal issues, and advice for future school and special education leaders. Challenges and issues are highlighted in Box 13.2.

BOX 13.1

Vignette: *"Jessica's IEP Conference"*

Everyone on the way to Jessica's IEP conference had different goals. Jessica's mother was thinking that she wants her daughter to spend less time on the bus. Her classroom teacher wants fewer special education students who are "included" in her class. Because she is fearful for her job, the special education inclusion teacher wants more students to be included in "regular" classrooms. The assistant principal has worked out a "perfect" master schedule and wants to maintain the parameters.

There are others who have concerns: The transportation supervisor wants to reduce total miles driven and therefore does not want another student added to the roster. The central office special education representative wants regulation compliance. And what about Jessica? She wants to be in class with her best friends, Carla and Yvonne.

The school principal needs to analyze the individual pieces of this puzzle and persuade the individuals into shifting their initial points of view into a composite amalgam that is possible, permissible, and promising for Jessica's educational growth.

1. What knowledge does the principal need?
2. What skills does the principal need to employ?
3. What is the principal's goal in this situation and what has to happen to attain that goal?
4. How does the principal strike an effective balance among collaboration, compromise, and compliance?
5. How does the principal judge whether the outcome is acceptable, adequate, equitable, or exceptional?
6. How does the principal know that the outcome will be compatible with future IEPs (there are three more scheduled for tomorrow)?

BOX 13.2

Challenges and Issues for School Leaders

- Information management with complex components of student databases, legislative mandates, financial regulations, compliance documentation, and the federalism of national, state, and local governance
- School leader positional responsibilities of being the coordinator, communicator, initiator, monitor, and arbiter of lots of moving parts
- Accomplishing both efficiencies and effectiveness, doing things quickly and correctly, without one compromising the other
- Matching resource availability with student need identification through appropriate diagnosis, prescription, delivery, and assessment practices
- Assigning costs to services delivered in the myriad of instructional settings
- Dealing with constant change across stakeholders, pedagogy, regulations, and scarcity of resources
- Discerning points of connectedness and points of separateness between general education and special education programs
- Progressing along the program continuum of adequacy, equity, and excellence for all children and constituencies
- Creating and expanding client trust through ideals, transparency, actions, and integrity.

To an average citizen it seems simple enough to understand: Provide a free and public education to all children. There is a complex array of definitions, regulations, philosophies, interpretations, and stakeholders. School leaders—be they superintendents, principals, or special education administrators—find themselves quickly in the vortex of competing values, high expectations, scarce resources, and murky cause/effect relationships. Add to this mix the dynamics of individual differences across staff, students, and parents, and one begins to understand the challenges faced by those entrusted to provide leadership toward the advancement of a child's educational experience. There are three policy issues: federalism, adequacy-equity-excellence, and accountability.

FEDERALISM: THREE STRUCTURAL STAGES

At the national level, Congress has the authority to promulgate legislation, such as the Individuals with Disabilities Education Act (1990, 1997, 2004), that sets in motion a flood of activity affecting everyone and everything downstream as it flows through statehouses, courthouses, district offices, and ebbs into classrooms. The legislation is always a product of the political process, which includes the inevitable compromises across powerful interest-group constituencies. Such legislation is subject to interpretation, needs to be applied to local settings, and changes over time. The school and special education leader have to transform those words on paper into behaviors between teachers and students. Although these congressional mandates are accompanied by implementational funding, recipients rarely believe that the funding levels are sufficient to accomplish the expressed desires of the decrees. Compliance regulations are firmly attached to the federal funds.

At the state level, a parallel set of activities occur within the individual statehouses as state legislatures wrestle with the federal legislation and funding package (Samuels, 2009). The resultant interpretation of the federal legislation is codified and provides the marching orders for state agencies. Concomitant funding is attached along with regulatory provisions that are to be followed at the local level. Again, this legislative package is the product of the political process with state-level interest groups participating. For the most part, these state-level machinations occur on a yearly basis and are prominent events in the state's budgetary process because of the vast sums of money involved. Education competes with other public services for the scarce resources of the state. Likewise, again, the school leader needs to transform these pronouncements into classroom behaviors across the state.

At the local school-district level, administrators (working with their respective elected Boards of Education) need to digest the content of the prescriptions of the federal and state regulations and match them to the programmatic needs of their students. There is no recipe as to how local districts devise their unique solution to this task, and variation is the norm within states and from state to state across the country. As at the two higher levels, the final product at the local level is again the result of the political process—this time with local players.

Occasionally, legislative interpretation requires the attention of the judicial branch of our government. Such adjudication can take place at the federal, state, or local level and, of course, such findings are binding on all parties. Thus, the court system is another arena of importance for the school and special education leader.

The U.S. system of federalism (Oates, 2008) structures the decision-making process directionally from the national level to the state level and then to the local school-district level. Lower levels must comply with the mandates of the higher levels. As things change in Washington, those changes are felt in state capitals, local board rooms, and school classrooms. The higher level *allocates* funds to the lower level, which *distributes* the funds across its units. This is the lay of the land that school leaders need to be cognizant of as they conduct their leadership activities. School and special education leaders need to be aware of the content of the political deliberations taking place at higher levels as well as those at their levels. The parameters of what they need to know and be able to do are inscribed by that which happens in their relevant environments, and their relevant environments include the political activities and actors of their Congress, statehouse, courthouse, and board rooms.

Changes will occur and should be expected across all three levels; therefore, school and special education leaders need to develop a systematic information-scanning technique to keep up to date with these changes. Professional association newsletters, intermediate school district workshops and communications, professional journals, and even newspapers can serve as conduits for change information. Do not assume that changes will be linear, consistent, compatible, or logical within or across the three levels.

Adequacy-Equity-Excellence

First, school and special education leaders need to be aware of how their decisions move students along the continuum of adequacy, equity, and excellence:

- Are the programs that are created and funded providing that which is adequate for responding to the identified needs of the student?
- If the program is implemented, will the student's individualized education plan (IEP)/individual transition plan (ITP)/individual family service plan (IFSP) goals be realized?
- Is the program compliant with the student's rights?

Second, equity needs to be considered:

- Are students with like needs or disabilities receiving like services?
- Are all categorizations of disabilities receiving appropriate services?

School and special education leaders who have access to all decision-making processes need to ensure that equity exists across all sectors of their programs. As such, that means that all students so identified across the state will be receiving the equally related services regardless of individual school district wealth considerations. Likewise, at the local level, all students with like identification categories will be receiving equally related services regardless of school site assignment.

Then, over time, excellence is sought:

- Is the special education program improving toward accomplishing demonstrated excellence in student achievement?
- Are school leaders motivating their staffs beyond the level of compliance to the more relevant realm of students flourishing and fulfilling their individual potentials?

Pertinent advice for school leaders is listed in Box 13.3.

Accountability

As will be discussed later in this chapter, the measurement point of intervention is shifting from the input side of the social processing model to the outcome side of the process. School and special education leaders will be confronted with accountability measures that examine student outcomes as opposed to teacher or program inputs. In other words, what will count is that which the student learned, not that which the teacher taught. This portends to raise the stakes of delivery

---

BOX 13.3

Advice for School and Special Education Leaders

- An awareness of historical events in the emergence of special education financing and transportation issues can aid in the understanding of current conditions and also help in the conceptualization of solutions to problems for future improvements.
- There are lots of moving parts in special education financing and transportation operations; therefore, the design of effective and efficient organizational structures and functions are crucial. Overcommunication is an oxymoron.
- Regulations and procedures are inevitable and historically necessary. Learn which apply to specific situations and then use them to your advantage. Complaining about how burdensome they are does not get the job done.
- The reach of mandates will always exceed the grasp of funding. Explore additional resource acquisition through grants and community partnerships.
- Remember that at the end of all of the red tape, there is a child who has some type of learning challenges that needs your creative expertise.
- Acknowledge the emotions that are attached to each case. If you can win over the family of the child, you can enlist very passionate supporters for your cause.
- Change has been a constant in special education funding and transportation laws, regulations, and standards. Devise a system of keeping abreast of these changes so that you can remain in compliance during both planning and implementing program services.
- Students will continue to present instructional needs, and resources will continue to be scarce. Be alert for any efficiencies that can be applied to your processes to improve services.
- Your most valuable resource is the trust that your clients bestow on you. Cultivate it with care, nurture it continuously, and treasure it with humility.
- Regardless of how large or complicated the delivery of special education financing and transportation services become, success begins and ends with individuals working together for the benefit of the child. Take ownership of your piece of the collective responsibility and make sure your fingerprints are all over the product.
- Leadership can transcend positional authority and responsibility. Expand your level of influence through initiative, competence, and teamwork.
- Remember, compliance spelled backwards is integrity. Well, not really, but the application of integrity, squeaky-clean honesty, and authentic transparency will always serve you well when helping children succeed in their school experiences.

---

expectations. It is a trend that general education has encountered and it will be applied to special education in the future.

This chapter introduction lays out the direction of that which will follow. School and special education leaders need to know content and practices that will serve them well as they exercise their leadership talents. The source of this knowledge, IDEA (2004), flows through the federalism structure of our governance system and is powered by the political process. The matching of students to programs needs to be adequate in terms of IEP/ITP/IFSP, equitable in application across all students, and striving toward individual student excellence. Measurement of student and program success will be extracted from outcomes as opposed to input efforts. With these policy issues established, attention shifts to specific content areas pertinent to school leaders' roles and responsibilities.

A STARTING POINT

An analogy may be drawn between the start of a vast river system and the promulgation of legislation. Everything flows from the origin and spreads across the landscape, affecting all sectors within which it comes in contact. IDEA (2004) sets forth the governance mandate that guides the operation of the special education programs across our country. School leaders do not need to become experts at interpreting the details of this tome, but they do need to become familiar with its basic tenets so that they can be conversant with a wide variety of stakeholders, such as legislators, lawyers, auditors, compliance officers, teachers, parents, advocates, and students. This can be accomplished through leaders attending workshops, reading professional journals, taking graduate level classes, or other professional development activities. Because the legislation is subject to judicial review, it is dynamic, and so school leaders need to develop a personal system of keeping up with present and future permutations of interpretations regarding the law's implementation. In essence, school leaders need to know the rules of the game—and there are lots of moving parts—including permissible use of funds, categories of student challenges, monitoring of student progress, and the interfaces of classroom-local-state educational agencies with federal operations.

A cursory glance at IDEA 2004's basic structural framework gives the school leader a glimpse at the complexity and far-reaching aspects of the law. A good vantage point is the U.S. Department of Education, Office of Special Education Programs (OSEP) self-professed one-stop shopping website (http://idea.ed.gov/explore/home). Full text of the law is available, as is a set of major topics and support materials such as training packets, model forms, video clips, webcasts, presentations, dialogue guides, and question and answer documents. Future plans include the capability to cross-reference IDEA (2004) with other legislation, such as the No Child Left Behind Act (NCLB, 2002), the Family Educational Rights and Privacy Act (FERPA; 1974), and links to OSEP's Technical Assistance and Dissemination Network (2007). The legislation is voluminous and spans over 300-plus pages of the Federal Registry. A cogent summary highlighting salient concepts related to the federal funding of special education can be found in Bateman, Bright, O'Shea, O'Shea, & Algozzine (2007). They comment on concepts such as "commingling, supplanting versus supplementing, excess cost, maintenance of effort, permissive use of funds, equitable participation, and allocations" (FERPA, pp. 151–160). They caution leaders to be aware of "pitfalls that can lead to unnecessary audit exceptions and possible sanctions" (p. 151) and suggest using the following tips:

1. When in doubt, use federal funds for clearly allowable expenditures and transfer questionable expenditures to local or state funding budget accounts.
2. Spend federal funds first because there is greater flexibility with state and local funds.
3. Be aware of obligations to charter schools in the area.
4. Be aware of other obligations such as residential facility placement; responsibility for providing assistive devices; and expenses associated with an extended school year (pp. 160–163).

The daily administrative demands of decision making, problem solving, and planning require a basic level of understanding of special education laws, regulations, and guidelines. Local school districts will have established Board of Education policies and administrative guidelines. These directives were accurate when they were published. The problem is the dynamism of special education practice and the constant changes that occur through judicial review and interpretation of regulations. The practicing school leader needs to develop a scanning mechanism wherein he or she can keep current with inevitable change. Periodicals such as *Education Week, The Chronicle of Higher Education, The School Administrator, Educational Leadership,* and *Phi Delta Kappan* publish news and commentary on current issues. Bateman and colleagues (2007) list additional organizational resources such as the American Association of School Administrators, the Center for Special Education Finance, The Council for Exceptional Children, the Council of Chief State School Officers, The Education Commission of the States, and the National Association of State Directors of Special Education.

Because the sums of money are so high and because the instructional decisions made concerning student learning are so crucial for the children involved, school leaders have tremendous responsibility to do their jobs right—the first time. The cost of audit-induced remediation is steep in both the loss of resources for districts and the loss of learning opportunities for students. School leaders would be well advised to make sure that all their staff members are afforded continuing professional development opportunities concerning the intersection of special education and school finance. Informed staff members have a better chance of conducting themselves appropriately and will reduce the number of "corrections" that an administrator would have to make. This is also fertile ground for school administrators to encourage leadership behavior in a nonhierarchical fashion among teachers, secretaries, and clerical staff (Goffee & Jones, 2006). Sending staff members to pertinent regional meetings and conferences and to state departments of instruction workshops should be seen as investments in the human capital of the school and district. Finally, when in doubt, school leaders need to seek and follow the advice of their districts' legal counsel. At times, administrators are inclined to shy away from the attorney's hourly rates but the endeavor should be seen as an investment instead of a cost. Attorney's fees at the front end can pale in comparison to the costs of an audit exception or possible sanctions for failure to comply with laws and regulations.

SPECIAL EDUCATION FORMULAS AND PRACTICE

The term *intergovernmental grants* describes the process of the higher-level unit passing funds to the lower-level unit. The manner through which states distribute their allocated special education funds to their respective school districts takes several forms. This reflects the complexity involved and it also illustrates the fact that there is no one solution that satisfies the needs of all situations. School leaders need to recognize that these formulae have evolved within states over time and that they continue to evolve as state political and economic conditions change. Basically there are six fundamental formulas in use and a couple states have developed their own unique systems (Parrish, Harr, Anthony, Merickel, & Esra, 2003):

1. *Pupil weights:* Funds are distributed to the respective school districts on a per-pupil basis relative to disability categories (e.g., Arizona).
2. *Flat grant:* The distribution of funds is made by a fixed amount per student that each district receives (e.g., North Carolina).
3. *Census-based:* The distribution of funds is made on a fixed amount that applies to a specifically identified group of students (e.g., California).
4. *Resource-based:* Funds are distributed on a specific educational resource, such as per teacher units or per classroom units (e.g., Delaware).
5. *Percent reimbursement:* Fund distribution is made to districts based on their actual expenditures (e.g., Michigan).
6. *Variable block grant:* Fund distribution is made to districts in areas of need as determined by the local officials (e.g., Arizona). (pp. 2–9)

Evaluative Criteria

With the various formula types constantly evolving, how does one judge the merits of the next "great idea" that might come down the pike? Parrish and colleagues (2003) offer the following list that can arm the school leader with rationale to be applied to policy discussions aimed at funding formula development:

- *Understandable:* Funding system and its underlying policy objectives and implementation procedures are straightforward and understood by all concerned parties (legislators, educators, parents, advocates, etc.).
- *Equitable:* Comparable students receive similar services regardless of district membership, district wealth.
- *Adequate:* Funding is sufficient for all districts to provide appropriate programs for special education students.
- *Predictable:* Local districts know allocation levels in time to plan for local services and can count on stable funding across years.
- *Flexible:* Local districts have latitude to deal with unique local conditions, changes affecting programs can be incorporated with minimum disruption.
- *Identification neutral:* The number of students identified as eligible for services is not affected by the type of formula used.
- *Reasonable reporting burden:* Costs to maintain the funding system are minimized and data requirements, recordkeeping, and reporting are kept at reasonable levels.
- *Fiscal accountability:* Conventional accounting procedures are followed and procedures are included to contain excessive or inappropriate costs.
- *Cost-based:* Funds received are linked to costs incurred by providing special education programs.
- *Cost control:* Conventional accounting procedures are followed and procedures are included to contain excessive or inappropriate costs.
- *Placement neutral:* District funding is not linked to where services are received, nor based on type of educational placement, nor disability category.
- *Outcome accountability:* State monitoring of local districts based on a variety of student outcome measures, a statewide system to demonstrate satisfactory progress, schools showing positive results given program and fiscal latitude to continue producing favorable results.
- *Connection to regular education funding:* Formula should have a clear conceptual link to the regular education system.
- *Political acceptability:* Implementation avoids any major short-term loss of funds or major disruption of existing services. (pp. 15–16)

It is important for school and special education leaders to be "up to speed" on these concepts so that they can participate effectively in policy discussions. Lacking such knowledge relegates the school leaders to the sidelines where they inevitably await passively for others to set the change agenda. Being in such a position is not in the best interests of the school leaders' clients—the children and their families. As such, this is a clear opportunity for understanding the role and responsibility of school leaders: They need to know the funding mechanisms of their state and district and they have to be active in its evolvement toward improvement. The school and special education leaders have more important roles than the lawyers and accountants in finance reform. The futures of school children across the country depend on their school and special education leaders' leadership talents being applied to the discussions for improvement.

Understanding Costs

Although "the IEP is to be established without regard to cost or present availability of services in the school district" (Bartlett, Weisenstein, & Etscheidt, 2007), school leaders need to understand the costs involved in the provision of special education services. Bartlett and colleagues (2007) point out that costs are influenced by the following factors:

- Type of disability
- Placement options selected
- Behavioral supports
- Adaptation of instructional program
- Medical supports
- Outsourcing of services
- Factors identified in the IEP

The rationale for school leaders to understand the costs involved with special education is anchored in the realities of scarce resources. Every dollar spent on one child cannot be spent on another, so the administrator must be careful not to overspend on one at the risk of underserving another. School leaders must have this knowledge to:

- Aid in planning and evaluation;
- Determine levels of financing to provide services;
- Avoid inappropriate student classification and placement;
- Monitor activities effectively;
- Participate as partners; and
- Obtain access to funds for innovation program development, special projects, teacher in-service training or other activities to improve the education of students with disabilities. (Bartlett et al., 2007)

In order to fulfill their roles and responsibilities, school leaders need to understand costs and must use that knowledge to inform their decision-making, problem-solving, and overall leadership activities. The prime application of this knowledge is the leaders' involvement in individual students' IEPs, but it should also guide the leaders' points of view throughout the day. Bartlett and colleagues (2007) point out that a "building principal with a solid understanding of special education finances often can (1) locate additional resources, (2) use existing resources more efficiently, (3) implement better planning, and (4) provide higher quality of services to students." There is a range of possible student disabilities across any school population, and the matching services vary in program costs. Distributing resources across the range of possibilities is often aided by a weighting formula that places program costs on a continuum. Brimley and Garfield (2008, p. 115) give an example of a theoretical structure for special education students:

Communicative disorder	1.1
Visually impaired	1.6
Other health impaired	1.8
Intellectually disabled	2.4
Learning disabled	2.4
Severely intellectually disabled	2.6
Hearing impaired, hard of hearing	2.7

Hard of hearing, deaf	2.9
Behavior disordered	2.9
Orthopedically disabled	2.9
Multiple disabilities	3.4

Weighted classification systems attempt to assign different dollar amounts to different special education conditions reflective of the relative costs associated with providing the necessary educations services for that particular learning challenge, special needs category, or disability. Frequently, there is a state distribution formula for funding students in the various categories.

Student placement decisions also carry with them cost differentials. Although the concept of least restrictive environment governs placement decisions, there are significant program cost implications across the continuum of possibilities, ranging from mainstreaming with regular education students to self-contained classes to partial-day attendance at center programs to residential out-of-district placements.

One can imagine the economies of scale that are involved with low incidence of a disability and a given district providing appropriate services. Intermediate school-district structures can assist in these cases, as can districts entering into cooperative agreements with neighboring school districts to pool resources. Picus and Miller (1995) raise questions about trade-offs involved in decisions made regarding the keeping of students in-district or sending them to center programs.

The salient point here is that the IEP decision carries with it budgetary implications in each and every individual case and, when taken together, the complete set of annual IEP decisions has major budget implications. School and special education leaders need to ensure the appropriateness of each and every IEP decision and should be guided by that which is in the best interests of the students involved. When the school leader is participating in making IEP decisions, it is always good to step back and ask the question, Who is my client in this situation? Such reflection increases the chances of students being well-served in the process (Arundel, 2009).

Reimbursement Procedures

Intergovernmental grants are often based on the concept of reimbursing the lower unit for the costs of providing the services *in the previous year*. Thus, the accuracy of record keeping, data generation/maintaining/retrieval, and information management protocols are crucial functions that need to be conceptualized, consistently implemented, and monitored very carefully by the school leader. Such data may be housed in several departments (Human Resources, Pupil Personnel, Guidance, Exceptional Services) and may be accessed by several staff categories (classroom teachers, special education teachers, special area teachers, school counselors, school social workers, school psychologists, administrators). Given the privacy requirements for all concerned, the necessary usage of the data must be governed by explicit, written, and published guidelines that will accomplish both cooperation among departments and privacy protection for students.

A fundamental tenet in special education financing is the concept of *excess costs*. Because public education in the United States is to be provided by the state, *free* for *all* children, reimbursement for mandated programs like special education is targeted at the costs that are incurred by these identified students that are above and beyond their regular educational costs. Bateman and colleagues (2007) declare that the intent of IDEA is to provide supplemental funding to the local school districts to assist in covering the costs of special education services. Thus, the federal funding was designed to be helpful but not complete. Goor (1995) points out that although federal funds are capped at a 40 percent level, they have never exceeded about 12 percent of program cost. As the funds go to the 50 states, 75 percent is earmarked for local educational agencies (LEAs). The state departments of public instruction (DPIs) are permitted to keep 5 percent for their administration of programming and are to use the remaining 20 percent for solving LEA problems, incentives, evaluation, and grants. Districts are required to ensure that IDEA funds are not used to supplant state and local funds. Accordingly, the maintenance of effort provision is included to assure that LEAs continue to provide at least the same level of support as they have done in prior years (Bateman, 2007). Although local districts have little direct impact on how much federal funding they receive, their focus is to know the rules for using federal funds in order to use them effectively to support programs and to protect local taxpayers' contributions to special education funding.

An important part of the regulatory compliance centers on a new glossary of terms with which the school leader must become conversant. Terms *such as supplanting and supplementing, excess costs, maintenance of effort, co-mingling of funds,* and *equitable participation* are examples of words that have specific connotations within each state's legislation and auditing procedures. The vocabulary must be understood and interpretations can be clarified through consultation with the department of public instruction, the intermediate school district, or the school attorney.

BUDGET PROCEDURES

Bartlett and colleagues (2007) identify five steps in the special education budgeting process:

1. *Identify educational needs.* This includes determining the classification of the disability.
2. *Analyze the service delivery options.* Consider staffing, grouping, placement possibilities, and instructional strategies.
3. *Explore funding sources.* Included all three funding levels and additional specialized sources such as local foundations, agencies, and so on.
4. *Match appropriate sources to cost items.* Be mindful of documentation compliance requirements.
5. *Prepare and submit budget requests.* These should iinclude department to school, school to district, district to state, and so on.

Keeping track of all of the funds is normally the responsibility of someone in the business office, but other school and special education leaders might want to create simple structures that enable them to "ballpark" these concepts so that they can be conversant in discussions. It might look something like Table 13.1.

TABLE 13.1 XYZ District Special Education Budget Form: John Doe Public Schools					
	Administration	Instruction (Personnel)	Instructional Support	Transportation	Total
Federal Sources					
State Sources					
Local Sources					
Other Sources					
Total					

School leaders need to be aware of their district's integrated budget-building calendar, which may call for the start of activities as early as late fall semester for the next school year. Master scheduling information is usually needed early and includes such items as classes offered, student and staff counts, and facility availabilities. The curriculum revision calendar may need program evaluation and program innovation data. Transportation supervisors begin the construction of their bus routes and vehicle specification requirements and will need pertinent data concerning student school assignment, pick-up/drop-off locations, and ridership safety requirements. Finally, the school calendars of any other placement sites for students need to be gathered and shared with all appropriate persons including parents and transportation officials.

COMPLIANCE DOCUMENTATION

The best time to become familiar with compliance documentation regulations is at the *start* of the process, not at the *end*. The adage "Being forewarned is being forearmed" holds true here. Compliance with special education finance regulations requires the management of information from several sources, including teachers, parents, bus drivers, administrators, and business office personnel. School leaders need to know what data are needed to be assembled and then must devise a plan to ensure its collection and analyses. Although these discrete tasks will be done by others, their involvement must be choreographed by someone and monitored for timeliness, accuracy, and completeness. Noncompliance will be very costly both in time and treasure and should be avoided at all costs.

Compliance procedures are specific to individual states and to districts within states and by governance level—federal, state, and local. Compliance procedures usually are tied to funding sources, which may be multiple and may not be well-coordinated with one another. For instance, reimbursement for transportation expenditures may span all student placement categories and may be calibrated to miles driven rather than number of students carried. Also, compliance procedures are ever-changing across these levels so the school leader has a formidable task to keep current in these important matters. Other legal concerns are listed in Box 13.4.

BOX 13.4

Legal Issues

Verstegen (1998) points out that courts have been involved in special education matters for a considerable time, including early cases like *PARC* v. *Commonwealth* in 1971, wherein the exclusion of mentally challenged children from public schools was struck down as unconstitutional, and *Mills* v. *Board of Education of Washington D.C.* in 1972 that extended coverage to all children with disabilities. "These two cases opened the door to the provision of a free and appropriate education for children with disabilities—a right enshrined into law and federal statute under IDEA" (p. 277). Themes under consideration by the courts seemed to have come in three waves of litigation. The first, between 1960 and 1972, argued that school finance disparities constituted a violation of the Fourteenth Amendment's equal protection clause. The second, between 1972 and 1988, focused on equity guarantee language in specific state constitutions, state education articles, or both. The third wave, beginning in 1989, centered not on equity but rather on adequacy of programs and services.

State Supreme Court decisions in Alabama, Wyoming, and Ohio raised important matters concerning the intersection of student rights, state school finance systems, and the provision of special education programs and services (Verstegen, 1998). The formulas that were used to distribute educational dollars were scrutinized and found to be arbitrary and irrational and not connected to student program needs or educational costs. Education was held as a fundamental right requiring the application of judicial strict scrutiny standards. Definitions were developed to describe program adequacy and the state was identified as the entity responsible for ensuring the coverage of excess cost of educating students with disabilities. These rulings portend broad parameters for future school finance systems:

1. Must be cost-based as determined through research—legitimate and justifiable.
2. Real costs of providing special education programs must be supported by the state either through full-state funding or shared with local districts (if shared, must be equitable across the state and consideration given to local ability to pay).
3. Provision of special education and related services must be uniform across the state regardless of whether the child resides in more or less affluent areas.
4. Facilities must be safe, healthy, and accessible to all children and these costs are a state and not a local responsibility. (Verstegen, 1998, pp. 307–308)

These cases make a strong argument that general case law related to school finance systems can be applied successfully to special education finance systems. The point of intervention is at each of the 50 states with their own unique set of constitutions and school finance systems and will be played out accordingly (and possibly repeated) over time. School leaders need to learn their state's set of circumstances and keep up to date with legislative and judicial action that impacts their operations. This can be done most efficiently through active membership in state professional associations.

Jordan, Weiner, and Jordan (1997) observe that school leaders are pressed for results while at the same time they are constrained by systems that change at different, uncoordinated rates. As school districts change delivery systems, changes in local district budgeting and cost accounting systems will be required to provide special education expenditure data. Thus, state funding approaches will need to accommodate these new instructional arrangements. The political crosswinds of reform measures come from many directions, and school leaders will need to be able to sort out implications for their respective districts. Jordan and colleagues (1997, pp. 67–68) offer the following propositions after reviewing the environment:

1. Referrals and regulations, not state funding levels, are the primary determinants for the number or percentage of students identified and serviced in special education;
2. If special education is underfunded, programs and services still must be provided and the result is that funds are taken from general education;
3. Free market theories of incentives and disincentives may not be relevant;
4. The effect of moving to population-based funding will be increased pressure to curtail programs and services in general education to cover agreed upon IEP decisions;
5. Strange bedfellows emerge among constituency groups; and,
6. Pressure for reform in special education funding systems suggest need for a new paradigm in system financing that is less manipulable by local districts, less dependent on traditional classification and program delivery systems, more flexible in permissive delivery systems, more supportive of placing students in general education classrooms, and more responsive to identifiable differences in the student population and district socio-demographic conditions.

Again, the degree to which these national trends show up in the local school leader's backyard will vary, but the administrator needs to be aware of them and needs to be cognizant of how other colleagues are dealing with them.

Summary

The provision of special education services involves huge sums of dollars. Attached to these funds are complicated and ever-changing regulations demanding compliance with standards as disparate as pedagogy and accounting. With everything else going on in a school district, special education might be nudged to the periphery. Administrators who tend to wear blinders and hope for the best do so at their own peril. Things can go wrong quickly with dire consequences from civil rights disputes to missed instructional opportunities. The old saying about doing it right the first time holds true in many instances of special education financing. This chapter has stressed the importance of individual professionals owning their responsibilities in the provision of special education services, while, at the same time, acting in concert with others under the leadership of informed, involved, and connected leaders. At the end of the day as the dust settles, it is imperative that school leaders have acted in ways that have advanced the chances of student success. The resolution to the vignette is given in Box 13.5.

Chapter Questions

1. How can school leaders keep up with ever-changing regulations and compliance procedures of financing special education?
2. Based on trends in general education, what policy changes can be expected in special education?
3. List the roles and responsibilities of the participating members of an IEP team. How can communication, cooperation, and consensus-building be fostered across the team and whose responsibility is this?
4. How can school leaders tap into potential local resources to enhance support for provision of special education services?
5. List resources, other than dollars, that can be used to support programs for children.
6. Positional leadership authority resides in the district superintendent, the district special education administrator, and the building principals. How can these three people work together in an interdependent, synergistic fashion that provides focused and consistent leadership toward goal attainment and excellence? Conversely, what pitfalls do they need to avoid bumping into each other and stepping on one another's toes?
7. Chart out how you will determine program success. How will this be communicated to stakeholders both inside and outside the school system? Be explicit with tasks, timelines, and named persons of responsibility.

BOX 13.5

Resolution to Vignette

The final resolutions reached at Jessica's IEP resembled a patch-quilt design of nuanced decisions reached after intense and, at times, heated discussion. The principal felt satisfied that, on balance, Jessica will be well-served by the committee's work. Every member of the IEP had a chance to express her or his concerns and hear the concerns of others. Not everyone attained what they specifically wanted, but the principal was pleased with its transparency, procedural compliance, and professional tone.

By reversing the bus route on the afternoon return trip, Jessica will spend 15 less minutes each day on the bus. Jessica's classroom assignment still leaves one more student slot on the classroom teacher's roll. By changing the time for reading support, the assistant principal was able to get Jessica into the same physical education and art classes as Carla and Yvonne. All the forms accompanying the meeting were in order and the necessary signatures were secured. The timeline for future meetings was reviewed.

CHAPTER 14

School Transportation

David M. Dunaway

INTRODUCTION

For any school leader, transportation issues raise difficult questions. How does the school maintain its behavioral expectations on a moving vehicle with dozens of students from multiple grades facing the back of the driver's head? How do school leaders handle altercations that might occur between students if the students are from different schools (often found in smaller districts)? When should a bus driver stop the bus to deal with a problem student? What if that student is served by an IEP? Do bus drivers have the authority or the knowledge to adequately deal with misbehavior on the bus? What are the ethical issues if a school leader suspends a student from the bus and that student has no other means of getting to school? Does school authority extend to issues at the bus stop? In difficult economic times, how do district leaders balance financial transportation surrounding special transportation issues involving extracurricular activities, co-curricular activities, after-school academic programs, and needs of special student populations?

According to the U.S. Department of Education, National Center for Education Statistics (2010), for the school year 2007–08 (the most recent data), 54.6 percent of all public students were transported at public expense for an average expense of $866 per student, or $21,836,398 nationwide expressed in constant 2008–09 dollars. Although the most recent figures are not available, it is reasonable to assume that the costs of transportation have increased far beyond the $866 per student given the current level of fuel costs. It should be noted that these figures do not include capital outlay costs of purchasing buses.

As school districts face economic hard times, there are few places where significant cuts can be made to balance a budget. Forsyth (2005) said that transportation costs, which make up 4 to 5 percent of the typical school district must be controlled. He wrote:

> With severe budget cuts, stringent demands for busing students with disabilities, and increasing service requirements for nontraditional modes of student transportation, it has become increasingly important to monitor and control student transportation costs. Student transportation is an important and complex school-support activity. . . . Administrators need a new methodology for measuring the performance of transportation

operations so they can better manage expenditures and maximize the ever-shrinking pool of federal, state and local dollars. (p. 1)

This chapter focuses on school and district leaders' responsibilities in the arena of transportation of students with disabilities. Special emphasis is placed on fulfilling both the letter and the spirit of the statutes and the regulations that flow from them.

Transportation challenges vary according to the level and responsibility of school leaders and the size of the school district (see Box 14.1). The school principal's challenges are often found in dealing with the day-to-day issues related to transportation, whereas the district leader looks more at districtwide policy level issues and transportation costs.

At the School Level

At the school level, the issues of school transportation focus on the following:

- Assignment of students to the proper bus to get them to and from home
- Student misbehavior while waiting for the bus at school or at the bus stop
- Misbehavior that occurs on the bus while it is moving
- Problems that fester on the bus and boil over at school or the bus stop
- Arranging buses for extracurricular activities
- Evaluating the performance of bus drivers
- Making recommendations for transportation of students with special needs

In the larger districts, all of these responsibilities may fall to the principal, as a fleet of buses may be assigned to a particular school as the cost/accountability center for that group of buses. In smaller districts, the district office may handle everything but student discipline.

BOX 14.1

Challenges and Issues for School and Special Education Leaders

- How to reduce overall student transportation cost and, at the same time, maintain or increase the cost to transport students with disabilities and special needs.
- How to promote and maintain appropriate student behavior on moving school buses carrying dozens of students of different ages, some of whom may have serious behavior problems
- How to recruit, employ, and educate school bus drivers so they can effectively transport students and resolve issues with students and parents, particularly those students who have disabilities and special needs
- How to resolve problems and issues involving students whose transportation to and from school is provided as a "related service" and is part these students' IEPs
- How to appropriately discipline a child with special needs for misbehavior on school buses or other vehicles when the child has no other means to get to and from school (Suspending these children from the bus is tantamount to suspending them from school.)
- How to balance the effort to provide children with disabilities the right to be transported with students without disabilities with the effort to provide children with specialized transportation or alternative transportation if they need it

At the District Level

For the district special education or general education leader, the issues around student transportation typically include financial, policy, legal, and even political considerations.

- Transportation costs occupy a significant part of school district expenses. Budgeting for transportation must include replacing worn-out buses with capital outlay costs of the buses themselves—typically at more than $75,000 on average.
- According to Forsyth (2005), "Depending on the region, one can expect approximate annual costs of up to $762 per transported student, and $41,000 to $43,000 per active (assigned) bus." Assuming a student population of 4,000 students and 30 buses, a small district would have a transportation budget exceeding $4,000,000.
- Other budgeting issues include bus driver salaries, benefits, and training, and the unpredictable, escalating cost of fuel.
- In some districts, the budgeting consists of placing the district's transportation needs out for bid. In small, rural midwestern districts, it is not unusual for each route to be bid separately.
- Political stresses on the district leadership and the board are produced when transportation is viewed by the public as an entitlement while the school district typically views it as a privilege.
- Of course, students in special education do have an entitlement to transportation when certain criteria are met. (See the vignette in Box 14.2; also see "Transportation Options" later in this chapter.)
- The district leadership must decide how much of the transportation budget is to be allocated to after-school programs including (1) remediation/tutoring; (2) extracurricular and co-curricular events (sports, band, or club trips); (3) transportation home from extra or co-curricular practices; and (4) transportation for after-school discipline such as daily detention or Saturday school.
- Providing funds for field trips can be a political issue for teachers, parents, and leaders.

Many of the issues raised in the preceding lists seem simple enough. Either a district has the funds to provide the services or they don't, and perhaps this is the mindset often at the district level. But take these same issues to the school and classroom level, and the picture becomes considerably murkier. For instance, many students from low-income families simply cannot participate in after-school programs if the district does not provide transportation. Participating in after-school tutoring may make the difference of passing or failing accountability testing. Participating in band, sports, or clubs is often the single factor that keeps students coming to school (Mahoney & Cairns, 1997; Special Education Report, 2009). Participation has beneficial effects in a number of other areas as well, including school grades, subjects selected, homework, educational and occupational ambitions, self-esteem, freedom from substance abuse, number of university applications, subsequent college enrollment, and highest educational level, and participation has stronger benefits for special populations (Kleitman & Marsh, 2002). For low-income students, field trips are not merely nice opportunities to get away from the school for the day; rather, they provide essential experiences that connect classroom learning to real-world experiences. When youngsters with disabilities participate in these events, the water becomes downright muddy for central office decision-makers.

Although the district directors of special education may be removed from the final decision on the transportation and related issues, they offer important input in the budget and

BOX 14.2

Vignette: *"Making Things Work"*

Adam Rowedder, 14 years old, suffers from cerebral palsy caused at birth. Adam does not fall into any easily definable disability. He is visually impaired but can see well enough to read large print. He is physically impaired and uses a wheelchair, but can walk short, flat distances with crutches, although his balance is not good at all. Socially, Adam performs significantly below his age peers.

Adam is now a seventh-grader and is a member of the middle school band; he plays the triangle and tambourine. Quickly approaching is an annual one-day fall band trip to perform at Six Flags. The band will be traveling on two large school system school buses. Unfortunately, neither is equipped for children with disabilities. James Thompson, the band director, has given a heads-up to Adam's parents about the issue with the buses.

Because Adam is the only child with physical disabilities in the small district, the district has not purchased a handicapped-equipped bus with a lift and wheelchair restraints. This has not been an issue to this point with Larry and Nancy, who both work in the school system and have transported Adam to and from school each day.

However, they view this middle school band trip to Six Flags differently (remember, Adam is a playing member). They requested that special accommodations consistent with Adam's IEP be granted. Specifically, they requested that a large capacity bus with a lift ramp and wheelchair restraints be provided for the Six Flags trip. The Rowedders' logic was simple: The school system should provide a bus in order to facilitate Adam's IEP goals.

The superintendent and special education director have proposed the rental of a disability accessible van to be driven by a district employee to transport Adam and his parents. Larry and Nancy, citing Adam's IEP, argued that the van would cause Adam to be viewed not as a typical band member, but to be singled out. Since building Adam's social skills with his peers was a specific IEP goal, the Rowedders disagreed with the use of the van. Additionally, a second IEP goal was that Adam function in the school environment as much as a nondisabled student as possible. The van, contended the Rowedders, would not meet the definition of a school environment, since the only people on the van would be Adam, his parents, and the driver.

Being longtime proponents of following established procedures, Adam's mom and dad decided to invoke their rights as parents to call for a special IEP conference to consider whether or not the superintendent's proposal of the handicapped accessible van was outside the expectations of Adam's IEP.

As you read through the chapter, think of these questions:

1. What are the legal requirements regarding transportation for special education students in general?
2. Do the legal requirements change for extracurricular and/or co-curricular events in which a student with disabilities may participate?
3. As a school leader, how can you meet the letter of the law while meeting the ethics/spirit of the law? Which tends to take precedence for school leaders? For parents? Why?
4. If you were a school leader, how would you approach Adam's IEP conference? Would you lead or defer to the director of special education, or the chair of your school's special education department? Defend your choice.
5. What is the superintendent's role?
6. What role should the director of transportation play, if any?

FIGURE 14.1   Transportation Challenges and Issues for School Leaders

- What the principal's role is in the day-to-day student issues, which typically include assignment to buses as well as misbehavior

- The responsibility of evaluating the drivers

- For the district level leader, the issues around student transportation typically include broader issues of financial, policy, legal, and politics

- Transportation costs of school district expenses

- Political stresses on leaders and the board when transportation is viewed by the public as an entitlement

- The transportation budget includes transportation to and from school as well as transportation for after-school programs, including: (1) remediation or tutoring, (2) extracurricular and co-curricular events (sports, band, or club trips), (3) transportation home from extra or co-curricular practices, and (5) transportation for after-school discipline such as daily detention or Saturday school

decision-making processes. The special education director is often the conduit that connects the child, the parents, and school personnel to the central office decision-makers (Education Daily, 2008; Lashley & Boscardin, 2003). In making recommendations for special transportation needs, district special education directors must balance, at least conceptually, the needs of the child, the state and federal statutes and policy requirements and issues, the district and community expectations and constraints, and the school-level needs and expectations (see Figure 14.1).

To parents, transportation seems to require little, if any, discussion—just get the kids to school and to school events. And, more times than not, it *is* just that simple. In the vignette, had Adam Rowedder been disabled but not wheelchair-bound, there would not have been any issue at all. As we will see in the discussion that follows, the goal of the Individuals with Disabilities Education Act (IDEA, 2004) and the acts that preceded it have been to include youngsters with disabilities in the everyday routines of the school. Only when that is not possible (as in the vignette) must more specific expectations take center stage. Although the profession must be careful to follow regulations, it must be equally vigilant in meeting the moral and ethical purposes found in the statutes and regulations.

LEGAL REQUIREMENTS FOR TRANSPORTATION

All discussions of legal requirements regarding special education begin with IDEA (2004). Transportation requirements are found in IDEA Regulations under "Related Services." According to the office of Assistance to States for the Education of Children with Disabilities (2004), *related services* means *transportation* and other services that are *required to assist a child with a disability to benefit from special education.* This includes:

- Speech-language and audiology services
- Interpreters for the deaf
- Psychological, physical, and occupational therapy
- *Recreation*, including therapeutic recreation
- Early identification and assessment of disabilities
- Counseling, including rehabilitation counseling
- Orientation and mobility services

FIGURE 14.2 Legal Requirements for Transportation

- The goal of IDEA 2004 and the acts that preceded it have been to include youngsters with disabilities in the everyday routines of the school.
- "Related services" means transportation and other services that are required to assist a child with a disability to benefit from special education.
- Transportation is travel to and from school; between schools; in and around school buildings; and specialized equipment if required to provide special transportation.
- School leaders have both ethical and legal obligations in the area of transportation.

FIGURE 14.3 Transportation and the IEP

- Leaders at district and school levels must be knowledgeable of the expectations of IDEA and transportation as a related service in the IEP.
- Transportation services in the IEP include services that allow the child to be involved in and to participate in extracurricular and other nonacademic activities.
- IEP goals are written for a related service just as they are for other special education services. They must specify when the service will begin, how often it will be provided and for what amount of time, and where it will be provided.
- Transportation directors may be members of the IEP team if requested by the school or the parent.

- Medical services for diagnostic or evaluation purposes, and school health and school nursing services
- Social work in schools, and parent counseling and training

Regulations specifically define transportation as the following (*emphasis added*):

- Travel *to and from school* and *between schools;*
- Travel *in and around school buildings;* and
- Specialized equipment (such as *special or adapted buses, lifts, and ramps*), if required *to provide special transportation* for a child with a disability (see Figure 14.2).

School and special education leaders have both ethical and legal obligations. The spirit of the regulations for related services clearly expects schools and districts to provide those nonacademic services that allow the child to most reasonably receive the most benefit from school attendance. The legal obligations to provide the services are spelled out in the regulations and/or in a child's individualized education program (IEP) (see Figure 14.3).

TRANSPORTATION AND THE INDIVIDUALIZED EDUCATION PROGRAM

School and special education leaders at both district and school levels must be knowledgeable of the expectations of IDEA (2004) regulations related to the requirements of transportation as a related service in the IEP. Specifically, the law requires a statement of the related services to be provided to each child as part of the IEP so that each student may reach IEP goals. Clearly, the spirit of the regulation is to provide those supplementary services that allow the student the greatest opportunities to be a member of the general school population. Toward this goal, as related to transportation, the regulation specifically requires that the statement include services that will allow the child to be involved in and to participate in extracurricular and other nonacademic activities (Assistance to States for the Education of Children with Disabilities, 2004).

The following recommendation is made by National Dissemination Center for Children with Disabilities (2009):

> It is the IEP team's responsibility to review all of the evaluation information, to identify any related services the child needs, and to include them in the IEP. Goals are written for a related service just as they are for other special education services. The IEP must also specify with respect to each service:
>
> - *When* the service will begin;
> - *How often* it will be provided and for *what amount of time*; and
> - *Where* it will be provided.

The law neither requires nor forbids the inclusion of related services providers such as transportation directors on the IEP team, but IDEA (2004) does provide that either the parent or the school may request that they be a part of the IEP team (National Dissemination Center for Children with Disabilities, 2009). Wise leaders purposefully include people with more expertise than their own in the make-up of decision-making teams.

TRANSPORTATION AND THE LEAST RESTRICTIVE ENVIRONMENT

Consistent with the IEP expectations, the law spells out expectations or the extent to which a child will participate with children without disabilities. Regulations require an explanation of the level at which students with disabilities will participate in academic and extracurricular activities. For school leaders, the spirit of the law is particularly strong here. The expectation is that youngsters with disabilities are treated as typical students without disabilities and that services and placements be individually established based on each child's individual abilities and needs to reasonably provide for the child's educational success academically and nonacademically (Assistance to States for the Education of Children with Disabilities, 2004).

For the school leader looking at transportation options, this means that students with disabilities should be transported with students without disabilities to every reasonable extent. As described in the vignette earlier in this chapter, transportation also is an issue of participation in extracurricular activities. Toward this end, the regulation requires: "In providing or arranging for *the provision of nonacademic and extracurricular services and activities (emphasis added),* including meals, recess periods, and the services and activities set forth in §300.306, each public agency shall ensure that each child with a disability participates with children without disabilities in those services and activities to the maximum extent appropriate to the needs of that child" (see Figure 14.4).

TRANSPORTATION OPTIONS

What options, then, do leaders have when transporting children with special needs with rights protected by IDEA? Generally, according to Bluth (2009), there are three questions to ask to determine if a district is required to provide transportation to students with disabilities:

- Does the student require transportation to access special education and related services?
- If yes, can the student utilize the same transportation services as students without a disability, or does the student require specialized services?

FIGURE 14.4 Transportation and the LRE

- Regulations require an explanation of the level at which students with disabilities will participate in academic and extracurricular activities.

- Youngsters with disabilities are to be treated as typical students, without disabilities, and services and placements are to be individually established based on each child's abilities and needs.

- Students with disabilities should be transported with students without disabilities to every reasonable extent.

- Participation in extracurricular activities with peers without disabilities is expected, and transportation must be provided if spelled out in the IEP.

FIGURE 14.5 Transportation Options

- Does the student require transportation to access special education and related services?

- Can the student use the same transportation services as students without a disability?

- Can the services be provided on the "regular" school bus with appropriate supplementary aids, or does the student a specially adapted bus?

- Transportation must be provided to students enrolled in private schools, if needed for the child to benefit from special education services provided to the child by the district.

- Districts are not required to provide transportation from the child's home to the private school.

- If a student requires specialized services (accommodations), can the services be provided on the same bus as children without disabilities with appropriate supplementary aids, or services, or does the child require these services on a separate bus with specialized equipment and trained personnel? (p. 14). Copyright © 2000 National Association for Pupil Transportation (NAPT). Reprinted with permission.

If necessary, transportation must be provided to students enrolled in private schools, if needed for the child to benefit from or participate in the services provided to the child by the district. The Individuals with Disabilities Education Act states that transportation must be provided "from the child's school or the child's home to a site other than the private school; and from the service site to the private school, or to the child's home, depending on the timing of the services." However, districts are not required to provide transportation from the child's home to the private school (Assistance to States for the Education of Children with Disabilities, 2004) (see Figure 14.5).

VEHICLE ACCESSIBILITY AND SPECIAL EQUIPMENT

It is probably the fully accessible, specialized van or small school bus that comes to mind when one first thinks of vehicle accessibility for youngsters with disabilities. And, as noted earlier, if this is what is required for the child to receive the fullest benefit of educational services, then the district must provide this level of service. The law requires "specialized equipment (such as special or adapted buses, lifts, and ramps), if required to provide special transportation for a child with a disability" (IDEA, 2004). However, according to the National Dissemination Center for Children with Disabilities (2009), this section isn't simply referring to a separate bus that only children with disabilities ride to school. Citing the Federal Register (71 Fed. Reg., 2006):

The Department of Education states, "It is assumed that most children with disabilities will receive the same transportation provided to nondisabled children" (*Id.*), in keeping

FIGURE 14.6   Vehicle Accessibility and Special Equipment

- Specialized equipment (special or adapted buses, lifts, and ramps) must be provided if required to provide transportation for a child with a disability to receive school services.

- Most children with disabilities can receive the same transportation provided to children without disabilities.

- Transportation may also mean providing modifications and support so that a student may ride the "regular" school bus.

- School and district officials must work diligently to provide a special education experience for youngsters with disabilities as close as possible to that of their peers without disabilities.

- Leaders must resist moving in two counterproductive directions: (1) doing nothing and (2) the quick fix of overproviding transportation equipment such as special or adapted buses.

with LRE requirements. Thus, transportation as a related service may also mean providing modifications and supports so that a child may ride the regular school bus transporting children without disabilities" (p. 46576).

The spirit of IDEA is again evident here. School and district officials must work diligently to provide a special education experience for youngsters with disabilities as close as possible to that of their peers without disabilities (see Figure 14.6). Leaders must resist moving in two counterproductive directions. First is the non-option of doing nothing to accommodate a youngster with disabilities, citing funding as a primary reason to resist purchasing special equipment or services. Clearly financial uncertainty diminishes proactivity. "Let's do nothing and see who complains" is not an uncommon thought, if not a publicly expressed one, and according to Birnbaum (2006), serving students with disabilities requires a proactive leadership perspective. Second, leaders must resist the quick fix of overproviding transportation equipment such as special or adapted buses when a far simpler choice may meet the needs.

Consider the elementary child with disabilities in a wheelchair whose regular education teacher is located upstairs in an older building without an elevator. Moving the child from one part of the building to another clearly falls under related services and would be part of the IEP (Assistance to States for the Education of Children with Disabilities, 2004). The district might opt for a chair lift or even a stair climber, but a far simpler and no-cost solution could be found in simply relocating the teacher's class to the first floor—a solution that also serves to keep the child functioning in a fashion much closer to that of the students without disabilities, thus meeting the spirit and the letter of the law.

TRANSPORTATION CHALLENGES AND POTENTIAL PROBLEMS

Transportation, whether of students with or without disabilities, will always present challenges to educational leaders. Those challenges typically fall into three categories: (1) financial considerations, (2) personnel considerations, (3) student considerations. Financial considerations have been discussed in greater detail in an earlier chapter, and personnel considerations will be discussed in the next section. So then, what are the challenges and potential problems related to transporting students with disabilities (see Figure 14.7)?

The first challenge is to compare student transportation needs to current transportation resources. If the district is small, the number of students with disabilities requiring special accommodations will also be small. The district may not currently have equipment on hand

FIGURE 14.7 Transportation Challenges and Potential Problems

- Comparing student transportation needs to current transportation resources
- Determining how much specialization is needed to meet the student's needs
- Managing the student's needs and behavior while being transported
- Meeting the other IDEA-related service of moving the child from one part of the building to another

to meet student needs, and it may be constrained by a small pool of resources from which to purchase needed equipment. In the larger district, the resources are likely to be on hand, but the number of students needing the specialized equipment may be widely dispersed throughout the district. Neither of these challenges removes the district from its obligations under IDEA.

The second challenge is how much specialization is needed to meet the student's needs. As discussed in the previous section, not only is there a statutory expectation that leaders must meet but there is an ethical one as well. The scenario at the beginning of this chapter paints a picture of this quandary: *School leaders can fail to meet the intent of the law by actually meeting the letter of the law*. The key to the challenge of how much specialization to provide begins and ends with the IEP. It is easily forgotten by both teachers and leaders that when the acronym *IEP* is used so frequently, that the heart of the process is *individualization using the least restrictive means possible*. In meeting this related services challenge, leaders, teachers, and parents would do well to emulate the response to intervention model which starts broadly and only ends up with specialized services when broader approaches have been documented as ineffective (Elliot, 2008).

The third challenge is managing students' needs and behavior while being transported. When the needs are very specialized, procedures for managing those needs are also specialized. It is when the student with a disability is provided transportation services with the general population that the most challenges arise. Issues may take the form of misbehavior by students with disabilities, or they may take the form of behavior of students without disabilities toward persons with disabilities. Both situations are fraught with complications. How can a bus driver best deal with the issues presented? Where do the rights of the persons with disabilities end and the rights of persons without disabilities begin if the misbehavior of students with disabilities is directed at students without disabilities? This is ultimately a personnel issue of the knowledge of intervention skills of the bus driver. You will find more on this topic in the next section.

Not all bus misbehavior issues can be anticipated, but school leaders can prevent many by taking a proactive approach. Agreeing on transportation options by the IEP team is the start, not the end, of the process for school leaders. The proactive leader will take steps to determine if the bus driver has the knowledge and skills to intervene successfully when misbehavior occurs on the bus or will procure the appropriate training for the driver. The final student issue does not involve transportation to school but meeting the other IDEA-related service of moving the child from one part of the building to another (Assistance to States for the Education of Children with Disabilities, 2004).

For the nonambulatory students with disabilities, barriers between areas of a building or campus may provide insurmountable obstacles. Steps are obvious barriers, but other not so obvious barriers include narrow doorways; doors with hardware that makes it difficult for the student to open the door and enter; lack of space to maneuver a wheelchair in confined spaces such as restroom stalls; lavatories or water fountains that are too high; and the arrangement of desks in classrooms or tables in the cafeteria. School and special education leaders must learn to view their buildings with an eye to accessibility for all students. Although some things like narrow doorways might require special solutions, most of the needed accommodations noted here can be accomplished at little or no cost.

SELECTION AND QUALIFICATIONS OF TRANSPORTATION PERSONNEL

In most situations, the selection of transportation personnel is a decision reserved for the superintendent in smaller districts or for the transportation director in larger districts. In a district where the bus contract is bid, the hiring of drivers is a function of the contractor, not the school district. In this situation, typically the district can set the qualifications, but the contractor does the actual hiring. Supervision and evaluation is likely to be a jointly shared responsibility of the school district and contractor.

What makes a good bus driver? A record of safe driving is often required before anyone is considered for the position of school bus driver. Drivers must be persons who understand the nature of the "cargo" they carry and who can drive safely and carefully in all weather and road conditions. Because bus drivers are communicating frequently with both students and parents, being good communicators ranks high on the list of skills needed to be a successful bus driver. Weishaar and Borsa (2001) wrote, "They must be able to communicate at a level appropriate to each child's level of development and communicative status" (p. 148). Drivers of buses that transport children with special needs often deliver students to the door of the student's home and have many opportunities to talk to parents or guardians. For instance, for wheelchair-bound students, the driver is often the first person to recognize when the chair needs adjustment or repair and can communicate that to the parent. Equally important, according to Weishaar and Borsa (2001), is that if a parent complains about something that happened on the bus, the driver must be able to communicate in a manner that allows clarification of the parents' concerns and to whom the parent may contact if the concern has not been resolved. Just as important, drivers must be able to communicate both in writing and orally to school administrators about behavioral or other issues occurring on the bus.

Drivers of buses of students with disabilities transported with students without disabilities should be well versed in the basics of techniques to encourage appropriate behavior on the bus and to manage misbehavior should it occur. Drivers must also be able to describe in writing to school leaders very specific details of incidents occurring on the bus so that the school personnel can take actions appropriate to the misbehavior and, in the case of youngsters with disabilities, consistent with their IEPs (Weishaar & Borsa, 2001).

Weishaar and Borsa (2001) also describe two other characteristics of good bus drivers: (1) a knowledge of emergency procedures and (2) a working knowledge of how to safely transport children with disabilities. Drivers who have a basic knowledge of emergency procedures may be hired and be trained further in state or district predriving training, but transporting students with disabilities requires a level of training beyond that for drivers transporting students without disabilities (see Figure 14.8).

As noted at the onset of this discussion, safety is every driver's first priority—however, drivers of students with disabilities have a greater obligation or duty than the typical driver. The following 10 recommendations are adapted from the American Academy of Pediatrics policy on bus

FIGURE 14.8 Selection and Qualifications of Transportation Personnel

Potential drivers should:
• Have a record of safe driving in all weather and road conditions.
• Understand the nature of the "cargo" they carry—especially students with disabilties.
• Be well versed in the basics of techniques needed to encourage appropriate behavior on the bus.
• Be able to manage misbehavior if it occurs.
• Be able to describe in writing to school leaders very specific details of incidents occurring on the bus.
• Be knowledgeable of emergency procedures.

transportation for students with special needs developed in 1994, revised in 2001, and reaffirmed in 2008 (School Bus Transportation of Children With Special Health Care Needs, 2008).

1. Children should be moved from a wheelchair or stroller to a forward-facing seat belted system, and the unoccupied chair or stroller should be secured.
2. Passenger seats with a seat belt or child restraint system should have a reinforced frame.
3. Children who weigh less than 50 pounds should be secured using a certified child restraint or safety vest.
4. Child restraints or safety vests should be secured to a school bus seat next to an emergency exit.
5. Children less than 20 pounds or younger than age 1 year should be attached in the rear-facing position.
6. When students must remain in wheelchairs, the wheelchairs should be secured in a forward-facing position.
7. Three-wheeled, cart-type strollers should not be occupied during transport unless secured to the floor.
8. Wheelchairs should be secured to the floor of the school bus. Any wheelchair attachment such as a lapboard or tray should be removed and secured during transport.
9. A restraint system including shoulder harness and lap belt should be provided for each wheelchair-seated rider.
10. Any liquid oxygen must be securely mounted and fastened. Signage indicating that oxygen is in use should be prominently placed on the bus.

TRANSPORTATION AND LEGALITIES

It is interesting to find in the policy- and procedure-heavy environment that is special education, that there are few legal opinions which give specific guidance in the area of transportation. The cases noted immediately below give such guidance. The Third Circuit Court of Appeals in 1984 (and later echoed by the Massachusetts Federal District Court in 1986) ruled that if transportation is indicated as a related service on the IEP, whether a change in transportation would be a change in placement is determined by whether or not the change is likely to affect the student's learning. He wrote, "In this case the [Third Circuit] court found that a minor change in the student's transportation arrangements was not a change in placement but warned that under some circumstances transportation could have an effect on the child's learning" (p. 51).

Two cases in 1997 reached two differing opinions on transportation. The Eleventh Circuit Court of Appeals ruled that a 7-year-old speech-impaired student did not require transportation services between his parochial school and the public school district to benefit from the speech therapy services since the age of the student and the three-block distance between schools meant that the child could easily traverse the distance to receive services (*Donald B. by Christine B. v. Board of School Commissioners of Mobile County*, 1997). The Federal District Court for the Northern District of Illinois ruled that a student required transportation between her parochial school and the public school to access and benefit from her special education program. The court said the 11-year-old child, suffering from attention deficit disorder, was too young to walk the two miles between the two schools and that the route was somewhat dangerous (*Board of Education v. Illinois,* 1997).

Other guidance for school leaders on transportation legal issues may be found in court opinions *not specifically directed at transportation* as an issue. The cases discussed next look at the important cases that tangentially address transportation.

In *Board of Education of Hendrick Hudson v. Rowley* (1982), the U.S. Supreme Court ruled, "We therefore conclude that the 'basic floor of opportunity' provided by the Act consists of access to specialized instruction and related services which are individually designed to provide educational benefit to the handicapped child" (p. 201), thus establishing the legal expectation for related services such as transportation.

In *Florence County School District v. Carter* (1993), the U.S. Supreme Court ruled that parents who unilaterally placed their child (Shannon Carter) in a private school in order to receive appropriate special education services not provided by the public school are eligible for reimbursement. Included in this reimbursement were transportation expenses. The school was some distance away from the student's home, and Carter lived with a family in Charleston, South Carolina, and traveled to attend the school each day. The court ruled that Carter's home district was responsible for these costs as well as the costs incurred in traveling home four times a year and for the costs of tuition and boarding costs to attend the private school. In *KDM v. Reedsport School District* (1999), the Ninth Circuit Court of Appeals ruled that the school district is not required to provide special education services on the site of a religious school. However, as noted earlier, the district would have to provide transportation from the private school if the IEP includes it as a related service.

In *Cedar Rapids Consolidated School District v. Garret F.* (1999), the Court ruled that if the services are related to keeping the child with disabilities in school and able to access educational opportunities available to others, school districts must provide such services. The Court further said that although the cost of the related services is not a determining factor in whether or not to provide the services, the costs can be discussed in coming to a final decision. The Court ruled that the provision of a personal nurse for Garret F., who was wheelchair-bound and dependent on a ventilator, was not excessive. Although the Court did not address transportation in the case, it is reasonable to conclude that the related service of a nurse would extend to providing the nurse during transportation if it were necessary.

Education leaders may want to approach each IEP as a potential lawsuit waiting to happen, but the dearth of case law simply points to the fact that this is not so. Leaders who see lawsuits around the corner of every IEP often immerse themselves in the minutia of administrative regulations in the belief that adhering without deviation to regulations will be their best protection. In fact, focusing on trivial regulations often results in trivial lawsuits. So what is the key? Stay familiar with regulations. Stay abreast of the latest court decisions. And learn the spirit of the law as well as the letter. Other legal concerns are summarized in Box 14.3.

BOX 14.3

Legal Issues

- There are few legal opinions that give specific guidance in the area of transportation.
- The U.S. Supreme Court established the legal expectation for related services.
- Parents who place their child in a private school in order to receive special education services not provided by the public school are eligible for reimbursement.
- The school district is not required to provide services on the site of a religious school.
- If the services are related to keeping the child with disabilities in school and being able to access educational opportunities available to others, districts must provide such services.
- If transportation is on the IEP, a change in transportation would be a change in placement as determined by whether or not the change is likely to affect the student's learning.
- Consider this example: A 7-year-old speech-impaired student did not require transportation services for three blocks between his parochial school and the public school district, however, an 11-year-old, suffering from attention deficit disorder, was too young to walk two miles between the two schools.

ESSENTIALS

Leaders must learn to view processes, proceedings, IEPs, needs, and obstacles relating to transportation from the perspective of parent and child. Parents almost always have little experience in raising a child with disabilities. Like school leaders, they are seeking answers. Understand that parents look to school leaders and teachers as the experts. When school people come across as confrontational or adversarial, parents will look elsewhere for answers. And when they look outside of the school, the results are almost always confrontational instead of collaborative. Remember a simple axiom: Most issues related to transportation or any other special education service can be solved by focusing on the *individual* needs of the child.

School leaders need to take the initiative in working with parents on transportation issues. Little is gained for the school or the district when the principal defers to the district special education director. That being said, school leaders need to build positive relationships with decision-makers at the district level. When transportation is involved, discussions may include the superintendent, director of finance, director of special education, and the director of transportation. All of these parties should be included in a consultative role so that the school leader has a solid working knowledge of both issues and solutions when transportation is discussed as an IEP-related service. Bluth (2009) describes instances where the district transportation director should be involved in an IEP meeting:

1. A child with disabilities rides the same bus as non-disabled peers; however, the child requires on-going assistance because of behavioral problems or requires specialized equipment and assistance from a trained bus attendant.
2. A child with disabilities rides a school bus exclusively with other children with disabilities to and from school, and requires any of the following: specialized equipment, bus attendant or a special behavior management program.
3. Special school bus equipment is required to provide transportation services, and these services are to be addressed on the IEP for the first time.

4. A child with disabilities has severe behavioral problems, impacting safe transportation, and transportation is an integral part of the school-based behavioral management program.
5. A child with disabilities is medically fragile and requires special handling and supervision including specific information from medical personnel.
6. A child with a disability has a technology-dependent condition.
7. A child has an infectious disease that requires precautions beyond typical universal precautions practiced.
8. A student with a disability rides to school with a nurse. (p. 17). Copyright © 2000 National Association for Pupil Transportation (NAPT). Reprinted with permission.

School leaders who forget that the IEP is the controlling document for all special education services in general and transportation specifically do so at their own peril. The IEP's transportation provisions may be modified only by the IEP committee. School leaders should think of the IEP as a legal document rather than as a school document.

School leaders should take a response to intervention approach with transportation. Start broadly (regular bus with children without disabilities) and move to specialized services (specially equipped bus or bus aide, etc.) based on very specific individual needs. Remember that parents want and the law requires that the schools treat youngsters with disabilities as close to "normal" as reasonable.

School and special education leaders should remember that related transportation services do not begin and end with just transporting the child to and from the school. The Individuals with Disabilities Education Act also regulates all school movement and participation in recreation and extracurricular activities when specified in the IEP, and remember that all decisions about whether to transport to an extracurricular activity can only be made by the IEP committee (Bluth, 2009).

Educational leaders working in the special education arena should work diligently and proactively to fulfill the spirit of IDEA which could easily be summarized in a phrase made popular by school reform pioneer, Larry Lezotte: *Learning for All— Whatever It Takes*. Pertinent advice for leaders is summarized in Box 14.4.

BOX 14.4

Advice for School and Special Education Leaders

- Learn to view processes, proceedings, IEPs, needs, and obstacles relating to transportation from the perspective of parent and child.
- Take the initiative in working with parents on transportation issues.
- Never forget that the IEP is the controlling document for all special education services.
- Remember that the IEP's transportation provisions may be modified only by the IEP committee.
- Think of the IEP as a legal document rather than as a school document.
- Take a response to intervention approach with transportation.
- Remember, IDEA also regulates all school movement and participation in recreation and extracurricular activities when specified in the IEP. (Remember the vignette!)
- Stay familiar with regulations. Stay abreast of the latest court decisions. And learn the spirit of the law as well as the letter.

Summary

This chapter has stressed the roles that transportation plays in allowing students with disabilities to fully access educational opportunities. The Individuals with Disabilities Education Act (2004) is clearly a law with precise rules and regulations. Many would say excessively so. But let's not forget that IDEA also has a well-defined spirit and heart. It is about children and their specific needs. It is about schools and leaders and specific expectations aimed at fully and functionally embracing and including youngsters with disabilities of all varying disabilities into the everyday life of every public school. The U.S. Supreme Court eloquently expressed the letter and the spirit of special education in *Board of Education of Hendrick Hudson* v. *Rowley* (1982):

Insofar as a State is required to provide a handicapped child with a "free appropriate public education," we hold that it satisfies this requirement by providing personalized instruction with sufficient support services to permit the child to benefit educationally from that instruction. Such instruction and services must be provided at public expense, must meet the State's educational standards, must approximate the grade levels used in the States regular education, and must comport with the child's IEP. (p. 26)

The resolution of the vignette is provided in Box 14.5.

BOX 14.5

Resolution of the Vignette

With the principal in charge of the meeting, this is good opportunity to involve the director of transportation, the director of special education, and perhaps even the superintendent. Clearly, the district wants to transport Adam to the event, and the van meets expectations of the IEP. The principal might suggest that parents travel separately directly behind the van in their own vehicle with mileage to be reimbursed by the district, which would allow Adam and several other classmates to travel together in the van. Given the option of riding on a school bus or in a van, it should not be difficult to find volunteers!

Chapter Questions

1. How would you describe the spirit of IDEA as it relates to transportation?
2. Educationally and procedurally, when is transportation as a related service required?
3. What should be the role of the principal, director of special education, and transportation director in transportation decisions for students with disabilities?
4. How would you describe the spirit of IDEA as it relates to transportation?
5. Educationally and procedurally, when is transportation as a related service required?
6. Can a district be required to transport students beyond transporting them to and from school? Under what conditions?
7. How can a leader best avoid confrontational issues regarding transportation of students with disabilities?

REFERENCES

Chapter 1

American Association of Research Association. (1999). *Standards for educational and psychological testing.* Washington, DC: American Educational Research Association, American Psychological Association.

Anthun, R., & Manger, T. (2006). Effects of special education teams on school psychology services. *School Psychology International, 27,* 259–280.

Barth, R. S. (1991). *Improving schools from within.* San Francisco: Jossey-Bass.

Bartlett, L. D., Weisenstein, G. R., & Etscheidt, S. (2002). *Successful inclusion for educational leaders.* Upper Saddle River, NJ: Merrill Prentice-Hall.

Bass, B. M. (1985). *Leadership and performance beyond expectation.* New York: Free Press.

Bass, B. M. (1990). *Bass and Stogdill's Handbook of Leadership* (3rd ed.). New York: Free Press.

Bass, B. M. (1998). *Transformational leadership: Industrial, military, and educational impact.* Mahwah, NJ: Erlbaum.

Bateman, D. (2007). Compensatory education. *TEACHING Exceptional Children, 39*(4), 69–71.

Bennis, W., & Nanus, B. (1985). *Leaders: The strategies for taking charge.* New York: Harper and Row.

Billingsley, B. S. (2005). *Cultivating and keeping committed special education teachers: What principals and district leaders can do.* Thousand Oaks, CA: Corwin.

Billingsley, B. S. (2010). Work contexts matter: Practical considerations for improving new special educators' experiences in schools. *Journal of Special Education Leadership, 23,* 41–49.

Blatchley, L., & Lau, M. (2010). Culturally competent screening and special education referral: A systematic approach. *Communique, 38*(7), 27–29.

Browder, D., Ahlgrim-Delzell, L., Courtade, G., Gibbs, S., & Flowers, C. (2008). Evaluation of the effectiveness of an early literacy program for students with significant developmental disabilities. *Exceptional Children, 75,* 33–52.

Browder, D., Wakeman, S. Y., & Flowers, C. (2006). Assessment of progress in the general curriculum for students with disabilities. *Theory Into Practice, 45,* 249–259.

Burns, J. M. (1978). *Leadership.* New York: Harper & Row.

Callahan, R. E. (1962). *Education and the cult of efficiency.* Chicago: University of Chicago Press.

Campbell, R. F., Fleming, T., Newell, L. J., & Bennion, J. W. (1987). *A history of thorough and practice in educational administration.* New York: Teachers College Press.

Crockett, J. B. (2002). Special education's role in preparing responsive leaders for inclusive schools. *Remedial and Special Education, 23,* 157–169.

Crockett, J. B., Becker, M. K., & Quinn, D. (2009). Reviewing the knowledge base of special education leadership and administration from 1970–2009. *Journal of Special Education Leadership, 22,* 55–67.

Dailey, B. E. (2002). A study of the relationship among individual education plan instructional objectives, Delaware student testing program scores, and class performance as depicting the achievement of fifth grade special education students in five Delaware intermediate grades. *Dissertation Abstracts International, 49,* 3041604/1.

Dailey, D., & Zantal-Wiener, K. (2000). Reforming high school learning: The effect of the standards movement on secondary students with disabilities. (*Center for Policy Research on the Impact of General and Special Education Reform). Special Education Programs (ED/OSERS),* Washington, DC.

Davidson, D. N., & Algozzine, B. (2002). Administrators' perceptions of special education law. *The Journal of Special Education, 15,* 43–48.

Deal, T. E., & Kennedy, A. A. (1982). *Corporate culture: The rites and rituals of corporate life.* Reading, MA: Addison-Wesley.

Defur, S. H. (2002). Education reform, high stakes assessment, and students with disabilities. *Remedial and Special Education, 23,* 203–212.

Dinnbeil, L., Mcinerney, W., & Hale, L. (2006). Least restrictive and natural environments for young children with disabilities: A legal analysis of issues. *Topics in Early Childhood Special Education, 26,* 167–178.

Dipaola, M., Tschannen-Moran, M., & Walter-Thomas, C. (2004). School principals and special education: Creating the context for academic success. *Focus on Exceptional Children, 37,* 1–10.

Ditkowsky, B., & Koonce, D. (2010). Predicting performance on high-stakes assessment for proficient students and students at risk with oral reading fluency growth. *Assessment for Effective Intervention, 35,* 159–167.

Education of the Deaf Act of 1986, 20 U.S.C. § 4301 *et seq.* (1986).

Education Week. (2006). *Special education financing system on trial in Washington state, 26*(11), 19–19.

Elmore, R. (2002). Local school districts and instructional improvement. In W. Hawley (Ed.), *The keys to effective schools: Educational reform as continuous improvement.* Thousand Oaks, CA: Corwin.

Epley, P., Gotto, I., Summers, J., Brotherson, M., Turnbull, A., & Friend, A. (2010). Supporting families of young children with disabilities: Examining the role of administrative structures. *Topics in Early Childhood Special Education, 30,* 20–31.

Etscheidt, S. (2006). Least restrictive and natural environments for young children with disabilities: A legal analysis of issues. *Topics in Early childhood Special Education, 26,* 167–178.

Fewster, S., & Macmillan, P. D. (2002). School based evidence for the validity of curriculum-based measurement of reading and writing. *Remedial and Special Education, 23,* 149–157.

Fox, E. (2004). Report cards provide more, or less, data. *Education Week, 24*(15), 10.

Gallagher-Browne, E. (2010). Guiding professional learning communities: Inspiration, challenge, surprise, and meaning. *Mentoring & Tutoring: Partnership in Learning, 18*(3), 321–325.

Goertz, M. E., & Duffy, M. C. (2001). *Assessment and accountability systems in the 50 states, 1999–2000.* Consortium for Policy Research in Education. Graduate School of Education, University of Pennsylvania.

Gravois, T. A., & Rosenfield, S. A. (2006). Impact of instructional consultation teams on the disproportionate referral and placement of minority students in special education. *Remedial and Special Education, 27,* 42–52.

Green, R. L. (2010). *Four dimensions of principal leadership: A framework for learning.* Upper Saddle River, NJ: Pearson.

Halvorsen, A. T. (2009). Building inclusive schools: Tools and strategies for success. New Jersey: Pearson.

Hancock, M., & Lamendola, B. (2005). A leadership journey. *Educational Leadership, 62,* 74–78.

Hanson, E. M. (2003). *Educational administration and organizational behavior* (5th ed.). Boston: Allyn & Bacon.

Harry, B., & Klinger, J. (2007). Discarding the deficit model. *Educational Leadership, 64,* 16–21.

Havelock, R. G., & Hamilton, R. G. (2004). *Guiding change in special education: How to help schools with new ideas and practices.* Thousand Oaks, CA: Corwin.

Heufner, D. S. (2000). The risks and opportunities of the IEP requirements under IDEA '97. *The Journal of Special Education, 33,* 195–205.

Hoy, W. K., & Miskel, C. G. (1996). *Educational administration: Theory, research, and* practice (5th ed.). New York: McGraw-Hill.

Hoy, W. K., & Miskel, C. G. (2005). *Educational administration: Theory, research, and practice* (7th ed.). New York: McGraw-Hill.

Idol, L. (2006). Toward inclusion of special education students in general education: A program evaluation of eight schools. *Remedial and Special Education, 27*, 77–94.

Individuals with Disabilities Education Act Amendments of 1997, PL 105-17, 20 U.S.C. §§ 1400 *et seq.*

Individuals with Disabilities Education Improvement Act of 2004, PL 108-466, 20 U. S. C. §1400, H. R. 1350.

Johnson, E., Kimball, K., Brown, S. O., & Anderson, D. (2001). A statewide review of the use of accommodations in large-scale, high stakes assessments. *Exceptional Children, 67*, 251–264.

Jorgensen, C. M. (1997). Curriculum and its impact on inclusion and the achievement of students with disabilities. *Policy Research Issue Brief, 2*(2), 144–167.

Katsiyannis, A., & Herbst, M. (2004). Minimize litigation in special education. *Intervention in School and Clinic, 40*, 106–110.

Klinger, J., & Harry, B. (2006). The special education referral and decision-making process for English Language learners: Child study team meetings and placement conferences. *Teachers College Record, 108*(11), 2247–2281.

Kowalski, T. J. (2003). *Contemporary school administration: An introduction.* Boston: Allyn & Bacon.

LaVenture, S. (2003). The individuals with disabilities education act (IDEA): Past and present. *Journal of Visual Impairment and Blindness, 97*, 517–518.

Lee-Tarver, A. (2006). A survey of teachers' perceptions of the function and purpose of student support teams. *Education, 126*(3), 525–533.

Little, M. E., & Houston, D. (2003). Comprehensive school reform. *Journal of Disability Policy Studies, 14*(1), 54–62.

Marshall, C., & Oliva, M. (2010). *Leadership for social justice: Making revolutions in education.* Upper Saddle River, NJ: Pearson.

McLaughlin, M. J., & Nolet, V. (2004). *What every principal needs to know about special education.* Thousand Oaks, CA: Corwin.

McLaughlin, M. J., & Rhim, L. M. (2007). Accountability frameworks and children with disabilities: A test of assumptions about improving public education for all students. *International Journal of Disability, Development, and Education, 54*(3), 24–49.

Measurement in Education & The American Association of Research Association. www.aera.net.

Meek, C. (2006). From the inside out: A look at testing special education students. *Phi Delta Kappan, 88*(4) 293–297.

Meier, D. (2001). Foreword. In S. Ohanian (Ed.), *Caught in the middle* (pp. v–vii). Portsmouth, NH: Heinemann.

Miskel C., & Ogawa, R. (1988). Work motivation, job satisfaction, and climate. In Norman J. Boyan, (Ed.), *Handbook of research on educational administration.* New York: Longman.

Moore-Brown, B. J., Montgomery, J., Bielinski, J., & Shubin, J. (2005). Responsiveness to intervention: Teaching before testing helps avoid labeling. *Top Language Disorders, 25*, 148–167.

National Research Council. (1999). *Testing, teaching, and learning: A guide for states and school districts.* Washington, DC: National Academy Press.

National Research Council. www.national-academies.org/nrc/.

No Child Left Behind Act of 2001, PL No. 107-110, 115, § 1425, 20 U.S.C. §§ 6301 *et seq.* (2002).

Northouse, P. G. (2007). Leadership: Theory and practice (4th ed.) Thousand Oaks, CA: Sage.

Orlich, D. C. (2004). No child left behind: An illogical accountability model. *Clearing House,* 6–11.

Ortiz, A., & Garcia. S. (2007). Preventing disproportionate representation: Culturally and linguistically responsive pre-referral interventions. *TEACHING Exceptional Children, 38*(4), 64–68.

Osborne, Jr. A. G. (1992). Legal standards for an appropriate education in the post-Rowley era. *Exceptional Children, 58*, 488–494.

Osborne Jr., A. G, & Russo, C. (2010). Attorney fees, school boards, and special education. *School Business Affairs, 76*(5), 36–38.

Owens, R. G. (1998). *Organizational behavior in education* (6th ed.). Boston: Allyn & Bacon.

Owens, W. A., & Kaplan, L. (Eds.). (2003). *Best practices, best thinking and emerging issues in school leadership*. Thousand Oaks: Corwin.

Podemski, R. S., Marsh, G. E., Smith, T. E. C., & Price, B. J. (1995). *Comprehensive administration of special education* (2nd ed.). Upper Saddle, NJ: Prentice-Hall.

Razik, T. A., & Swanson, A. D. (2010). *Fundamental concepts of educational leadership and management*. Upper Saddle River, NJ: Pearson.

Riley, K. (2010). Special education accountability scores affect schools' AYP. *Education Daily, 43*(148), 2.

Roach, V. (2000). *Center for policy research on the impact of general and special education reform on student with disabilities*. Final Report. (Center for Policy Research). Special Education Programs (ED/OSERS), Washington, DC.

Salend, S., & Garrick-Duhaney, L. M. (2005). Understanding and addressing the disproportionate representative of students of color in special education. *Intervention in School and Clinic, 40*, 213–221.

Scheffel, D., Rude, H. A., & Bole, P. T. (2005). Avoiding special education litigation in rural school districts. *Rural Special Education Quarterly, 24*(4), 3–8.

Scherer, M. (2003). Miles to go. *Educational Leadership, 61*, 5.

Schwarz, P. (2007). A service, not a sentence. *Educational Leadership, 64*, 39–42.

Short, P. M., & Greer, J. T. (2002). *Leadership in empowered schools: Themes from innovative efforts*. Upper Saddle River, NJ: Merrill.

Smartt, S., & Fuchs, L. (2000). *The validity of test accommodations for students with learning disabilities: Differential item performance on reading and mathematics tests as a function of test accommodations and disability status*. (Grant # R279A50022). Delaware Department of Education: U.S. Department of Education.

Smircich, L. (1983). Concepts of culture and organizational analysis. *Administrative Science Quarterly, 28*, 339–358.

Snell, D. (2007). The consequences of IDEA. *American Board Journal*, 14–15.

Sugai, G., Guardino, D., & Lathrop, M. (2007). Response to intervention: Examining classroom behavior support in second grade. *Exceptional Children, 73*, 288–310.

Tagiuri, R. (1968). The concept of organizational climate. In Renato Tagiluri & George H. Litwin, (Eds.), *Organizational climate: Exploration of a concept*. Boston: Harvard University, Graduate School of Business Administration.

Thurlow, M. L., Lazarus, S. S., Thompson, S. J., & Morse, A. B. (2005). State policies on assessment participation and accommodations for students with disabilities. *The Journal of Special Education 38*, 232–235.

Trainor, A. (2010). Reexamining the promise of parent participation in special education: An analysis of cultural and social capital. *Anthropology & Education Quarterly, 41*, 245–263.

Walsh, D., & Matlock, L. (2000). Demonstrating achievement in special education. *Thrust for Educational Leadership, 29*(4), 34–36.

Washburn-Moses, L. (2003). What every special educator should know about high-stakes testing. *TEACHING Exceptional Children, 35*(4), 12–16.

Weishaar, M. K., & Borsa, J. C. (2001). *Inclusive educational administration: A case study*. Boston: McGraw-Hill.

Yeh, S. (2006). Can rapid assessment moderate the consequences of high-stakes testing? *Education and Urban Society, 39*(1), 1–2.

Zaretsky, L. (2004). Responding ethically to complex school-based issues in special education. *International Studies in Educational Administration, 32*, 63–78.

Zirkel, P. A. (2005). The paralyzing fear of education litigation. *The Education Standard*, 43–44.

Chapter 2

American Recovery and Reinvestment Act of 2009. http://frwebgate.access.gpo.gov/cgiin/getdoc.cgi?dbname=111_cong_bills&docid=f:h1enr.pdf

Americans with Disabilities Act of 1990, 42 U.S.C. § 12101 *et seq.* (1990).

Baily, D. S. (2003). Who is learning disabled? *Monitor on Psychology, 34*(8), 58.

Bar, L., & Galluzzo, J. (1999). The accessible school: *Universal design for educational settings.* Berkeley, CA: MIG Communications.

Boehner, J., & Castle, M. (2005). Committee on Education and the Workforce, Subcommittee of Education Reform. *Individuals with Disabilities Act: Guide to frequently asked questions.* Washington, DC: U.S. Government Printing Office.

Brozo, W. G. (2009). Response to intervention or instruction: Challenges and possibilities of response to intervention for adolescent literacy. *Journal of Adolescent and Adult Literacy, 53,* 277–281.

Cohen, M. (2001). *Transforming the American high school: New directions or state and local policy.* Washington, DC: Aspen Institute

Comparison of IDEA 94 and IDEA 97. *NICHCY News Digest 26.* Retrieved April 29, 2005, from www.nichcy.org/idealist.htm#transition.

Cortiella, C. (n.d.). *The discrepancy dilemma: Congress ponders a better way to identify learning sisabilities.* www.schwablearning.org/articles.asp?r=703&g=2.

Council for Exceptional Children. (2004). *The new IDEA* [Brochure]. Arlington, VA.

Council for Exceptional Children. (2004, November). *The new idea: CEC's summary of significant issues,* Arlington, VA.

Crabtree, R. K. (2005). Due process hearings: Powerful but costly. *Family Education.* Retrieved April 27, 2005, from www.familyeducation.com/article/0,1120,23-8149,00.html.

Finn, C. (2002). *What ails U.S. high schools? How should they be reformed? Is there a federal role?* Washington, DC: U.S. Department of Education.

Hazelkorn, M., Packard, A. L., & Douvanis, G. (2008). Alternative dispute resolution in special education: A view from the field. *Journal of Special Education Leadership, 21,* 32–38.

Hitchcock, C., Meyer, A., Rose, D., & Jackson, R. (2002). Providing access to the general education curriculum: Universal Design for Learning. *TEACHING Exceptional Children, 35*(2), 8–17.

Individuals with Disabilities Education Act Amendments of 1997, PL 105-17, 20 U.S.C. §§ 1400 *et seq.*

Individuals with Disabilities Education Improvement Act of 2004, PL 108-466, 20 U.S.C. §1400, H.R. 1350.

Kame'enui, E., & Simmons, D. (1999). *Toward successful inclusion of students with disabilities: The architecture of instruction.* (ERIC/OSEP Mini Library on Adapting Curricular Materials, Vol. 1). Reston, VA: ERIC Clearinghouse on Disabilities and Gifted Education.

King-Sears, M. (2009). Universal design for learning: Technology and pedagogy. *Learning Disabilities Quarterly, 32,* 199–201.

Klotz, M. B., & Nealis, L. (2004). The New IDEA: A summary of significant reforms. *National Association of School Psychologists.*

Kohler, P. D., & Hood, L. K. (2000). *Improving student outcomes: Promising practices and programs for 1999–2000.* www.ed.unic.edu/sped/tri/kohlerdirectory2000.htm.

McNeil, P. (2003). *Rethinking high school: The next frontier for state policymakers* Washington, DC: Aspen Institute.

Meyer, A., & Rose, D. (2000). Universal design for individual differences. *Educational Leadership 58*(3), 39–43.

Latham, P. H., Latham, P. S., & Mandlawitz, M. (2008). *Special education law.* Upper Saddle River, NJ: Merrill.

Luecking, R., & Gramlich, M. (2003). Quality work-based learning and post-school employment succeeds. Retrieved April 29, 2005, from www.ncset.org/publications/printresource.asp?id=1192.

Mellard, D., & Johnson, E. (2007). *A practitioner's guide to response to intervention.* Thousand Oaks, CA: Corwin.

Mercer, C. D., & Pullen, P. C. (2009). *Students with learning disabilities.* Upper Saddle River, NJ: Merrill.

National Center on Secondary Education and Transition. (2005). *Key provisions on transition: IDEA 1997 compared to H. R. 1350* (IDEA 2004). Retrieved April 28, 2005, from www. ncset.org/publications.

North Carolina Department of Public Instruction. (2001a). *Four courses of study, one diploma.* Retrieved April 29, 2005, from www.ncpublic-shoolsl.org/student_promotion/gradreq.html.

North Carolina Department of Public Instruction. (2001b). *Raising the bar: North Carolina high school diploma requirements.* Retrieved April 29, 2005, from www.ncpublicshoolsl.org/student_promotion/diploma_req.html.

O'Leary, E. (2005). *Overview, comments, and recommended action for transition services: P.L. 108-446, Individuals with disabilities education improvement act of 2004.* Resources available from www.wsti.org/resroucepdf.cfm.

Rehabilitation Act of 1973, 29 U.S.C. § 701 *et seq.* (1973).

Rose, D., & Meyer, A. (2002). *Teaching every student in the digital age: Universal Design for Learning.* Alexandria, VA: Association for Supervision and Curriculum Development. Retrieved July 28, 2003, from www.cast.org/teachingeverystudent/.

Steenwyk, B. (2005). *IDEIA monitoring priorities.* Office of Special Education and Early Intervention Services, Department of Education, Michigan. Retrieved April 28, 2005, from www.cenmi.org/tspmi/downloads/MTSA05Leadership.ppt.

Transition Technical Assistance Centers. (2005). Retrieved April 29, 2005, from www.uncc.edu/ttac/ttac.asp?FileName=profiles_and_contacts.

Visser, R. (2002, April). *Texas Center for the Advancement of Literacy & Learning.* Retrieved April 25, 2005, from www-tcall.tamu.edu/research/diagnog.htm.

Williams, J. M. (2005, March). *Transcript of questions on transition.* Retrieved from www.special-edconnection.com.

Zirkel, P. A., & Gischlar, K. L. (2008). Due process hearings under the IDEA: A longitudinal frequency analysis. *Journal of Special Education Leadership, 21,* 22–31.

Chapter 3

Allen, L. A. (2006). The moral life of schools revisited: Preparing educational leaders to "build a new social order" for social justice and democratic community. *International Journal of Urban Educational Leadership, 1,* 1–13.

Americans with Disabilities Act of 1990, 42 U.S.C. § 12101 *et seq.* (1990).

Anyon, J. (1980). Social class and the hidden curriculum of work. *Journal of Education, 162,* 67–92.

Biesinger, K., Crippen, K., & Muis, K. (2008). The impact of block scheduling on student motivation and classroom practice in mathematics. *NASSP Bulletin, 92*(3), 191–208.

Browder, D., Flowers, C., Ahgrim-Delzell, L., Karvonen, M., Spooner, F., & Algozzine, R. (2004). The alignment of alternative assessment and content with academic and functional curricula. *The Journal of Special Education, 37,* 211–219.

Buckman, D., King. B., & Ryan. S. (1995). Block scheduling: A means to improve school climate. *NASSP Bulletin, 79*(571), 9–18.

Chappell, T. (2008). Getting serious about inclusive curriculum for special education. *Primary & Middle Years Educator, 6,* 28–31.

Council for Exceptional Children. (2007). *CASE special education administrator performance-based standards validation study.* Arlington, VA: Author.

Council for Exceptional Children. (2009). *What every special educator must know: Ethics, standards, and guidelines for special educators* (5th ed.). Arlington, VA: Author.

Crockett, J. (2007). The changing landscape of special education administration. *Exceptionality, 8,* 139–142.

Crockett, J., & Kauffman, J. M. (1999). *The least restrictive environment: Its origins and interpretations in special education.* Mahwah, NJ: Erlbaum.

Darling-Hammond, L. (2009). A future worthy of teaching for America. *Education Digest, 74,* 11–16.

Darling-Hammond, L., & Ascher, C. (1991). *Accountability mechanisms in big city school systems* (Digest No. 71). New York: ERIC Clearinghouse on Urban Education. (ERIC Document Reproduction Service No. ED334311)

Education for All Handicapped Children Act of 1975, 20 U.S.C. § 1400 *et seq.* (1975).

Educational Leadership Constituent Council. (2001). Reston, VA: National Board for Education Administration.

Elliott, J., Erickson, R., Thurlow, M., & Shriner, J. (2000). State-level accountability for the performance of students with disabilities: Five years of change. *The Journal of Special Education, 34,* 39–40.

Fisher, D., & Frey, N. (2002). Access to the core curriculum. *Remedial and Special Education, 22,* 148.

Fisher, D., Frey, N., & Lapp, D. (2009). Meeting AYP in a high-need school: A formative experiment. *Journal of Adolescent and Adult Literacy, 52*(5), 386–396.

Fogarty, R. (1995). Think about block scheduling: It's not a question of time. Palatine, IL: Skylight Training and Publishing.

Fuhrman, S. H. (2001). Introduction. In S. H. Fuhrman (Ed.), *From the capitol to the classroom: Standards-based reform in the states* (pp. 1–12). Chicago: University of Chicago.

Garber, M. G. (1997). *Parallel block scheduling: A study of integrated services and funding resulting in improved student achievement.* Unpublished doctoral dissertation. University of Virginia, Charlottesville.

Gullatt, D. (2006). Block scheduling: The effects on curriculum and student productivity. *NASSP Bulletin, 90*(3), 250–266.

Hallahan D. P., Kauffman J. M., & Pullen, P. C. (2009). *Exceptional learners: Introduction to special education* (11th ed.). Boston: Allyn & Bacon.

Hopkins H. J. (1990). *A comparison of the effectiveness of pull out programs in a parallel block scheduled school and in a traditionally scheduled school.* Unpublished doctoral dissertation. University of Virginia, Charlottesville.

Individuals with Disabilities Education Act Amendments of 1997, PL 105-17, 20 U.S.C. §§ 1400 *et seq.*

Individuals with Disabilities Education Improvement Act of 2004, PL 108-466, 20 U.S.C. §1400, H.R. 1350.

Jackson, B. T. (1994). Foreword. In R. F. Elmore & S. H. Fuhrman, S. H. *The governance of curriculum: 1994 yearbook of the association for supervision and curriculum development* (pp. v–vi). Alexandria, VA: ASCD.

Kendall, D. (2010). *Social problems in a diverse society* (5th ed.). Upper Saddle River, NJ: Pearson.

Kentucky Department of Education. Results that matter: A decade of difference in Kentucky's public schools, 1990–2000. Frankfurt, KY: Author.

Kode, K. (2002). *Elizabeth Farrell and the history of special education.* Arlington, VA: Council for Exceptional Children.

Latham, P., Latham, P. S., & Mandlawitz, M. (2008). *Special education law.* Upper Saddle River, NJ: Pearson.

Leif, B. (2001). The children's school: Lessons for inclusion, leadership, and school success. *Fordham Urban Law Journal, 29,* 705.

Lessinger, L. M., & Tyler, R. W. (Eds.). (1971). *Accountability in education.* Worthington, OH: Charles A. Jones Publishing.

Marshall, J. D., Sears, J. T., Allen, L. A., Roberts, P., & Schubert, W. (2007). *Turning points in curriculum: A contemporary American memoir* (2nd ed.). Upper Saddle River, NJ: Prentice-Hall.

McGrew, K. S., Thurlow, M. L., & Spiegel, A. N. (1993). An investigation of the exclusion of students with disabilities in national data collection programs. *Educational Evaluation and Policy Analysis, 15,* 339–352.

McLaughlin, M., & Rhim, L. M. (2007). Accountability frameworks and children with disabilities: A test of assumptions about improving public education for all students. *International Journal of Disability, Development and Education, 54,* 24–49.

Murphy, J. (2001). The changing face of leadership preparation. *School Administrator, 58*(10), 14.

Nagle, K., Yunker, C., & Malmgren, K. (2006). Students with disabilities and accountability reform. *Journal of Disability Policy Studies, 17,* 28–39.

National Commission on Excellence in Education. (1983). *A nation at risk: The imperative for educational reform.* Washington, DC: U.S. Government Printing Office.

National Council on Education Standards and Testing. (1992). *Raising standards for American education.* Washington, DC: U.S. Government Printing Office.

National Education Goals Panel. (1993). *Promises to keep: Creating high standards for American students.* Washington, DC: U.S. Government Printing Office.

National Governors' Association Center for Policy Research and Analysis. (August 1986). *Time for results: The governors' 1991 report on education.* Washington, DC: Author.

Nilholm, C. (2006). Special education, inclusion and democracy. *European Journal of Special Needs Education, 21,* 431–445.

Nolet, V., & McLaughlin, M. J. (2005). *Accessing the general curriculum: Including students with disabilities in standards-based reform* (2nd ed.). Thousand Oaks, CA: Corwin.

Oakes, J. (1985). *Keeping track: How schools structure inequality.* New Haven, CT: Yale.

Olson, L. (2006). A decade of effort. *Education Week, 25*(17), 8–16.

Olson, L. (2008). Standards for school leaders get new thumbs-up. *Education Week, 27*(25), 1–14.

Pugach, M., & Warger, C. (2001). Curriculum matters: Raising expectation for students with disabilities. *Remedial and Special Education, 22,* 213–220.

Ravitch, D. (1992). A culture in common. *Educational Leadership, 49*(8-4), 11.

Ravtich, D., & Finn, C. E., Jr. (1987). *What do our 17-year-olds know? A report on the first national assessment of history and literature.* New York: Harper & Row.

Rice, N. (2006). Opportunities lost, possibilities found: shared leadership and inclusion in an urban high school. *Journal of Disability Policy Studies, 17,* 88–100.

Roaf, C. (2008). Deconstructing special education and constructing inclusion. *Support for Learning, 23,* 95–96.

Salvaterra, M., & Adams. D. (1995). Departing from tradition: Two schools' stories. *Educational Leadership, 53,* 32–35.

Schoenstein, R. (1994). Block schedules: Building the high schools of the future? *Virginia Journal of Education, 87,* 7–13.

Shipman, N. J., Queen, J. A., & Peel, H. A. (2007). *Transforming school leadership with ISLLC and ELCC.* New York: Eye on Education.

Shortt, T., & Thayer, Y. (1995). What can we expect to see in the next generation of block scheduling? *NASSP Bulletin, 79*(571), 53–62.

Suk-Hyang, L., Wehmeyer, M. H., Soukup, J. H., & Palmer, S. B. (2010). Impact of curriculum modifications on access to the general curriculum for students with disabilities. *Exceptional Children, 76*(2), 213–233.

Tanner, D. (1998). The social consequences of bad research. *Phi Delta Kappan, 79*(5), 345–349.

Tyack, D. (1974). *The one best system: A history of American urban education.* Cambridge, MA: Harvard University Press.

United States Department of Education. (1998). *A nation 'still' at risk: An education manifesto.* Washington, DC: Thomas Fordham Foundation.

Viadero, D. (2003, February 5). Researchers debate impact of tests. *Education Week.* Retrieved April 7, 2003, from www. edweek.org/ew/ew_printstory.cfm?slug=21carnoy.h22.

Walker, R. (1989, June 14). Bush to appoint group to proffer education ideas. *Education Week.* Retrieved February 10, 2003, from www.edweek. org/ew/ewstory. cfm?slug=08340005.h08.

Weller, D., & McLeskey, J. (2002). Block scheduling and inclusion in a high school. *Remedial and Special Education, 21,* 29.

Weisman, J. (1991a). Educators watch with a wary eye as business gains policy muscle. *Education Week*. Retrieved February 10, 2003, from www.edweek.org/ew/ewstory.cfm?slug=10350004.h10.

Weisman, J. (1991b). Business Roundtable assessing state progress on reforms. *Education Week*. Retrieved February 10, 2003, from www.edweek.org/ew/ewstory.cfm?slug=12table.h11.

Williams, J., Williams, S., Metcalf, D., Smith Canter, L., Zambone, A., & Jeffs, T. (2009). From "Big Ideas" to deliberate action: Curriculum revision and alignment in an American special education teacher preparation program. *Teaching & Teacher Education, 25*, 128–133.

Wilson L. J. (1993). *The effects of parallel block scheduling versus surface scheduling on reading and mathematics achievement on students' attitudes toward school and learning*. Unpublished doctoral dissertation, Ball State University, Muncie, IN.

Woolfolk-Hoy, A., & Hoy, W. (2003). *Instructional leadership: A learning-centered guide*. Upper Saddle River, NJ: Pearson.

Chapter 4

Americans with Disabilities Act of 1990, 42 U.S.C. § 12101 *et seq.* (1990).

Anderson, M. G., & Webb-Johnson, G. (1995). Cultural contexts, the seriously emotionally disturbed classification, and African American learners. In B. A. Ford, F. E. Obiakor, & J. M. Patton (Eds.), *Effective education of African-American exceptional learners: New perspectives* (pp. 151–188). Austin TX: Pro-Ed.

Anderson-Butcher, D. (2004). Innovative models of collaboration to serve children, youths, families, and communities. *Children and Schools 26*(1), 39–54.

Andrews, T. J., Wisnieswski, J. J., & Mulick, J. A. (1997). Variables influencing teachers' decisions to refer children for psychological assessment services. *Psychology in the Schools, 34*, 239–244.

Artiles, A. J. (1998). The dilemma of difference: Enriching the disproportionality discourse with theory and content. *The Journal of Special Education, 32*, 32–36.

Artiles, A. J., & Bal, A. (2008). The next generation of disproportional research: Toward a comparative model in the study of equity in ability differences. *The Journal of Special Education, 42*, 4–14.

Artiles, A. J., Reschly, D. J., & Chinn, P. C. (2002). Overidentification of students of color in special education: A critical overview. *Multicultural Perspectives, 4* (1), 3–12.

Artiles, A. J., & Trent, S. C. (1994). Over-representation of minority students in special education: A continuing debate. *The Journal of Special Education, 27*, 410–437.

Bartlett, L. D., Etscheidt, S., & Weisenstein, G. R. (2007). *Special education law and practice in public schools*. Columbus, OH: Pearson.

Boyle, J. R., & Weishaar, M. (2001). *Special education law with cases*. Needham Heights, MA: Allyn and Bacon.

Connolly, A. J. (2007). *Key math-revised: A diagnostic inventory of essential mathematics*. Circle Pines, MN: American Guidance Service.

Coutinho, M., & Malouf, D. (1993). Performance assessment and children with disabilities: Issues and possibilities. *TEACHING Exceptional Children, 25*(4), 62–67.

Coutinho, M., Oswald, D. P., & Best, A. M. (2002). The influence of sociodemographics and gender on the disproportionate identification of minority students as having learning disabilities. *Remedial and Special Education, 23*, 49–60.

Curran, B. (1999). *Focusing on results: Toward an education accountability system*. Washington. DC: National Governor's Association.

Defur, S. H. (2002). Education reform, high stakes assessment, and students with disabilities. *Remedial and Special Education 23*, 203–212.

Defur, S. H. (2003). IEP transition planning—From compliance to quality. *Exceptionality 11*, 115–128.

Deno, S. L. (2003). Developments in curriculum based measurement. *The Journal of Special Education, 37*, 184–193.

Edwards, O. W. (2006). Special education disproportionality and the influence of intelligence test selection. *Journal of Intellectual and Developmental Disabilities, 31,* 246–248.

Fewster, S., & Macmillan, P. D. (2002). School based evidence for the validity of curriculum-based measurement of reading and writing. *Remedial and Special Education, 23,* 149–157.

Fradd, S., & Hallman, C. (1983). Implications of psychological and educational research for assessment and instruction of culturally and linguistically different students. *Learning Disabilities Quarterly, 6,* 468–477.

Fuchs, L., Fuchs, D., & Hamlett, C. (1989). Effects of instrumental use of curriculum-based measurement to enhance instructional programs. *Remedial and Special Education, 10,* 43–52.

Furney, K. S., Hasazi, S. B., Clark/Keefe, K., & Hartnett, J. (2003). A longitudinal analysis of shifting policy landscapes in special and general education reform. *Exceptional Children, 70,* 81–95.

Gable, R. A., Mostert, M., & Tonelson, S. W. (2004). Assessing professional collaboration in schools: Knowing what works. *Preventing School Failure 48,* 4–9.

Gartner, A., & Lipsky, D. K. (1987). Beyond special education: Toward a quality system for all students. *Harvard Educational Review, 57,* 367–395.

Gerstmyer v. Howard County Public Schools, 850 F. Supp. 361 (D. Md. 1994).

Gotsch, T. (2000, April 11). More N.Y. special ed kids take, pass high-stakes test. *Education Daily, 33*(68), 2–3.

Hardman, M. L., & Dawson, S. (2008). The impact of federal policy on curriculum and instruction for students with disabilities in the general classroom. *Preventing School Failure, 52,* 5–11.

Hart, K. E., & Scuitto, M. J. (1996). Criterion-referenced measurement of instructional impact on cognitive outcomes. *Journal of Instructional Psychology, 23,* 26–34.

Harry, B. (1995). African-American families. In B. A. Ford, F. E. Obiakor, & J. M. Patton (Eds.). *Effective education of African American exceptional learners: New perspectives* (pp. ix–xvi), Austin, TX: Pro-Ed.

Harry, B. (2008). Collaboration with culturally and linguistically diverse families: Ideal versus reality. *Exceptional Children, 74,* 372–388.

Harry, B., Allen, N., & McLaughlin, M. (1995). Communication versus compliance: African-American parents' involvement in special education. *Exceptional Children, 61,* 364–377.

Harry, B., Arnaiz, P., Klingner, J., & Sturges, K. (2008). Schooling and the construction of identity among minority students in Spain and the United States. *The Journal of Special Education, 42,* 15–25.

Haws, M. (2004). What we know and need to know about the consequences of high-stakes testing for students with disabilities. *Exceptional Children, 71,* 75–94.

Heshusius, L. (1991). Curriculum-based assessment and direct instruction: Critical reflections on fundamental assumptions. *Exceptional Children, 57,* 315–328.

Hewitt, G. (1995). *A portfolio primer.* Portsmouth, NH: Heinemann.

Hilliard, A. S. (1995). Culture, assessment, and valid teaching for the African-American student. In B. A. Ford, F. E. Obiakor, & J. M. Patton (Eds.), *Effective education of African American exceptional learners: New perspectives* (pp. ix–xvi). Austin, TX: Pro-Ed.

Hilton, A. (March/April 2007). Response to intervention: Changing how we do business. *Leadership, 36,* 16–19.

Hintz, J. M., Shapiro, E. S., & Lutz, J. G. (1994). The effects of curriculum on the sensitivity of curriculum-based measurement in reading. *The Journal of Special Education, 28,* 188–202.

Hobbs, R. (1993). Portfolio use in learning disabilities resource room. *Reading and Writing Quarterly: Overcoming Learning Difficulties, 9,* 249–261.

Hobson v. Hansen, 269 F. Supp. 401 (D.D.C. 1967), 393 U.S. 801 (1968).

Hoffman v. The Board of Education, 49 N. Y. 2d 121, 4000 N.E. 2d 317, 424 N.Y. S. 2d 376 (1979).

Improving America's Schools Act, *No Child Left Behind,* 20 U. S. C. § 1111 et seq.

Individuals with Disabilities Education Act Amendments of 1997, PL 105-17, 20 U.S.C. §§ 1400 *et seq.*

Individuals with Disabilities Education Improvement Act of 2004, PL 108-466, 20 U.S.C. §1400, H.R. 1350.

Johnson, E., Kimball, K., Brown, S. O., & Anderson, D. (2001). A statewide review of the use of accommodations in large-scale, high stakes assessments. *Exceptional Children, 67,* 251–264.

Kamens, M. W. (2004). Learning to write IEPs: A personalized, reflective approach for preservice teachers. *Intervention in School and Clinic, 40*(2), 76–80.

Larry P. v. Riles, 343 F. Supp. 1306, aff'd., 502 F 2d 963 (1972), further proceedings, 495 F. Supp. 926, aff'd., 502 F 2d 693 (9th Cir. 1984).

Little, M. E., & Houston, D. (2003). Comprehensive school reform. *Journal of Disability Policy Studies,* 14, 54–62.

Lynch, S., & Adams, P. (2008). Developing standards-based individualized education program objectives for students with significant needs. *TEACHING Exceptional Children, 40*(3), 36–39.

Madelaine, A., & Wheldall, K. (2004). Curriculum-based measurement of reading: Recent Advances. *International Journal of Disability, Development & Education 51*(1), 57–83.

Marston, D., Fuchs, L., & Deno, S. (1986). Measuring pupil progress: A comparison of standardized achievement tests and curriculum related measures. *Diagnostique, 11,* 77–90.

Mastropieri, M. A., & Scruggs, T. E. (2007). *The inclusive classroom: Strategies for effective instruction.* Upper Saddle River, NJ: Prentice-Hall.

McGlinchey, M. T., & Hixson, M. D. (2004). Using curriculum-based measurement to predict performance on state assessments in reading. *School Psychology Review, 33,* 204.

Meek, C. (December 2006). From the inside out: A look at testing special education students. *Phi Delta Kappan,* 293–297.

Murdick, N., Gartin, B., & Crabtree, T. (2007). *Special education law.* Upper Saddle River, NJ: Prentice-Hall.

National Center on Response to Intervention: RTI State Database. http://state.rti4success.org/index.php?option=com_chart.

National Governors' Association. Debra P. v. *Turlington,* 644 F. 2d 397 (5th Cir. 1981).

Nolet, V. (1993). Curriculum based assessment and portfolio assessment. *Diagnostique, 18,* 5–26.

Ortiz, A. A. (1997). Learning disabilities occurring concomitantly with linguistic differences. *Journal of Learning Disabilities, 30,* 321–332.

Ortiz, A. A., & Yates, J. R. (1983). Incidence of exceptionality among Hispanics: Implications for manpower training. *NAEB Journal, 7,* 41–51.

Oswald, D. P., Coutinho, M. J., Best, A. M., & Nguyen, N. (2001). Impact of sociodemographic characteristics on the identification rates of minority students. *Mental Retardation, 39,* 351–368.

Overton, T. (2009). *Assessment in special education: An applied approach* (6th ed.). Upper Saddle River, NJ: Prentice-Hall.

Parents in Action on Special Education (PASE) v. *Hannon,* 506 F. Supp. 831 (N.D. III. 1980).

Patton, J. (1998). The disproportionate representation of African Americans in special education: Looking behind the curtain for understanding and solutions. *The Journal of Special Education, 32,* 25–32.

Paulson, F. L., Paulson, P. R., & Meyer, C. A. (1991). What makes a portfolio? *Educational Leadership, 48*(5), 60–63.

Poteet, J. A., Choate, J. S., & Stewart, S. C. (1993). Performance assessment and special education: Practices and prospects. *Focus on Exceptional Children, 26*(1), 1–20.

Rehabilitation Act of 1973, 29 U.S.C. § 701 *et seq.* (1973).

Reynolds, C. (1992). The problems of bias in psychological assessment. In C. R. Reynolds & T. Gutkin (Eds.), *The handbook of school psychology* (pp. 179–180). New York: Wiley.

Rothstein, L. F. (2000). *Special education law.* New York: Longman.

Russo, C. J., & Talbert-Johnson, C. (1997). The overrepresentation of African-American children in special education: The resegregation of educational programming? *Education & Urban Society, 29*, 136–149.

Salend, S. J. (2008). Determining appropriate testing accommodations: Complying with NCLB and IDEA. *TEACHING Exceptional Children, 40*, 14–22.

Saland, S. J., & Duhaney, L. M. (2005). *Intervention in School and Clinic, 40*, 213–221.

Seals v. Loftis, 614 F. Supp. 302 (D.C. Tenn. 1985).

Sergiovanni, T. J. (2009). *The principalship: A reflective practice perspective.* Boston: Allyn & Bacon.

Shapiro, E. S. (1996). *Academic skills problems: Direct assessment and intervention* (2nd ed.). New York: Guilford.

Shriner, J. G. (2000). Legal perspectives on school outcomes assessment for students with disabilities. *Journal of Special Education, 33*, 232–240.

Shriner, J. G., & Destefano, L. (2003). Participation and accommodation in state assessment: The role of individualized education programs. *Exceptional Children, 69*, 147–161.

Shulte, A. C., Villwock, D. N., Whichard, S. M., & Stallings, C. F. (2001). High stakes testing and expected progress standards for students with learning disabilities: A five-year study. *School Psychology Review, 30*, 487–507.

Skiba, R. J., Simmons, A. B., Ritter, S., Gibb, A. C., Rausch, M. K., Cuadrado, J., Chung, G. (2008). *Exceptional Children, 74*, 264–288.

Smuck v. Hobson, 408 F. 2d 175, 132 D.C. 372(D.C. Cir. 1969).

Sparrow, S. S., Balla, D. A., & Cicchetti, D. V. (1984). *Vineland Adaptive Behavior Scales.* Circle Pines, MN: American Guidance Service.

Stecker, P. M., & Fuchs, L. S. (2000). Effecting superior achievement using curriculum-based measurement: The importance of individual progress monitoring. *Learning Disabilities Research and Practice, 15*, 128–135.

Swicegood, P. (1994). Portfolio-based assessment practice. *Intervention, 30* (1), 6-15.

Taylor, R. L. (2009). *Assessment of exceptional students: Educational and psychological procedures.* Boston: Allyn & Bacon.

Taylor, R. L., Smiley, L. R., & Richards, S. B. (2009). *Exceptional students.* Boson: McGraw-Hill.

Thurlow, M. L. (2002). Positive educational results for all students: The promise of standards based reform. *Remedial and Special Education, 23*, 195–203.

Thurlow, M. L., Christenson, S., & Yssledyke, J. (1983). *Referral research: An integrative summary of findings (Research Report No. 141).* Minneapolis: University of Minnesota, Institute for Research on Learning Disabilities.

Thurlow, M. L., Lazarus, S. S., Thompson, S. J., & Morse, A. B. (2005). State policies on assessment participation and accommodations for students with disabilities. *The Journal of Special Education, 38*, 232–235.

Tindal, G. (1991). Operationalizing learning portfolios: A good idea in search of a method. *Diagnostique, 2*, 127–133.

Townsend, B. L. (2002). Testing while Black. *Remedial and Special Education, 23*, 222–230.

Turnbull, A., Turnbull, A., Truscott, S. D., Meyers, B., Gelzheiser, L., & Grout, C. B. (2004). Do shared decision-making teams discuss special education in educational reform meetings? *Journal of Disability Policy Studies, 15*, 112–126.

Turnbull, A., Turnbull, A., & Wehmeyer, M. (2009). *Exceptional lives: Special education in today's schools* (6th ed.). Upper Saddle River, NJ: Prentice-Hall.

Turnbull, H. R., Huerta, N., & Stowe, M. (2009). *What every teacher should know about the individuals with disabilities education act in 2004* (2nd ed.). Upper Saddle River, NJ: Prentice-Hall.

Vavrus, L. (1990). Put portfolios to the test. *Instructor, 100*(1), 48–53.

Venn, J. J. (2007). *Assessing students with special needs* (4th ed.). Upper Saddle River, NJ: Prentice-Hall.

Warner, T. D., Dede, T. E., Garvan, C. W., & Conway, T. W. (2002). One size does not fit all in specific learning disability assessment across ethnic groups. *Journal of Learning Disabilities, 35,* 500–508.

Weinstein, D. F. (1997). *The special education audit handbook.* Lancaster, PA: Technomic Publication.

Wesson, C. L., & King, R. P. (1996). Portfolio assessment and special education students. *TEACHING Exceptional Children, 28,* 44–48.

Wiig, E. H. (2000). Authentic and other assessments of Language disabilities: When is fair fair? *Reading and Writing Quarterly, 16,* 179–211.

Wiles, J., & Bondi, J. (2004). *Supervision: A guide to practice.* Upper Saddle River, NJ: Merrill/Prentice-Hall.

Wilkinson, G. S. (1993). *Wide Range Achievement Test–3.* Wilmington, DE: Wide Range, Inc.

Woodcock, R. (1998). *Woodcock Reading Mastery Test–Revised.* Circle Pines, MN: American Guidance Service.

Yell, M. (2006). *The law and special education.* Upper Saddle River, NJ: Merrill/Prentice-Hall.

Yell, M., & Katsiyannis, A. (2004). Placing students with disabilities in inclusive settings: Legal guidelines and preferred practices. *Preventing School Failure, 49,* 28–36.

Ysseldyke, J. E., Algozzine, B., Shinn, M. and McGue, M. (1982). Similarities and differences between low achievers and students labeled learning disabled. *The Journal of Special Education, 16,* 73–85.

Ysseldyke, J., Nelson, J., Christenson, S., Johnson, D., Dennison, A., Triezenberg, H., et al. (2004). What we know and need to know about the consequences of high-stakes testing for students with disabilities. *Exceptional Children, 71,* 75–95.

Ysseldyke, J., Thurlow, M., Bielinski, J., House, A., Moody, M., & Haigh, J. (2001). The relationship between instructional and assessment accommodations in an inclusive state accountability system. *The Journal of Learning Disabilities, 34,* 212–218.

Chapter 5

Anderson, C. M., & Kincaid, D. (2005). Applying behavior analysis to school violence and discipline problems: Schoolwide Positive Behavior Support. *The Behavior Analyst, 28,* 49–63.

Beyda, S. D., Fentall, S. S., & Zerco, D. J. (2002). The relationship between teacher practices and the task appropriate and social behavior of students with behavioral disorders. *Behavioral Disorders, 27,* 236–255.

Blair, K. C., Umbreit, J., Dunlap, G., & Jung, G. (2007). Promoting inclusion and peer participation through assessment-based intervention. *Topics in Early Childhood Special Education, 27,* 134–147.

Bohanon, H., Fenning, P., Carney, K. L., Minnis-Kim, M. J., Anderson-Harriss, S., Moroz, K. B., . . . Pigott, T. D. (2006). Schoolwide application of positive behavior support in an urban high school: A case study. *Journal of Positive Behavior Interventions, 8,* 131–145.

Carr, E. G., Dunlap, G., Horner, R. H., Koegel, R. L., Turnbull, A. P., & Sailor, W. (2002). Positive behavior support: Evolution of an applied science. *Journal of Positive Behavior Interventions, 4,* 4–16, 20.

Cartledge, G., & Dukes, C. (2008). Disproportionality of African American children in special education. In L. C. Tillman (Ed.), *The SAGE handbook of African American education* (pp. 383–398). Thousand Oaks, CA: Sage.

Chitiyo, M., & Wheeler, J. (2009). Challenges faced by school teachers in implementing positive behavior support in their school systems. *Remedial and Special Education, 30,* 58–63.

Christle, C. A., & Schuster, J. W. (2003). The effects of using response cards on student participation, academic achievement, and on-task behavior during whole-class, math instruction. *Journal of Behavioral Education, 12,* 147–165.

Conroy, M. A., Sutherland, K. S., Snyder, A., Al-Hendawi, M., & Vo, A. (2009). Creating a positive classroom atmosphere: Teacher's use of effective praise and feedback. *Beyond Behavior, 18,* 18–26.

Conroy, M. A., Sutherland, K. S., Snyder, A., & Marsh, S. (2008). Classwide interventions: Effective instruction makes a difference. TEACHING Exceptional Children, 40(6), 24–30.

Dunlap, G., Kern, L., dePerczel, M., Clarke, S., Wilson, D., Childs, K. E., . . . Falk, G. D. (1993). Functional analysis of classroom variables for students with emotional and behavioral disorders. Behavioral Disorders, 18, 275–291.

Ellingson, S. A., Miltenberger, R. G., Stricker, J., Galensky, T. L., & Garlinghouse, M. (2000). Functional assessment and intervention for challenging behaviors in the classroom by general classroom teachers. Journal of Positive Behavior Interventions, 2, 85–97.

Ervin, R. A., Schaughency, E., Matthews, A., Goodman, S. D., & McGlinchey, M. T. (2007). Primary and secondary prevention of behavior difficulties: Developing data-informed problem-solving model to guide decision making at a school-wide level. Psychology in the Schools, 44, 7–18.

Filter, K. J., & Horner, R. H. (2009). Function-based academic interventions for problem behavior. Education & Treatment of Children, 32, 1–19.

Gregory, A., & Mosely, P. M. (2004). The discipline gap: Teacher's views on the over-representation of African American students in the discipline system. Equity & Excellence in Education, 37, 18–30.

Hayden, T., Borders, C., Embury, D., & Clarke, L. (2009). Using effective classroom delivery as a classwide management tool. Beyond Behavior, 18, 12–17.

Heward, W. L. (1994). Three "low-tech" strategies for increasing the frequency of active student response during group instruction. In R. Gardner III, D. M. Sainato, J. O. Cooper, T. E. Heron, W. L. Heward, J. Eshleman, & T. A. Grossi (Eds.), Behavior analysis in education: Focus on measurably superior instruction (pp. 283–320). Pacific Grove, CA: Brooks/Cole.

Horner, R. H., Dunlap, G., Koegel, R. L., Carr, E. G., Sailor, W., Anderson, J., et al. (1990). Toward a technology of "non-aversive" behavior support. Journal of the Association for Persons with Severe Handicaps, 15, 125–132.

Houchins, D., Puckett-Patterson, D., Crosby, S., Shippen, M., & Jolivette, K. (2009). Barriers and facilitators to providing incarcerated youth with a quality education. Preventing School Failure, 53, 159–166.

Individuals with Disabilities Education Act Amendments of 1997, Pub. L. No. 105-17, 20 U.S.C. § 1400 et seq. (1997).

Individuals with Disabilities Education Improvement Act of 2004, Pub. L. No. 108-446, 20 U.S.C. § 1400 et seq. (2004).

Ingram, K., Lewis-Palmer, T., & Sugai, G. (2005). Functional-based intervention planning: Comparing the effectiveness of FBA function-based and non-function-based intervention plans. Journal of Positive Behavior Interventions, 7, 224–236.

Lambert, M. C., Cartledge, G., Heward, W. L., & Lo, Y.-y. (2006). Effects of response cards on disruptive behavior and academic responding during math lessons by fourth-grade urban students. Journal of Positive Behavior Interventions, 8, 88–99.

Lo, Y.-y., Algozzine, B., Algozzine, K., Horner, R., & Sugai, G. (2010). Schoolwide positive behavior support. In B. Algozzine, A. P. Daunic, & S. W. Smith (Eds.), Preventing problem behaviors (2nd ed., pp. 33–51). Thousand Oaks, CA: Corwin.

Lo, Y.-y., & Cartledge, G. (2006). FBA and BIP: Increasing the behavior adjustment of African American boys in schools. Behavioral Disorders, 31, 147–161.

Meyer, L. H., & Evans, I. M. (1993). Science and practice in behavioral intervention: Meaningful outcomes, research validity, and usable knowledge. Journal of the Association for Persons with Severe Handicaps, 18, 224–234.

Miller, D. N., George, M. P., & Fogt, J. B. (2005). Establishing and sustaining research-based practices at Centennial School: A descriptive case study of systemic change. Psychology in the Schools, 42, 553–567.

MotivAider® (2011). Thief River Falls, MN: Behavioral Dynamics.

Muscott, H. S., Mann, E. L., & LeBrun, M. R. (2008). Positive behavioral interventions and supports in New Hampshire: Effects of large-scale implementation of schoolwide positive behavior support on student discipline and academic achievement. *Journal of Positive Behavior Interventions, 10*, 190–205.

Nelson, J. R., Martella, R. M., & Marchand-Martella, N. (2002). Maximizing student learning: The effects of a comprehensive school-based program for preventing problem behaviors. *Journal of Emotional and Behavioral Disorders, 10*, 136–148.

No Child Left Behind Act of 2001, Pub. L. No. 107-110, 20 U.S.C. § 6301 et seq. (2002).

O'Neill, R. E., Horner, R. H., Albin, R. W., Sprague, J. R., Storey, K., & Newton, J. S. (1997). *Functional assessment and program development for problem behavior: A practical handbook* (2nd ed.). Pacific Grove, CA: Brooks/Cole.

O'Shea, D., & Drayden, M. (2008). Legal aspects of preventing problem behavior. *Exceptionality, 16*, 105–118.

Payne, L. D., Scott, T. M., & Conroy, M. (2007). A school-based examination of the efficacy of function-based intervention. *Behavioral Disorders, 32*, 158–174.

Public Schools of North Carolina. (2008). *Positive Behavior Support training modules.* Retrieved October 28, 2009 from www.ncpublicschools.org/positivebehavior/implementation/modules/.

Reid, R., & Nelson, J. R. (2002). The utility, acceptability, and practicality of functional behavioral assessment for students with high-incidence problem behaviors. *Remedial and Special Education, 23*, 15–23.

Robers, S., Zhang, J., & Truman, J. (2010). *Indicators of school crime and safety: 2010* (NCES 2011-002/NCJ 230812). National Center for Education Statistics, U.S. Department of Education, and Bureau of Justice Statistics, Office of Justice Programs, U.S. Department of Justice. Washington, DC. http://nces.ed.gov/pubs2011/2011002.pdf.

Rose, L. C., & Gallup, A. M. (2006). The 38th annual Phi Delta Kappa/Gallup poll of the public's attitudes toward the public schools. *Phi Delta Kappan, 88*(1), 41–56.

Scott, T. M., & Nelson, C. M. (1999). Using functional behavioral assessment to develop effective intervention plans: Practical classroom applications. *Journal of Positive Behavioral Intervention, 1*, 242–251.

Shaw, S. R., & Braden, J. P. (1990). Race and gender bias in the administration of corporal punishment. *School Psychology Review, 19*, 378–383.

Simonson, B., Sugai, G., & Negron, M. (2008). Schoolwide positive behavior supports: Primary systems and practices. *TEACHING Exceptional Children, 40*(6), 32–40.

Skiba, R. J., Michael, R. S., Nardo, A. C., & Peterson, R. (2002). The color of discipline: Sources of racial and gender disproportionality in school punishment. *Urban Review, 34*, 317–342.

Skiba, R. J., & Peterson, R. L. (1999). The dark side of zero tolerance. *Phi Delta Kappan*, 372–382.

Skiba, R. J., & Peterson, R. L. (2000). School discipline at a crossroads: From zero tolerance to early response. *Exceptional Children, 66*, 335–346.

Skiba, R. J., Poloni-Staudinger, L., Simmons, A. B., Feggins-Azziz, R., & Chung, C.-G. (2005). Unproven links: Can poverty explain ethnic disproportionality in special education? *The Journal of Special Education, 39*, 130–144.

Skiba, R. J., Simmons, A. B., Ritter, S., Gibb, A. C., Rausch, M. K., Cuadrado, J., & Chung, C. (2008). Achieving equity in special education: History, status, and current challenges. *Exceptional Children, 74*, 264–288.

Stage, S. A., Jackson, H. G., Jensen, M. J., Moscovitz, K. K., Bush, J. W., Violette, H. D., et al. (2008). A validity study of functionally-based behavioral consultation with students with emotional/behavioral disabilities. *School Psychology Quarterly, 23*, 327–353.

Sterling-Turner, H. E., Robinson, S. L., & Wilczynski, S. M. (2001). Functional assessment of distracting and disruptive behaviors in the school setting. *The School Psychology Review, 30*, 211–226.

Sugai, G., & Horner, R. H. (1999–2000). Including the functional behavioral assessment technology in schools. *Exceptionality, 8*, 145–148.

Sugai, G., & Horner, R. H. (2002). Introduction to the special series on positive behavior support in schools. *Journal of Emotional and Behavioral Disorders, 10*, 130–135.

Sugai, G., & Horner, R. H. (2008). What we know and need to know about preventing problem behavior in schools. *Exceptionality, 16*, 67–77.

Sugai, G., Horner, R. H., Dunlap, G., Hieneman, M., Lewis, T. J., & Nelson, C. M. (2000). Applying positive behavioral support and functional behavioral assessment in schools. *Journal of Positive Behavior Interventions, 2*, 131–143.

Sugai, G., Lewis-Palmer, T., & Hagan-Burke, S. (1999–2000). Overview of the functional behavioral assessment process. *Exceptionality, 8*, 149–160.

Sutherland, K. S., Wehby, J. H., & Copeland, S. R. (2000). Effect of varying rates of behavior-specific praise on the on-task behavior of students with emotional or behavioral disorders. *Journal of Emotional or Behavioral Disorders, 8*, 2–8.

Vollmer, T., & Northup, J. (1996). Some implications of functional analysis for school psychology. *School Psychology Quarterly, 11*, 76–92.

Walker, H. M., Ramsey, E., & Gresham, R. M. (2004). *Antisocial behavior in school: Evidence-based practices* (2nd ed.). Belmont, CA: Wadsworth/Thomson Learning.

Wood, B. K., Umbreit, J., Liaupsin, C. J., & Gresham, F. M. (2007). A treatment integrity analysis of function-based intervention. *Education & Treatment of Children, 30*, 105–120.

Chapter 6

Anderson, K. J., & Minke, K. M. (2007). Parent involvement in education: Toward an understanding of parents' decision making. *Journal of Education Research, 100*, 311–323.

Applequist, K. (2009). Parent perspectives of special education: Framing of experiences for prospective special educators. *Rural Special Education Quarterly, 28*, 3–16.

Barbour, C., Barbour, N. H., & Scully, P. A. (2010). *Families, schools, and communities: Building partnerships for educating children* (5th ed.). Upper Saddle River, NJ: Prentice-Hall.

Bateman, D., & Bateman, C. F. (2001). *A principal's guide to special education.* Arlington, VA: Council for Exceptional Children.

Berger, E. H. (2008). *Parents as partners in education: Families and schools working together* (7th ed.). Upper Saddle River, NJ: Pearson.

Crockett, J. (2002). Special education's role in preparing responsive leaders for inclusive schools. *Remedial and Special Education, 39*, 157–168.

Crockett, J., Becker, M., & Quinn, D. (2009). Reviewing the knowledge base of special education leadership and administration from 1970–2009. *Journal of Special Education Leadership, 22*, 55–67.

Darch, C. Y., Miao, Y., & Shippen, P. (2004). A model for involving parents of children with learning and behavior problems in schools. *Preventing School Failure, 48*, 24–34.

Davern, L. (1996). Listening to parents of children with disabilities. *Educational Leadership, 53*, 61–63.

DiPaola, M. F., & Tschannen-Moran, M. (2003). The principalship at a crossroads: A study of the conditions and concerns of princpals. *NASSP Bulletin, 87*, 43–65.

Dodd, A. (1996). Involving parents, avoiding gridlock. *Educational Leadership, 53*, 44–47.

Epstein, J. L. (1995). School/family/community partnerships. *Phi Delta Kappan, 76*(9): 701–712.

Epstein, J. L. (2001). Building bridges of home, school, and community: The importance of design. *Journal of Education for Students at Risk, 6*, 161–168.

Epstein, J. L. (2005). Attainable goals? The spirit and letter of the No Child Left Behind Act on parental involvement. *Sociology of Education, 78*, 179–182.

Epstein, J. L. & Salinas, K. C. (2004). Partnering with families and communities. *Educational Leadership, 61,* 12–18.

Epstein, J. L., Sanders, M. G., Simon, B. S., Salinas, K. C., Jansorn, N. R., & Van Voorhis, F. L. (2002). *School, family, and community partnerships: Your handbook for action* (2nd ed.). Thousand Oaks, CA: Corwin.

Evans, A. (2003). Empowering families, supporting students. *Educational Leadership, 61,* 35–37.

Ferguson, P. (2002). A place in the family: An historical interpretation of research on parental reactions to having a child with a disability. *The Journal of Special Education, 36,* 124–130.

Finders, M., & Lewis, C. (1991). Why some families don't come to school. *Educational Leadership, 51,* 50–54.

Fox, L., Vaughn, B. J., Wyatte, M. L., & Dunlap, G. (2002). We can't expect other people to understand: Family perspectives on problem behavior. *Exceptional Children, 68,* 437–450.

Gersten, R., Irvine, L., & Keating, T. (2002). Critical issues in research on families: Introduction to the special issue. *The Journal of Special Education, 36,* 122–123.

Gersten, R., Keating, T., Yovanhoff, P., & Harniss, M. K. (2001). Working in special education: Factors that enhance special educators' intent to stay. *Exceptional Students, 67,* 449–453.

Gonzalez-DeHass, A., Willems, P., & Doan-Holbein, M. (2005). Examining the relationship between parental involvement and student motivation. *Educational Psychology Review, 17,* 99–123.

Hornby, G. (2000). *I.* New York: Cassell.

Individuals with Disabilities Education Act Amendments of 1997, PL 105-17, 20 U.S.C. §§ 1400 et seq.

Individuals with Disabilities Education Improvement Act of 2004, PL 108-466, 20 U.S.C. S. C. §1400, H.R. 1350.

Johnson, L. J., Pugach, M. C., & Hawkins, A. (2004). School-family collaboration: A partnership. *Focus on Exceptional Children, 36,* 1–12.

Kozik, P. L. (2005). *Positive leadership for family engagement: Preparing educators to communicate and connect with families and communities.* Greenwich, CT: Information Age Publishing.

Kozleski, E., Engelbrecht, P., Hess, R., Swart, E., Eloff, I., Oswald, M., et al. (2008). Where differences matter: A cross-cultural analysis of family voice in special education. *Journal of Special Education, 42,* 26–35.

López, G. R. (2001a). Redefining parental involvement: Lessons from high-performing migrant-impacted schools. *American Educational Research Journal, 38,* 253–288.

López, G. R. (2001b). The value of hard work: Lessons on parent involvement from an (Im)migrant household. *Harvard Educational Review, 71,* 416–437.

Lynch, E. W., & Stein, R. (1987). Perspectives on parent participation in special education. *Exceptional Education Quarterly, 3*(2), 56–63.

Mostert, M. P. (1998). *Interprofessional collaboration in schools.* Boston: Allyn Bacon.

Murray, M., Christensen, K., Umbarger, G., Rade, K., Aldridge, K., & Niemeyer, J. (2007). Supporting family choice. *Early Childhood Education Journal, 35,* 111–117.

Noddings, N. (2005). *The challenge to care in schools: An alternative approach to education* (2nd ed.). New York: Teachers College Press.

O'Shea, L., Algozzine, R., Hammitte D., & O'Shea, D. L. (2001). *Families and teachers of individuals with disabilities: Collaborative orientations and responsive practices.* Boston: Allyn & Bacon.

Parette, H., & Petch-Hogan, B. (2000). Approaching families: Facilitaing culturally/linguistically diverse family involvement. *TEACHING Exceptional Children, 33,* 4–10.

Pogoloff, S. M. (2004). Facilitate positive relationships between parents and professionals. *Intervention in School and Clinic, 40,* 116–119.

Ramirez, A., & Soto-Hinman, I. (2009). A place for all families. *Educational Leadership, 66,* 79–82.

Runswick-Cole, K. (2007). The Tribunal was the most stressful thing—More stressful than my son's diagnosis or behaviour: The experiences of families who go to the Special Educational Needs and Disability Tribunal (SENDisT). *Disability & Society, 22,* 315–328.

Russell, P. (2008). Building brighter futures for all our children—A new focus on families as partners and change agents in the care and development of children with disabilities or special educational needs. *Support for Learning, 23,* 104–112.

Ryan, J. B., Katsiyannis, A., Peterson, R., & Chemler, R. (2007a). IDEA 2004 and disciplining students with disabilities. *NASSP Bulletin, 91,* 130–140.

Ryan, J. B., Sanders, S., Katsyiannis, A., & Yell, M. L. (2007b). Using time-out effectively in the classroom. *TEACHING Exceptional Children, 39*(4), 60–67.

Schmidt, P. R. (2005). *Preparing educators to communicate and connect with families and communities.* Greenwich, CT: Information Age Publishing.

Turnbull, A. P., Taylor, R. L., Erwin, E. J., & Soodak, L. C. (2011). *Families, professionals, and exceptionality: Positive outcomes through partnerships and trust* (6th ed.). Upper Saddle River, NJ: Pearson/Merrill-Prentice Hall.

United States Department of Education. (1999). *Parent involvement in educating children with disabilities:Theory and practice.* Twenty-First Annual Report to Congress on the Implementation of IDEA. Washington, DC: Author.

Walker, H., Colvin, G., & Ramsey, E. (1995). *Antisocial behavior in school: Strategies and best practices.* Pacific Grove, CA: Brooks/Cole.

Walther-Thomas, C. S., Korinek, L., McLaughlin, V. L., & Williams, B. T. (2000). *Collaboration for inclusive education.* Boston: Allyn & Bacon.

Yell, M. L. (2006). *The law and special education* (2nd ed.). Upper Saddle River, NJ: Pearson.

Yell, M. L., Shriner, J. G., & Katsiyannis, A. (2006). Individuals with Disabilities Education Improvement Act of 2004 and IDEA Regulations of 2006: Implications for educators, administra-

tors, and teacher trainers. *Focus on Exceptional Children, 39,* 1–24.

Zinn, M. B., Eitzen, S., & Wells, B. (2011) *Diversity in families.* Upper Saddle River, NJ: Pearson.

Chapter 7

Baugher, R., & Nichols, J. (2008). Conducting a rural school district transition fair: Successes and challenges for students with disabilities. *Education, 129*(2), 216–223.

Blalock, G. (1996). Community transition teams as the foundation for transition services for youth with learning disabilities. *Journal of Learning Disabilities, 29,* 145–159.

Cameto, R. (April 2005). The transition planning process. *NLTS Data Brief, 4*(1). Retrieved May 22, 2008, from www.ncset.org/publications/printresource.as?id=2130.

Education for All Handicapped Children Act of 1975, 20 U.S.C. § 1400 *et seq.* (1975) (amended 1986).

Fabian, E. S., Luecking, R. G., & Tilson, G. P. (1994). *A working relationship: The job development specialist's guide to successful partnerships with businesses.* Baltimore, MD: Brookes.

Follari, L. (2011). *Foundations and best: Practices in early childhood education: History, theories and approaches to learning.* Upper Saddle River, NJ: Pearson.

Garwood, S. G., Fewell, R. R., & Neisworth, J. T. (1988). Public Law 94-142: You can get there from here! *Topics in Early Childhood Special Education, 8,* 1–11.

Goodwill Industries. (n.d.). Retrieved June 13, 2009, from www.goodwill.org/page/guest/about.

Heward, W. L. (2009). *Exceptional children.* Upper Saddle River, NJ: Pearson.

Individuals with Disabilities Education Act of 1986, PL No. 99-457.

Individuals with Disabilities Education Act of 1990, 20 U.S.C. § 1400 *et seq.* (1990).

Individuals with Disabilities Education Act Amendments of 1997, PL 105-17, 20 U.S.C. §§ 1400 *et seq.*

Individuals with Disabilities Education Improvement Act of 2004, PL 108-466, 20 U.S.C. §1400, H.R. 1350.

Kochhar-Bryant, C. A., Shaw, S., & Izzo, M. (2007). *What every teacher should know about transition and IDEA 2004.* Boston: Pearson.

Kohler, P. D. (1993). Best practices in transition: Substantiated or implied? *Career Development for Exceptional Individuals, 16,* 107–121.

Kohler, P. D. (1996). *A taxonomy for transition programming: Linking research and practice.* Champaign: Transition Research Institute, University of Illinois.

Kohler, P. D., & Field, S. (2003). Transition-focused education: Foundation for the future. *The Journal of Special Education, 37,* 174–183.

Kortering, L. (2009). School completion issues in special education. *Exceptionality, 17*(1), 1–4.

Kortering, L., Braziel, P., & McClannon, T. (2010). Career ambitions. *Remedial and Special Education, 31,* 230–240.

Kraemer, B. R., McIntyre, L. L., & Blacher, J. (2003). Quality of life for young adults with mental retardation during transition. *Mental Retardation, 41,* 250–262.

Kramer, T., Caldarella, P., Christensen, L., & Shatzer, R. (2010). Social and emotional learning in the kindergarten classroom: Evaluation of the Strong Start Curriculum. *Early Childhood Education Journal, 37,* 303–309.

Marion, M. C. (2010). *Introduction to early childhood education: A developmental perspective.* Upper Saddle River, NJ: Merrill.

Morrison, G. S. (2011). *Fundamentals of early childhood education.* Upper Saddle River, NJ: Pearson.

Meisels, S. J., & Shonkoff, J. P. (2000). Early childhood interventions: A continuing evolution. In J. P. Shonkoff & S. J. Meisels (Eds.), *Handbook of early childhood intervention* (2nd ed., pp. 3–31). New York: Cambridge University Press.

National Center on Secondary Education and Transition (NCSET). (2007). Key provisions on transition: IDEA 1997 compared to H. R. 1350 (IDEA 2004). Retrieved October 5, 2008, from www.ncset.org/publications/related/ideatransition.asp.

National Secondary Transition Technical Assistance Center (NSTTAC) (2008). Personnel Development #1: Using NSTTAC Indicator-13 Resources. Charlotte, NC: NSTTAC.

Noonan, M. J., & McCormick, I. (2006). *Young children with disabilities in natural environments: Methods and Procedures.* Baltimore, MD: Brookes.

North Central Regional Educational Library. (n.d.). School to Work Opportunities Act of 1994. Retrieved on June 13, 2009, from www.ncrel.org/sdrs/areas/issues/envrnmnt/stw/sw3swopp.htm.

Odom, S. L. (2000). Preschool inclusion: What we know and where we go from here. *Topics in Early Childhood Special Education, 20,* 20–27.

Reedy, C., & McGrath, W. (2010). Can you hear me now? Staff-parent communication in child care centres. *Early Child Development & Care, 180,* 347–357.

Repetto, J. B., Webb, K. W., Garvan, C. W., & Washington, T. (2002). Connecting student outcomes with transition practices in Florida. *Career Development for Exceptional Individuals, 25,* 123–139.

Richards, C., & Leafstedt, J. (2010). *Early reading intervention: Strategies and methods.* Upper Saddle River, NJ: Pearson.

Social Security Administration. (n.d.). *Social Security online.* Retrieved June 13, 2009, from www.ssa.gov/.

Steere, D. E., & Rose, E., & Cavaiuolo, D. (2007). *Growing up transition to adult life for students with disabilities.* Boston: Pearson.

Test, D. W. (2000). Implementing the transition mandate: The relationship between programs, personnel, and services. *Special Services in the Schools, 16,* 23–34.

Test, D. W. (2004). Invited commentary on Rusch and Braddock (2004): One person at a time. *Research and Practice for Persons with Severe Disabilities, 29,* 248–252.

Test, D. W., Aspel, N. P., & Everson, J. M. (2006). Transition methods for youth with disabilities. Upper Saddle River, NJ: Pearson Merrill/Prentice-Hall.

Test, D. W., Fowler, C. H., White, J., Richter, S. M., & Walker, A. R. (2009). Evidence-based secondary transition practices for enhancing school completion. *Exceptionality, 17,* 16–29.

Test, D. W., Fowler, C. H., Richter, S. M., White, J., Mazzotti, V. L., Walker, A. R., et al. (2008). Evidence-based practices in secondary transition. *Exceptionality, 17,* 16–29.

Test, D. W., Mazzotti, V. L., Mustian, A., Fowler, C. H., Kohler, P., & Kortering, L. (2009). *Evidence-based secondary transition predictors for improving post-school outcomes for students with disabilities.* Unpublished manuscript.

Turnbull, A., Turnbull, A., & Wehmeyer, M. (2009). *Exceptional lives: Special education in today's schools* (6th ed.). Upper Saddle River, NJ: Prentice-Hall.

U.S. Department of Education. (n.d.). *Elementary and secondary education legislation.* Retrieved June 13, 2009, from www.ed.gov/policy/elsec/leg/edpicks.jhtml?src=ln.

U.S. Department of Education, Office of Civil Rights. (2007). *Students with disabilities preparing for postsecondary education: Know your rights and responsibilities.* Retrieved September 24, 2008, from www.ed.gov/about/offices/list/ocr/transition.html.

U.S. Department of Education, Office of Special Education Programs, Data Analysis System (DANS), *Infants and toddlers receiving early intervention services in accordance with Part C 1998-2007.* Data updated July 15, 2008. Washington, DC: Author.

U.S. Department of Education. (n.d.). *Special education and rehabilitative services: The Rehabilitation Act.* Retrieved June 11, 2009, from www.ed.gov/policy/speced/reg/narrative.html.

U.S. Department of Education, Office of Vocational and Adult Education. (n.d.). Retrieved June 11, 2009, from www.ed.gov/about/offices/list/ovae/pi/cte/index.html.

U.S. Department of Justice, Civil Rights Division. (n.d.). *Work Force Investment Act.* Retrieved June 11, 2009, from www.usdoj.gov/crt/508/508law.php.

U.S. Department of Labor. (n.d.). *Job Corps.* Retrieved on June 13, 2009, from www.jobcorps.gov/home.aspx.

U.S. Department of Veteran Affairs. (n.d.) *Vocational rehabilitation.* Retrieved June 11, 2009, from www.vba.va.gov/bln/vre/.

Williamson, R., Robertson, J., & Casey, L. (2010). Using a dynamic systems approach to investigating postsecondary education and employment outcomes for transitioning students with disabilities. *Journal of Vocational Rehabilitation, 33,* 101–111.

Zhang, C., Fowler, S., & Bennett, T. (2004). Experiences and perceptions of EHS staff with the IFSP process: Implications for practice and policy. *Early Childhood Education Journal, 32,* 179–186.

Chapter 8

Alberto, P. A. & Troutman, A. C. (2009). *Applied behavior analysis for teachers.* Upper Saddle River, NJ: Pearson.

Aldeman, H. H. (1996). *Restructuring education support services: Toward the concept of an enabling component.* Kent, OH: American School Health Association.

Barton, W. (2010). RTI in the classroom: Guidelines and recipes for success. *Childhood Education, 86,* 340.

Bouck, E. C. (2007). Co-teaching . . . Not just a textbook term: Implications for practice. *Preventing School Failure, 51,* 46–51.

Bradley, R., Danielson, L., & Doolittle, J. (2005). Response to intervention. *Journal of Learning Disabilities, 38,* 485–486.

Carnahan, C., Williamson, P., Clarke, L., & Sorensen, R. (2009). A systematic approach for supporting paraeducators in educational settings. *TEACHING Exceptional Children, 41*(5), 34–43.

Cesar, M., & Santos, N. (2006). From exclusion to inclusion: Collaborative work contributions to more inclusive learning settings. *European Journal of Psychology of Education, 21*, 333–346.

Cox, S. G. (2008). Differentiated instruction in the elementary classroom. *Education Digest, 73*, 52–54.

Cummings, K. D., Atkins, T., Allison, R., & Cole, C. (2008). Response to intervention. *TEACHING Exceptional Children, 40*(4), 24–31.

Danielson, L., Doolittle, J., & Bradley, R. (2007). Professional development, capacity building, and research needs: Critical issues for response to intervention Implementation. *School Psychology Review, 36*, 632–637.

Dettmer, P. A., Thurston, L. P., & Dyck, N. J. (2004). *Consultation, collaboration, and teamwork* (5th ed.). Boston:Allyn & Bacon.

Dettmer, P. A., Thurston, L. P., Knackendoffel, A., & Dyck, N. J. (2009). *Collaboration, consultation, and teamwork* (6th ed.). Columbus, OH: Pearson.

DuFour, R. P. (1997). The school as a learning organization: Recommendations for school improvement. *NASSP Bulletin, 81*, 81–87.

Dufrene, B., Reisener, C., Olmi, D., Zoder-Martell, K., McNutt, M., & Horn, D. (2010). Peer tutoring for reading fluency as a feasible and effective alternative in response to intervention systems. *Journal of Behavioral Education, 19*(3), 239–256.

Education for All Handicapped Children Act of 1975, PL No. 94-142, 89 Stat. 773 (1975).

Elliott, D., & McKenney, M. (1998). Four inclusion models that work. *TEACHING Exceptional Children, 30*(4), 25–30.

Floyd, L., & Vernon, L. (2007). *Relationships in and outside the classroom. Integrating curriculum in the inclusive K–3 classroom.* Boston: Allyn & Bacon.

Friend, M., & Bursuck, W. (2009). *Including students with special needs: A practical guide for classroom teachers.* Boston: Allyn & Bacon.

Friend, M., & Cook, L. (2007). *Interactions: Collaboration skills for school professionals* (5th ed.). Boston: Allyn & Bacon.

Friend, M., & Pope, K. (2005) Creating schools in which all students can succeed. *Kappa Delta Pi Record, 41*(2), 56–61.

Fullan, M. (1993). *Change forces. Probing the depths of education reform.* Bristol, PA: Palmer Press.

Gadfly, S. E., & Gately, F. J. (2001). Understanding co-teaching components. *TEACHING Exceptional Children, 33*(4), 25–30.

Giangreco, M., Suter, J., & Doyle, M. (2010). Paraprofessionals in inclusive schools: A review of recent research. *Journal of Educational & Psychological Consultation, 20*, 41–57.

Graden, J. L., Casey, A., & Bonstrom, I. (1985). Implementing a prereferral intervention system: Part II. The data. *Exceptional Children, 51*, 487–496.

Grande, M. (2004). Increasing parent participation and knowledge using home literacy bags. *Intervention in School and Clinic, 41*, 290–294.

Hands, C. (2010). Why collaborate? The differing reasons for secondary school educators' establishment of school-community partnerships. *School Effectiveness & School Improvement, 21*, 189–207.

Hoover, J., & Patton, J. (2008). The role of special educators in a multitiered instructional system. *Intervention in School & Clinic, 43*, 195–202.

Individuals with Disabilities Education Act of 1990, 20 U.S.C. § 1400 *et seq.* (1990).

Individuals with Disabilities Education Act Amendments of 1997, PL 105-17, 20 U.S.C. §§ 1400 *et seq.*

Individuals with Disabilities Education Improvement Act of 2004, PL 108-466, 20 U.S.C. §1400, H.R. 1350.

Jenkins, T. (2007). *When a child struggles in school: Everything parents and educators should know about getting children the help they need.* Charleston, SC: Advantage.

Lehr, A. E. (1999). The administrative role in collaborative teaching. *NASSP, 83*, 1.

Lembke, E., Garman, C., Deno, S., & Stecker, P. (2010). One elementary school's implementation of response to intervention (RTI). *Reading & Writing Quarterly, 26*, 361–373.

McKenzie, R. (2010). The insufficiency of response to intervention in identifying gifted students with learning disabilities. *Learning Disabilities*

Research & Practice (Blackwell Publishing Limited), *25*, 161–168.

McLeskey, J., Hoppey, D., Williamson, P., & Rentz, T. (2004). Is inclusion an illusion? An examination of national and state trends toward the education of students with learning disabilities in general education classrooms. *Learning Disabilities Research and Practice, 19*, 12–15.

Mellard, D., & Johnson, E. S. (2008). *A practitioner's guide to implementing response to intervention.* Thousand Oaks, CA: Corwin.

National Center for Educational Statistics, http://nces.ed.gov/programs/coe/indicator_cwd.asp.

National Center for Response to Intervention, www.rti4success.org/.

No Child Left Behind Act of 2001, PL 107-110, 115, § 1425, 20 U.S.C. §§ 6301 *et seq.* (2002).

105th Congress. (August, 1997). *The IDEA amendments of 1997.* Washington, DC: National Information Center for Children and Youth with Disabilities, pp. 1–39.

Ormsbee, C. K., Myles, B. S., & Simpson, R. L. (1999). General and special educators' perception of preassessment team operating procedures. *Journal of Developmental and Physical Disabilities, 11*, 327–338.

Pinchot, G. (1998). Building community in the workplace. In F. Hesselbein, M. Goldsmith, R. Becjhard, & R. F. Schubert (Eds.), *The community of the future* (pp. 125–137). San Francisco: Jossey-Bass.

Reedy, C., & McGrath, W. (2010). Can you hear me now? Staff-parent communication in child care centres. *Early Child Development & Care, 180*, 347–357.

Reschly, A., Busch, T., Betts, J., Deno, S., & Long, J. (2009). Curriculum-based measurement oral reading as an indicator of reading achievement: A meta-analysis of the correlational evidence. *Journal of School Psychology, 47*, 427–469.

Rock, M., Gregg, M., Ellis, E., & Gable, R. (2008). REACH: A Framework for differentiating classroom instruction. *Preventing School Failure, 52*, 31–47.

Rouse, H. L., & Fantuzzo, J. W. (2006). Validity of the dynamic indicators for basic early literacy skills as an indicator of early literacy for urban kindergarten children. *School Psychology Review, 35*, 341–355.

Salend, S. J. (2008). *Creating inclusive classrooms: Effective and reflective practices for all students* (6th ed.). Columbus, OH: Prentice-Hall.

Smith, E. C., Gartin, B. C. Murdurdick, N. L., & Hilton, A. (2006). *Families and children with special needs.* Columbus, OH: Pearson.

Tomlinson, C. A. (2003). *Fulfilling the promise of the differentiated classroom: Strategies and tools for responsive teaching.* Alexandria, VA: Association for Supervision and Curriculum.

Tuckwiller, E., Pullen, P., & Coyne, M. (2010). The use of the regression discontinuity design in tiered intervention research: A pilot study exploring vocabulary instruction for at-risk kindergartners. *Learning Disabilities Research & Practice* (Blackwell Publishing Limited), *25*, 137–150.

Turnbull, A., Turnbull, R., Erin, E., & Soodak, L. (2006). *Families, professionals, and exceptionality.* Columbus, OH: Pearson.

U.S. Department of Education. (2004). *Twenty-sixth annual report to Congress on the implementation of the Individuals with Disabilities Education Act.* Washington, DC: Author.

Vaughn, S., Bos, C., & Schumm, J. (2000). *Teaching exceptional, diverse, and at-risk students in the general education classroom.* Boston: Allyn & Bacon.

Vaughn, S., Bos, C., & Schumm, J. (2003). *Teaching exceptional, diverse, and at-risk students in the general education classroom* (3rd ed.). Boston: Pearson Education.

Villa, R. A., Thousand, J. S., & Nevin, A. I. (2008). *A guide to co-teaching: Practical tips for facilitating student learning.* Thousand Oaks, CA: Corwin.

Walther-Thomas, C., Korinek, L., McLaughlin, V. L., & Williams, B. T. (2000). *Collaboration for inclusive education: Developing successful programs.* Boston: Allyn & Bacon.

Warren, L. L., & Peel, H. A. (2005). Collaborative model for school reform through a rural school/university partnership. *Education, 126,* 246–352.

Wilson, G. L. (2008). Be an active co-teacher. *Intervention in School and Clinic, 43,* 240–243.

Zirkel, P., & Krohn, N. (2008). RTI after IDEA. *Teaching Exceptional Children, 40,* 71–73.

Chapter 9

Artiles, A. (2009). Re-framing disproportionality research: Outline of a cultural-historical paradigm. *Multiple Voices for Ethnically Diverse Exceptional Learners, 11,* 24–37.

Banks, J. A. (1993). Approaches to multicultural curriculum reform. In J. A. Banks & C. A. M. Banks (Eds.), *Multicultural education: Issues and perspectives* (pp. 195–214). Boston: Allyn & Bacon.

Banks, J. A. (1994). Multicultural education: History and revitalization movements. In J. A. Banks (Ed.). *Multiethnic education: Theory and practice* (3rd ed., pp. 19–39). Boston: Allyn & Bacon.

Barry, N. H., & Lechner, J. V. (1995). Preservice teachers' attitudes about and awareness of multicultural teaching and learning. *Teaching and Teacher Education, 11,* 149–161.

Blanton, L.L., & Lee, L. (1995). *The multicultural workshop: A reading and writing program.* Boston: Heinle & Heinle.

Capella-Santana, N. (2003). Voices of teacher candidates: Positive changes in multicultural attitudes and knowledge. *The Journal of Educational Research, 96,* 182–190.

Cartledge, G., Gardner, R., & Ford (2009). *Diverse learners with exceptionalities.* Upper Saddle River, NJ: Pearson.

Cirino, P., Vaughn, S., Linan-Thompson, S., Cardenas-Hagan, E., Fletcher, J., & Francis, D. (2009). One-year follow-up outcomes of Spanish and English interventions for English language learners at risk for reading problems. *American Educational Research Journal, 46*(3), 744–781.

Cockrell, K. S., Placier, P. L., Cockrell, D. H., & Middleton, J. N. (1999). Coming to terms with "diversity" and "multiculturalism" in teacher education: Learning about our students, changing our practice. *Teaching and Teacher Education, 15,* 351–366.

Cummins, J. (2009). Transformative multiliteracies pedagogy: School-based strategies for closing the achievement gap. *Multiple Voices for Ethnically Diverse Exceptional Learners, 11*(2), 38–56.

Dee, J. R., & Henkin, A. B. (2002). Assessing dispositions toward cultural diversity among preservice teachers. *Urban Education, 37,* 22–40.

Duesterberg, L. M. (1998). Rethinking culture in the pedagogy and practices of preservice teachers. *Teaching and Teacher Education, 14,* 497–512.

Edgar, E., Patton, J. M., & Day-Vines, N. (2002). Democratic dispositions and cultural competency: Ingredients for school renewal. *Remedial and Special Education, 23,* 231–241.

Gay, G. (2002a). Preparing for culturally responsive teaching. *Journal of Teacher Education, 53,* 106–116.

Gay, G. (2002b). Culturally responsive teaching in special education for ethnically diverse students: Setting the stage. *Qualitative Studies in Education, 15,* 613–629.

Gollnick, D. M., & Chinn, P. C. (2002). *Multicultural education in a pluralistic society* (6th ed.). Upper Saddle River, NJ: Prentice-Hall.

Grant, C., & Sleeter, C. (2011a). *Doing multicultural education for achievement and equity.* San Francisco: Jossey-Bass.

Grant, C., & Sleeter, C. (2011b). *Turning on learning: Five approaches for multicultural teaching plans for race, class, gender, and disability.* San Francisco: Jossey-Bass.

Grant, C. A., & Tate, W. F. (1995). Multicultural education through the lens of the multicultural education research literature. In J. A. Banks & C. A. M. Banks (Eds.), *Handbook of research on multicultural education* (pp. 145–166). New York: Macmillan.

Green, M. F. (Ed.). (1989). *Minorities on campus: A handbook for enhancing diversity.* Washington, DC: American Council on Education.

Green, S. (2010). Multicultural education: A necessary tool for general and special education. *Advances in Special Education, 20,* 107–122.

Green, V. (2010). Global perspectives on learning disabilities and emotional/behavioral disorders. *Intervention in School & Clinic, 45,* 51–53.

Harry, B., & Anderson, M. G. (1994). The disproportionate placement of African American males in special education programs: A critique for the process. *Journal of Negro Education, 63,* 602–619.

King, J. E. (1991). Dysconsious racism: Ideology, identity, and the miseducation of teachers. *Journal of Negro Education, 60,* 133–146.

Kitano, M. K., & Pedersen, K. S. (2002). Action research and practical inquiry: Multicultural content integration in gifted education: Lessons from the field. *Journal for the Education of the Gifted, 25,* 269–289.

Ladson-Billings, G. (1992). Liberatory consequences of literacy: A case of culturally relevant instruction for African American students. *Journal of Negro Education, 61,* 378–391.

Ladson-Billings, G. (1994). *The dreamkeepers.* San Francisco: Jossey-Bass.

Levine, D. R., & Adelman, M. B. (1993). *Beyond languages: Cross cultural communication.* Englewood Cliffs, NJ: Prentice-Hall Regents.

Lumpkin, B., Strong, D., & Earle, S. W. (1995). *Multicultural science and math connections: Middle school projects and activities.* Portland, ME: J. Weston Walch, Publisher.

Lynn, M. (1999). Toward critical race pedagogy: A research note. *Urban Education, 33,* 606–626.

Marshall, P. L. (1996). Multicultural teaching concerns: New dimensions in the area of teacher concerns research? *The Journal of Educational Research, 89,* 371–379.

Morey, A. I., & Kitano, M. K. (Eds.). (1997). *Multicultural course transformation in higher education: A broader truth.* Boston: Allyn & Bacon.

Muschla, J. A., & Muschla, G. R. (2006). *Hands-on math projects with real-life applications.* San Francisco: Jossey-Bass.

National Council for the Accreditation of Teacher Education. (2001). *Professional standards for the accreditation of schools, colleges, and departments of education.* Washington, DC: Author.

Nieto, S. (1998). Fact and fiction: Stories of Puerto Ricans in U.S. schools. *Harvard Educational Review, 68,* 133–163.

Obiakor, F. E. (2001). Multicultural education: Powerful tool for preparing future general and special educators. *Teacher Education and Special Education, 24,* 241–255.

Obiakor, F. E., & Utley, C. A. (2001). Culturally responsive teacher preparation programming for the twenty-first century. In C. A. Utley and F. E. Obiakor (Eds.). *Special education, multicultural education, and school reform: Components of quality education for learners with mild disabilities* (pp. 188–207). Chicago: Charles C. Thomas.

Ognibene, E. R. (1989). Integrating the curriculum: From impossible to possible. *College Teaching, 37,* 105–110.

Overholt, J. L., Aaberg, N. H., & Lindsey, J. (2008). *Math stories for problem solving success: Ready-to-use activities Based on real-life situation, grades 6–12.* San Francisco: Jossey-Bass.

Ramsey, P. G., Williams, L. R., & Vold, E. B. (2003). *Multicultural education: A source book* (2nd ed.). New York: Routledge Falmer.

Rosas, C., & West, M. (2009). Teachers beliefs about classroom management: Pre-service and inservice teachers' beliefs about classroom management. *International Journal of Applied Educational Studies, 5,* 54–61.

Schoem, D., Frankel, L., Zúñiga, X., & Lewis, E. A. (1993). The meaning of multicultural teaching: An introduction. In D. Schoem, L. Frankel, X. Zúñiga, & E. A. Lewis (Eds.), *Multicultural teaching in the university* (pp. 1–12). Westport, CT: Praeger.

Seidl, B., & Pugach, M. (2009). Support and teaching in the vulnerable moments: preparing special educators for diversity. *Multiple Voices for Ethnically Diverse Exceptional Learners, 11,* 57–75.

Sleeter, C. E. (1991). Multicultural education and empowerment. In C. E. Sleeter (Ed.),

Empowerment through multicultural education (pp. 1–23). New York: State University of New York Press.

Sleeter, C. E., & Grant, C. A. (1987). An analysis of multicultural education in the United States. *Harvard Educational Review, 57,* 421–444.

Sleeter, C. E., & Grant, C. A. (1999). *Making choices for multicultural education: Five approaches to race, class, and gender* (3rd ed.). Upper Saddle River, NJ: Prentice-Hall.

Sullivan, A., A'Vant, E., Baker, J., Chandler, D., Graves, S., McKinney, E., et al. (2009). Promising practices in addressing disproportionality. *Communique, 38*(2), 1–18.

Teel, K. M., Debruin-Parecki, A., & Covington, M. V. (1998). Teaching strategies that honor and motivate inner-city African-American students: A school/university collaboration. *Teaching and Teacher Education, 14,* 479–495.

Udvari-Solner, A., & Thousand, J. S. (1996). Creating a responsive curriculum for inclusive schools. *Remedial and Special Education, 17,* 182–193.

U.S. Census Bureau. (2001). *State profiles: 2000 census.* Washington, DC: U.S. Department of Commerce, Economics and Statistics Division. Retrieved from www.census.gov/statab/.

U.S. Department of Education. (2000). *Twenty-second annual report to Congress on the implementation of the Individuals with Disabilities Education Act.* Washington, DC: Author.

U.S. Department of Education. (2001). *Twenty-third annual report to Congress on the implementation of the Individuals with Disabilities Education Act.* Washington, DC: Author.

Utley, C. A., & Obiakor, F. E. (2001). Multicultural education and special education: Infusion for better schooling. In C. A. Utley & F. E. Obiakor (Eds.), *Special education, multicultural education, and school reform: Components for quality education for learners with mild disabilities* (pp. 3–29). Chicago: Charles C. Thomas.

Villegas A. M., & Lucas, T. (2002a). *Educating culturally responsive teachers.* New York: State University of New York Press.

Villegas, A. M., & Lucas, T. (2002b). Preparing culturally responsive teachers: Rethinking the curriculum. *Journal of Teacher Education, 53,* 20–32.

Webb-Johnson, G. (2002). Are schools ready for Joshua? Dimensions of African-American culture among students identified as having behavioral/emotional disorders. *Qualitative Studies in Education, 15,* 653–671.

Winzer, M. A., & Mazurek, K. (1998). *Special education in multicultural contexts.* Upper Saddle River, NJ: Merrill.

Wlodkowski, R. J., & Ginsberg, M. B. (1995). A framework for culturally responsive teaching. *Educational Leadership, 53,* 17–21.

Yellin, D., & Mokhtari, K. (2010). Learning from our students: ELL alternatives to special ed and grade retention. *English Leadership Quarterly, 32*(3), 8–12.

Zaslavsky, C. (1993). *Multicultural mathematics: Interdisciplinary cooperative-learning activities.* Portland, ME: J. Weston Walch.

Zaslavsky, C. (1996). *The multicultural math classroom: Bringing in the world.* Portsmouth, NH: Heinemann.

Zaslavsky, C. (1998). *Math games and activities from around the world.* Chicago: Chicago Review Press.

Chapter 10

Assistive Technology Act of 1998, 29 U.S.C. § 3001 et seq. (1998). Retrieved November 20, 2008, from www.section508.gov/docs/AT1998.html.

Bashan, J., & Gardner, J. (2010). Measuring universal design for learning. *Special Education Technology Practice, 12,* 15–19.

Bauwens, J., & Hourcade, J. J. (1991). Making co-teaching a mainstreaming strategy. *Preventing School Failure, 35*(4), 19–24.

Betts, F. (1992). How systems thinking applies to education. *Educational Leadership, 50*(3), 38–41.

Blue, E. (2010). UDL: Paving the way toward 21st century literacies for special needs learners. *School Talk, 15*(3), 1–3.

Bouck, E. (2010). Technology and students with disabilities: Does it solve all the problems? *Advances in Special Education, 20,* 91–104.

Cook, B. G., & Schirmer, B. R. (2003). What is special about special education? *Journal of Special Education, 37*(3), 139.

Cook, L., & Friend, M. (1995). Co-teaching: Guidelines for creating effective practices. *Focus on Exceptional Children, 28*(3), 1–16.

Dalton, B., Pisha, B., Eagleton, M., Coyne, P., & Deysher, S. (2001). *Engaging the text: Reciprocal teaching and questioning strategies in a scaffolded learning environment. Final report to the U.S. Department of Education.* Peabody, MA: Center for Applied Special Technology.

Delano, M. E. (2007). Video modeling interventions for individuals with autism. *Remedial & Special Education, 28*(1), 33–42.

Edyburn, D. (2003). *Technology-Enhanced Performance Intervention Menu (TEPIM) Model Overview.* www.uwm.edu/~edyburn/.

Edyburn, D. (2008). *A primer on universal design (UD) in education.* Retrieved December 2, 2008, from www.uwm.edu/~edyburn/ud.htm.

Ellis, E. S. (2000). *The LINCS Vocabulary Strategy.* Lawrence, KS: Edge Enterprises.

Fuchs, D., Fuchs, L. S., Mathes, P., & Simmons, D. C. (1997). Peer-assisted learning strategies: Making classrooms more responsive to diversity. *American Educational Research Journal, 34*(1), 174–206.

Gersten, R. (1998). Recent advances in instructional research for students with learning disabilities: An overview. *Learning Disabilities Research and Practice, 13*(3), 162–170.

Gersten, R., Baker, S. K., Smith-Johnson, J., Dimino, J., & Peterson, A. (2006). Eyes on the prize: Teaching complex historical content to middle school students with learning disabilities. *Exceptional Children, 72*(3), 264–280.

Greenwood, C. R., & Delquadri, J. (1995). Classwide peer tutoring and the prevention of school failure. *Preventing School Failure, 39*(4), 21–25.

Greenwood, C. R., & Terry, B. (1993). Achievement, placement, and services: Middle school benefits of classwide peer tutoring used at the elementary school. *School Psychology Review, 22*(3), 20–39.

Hall, T., Meyer, A., & Strangman, N. (2005). UDL implementation: Examples using best practices and curriculum enhancements. In D. Rose, A. Meyer, & C. Hitchcock (Eds.), *The universally designed classroom: Accessible curriculum and digital technologies* (pp. 149–197). Cambridge, MA: Harvard Education Press.

Hall, T., Strangman, N., & Meyer, A. (2003). Differentiated instruction and implications for UDL implementation. Retrieved December 2, 2008, from www.cast.org/publications/ncac/ncac_diffinstructudl.html.

Heward, W. (2006). *Exceptional children: An introduction to special education* (8th ed.). Upper Saddle River, NJ: Prentice-Hall.

Horner, R. H., & Sugai, G. (2005). School-wide positive behavior support: An alternative approach to discipline in schools. In L. Bambara & L. Kern (Eds.), *Positive behavior support* (pp. 359–390). New York: Guilford.

Jackson, R., & Harper, K. (2005). Teacher planning for accessibility: The universal design of learning environments. In D. Rose, A. Meyer, & C. Hitchcock (Eds.), *The universally designed classroom: Accessible curriculum and digital technologies* (pp. 101–123). Cambridge, MA: Harvard Education Press.

King-Sears, M. E. (1997). Best academic practices for inclusive classrooms. *Focus on Exceptional Children, 29*(7), 1–22.

King-Sears, M. E., & Mooney, J. F. (2004). Teaching content in an academically diverse class. In B. K. Lenz, D. Deshler, & B. R. Kissam (Eds.), *Teaching content to all: Evidence-based practices in middle and secondary schools.* Boston: Pearson.

Lenz, B. K., Deshler, D. D., & Kissam, B. R. (2004). *Teaching content to all: Evidence-based inclusive practices in middle and secondary schools.* Boston: Pearson.

Maheady, L. (1988). Peer-mediated instruction: A promising approach to meeting the diverse needs of LD adolescents. *Learning Disability Quarterly, 11*(2), 108–113.

Maheady, L., Harper, G. F., & Mallette, B. (2001). Peer-mediated instruction and interventions and students with mild disabilities. *Remedial and Special Education, 22*(1), 4–14.

McMaster, K. N., & Fuchs, D. (2002). Effects of cooperative learning on the academic achievement of students with learning disabilities: An update of Tateyama-Sniezek's review. *Learning Disabilities Research and Practice, 17*(2), 107–117.

Messinger-Willman, J., & Marino, M. T. (2010). Universal Design for Learning and assistive technology: Leadership considerations for promoting inclusive education in today's secondary schools. *NASSP Bulletin, 94*(1), 5–16.

Meyer, A., & Rose, D. H. (2000). Universal design for individual differences. *Educational Leadership, 58*(3), 39.

O'Brien, C. (2007). Using collaborative reading groups to accommodate diverse learning and behavior needs in the general education classroom. *Beyond Behavior, 16*(3), 7–15.

O'Brien, C., Aguinaga, N., & Mundorf, J. (2009, March). Preparing the next generation of teachers to integrate special education technology in inclusive classrooms. In I. Gibson et al. (Eds.), *Proceedings of Sociedty for Information Technology & Teacher Education International Conference 2009* (pp. 3189–3194). Chesapeake, VA: AACE.

O'Brien, C., & Dieker, L. A. (2008). Effects of video modeling on implementation of literature circles by students with learning disabilities and their peers in inclusive content classrooms. *Journal of Curriculum and Instruction, 2*(2), 52–73.

Palincsar, A., & Brown, A. L. (1984). Reciprocal teaching of comprehension-fostering and comprehension-monitoring activities. *Cognition and Instruction, 1*(2), 117–175.

Pisha, B., & Coyne, P. (2001). Jumping off the page: Content area curriculum for the Internet age. *Reading Online, 5*(4). www.readingonline.org/articles/art_index.asp?HREF=pisha/index.html.

Rose, D., & Dalton, B. (2007). *Plato revisited: Learning through listening in the digital world.* Recording for the Blind and Dyslexic.

Rose, D., & Meyer, A. (2000). Universal design for learning. *Journal of Special Education Technology, 15*(1), 67.

Rose, D., & Meyer, A. (2002). *Teaching every student in the digital age: Universal design for learning.* Alexandria, VA: ASCD.

Rose, D., Meyer, A., & Hitchcock, C. (2005). Introduction. In D. Rose, A. Meyer, & C. Hitchcock (Eds.), *The universally designed classroom: Accessible curriculum and digital technologies.* (pp. 1–12). Cambridge, MA: Harvard Education Press.

Sabia, R. (2008, April). The national UDL task force. *Presented at the Council for Exceptional Children National Convention, Boston.*

Salazar, P. (2010). In this issue. *NASSP Bulletin, 94*(1), 3–4.

Skrtic, T. M. (1995). Theory/Practice and objectivism: The modern view of the professions. In T. M. Skrtic (Ed.), *Disability and democracy: Reconstructing (special) education for postmodernity* (pp. 3–24). New York: Teachers College Press.

Spooner, F., Baker, J. N., Harris, A. A., Ahlgrim-Delzell, L., & Browder, D. M. (2007). Effects of training in universal design for learning on lesson plan development. *Remedial and Special Education, 28*(2), 108–116.

Stahl, S. (2003). The NFF: A national file format for accessible instruction materials. *Journal of Special Education Technology, 18*(2), 65–67.

Tomlinson, C. (2001). *How to differentiate instruction in mixed-ability classrooms* (2nd ed.). Alexandria, VA: ASCD.

U.S. Department of Education. (2004). *Individuals with Disabilities Education Adt, 20* U.S.C. 1400 et seq.

Villegas, A. M., & Lucas, T. (2002). Preparing culturally responsive teachers: Rethinking the curriculum. *Journal of Teacher Education, 53*(1), 20–32.

Vygotsky, L. (1962). *Thought and language.* Cambridge, MA: MIT Press.

Chapter 11

American Educational Research Association, (2009, July 9). *Ethical standards.* www.aera.net/AboutAERA/./

American Evaluation Association. (2009, July 9). *Guiding principles for evaluators.* www.eval.

org/GPTraining/GP%20Training%20Final/gp.principles.pdf.

Bagley, S. (2010). Students, teachers and alternative assessment in secondary school: Relational models theory (RMT) in the field of education. *Australian Educational Researcher, 37*, 83–106.

Berliner, D. C. (2002). The hardest science of all. *Educational Researcher, 31(8)*, 18–20.

Fitzpatrick, J. L., Sanders, J. R., & Worthen, B. R. (2010). *Program evaluation: Alternative approaches and practical guidelines.* Upper Saddle River, NJ: Pearson.

Gall, M. D., & Borg, W. R. (2010). *Applying educational research: How to read, do, and use research to solve problems of problems of practice.* Upper Saddle River, NJ: Pearson.

Gallagher, P., & Lambert, R. (2006). Classroom quality, concentration of children with special needs, and child outcomes in head start. *Exceptional Children, 73*, 31–52.

Gorard, S. (2010). Serious doubts about school effectiveness. *British Educational Research Journal, 36*, 745–766.

Kaestle, C. F. (1993). The awful reputation of education research. *Educational Researcher, 22*, 26–31.

Kimball, S. M., & Milanowski, A. (2009). Examining teacher evaluation validity and leadership decision making within a standards-based evaluation system. *Educational Administration Quarterly, 45*, 34–70.

Kirkpatrick, D. L. (1998). *Evaluating training programs* (2nd ed.). San Francisco: Berrett-Koehler Publishers.

Isomursu, M., Tähti, M., Väinämö, S., & Kuutti, K. (2007). Experimental evaluation of five methods for collecting emotions in field settings with mobile applications. *International Journal of Human-Computer Studies, 65(4)*, 404–418.

McMillan, J. H., & Wergin, J. F. (2010). *Understanding and evaluating educational research.* Upper Saddle River, NJ: Pearson.

Praslova, L. (2010). Adaptation of Kirkpatrick's four level model of training criteria to assessment of learning outcomes and program evaluation in higher education. *Educational Assessment, Evaluation and Accountability, 22*, 215–225.

Sales, B. D., & Folkman, S. (Eds.). (2000). *Ethics in research with human participants.* Washington, DC: American Psychological Association.

Sanders, J. R. (1994). *The program evaluation standards: How to assess evaluations of educational programs* (2nd ed.). Thousand Oaks, CA: Sage.

Schneider, B., Carnoy, M., Kilpatrick, J., Schmidt, W., & Shavelson, R. (2007). *Estimating causal effects.* Washington, DC: American Educational Research Association.

Shadish, W. R., Cook, T. D., & Campbell, D. T. (2002). *Experimental and quasi-experimental design for generalized causal inference.* Boston: Houghton Mifflin.

Shadish, W. R., Cook, T. D., & Leviton, L.C. (1991). *Foundations of program evaluation: Theories of practice.* Newbury Park, CA: Sage.

Sroufe, G. E. (1997). Improving the "awful reputation" of educational research. *Educational Researcher, 26*, 26–28.

Stufflebeam, D. L., Madaus, G. F., & Kellaghan, T. (2000). *Evaluation models: Viewpoints on educational and human services evaluation* (2nd ed.). Norwell, MA: Kluwer.

Stufflebeam, D. L., & Shinkfield, A. J. (2007). *Evaluation, theory, models, and applications.* San Francisco: Jossey-Bass.

Thurston, P. W. (1984). Legal and professional standards in program evaluation. *Educational Evaluation and Policy Analysis, 6*, 15–26.

U.S. Department of Education. (2009, July 9). *Family Educational Rights and Privacy Act (FERPA).* www.ed.gov/policy/gen/guid/fpco/ferpa/index.html.

United Way of America. (1996). *Measuring program outcomes: A practical approach.* Alexandria, VA: Author.

Van de Pol, J., Volman, M., & Beishuizen, J. (2010). Scaffolding in teacher–student interaction: A decade of research. *Educational Psychology Review, 22*, 271–296.

W. K. Kellogg Foundation. (2004). *Logic model development guide.* Battle Creek, MI: Author.

Chapter 12

Angelides, P. (2002). A collaborative approach for teachers' in-service training. *Journal of Education for Teaching, 28,* 81–82.

Assistance for Education of All Children with Disabilities. (2000). 34 Code of Federal Regulations, Part 300.

Bartlett, L. D., Weisenstein, G. R., & Etscheidt, S. (2002). *Successful inclusion for educational leaders.* Upper Saddle River, NJ: Merrill/Prentice-Hall.

Bateman, D., & Bateman, C. F. (2001). *A principal's guide to special education.* Arlington, VA: Council for Exceptional Children.

Bateman, D. F., Bright, K. L., O'Shea, L. J., & Algozzine, B. (2007). *The special education program: Administrator's handbook.* Boston: Pearson.

Billingsley, B. S. (2005). *Cultivating and keeping committed special education teachers: What principals and district leaders can do.* Thousand Oaks, CA: Corwin.

Billingsley, B. S., & Tomchin, E. M. (1992). Four beginning LD teachers: What their experiences suggest for trainers and employers. *Learning Disabilities Research and Practice, 7,* 104–112.

Bingham, J. (2005). Prince Harry's former teacher wins case for unfair dismissal. *Times Educational Supplement, 4642,* 8.

Boe, E. E., Cook, L. H., Bobbitt, S. A., & Terbanian, G. (1998). The shortage of fully certified teachers in special and general education. *Teacher Education and Special Education, 21,* 1–21.

Bright Futures Technical Report Part 5. (2000). *Special education teaching initiatives.* Reston, VA: Council for Exceptional Children.

Brown, S. W. (2005). Emily and Rebecca: A tale of two teachers. *Teaching & Teacher Education, 21,* 637–648.

Bureau of Labor Statistics, U.S. Department of Labor. (2004). *Occupational outlook handbook.* Washington, DC: Author.

Burrello, L. C., & Greenburg, D. E. (1988). *Leadership and supervision in special services: Promising ideas and practices.* New York: Hawthorne Press.

Campbell-Whatley, G. D. (2003). Recruiting culturally and linguistically diverse groups in special education: Defining the problem. *Teacher Education and Special Education, 26,* 255–261.

Capper, C. A., Frattura, E., & Keys, M. (2002). *Meeting the needs of students of all abilities: How leaders go beyond inclusion.* Thousand Oaks, CA: Corwin.

Castetter, W. B., & Young, I. P. (2000). *The human resource function in educational administration* (7th ed.). Upper Saddle River, NJ: Merrill/Prentice Hall.

Cloud, J., & Fastenberg, D. (2010). How to recruit better teachers. *Time, 176*(12), 46–52.

Cogan, M. (1973). *Clinical supervision.* Boston: Houghton Mifflin.

Connolly, A. J. (1998). *Key math-revised: A diagnostic inventory of essential mathematics.* Circle Pines, MN: American Guidance Service.

Cooper, B. S., Ehrensal, P. A. L., & Bromme, M. (2005). School-level politics and professional development: Traps in evaluating the quality of practicing teachers. *Educational Policy, 19,* 112–125.

Cox, L. (2001). Retaining special educators: Comment on Ax, Conderman, and Stephens. *National Association of Secondary School Principals, 85*(621), 4–5.

Curriculum Review. (1999). Making the most of professional development, *8,* 4.

Danielson, C. (2007). *Enhancing professional practice: A framework for teaching* (2nd ed.). Alexandria, VA: ASCD.

DiBello, L., Harlin, R. P., & Hall, L. (2007). Mentoring teachers toward excellence. *Childhood Education, 83,* 246–247.

Duffy, M. L., & Forgan, J. (2005). *Mentoring new special education teachers: A guide for mentors and program developers.* Thousand Oaks, CA: Corwin.

Edds, D. B. (2001). Is anyone listening? *School Planning and Management, 40*(26), 13.

Education USA. (2000). CEC: Special ed teachers overwhelmed with demands, *42*(22), 7–8.

Egyed, C., & Short, R. J. (2006). Teacher self-efficacy, burnout, experience, and decisions to refer a disruptive student. *School Psychology International, 27,* 462N474.

Gersten, R., Keating, T., Yovanoff, P., & Harniss, M. K. (2001). Working in special education factors that enhance special educators' intent to stay. *Exceptional Children, 67,* 549–567.

Glickman, C. D., Gordon, S. P., & Ross-Gordon, J. (2010). *Supervision and instructional leadership: A developmental approach* (8th ed.). Boston: Allyn & Bacon.

Goldhammer, R. (1969). *Clinical supervision: Special methods for the supervision of teachers.* New York: Holt, Rinehart, and Winston.

Goor, M. B., Schwenn, J. O., & Boyer, L. (1997). Preparing principals for leadership in special education. *Intervention in School and Clinic, 32,* 133–141.

Hill, R., Carjuzaa, J., Aramburo, D., & Baca, L. (1993). Culturally and linguistically diverse teachers in special education: Repairing or redesigning the leaky pipeline. *Teacher Education and Special Education, 16,* 258–269.

Hoy, A., & Hoy, W. (2006). *Instructional leadership: A learning-centered guide* (2nd ed.). Boston: Allyn & Bacon.

Hoy, W. K., & Miskel, C. G. (2007). *Educational administration: Theory, research, and practice.* New York: McGraw-Hill.

Individuals with Disabilities Education Improvement Act of 2004, PL 108-466, 20 U.S.C. §1400, H.R. 1350.

Irinaga-Bistolas, C., Schalock, M., Marvin, R., & Beck, L. (2007). Bridges to success: A developmental induction model for rural early career special educators. *Rural Special Education Quarterly, 26*(1), 13–22.

Karge, B., & Lasky, B. (2009). SPOTLIGHT on special education. *Journal of Staff Development, 30*(3), 49–52.

Keller, B. (2004). States receive poor marks for teacher-quality standards. *Education Week, 23*(32), 21.

Lee, S., Theoaris, R., Fitzpatrick, M., Liss, J. M., Nix-Williams, T., Griswoald, D. E., & Walther-Thomas, C. (2006). Create effective mentoring relationships: Strategies for mentor and mentee success. *Intervention in School and Clinic, 41,* 233–240.

Leko, M., & Brownell, M. (2009). Crafting quality professional development for special educators. *TEACHING Exceptional Children, 42*(1), 64–70.

Littrell, P. C., Billingsley, B. S., & Cross, J. H. (1994). The effects of principal support on special and general educator's stress, job satisfaction, and school commitment, health, and intent to stay in teaching. *Remedial and Special Education, 15,* 297–309.

Lloyd, S. R., Wood, T. A., & Moreno, G. (2000). What's a mentor to do? *TEACHING Exceptional Children, 33*(1), 38–42.

Lucas, S. (2004). Accused wins sum for unfair dismissal. *Times Educational Supplement, 4614,* 9.

Lunenburg, F. C., & Ornstein, A. C. (1991). *Educational administration.* Belmont, CA: Wadsworth.

Mastropieri, M. A. (2001). Is the glass half full or half empty? Challenge encountered by first-year special education teachers. *The Journal of Special Education, 35,* 66–74.

McIntire, J. (2001). Market forces and special education. *Education Week, 20*(40), 37.

McLaughlin, M. J., & Nolet, V. (2008). *What every principal needs to know about special education.* Thousand Oaks, CA: Corwin.

Miros, R. (2001). How to select and evaluate special education staff. In D. Bateman & C. F. Bateman (Eds.). *A principal's guide to special education.* Arlington, VA: Council for Exceptional Children.

Mullen, C. A. (2007). Supporting the professional development of new and seasoned practitioners. *Mentoring and Tutoring: Partnership in Learning, 15,* 219–221.

Murawski, W., & Dieker, L. (2008). 50 ways to keep Your co-teacher. *TEACHING Exceptional Children, 40*(4), 40–48.

National Clearinghouse for Professionals in Special Education. (2002). Reston, VA: Council for Exceptional Children.

Nolet, V., & McLaughlin, M. J. (2005). *Accessing the general curriculum: Including students with disabilities in standard-based reform* (2nd ed.). Thousand Oaks, CA: Corwin.

Norton, M. S. (2008). *Human resources administration for educational leaders.* Thousand Oaks, CA: Sage.

Odden, A. (2004). Lessons learned about standards-based teacher evaluation systems. *Peabody Journal of Education, 79,* 126–137.

Osborne, A. G., DiMattia, P., & Curran, F. X. (1993). *Effective management of special education programs: A handbook for school administrators.* New York: Teachers College Press.

Osborne, A. G., Jr., & Russo, C. J. (2006). *Special education and the law: A guide for practitioners* (2nd ed.). Thousand Oaks, CA: Corwin.

Ottesen, E. (2007). Teachers in the making: Building accounts of teaching: *Teaching and Teacher Education, 43,* 612–623.

Otto, S. J., & Arnold, M. (2005). A study of experienced special education teachers' perceptions of administrative support. *College Student Journal, 39,* 253–259.

Podemski, R. S., Marsh, G. E., Smith, T. E. C., & Price, B. J. (1995). *Comprehensive administration of special education.* Englewood Cliffs, NJ: Prentice-Hall.

Razik, T. A., & Swanson, A. D. (2010). *Fundamental concepts of educational leadership and management* (3rd ed.). Upper Saddle River, NJ: Pearson.

Rebore, R. W. (2011). *Human resources administration in education: A management approach.* Upper Saddle River, NJ: Pearson.

Rosenberg, M. S., Griffin, C. G., Kilgore, K. L., & Carpenter, S. L. (1997). Beginning teachers in special education: A model for providing individualized support. *Teacher Education and Special Education, 20,* 301–321.

Schilchte, J., Yssel, N., & Merbler, J. (2005). Pathways to burnout: Case studies in teacher isolation and alienation. *Preventing School Failure, 50,* 35–40.

Sergiovanni, T. J. (2009). *The principalship: A reflective practice perspective.* Boston: Allyn & Bacon.

Sergiovanni, T. J., Kelleher, P., McCarthy, M. M., & Wirt, F. M. (2004). *Educational governance and administration.* Boston: Allyn & Bacon.

Shelton, C. F., & Pollingue, A. (2000). *The exceptional teacher's handbook: The first year teachers guide for success.* Thousand Oaks, CA: Corwin.

Special Education Report. (2000). Special education teacher shortage hits districts hard, *26*(19), 1–3.

Special Education Report. (2002). ED: Special Ed is tops in certified instructors, *28*(14), 3–4.

Special Education Report. (2002). New thinking needed to lure special education teachers, *28*(8), 1–3.

Spencer, S. A. (2005). Lynne Cook and June Downing: The practicalities of collaboration in special education service delivery. *Intervention in School & Clinic, 40,* 296–300.

Stempien, L. R., & Loeb, R. C. (2002). Differences in job satisfaction between general education and special education teachers: Implications for retention. *Remedial and Special Education, 23,* 258–267.

Sylar, A. A., Higgins, K., & Boone, R. (2007). Strategies for adapting WebQuests for students with learning disabilities. *Intervention in School and Clinic, 43*(1), 20–28.

Talmor, R., Reiter, S., & Feigin, N. (2005). Factors relating to regular education teacher burnout in inclusive education. *European Journal of Special Needs Education, 20,* 215–229.

Times Educational Supplement. (2004). Unfair sacking compensation, *4613,* 4.

Ubben, G. C., Hughes, L. W., & Norris, C. J. (2004). *The principal: Creative leadership for excellence in schools.* Boston: Allyn & Bacon.

U.S. Department of Education. (1997). National Center for Education Statistics. *Digest of Education Statistics.*

U.S. Department of Education. (1998). To assure the free appropriate public education of all children with disabilities: *Twentieth annual report to Congress on the implementation of the Individuals with Disabilities Education Act of 1990.*

U.S. Department of Education. (2000). To assure the free appropriate public education of all children with disabilities: *Twenty-Second annual report to Congress on the implementation of the Individuals with Disabilities Education Act of 1990.*

U.S. Department of Education. (2002). National Center for Education Statistics. *Digest of Education Statistics.*

Useem, E. (2005). Supporting new teachers in the city. *Educational Leadership, 62,* 44–47.

Webb, L. D., & Norton, M. S. (2009). *Human resources administration: personnel issues and needs in education.* Upper Saddle River, NJ: Pearson.

Weishaar, M. K., & Borsa, J. C. (2001). *Inclusive educational administration: A case study approach.* Boston: McGraw-Hill.

Whitaker, S. D. (2000). Mentoring beginning special education teachers and the relationship to attrition. *Exceptional Children, 66,* 546–566.

Williams, J., & Warren, S. H. (2007). E-Mentoring: Supporting first-year educators and rejuvenating veteran teachers. *The Delta Kappa Gamma Bulletin,* 9–11.

Winerip, M. (2005). New York's revolving door of good teachers driven out. *New York Times, 154* (53232), B10–B10.

Woodcock, R. W. (1998). *Woodcock Reading Mastery Test-Revised.* Circle Pines, MN: American Guidance Service.

Woodcock, R. W., & Johnson, M. B. (2001). *Woodcock-Johnson Psycho-Educational Battery* (rev. ed.). Allen, TX: DLM Teaching Resources.

Young, P. (2008). *Human resources function in educational administration* (9th ed.). Upper Saddle River, NJ: Pearson.

Wynn, S. R., Carboni, L. W., & Patall, E. A. (2007). Beginning teacher's perceptions of mentoring climate, and leadership: Promoting retention through a learning communities perspective. *Leadership and Policy in Schools, 6,* 209–229.

Chapter 13

Arundel, K. (2009). Districts express concerns over future-year budgets, services. *Education Daily, 42*(183), 3.

Assistance to States for the Education of Children with Disabilities and Preschool Grants for Children with Disabilities, 71 Fed. Reg. 46, 540–46, 845.

Bartlett, L. W., Weisenstein, L. D., & Etscheidt, S. (2007). *Successful inclusion for educational leaders* (2nd ed.). Columbus, OH: Merrill/Prentice-Hall.

Bateman, D. F., Bright, K. L., O'Shea, D. J., O'Shea, L. J., & Algozzine, B. (2007). *The special education program: Administrator's handbook.* Boston: Pearson.

Brimley, V., & Garfield, R. R. (2008). *Financing education in a climate of change.* Boston: Pearson/Allyn and Bacon.

Family Education Rights and Privacy Act (FERPA). (1974). www2.ed.gov/policy/gen/quid/fpco/ferpa/index/html.

Goffee, R., & Jones, G. (2006). *Why should anyone be led by you? What it takes to be an authentic leader.* Boston: Harvard Business Press.

Goor, M. B. (1995). *Leadership for special education administration: A case-based approach.* New York: Harcourt Brace.

Guthrie, J. W., Springer, M. G., Rolle, R. A., & Houck, E. A (2007). *Modern education finance and policy.* Upper Saddle River, NJ: Pearson.

Individuals with Disabilities Education Act of 1990, 20 U.S.C. § 1400 *et seq.* (1990).

Individuals with Disabilities Education Act Amendments of 1997, PL 105-17, 20 U.S.C. §§ 1400 *et seq.*

Individuals with Disabilities Education Improvement Act of 2004, PL 108-466, 20 U.S.C. §1400, H.R. 1350.

Jordan, T. S., Weiner, C. A., & Jordan, K. F. (1997). The interaction of shifting special education policies and state funding practices. *Journal of Education Finance, 23*(1), 43–68.

Jordan, T. S., & Weiner, C. A. (1997). The interaction of shifting special education policies and state funding practices. *Journal of Education Finance, 23*(1), 43–68.

North Carolina Public Schools. (2009). *Statistical profile of 2009* (Public Schools of North Carolina. State Board of Education, Department of Public Instruction). Raleigh, NC.

Oates, W. E. (2008). On the evolution of fiscal federalism: Theory and institutions. *National Tax Journal, 61,* 313–334.

Parrish, T., Harr, J., Anthony, J., Merickel, A., & Esra, P. (2003). *State special education fund-*

ing systems, 1999–2000. Palo Alto, CA: The Center for Special Education Finance, American Institutes for Research.

Picus, L. O., & Miller, C. J. (1995). Costs and service delivery trade-offs in providing educational services for students with severe disabilities. *Educational Administration Quarterly, 31,* 268–293.

Samuels, C. (2009). Stimulus spurs shifts of special education funding. *Education Week, 28*(37), 9.

South Carolina Department of Public Instruction. (2009). *Weighted pupil unit (WPU): Pupil classifications and weightings.* Finance and Operations Paper.

Special Education Report. (2010). Consider accessibility issues when distributing federal funds, *36*(3), 9.

Verstegen, D. A. (1998). New directions in special education finance litigation. *Journal of Education Finance, 23*(3), 277–308.

Chapter 14

American Academy of Pediatrics: Committee on Injury and Poison Prevention. (2001). School bus transportation of children with special health care needs. *Pediatrics, 108,* 516–518.

Assistance to States for the Education of Children with Disabilities and the Early Intervention Program for Infants and Toddlers with Disabilities: Final Regulations (Transportation). (2006). 71 Fed. Reg., 46540-46576 (to be codified at 34 CFR Parts §300 and 301).

Assistance to States for the Education of Children with Disabilities: Related Services. (2004). 34 C.F.R. § 300.34(c)(16).

Bluth L. (2009). *Transporting students with disabilities* (4th ed.). Presented by the NAPT Foundation.

Birnbaum, B. (2006). *Foundations of special education leadership: Administration, assessment, placement, and the law.* Ceredigion, United Kingdom: Edwin Mellen Press.

Board of Educ. of the Dist. 130 Pub. Sch. v. Illinois State Bd. of Educ., 1997 U.S. Dist. LEXIS 12921 (N.D. Ill. Aug. 25, 1997).

Board of Education of Hendrick Hudson v. Rowley, 458 U.S.176 (1982).

Cedar Rapids Consolidated School District v. Garret F., 526 U.S. 66 (1999). www.law.cornell.edu/supct/html/96-1793.ZO.html.

Donald B. by Christine B. v. Board of School Commissioners of Mobile County, 117 F.3d 1371 (11th Cir. 1997).

Education Daily. (2008). Fewer buses to transport NYC special education students, *41*(157), 6.

Elliott, J. (2008). Response to intervention: What and why. *The School Administrator.* www.scred.k12.mn.us/School/documents/RtI%20Final.pdf.

Florence County School District v. Carter, 510 U.S. 7 (1993).

Forsyth, A. (2005). Timely transport. *American School and University.* http://asumag.com/mag/university_timely_transport/.

KDM v. Reedsport School District, 196 F.3d 1046 (9th Cir. 1999).

Kleitman, S., & Marsh, H. (2002). Extracurricular school activities: The good, the bad, and the nonlinear. *Harvard Educational Review.* https://connect2.uncc.edu/harvard02/2002/wi02/, DanaInfo=www.edreview.org+w02marsh.htm.

Lashley, C., & Boscardin, M. L. (2003). *Special education administration at a crossroads: Availability, licensure, and preparation of special education administrators.* Gainesville, FL: University of Florida, Center on Personnel Studies in Special Education. (ERIC Document Reproduction Service No. ED477116)

Mahoney, J., & Carins, R. (1997). Do extracurricular activities protect against early school dropout? *Developmental Psychology, 33*(2), 241–253.

National Dissemination Center for Children with Disabilities. (2009). *Related services.* www.nichcy.org/educatechildren/iep/pages/related-services.aspx.

Special Education Report. (2009). Make sure transportation offer reflects child's unique needs. *LRP Publications, 35*(10), 7.

U.S. Department of Education, National Center for Education Statistics. (2008). *Digest of Education Statistics, 2007* (NCES 2008-022), Table 176.

Weishaar, M. K., & Borsa, J. C. (2001). *Inclusive educational administration: A case study approach.* Boston: McGraw-Hill.

INDEX